The UP Saga

Also from NIAS Press

NATURE AND NATION
Forests and Development in Peninsular Malaysia
Jeya Kathirithamby-Wells

The Nordic Institute of Asian Studies (NIAS) is funded by the governments of Denmark, Finland, Iceland, Norway and Sweden via the Nordic Council of Ministers, and works to encourage and support Asian studies in the Nordic countries. In so doing, NIAS has been publishing books since 1969, with more than one hundred titles produced in the last ten years.

Nordic Council of Ministers

The UP Saga

Susan M. Martin

NIAS
Press

First published in 2003 by NIAS Press
Nordic Institute of Asian Studies
Leifsgade 33, DK–2300 Copenhagen S, Denmark
tel: (+45) 3532 9501 • fax: (+45) 3532 9549
E–mail: books@nias.ku.dk • Website: www.niaspress.dk

British Library Cataloguing in Publication Data
Martin, Susan M.
    The UP saga. - (NIAS monograph ; 94)
    1.United Plantations Berhad - History 2.Plantations -
    Malaysia - History 3.Palm oil industry - Malaysia - History
    I.Title II.Nordic Institute of Asian Studies
    338.4'766535'09595

ISBN 87-91114-33-0 (deluxe edition)
ISBN 87-91114-20-9 (printed papercase edition)

Typesetting by NIAS Press
Printed on acid-free paper in Singapore
by Bestprint Printing Company

Contents

Contents

LIST OF ILLUSTATIONS

LIST OF MAPS

LIST OF TABLES

COLOUR SECTION (DELUXE EDITION ONLY)

Tan Sri Dato' Seri Børge Bek-Nielsen: A Life in Pictures

Young Børge Bek-Nielsen as a scout member in Holstebro

Bek-Nielsen prior to his departure to the Far East in 1951

Bek-Nielsen with his submachine gun during the Emergency

Rolf and Rothes Grut with Bek-Nielsen in front of United Plantations Research Centre

The Sultan of Perak awarding Bek-Nielsen the title of Dato' in 1976

Bek-Nielsen after acquiring the land for Australia's biggest organic farm

Dato' Seri Dr Mahathir Mohamad visiting United Plantations in 1985

Bek-Nielsen receives the title of 'BAPA United Plantations' in 1986

The Menteri Besar of Perak signing a fresh land agreement with Bek-Nielsen in 1987

The Sultan of Perak awarding Bek-Nielsen the title of Dato' Seri in 1989

Tan Sri Dato' Seri B. Bek-Nielsen receiving the Award 'Commander of the Most Esteemed Order of the Crown of Malaysia' from the King in 1996

Bek-Nielsen with his two sons, Carl and Martin

Bek-Nielsen's family home 'Aahuset' in Holstebro, Denmark

Bek-Nielsen's bust at the entrance to the Municipal Gardens, Holstebro

Martin Bek-Nielsen at the Petra-Andrea Church on Margrethe Hill, Perak

Preface

This book tells an amazing story, the saga of United Plantations (UP), a European firm founded in early colonial Malaya, which dared to do things differently. As a Scandinavian enterprise with a strong culture of co-operation and good corporate citizenship, this firm was able to thrive even better after independence than it had done under colonialism, and made a distinctive contribution to the development process. In recent years the UP success story has also been the story of Malaysia's success in export-led industrialization, a rare and spectacular case of industrial growth based on tropical agricultural foundations.

Within the context of both imperial economic history and development studies, this is such a remarkable story that no researcher could have been expected to go out looking for it. Nor could it have been found and understood by one person without a great deal of help. Indeed, so many people have helped in the writing of this book that it is impossible to list them all in one short preface. Most of them appear in the list of interviews and correspondents in the Bibliography, and several more may be found as authors discussed in the Introduction. Special thanks must be given to the School of Oriental and African Studies (SOAS), University of London, and to the Nuffield Foundation, which funded the initial fieldwork in Malaysia and Denmark, and to Tan Sri Dato' Seri Børge Bek-Nielsen, who offered hospitality and full access to company archives both in Malaysia and Denmark, and who has supported the project consistently without ever seeking to determine my analysis or change the text. He has also supplied photographs from his own collection for the colour section, and copies of the documents reproduced there and in the appendix.

Thanks are also due to Datuk Dr Yusof Basiron and his staff at the Malaysian Palm Oil Board's Head Office, especially Dr N. Rajanaidu and Jaya Gopal, who helped to get the project off to a flying start, and to Dr B.A. Elias, Mohd. Jaaffar Ahmad, and the staff of the Malaysian Palm Oil Board's European office in Hertford, without whom the industry trends of the past thirty years would have remained baffling to this classically trained historian. Colin Barlow and Ria

Gondowarsito of the International Oil Palm Study Group, Canberra, have provided further insights into current events. All responsibility for the analysis and conclusions below remains, however, my own.

How, then, did the idea of the *UP Saga* come to be? It has its roots in a first degree in History with Economics at the University of York, where one tutor in particular, Bob Sugden, inspired me with the idea of seeking the causes of big macroeconomic changes in the choices of individual people. Both in this book and in my earlier study of the Nigerian palm oil industry, I have chosen to tell the story through the experiences of a community of people involved in producing this commodity for export. The aim has been to breathe life into the trade statistics, and to show familiar events of the twentieth century from an unfamiliar angle. The First and Second World Wars, the inter-war depression and popular protests, the Malayan Emergency and the Nigerian Civil War, may all be seen through the eyes of ordinary people in rural areas, rather than those of colonial officials or city dwellers. This approach is rooted above all in lessons learnt in the late 1970s from Ian Brown, then at the University of Birmingham, while taking his Masters' course in South-East Asian economic and social history. Later on, while we were colleagues in the History Department at SOAS, Ian helped me to understand the Scandinavian side of the *UP Saga* by providing references on Aage Westenholz's early career in Siam. Together with Rajeswary Ampalavanar Brown, Gareth Austin, Kirti Chaudhuri, William and Keiko Clarence-Smith, Kent Deng, Janet Hunter, John Latham, Colin Lewis, Peter Robb and Kaoru Sugihara, he provided many stimulating ideas on the scope for comparative tropical economic history.

Peter Cain and Tony Hopkins, through their own Masters' courses in economic imperialism at the University of Birmingham in the late 1970s, provided further vital links in the chain of ideas which led to the writing of this book. They highlighted the concept of national styles in economic imperialism, and showed how much the discipline of business history had to contribute to the understanding both of imperialism and of post-colonial development, including development failures and underdevelopment. Having heard their laments on how little was being done by business historians to contribute in this way, it became my ambition to help fill that gap. The task has proved by no means easy, but further help has come from John Stopford, of London Business School, an inspiration not least because of his personal involvement in the development process through consultancy to the Thai government; and the business historians

David Fieldhouse, who introduced me to Unilever, and Geoff Jones, who provided much-needed moral support as the book neared completion.

A trip with fellow MBA students to Singapore with the London Business School in 1987 provided the final link in the chain. The dynamism and optimism which we experienced both in Singapore and in neighbouring countries took us all by surprise. Like the success of the Malaysian palm oil industry, on which this book focuses, the vibrancy of the regional economy is something not often stressed in the lecture halls and senior common rooms of Western universities. A chance encounter some months earlier with Sally Stewart of the University of Hong Kong, who had previously worked for the Palm Oil Research Institute of Malaysia, had given me some idea of what to expect, but it had to be seen to be believed. Special thanks are due to Sally and to her friends Kurt and Margaret Berger, and Datin Liz and Datuk Leo Moggie, for arranging a series of visits to Malaysian palm oil producers, and for providing hospitality in Kuala Lumpur and constant moral support throughout the long years of research and writing which followed.

Among the many people who then welcomed me at United Plantations were a few who made an especially direct contribution to the process of research and writing. Andal Krishnan and A. Arikiah provided invaluable help in understanding workforce views of the company history, both through translating interviews and through more general conversations. Munusamy and Chong Cho Tan (Mrs C.T. Kerk) guided me through the archives held in Jendarata's Head Office buildings and in the old pineapple factory. Carrie Jørgensen gave me a copy and allowed me to make full use of her unpublished history of UP; and Mogens Jensen, Cliff Dennis, Kenneth Nilsson and all in the Copenhagen office have provided unfailing support, not least by supplying black-and-white photographs for the main text. Invaluable insights into the shareholders' point of view, and into the lives of planters, engineers and their families, have been provided by Knud Gyldenstierne Sehested and Dr Val Lindquist, who have remained keen and supportive readers as the manuscript progressed. Dr Val also supplied two of the black-and-white illustrations from his own collection.

Finally, it would be impossible to overstate the contribution of Martin Lockett, whose commitment to Asia and to the co-operative movement and other forms of ethical business enterprise has been a constant inspiration. Without his support for my decision to give up teaching and focus on this project while bringing up our daughters Helen and Anna, the book would never have been completed and a wonderful story would have remained untold.

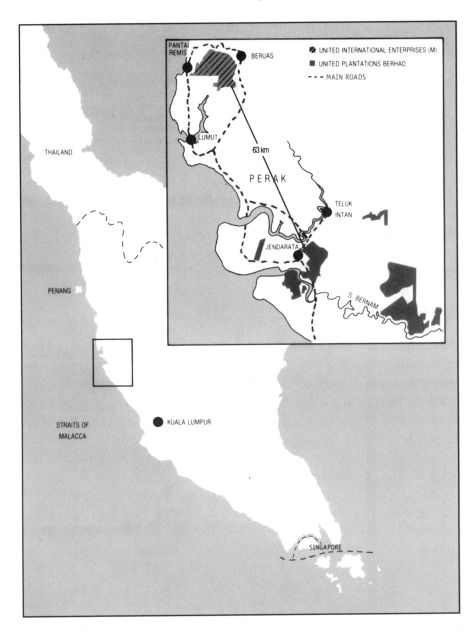

Map 1: Peninsular Malaysia, 2001: location of plantations, United Plantations Berhad and United International Enterprises (M) Berhad.

Source: Annual Report, United International Enterprises Ltd, 1994.

Introduction

*M*ore than ten years after the fall of the Berlin Wall and nearly 50 after *Merdeka* (Malaysian independence), one might be forgiven for supposing that the forces of globalization were sweeping all before them, both in Asia and in Europe. As Merrill Lynch boldly declared in October 1998, 'The World is 10 Years Old.' The new world is centred on one dominant power, America, and on the common pursuit of service-sector wealth. The prosperous groups within each nation are becoming ever more closely bound to each other by this shared pursuit, by shared and increasingly ruthless business norms and values, and by increasingly effective electronic ties. What place can there be in this brave new world for the businesses founded in an earlier era of globalization, the steamship and telegraph era of colonial expansion between 1870 and 1914? And what hope is there for the primary commodity producers on whom colonial prosperity was founded, but who are now facing falling prices and an uncertain future?[1]

Against this background the story of United Plantations shines forth as a beacon of hope. United Plantations, a Danish firm founded in Malaysia in 1906, continues to thrive in the era of globalization. It has continued to expand, and to involve Danish managers and investors, following the purchase of a controlling interest by Malaysians in 1982. During the 1990s the Danish-Malaysian partnership took on fresh life with the involvement of the Danish firm Aarhus Oliefabrik A/S as a major shareholder in United Plantations Berhad. As the story to be told in this book concludes in 2002, the ties between Danes and Malaysians are about to deepen further with the merger of United Plantations and its much younger sister company, United International Enterprises (see Map 1).

1

A distinctive culture of enthusiasm for innovation and an imaginative approach to business strategy have enabled United Plantations not only to survive the many political and economic upheavals of the twentieth century but also to inspire others within the Malaysian palm oil industry. Over a period of 50 years one man in particular, Børge Bek-Nielsen, has been exceptionally successful in sharing his passion for quality and his vision of growth through intra-Asian, and not just Western-orientated trade. His success contributed greatly to that of the Malaysian palm oil industry as a whole that in turn represents one of the brightest icons for primary producers elsewhere, demonstrating that it is possible for industrial growth to be built on tropical agricultural foundations and to be sustained over generations. [2]

Bek-Nielsen's successes have brought him high personal honours, including the Malaysian titles of Tan Sri and Dato' Seri. However, he has been the first to acknowledge that his successes are founded upon the lessons he learnt from his colleagues and predecessors at United Plantations, and from colleagues elsewhere in the industry. The remarkable collaborative spirit within the Malaysian palm industry is one of its most attractive features, not least to the Danes within United Plantations (UP) with their strong national tradition of enthusiasm for the co-operative form of business enterprise. A further aspect of Danish culture, which appeals especially strongly to the modern Malaysian government, is the enthusiasm shown by successive company leaders – beginning with the founder, Aage Westenholz – for setting the highest possible welfare standards for the work-force, within the conventions of the day. [3]

For all these reasons the UP saga can be seen as an icon, not only of effective innovation but also of ethical conduct within plantation agriculture. This view was reflected in the landmark Malaysian government decision of 1991 that allowed the original Danish shareholders, in their new role as investors in Aarhus Oliefabrik A/S, to buy back a substantial stake in the firm. Like the shareholders of all other foreign firms owning plantations in Malaysia, United Plantations had been obliged to sell a controlling interest to 'sons of the soil', or *Bumiputeras*, in the early 1980s. Yet UP, unlike all the rest, were allowed – and chose – to return, this time as business partners with Malaysians rather than as sole owners, just a decade later. They bucked the 'globalization' trend of the 1990s, within which all new FDI (foreign direct investment) in South-East Asia was being made by new entrants. They also bucked the 'decolonization' trend, through which businesses set up in the colonial period withdrew their executives as well as their capital when faced with pressures for localization.[4]

Academic views on the 'decolonization' trend have been sharply divided. James Puthucheary, in his classic book written while in detention in Singapore's Changi jail in the late 1950s, argued that foreign ownership of the commanding heights of the Malayan economy was a serious weakness and a glaring injustice which should be rectified as soon as possible. Mohamed Amin and Malcolm Caldwell, in a hugely influential collection of essays published nearly two decades later, reinforced this view. They tried to explain why independent Malaysia had delayed far longer than most other Asian and African states in nationalizing foreign enterprises, largely by arguing that foreign firms in Malaya had inherited exceptional power from the colonial era.[5]

During the late 1970s and 1980s, as the trend towards localization gathered strength in Malaysia, and as Tony Stockwell led a fresh wave of empirical research into the era of decolonization, academic opinion began to shift. Both the late colonial administration 'on the spot' and the foreign firms then operating in Malaya came to be seen as being weakened by their social and political, as well as geographical, distance from the metropolitan centre of power. Peter Cain and Tony Hopkins's analysis of 'gentlemanly capitalism' and the wellsprings of imperial action, while not applied by the authors to the Malayan case, nevertheless inspired Nicholas White to see that the gentlemanly club of the City was one to which few Malayan planters belonged. For a time the economic interests of the City and of the imperial adventurers had coincided, but by the mid-1950s this was no longer the case.[6]

Once the economic interests of the metropolitan and peripheral capitalists began to diverge, there was no special reason for metropolitan strategists to insist that incoming leaders of former colonies should tailor their economic policies to suit the wishes of long-established European-owned businesses. Indeed, the 'development' orthodoxies of the 1950s suggested that local smallholders, working under the direction of an enlightened state, might well prove far better agents of economic growth – and welfare gains – than the old colonial firms. Tate's recent study of the Agency Houses, British-owned firms whose directors formed the backbone of the Malayan Rubber Growers' Association, provides ample evidence to support the view that, as early as the 1920s, these organizations were reluctant innovators who despised their smallholder competitors, but believed

3

that their own survival depended on state policies defending them against the smallholder threat.[7]

Fresh support for the view of British planters in Malaya (and their Agency House backers) as being fragile dinosaurs who came very close to extinction and to being blown away altogether by the 1950s winds of change has come from recent studies of the Malayan Emergency and of Malay politics in the era of decolonization. These accounts certainly have the ring of truth for anyone who has either lived through the events described or listened to the memories and read the memoirs of those who did. The authors show persuasively how the fear of more radical change helped to draw together the last colonial administrators, and the first Malay leaders of the state that was born in 1957 through *Merdeka* (independence). The conservative policies which resulted effectively preserved foreign ownership and the established management structures of the plantations sector for decades, despite all the arguments both of protesters and of Western development planners in favour of change.[8]

In all the debate over decolonization and development, few voices have emerged to challenge the academic consensus that the survival of the foreign firms through nearly 25 years of independent nationhood was a developmental disadvantage for Malaysia. This silence persists despite the mounting evidence that rapid nationalization, coupled with inadequate prior development of local managers, can cause a disastrous waste of the capital assets so painfully (and, as many would argue, expensively) built up in the form of estates, factories or trading operations at a local level under colonial rule. There are two main exceptions to this rule. At a general level, Gerold Krozewski has recently drawn attention to the fact that, while radical state-sponsored development projects failed elsewhere, the Malayan economy was going from strength to strength and continued to be the British Empire's main dollar earner throughout the 1950s. Since their economy wasn't broken, was it a great loss to the Malayan people if the development planners didn't fix it? Second, within the field of business history, the outstanding studies of Unilever by Charles Wilson and David Fieldhouse are soon to be brought up to date by Geoff Jones. Jones's recent study of the Agency Houses, in Malaya and elsewhere, has emphasized that their survival was due to their imaginative and flexible use of real business strengths, and not only to colonial discrimination and patronage.[9]

If Jones is right in arguing that the Agency Houses survived, and indeed continued to thrive after Merdeka, essentially because they were doing business effectively, then their survival is to be celebrated. The saga of United Plantations lends strength to this view, especially because the records of this firm, unlike those of the Agency Houses that have formed the main focus of the academic debate to date, lend themselves to the reconstruction of real cash flows and of developments at the level of production rather than trade.[10]

The picture which emerges from these records is entirely positive. United Plantations' shareholders, whether Scandinavian or Malaysian, have consistently ploughed back a substantial part of their profits into assets located in or firmly linked to Malaysia rather than expatriating the cash generated locally in the form of dividends or reverse investment flows. Furthermore, the investments which they have made have often embodied striking technical improvements, both in planting materials and in processing machinery, that have been successfully linked to an innovative and flexible marketing strategy. The wealth generated by the firm has thus been produced through real economic progress, and not as a byproduct of colonial patronage. Furthermore, work-force welfare has always been a priority for the management, and consistent attempts have been made to improve living conditions on the estates, quite apart from maintaining pay levels sufficient to attract and retain people in an increasingly competitive recruitment market.[11]

One of the reasons why the UP saga is such a positive story, and one of the main features which differentiate it from that of the more widely studied Agency House operations, is that United Plantations was among the earliest enterprises to realize the potential of the oil palm. Palm oil and kernels accounted for just 10 per cent of world trade in all oils and fats in 1962–65, as measured by volume. This share rose to 20 per cent in 1982–85 and 40 per cent in 1997–2000. Underpinning this rise in market share was a continuous development of new markets and processing methods that underpinned a spectacular increase in the range of applications for the more versatile of the two main palm products, palm oil. Palm oil, indeed, accounted for most of the growth in market share outlined above. In 1962–65, world exports of palm oil alone accounted for just 6 per cent of the total volume of trade in oils and fats. This proportion had grown to 17 per cent by 1982–85 and 38 per cent by 1997–2000. In the final period, world exports of palm oil averaged 13 million tonnes per annum, of which Malaysia accounted for 8 million tonnes, or just over 60 per cent.[12]

Many writers have noted that the oil palm has proved the economic salvation of Malaysia's plantations sector since the 1960s, without exploring the topic in any great depth. Yet the fact that, having switched to palm oil, the Agency House plantations thrived, raises at least one obvious and highly intriguing question. Could it be that the mid-twentieth century profitability problems, which underpinned the endless lobbying attempts of the RGA for colonial government support, arose not – as the 1950s development planners supposed – from the economic inefficiency of plantation enterprises in general but from the specific characteristics of the natural rubber industry in particular? The Malaysian rubber industry has been exhaustively studied by both economists and historians, and it is clear that smallholders were relatively efficient producers within it while the competition from synthetics drastically eroded the market for natural rubber, whether smallholder- or estate-produced, after 1940.[13]

The palm oil industry, by contrast, has offered substantial economies of scale ever since the 1940s, when technical innovation gave producers access to improved planting materials and mill-based processing machinery, and when developments in the world food industry created an expanding market, willing to pay a premium for the standardized, high-quality product of mill-based processing. Technical change, allied to a creative marketing strategy on the part of Bek-Nielsen and his fellow planters, effectively changed the rules of the game in this one branch of tropical agriculture. At the level of production within the oil palm industry, although not within the rubber industry in which no comparable changes occurred, the new rules of the game finally gave planters the edge over the smallholders who, since the 1920s, had been their highly effective rivals. At the level of international trade, the fortunes of the two agricultural export industries once again diverged. Unlike natural rubber, where technical change in the industrial West since 1940 has introduced new and effective competition from alternative products, a parallel set of changes in the case of palm oil has strengthened the Malaysian product's ability to compete with rivals on the world oils and fats market. Since 1960 the Malaysian palm oil industry has expanded dramatically to become both a major source of export revenues for the country and a major source of food for the world; and this expansion has been led by the plantations sector.[14]

While there is an extensive technical literature and a small body of economic work on the Malaysian palm oil industry, it has so far escaped the attention of historians. I came across it by chance while visiting the region in 1987, on a field study trip with fellow MBA students from the London Business School. At the time I was about to publish a book on the history of smallholder palm oil production in Nigeria. It was a shock to discover that, at the very same time as the Nigerian palm oil export industry had been entering a phase of terminal decline, the Malaysian plantations were embarking on a highly successful and innovative phase of expansion that continues to this day.[15]

With help from scholars associated with the Palm Oil Research Institute of Malaysia (PORIM: now part of the Malaysian Palm Oil Board), I was able to arrange visits to a number of plantations in 1987. These brought me into contact with United Plantations for the first time, renowned throughout the industry as an extremely well-managed operation with 'state-of-the-art' technology that welcomes visitors from all backgrounds. On the initial visit it quickly emerged that United Plantations' managers were extremely proud, not only of their current operations but also of their firm's innovative track record. The workers too, many of whom were second or third generation, took a keen interest in the estate communities' past. Hence, the remembered experiences of the workers, and the stories still told about the two charismatic founders, Aage Westenholz and Lennart Grut, and their successors, form a vital part of United Plantations' community life and culture today. Many people were keen to talk and even write about their past experiences, and the company records were well preserved. The wife of a former executive, Carrie Jørgensen, who has a degree in history, had already edited an excellent collection of materials on the early history of the company (to the late 1940s) which she generously made available to me.[16]

A further four-month visit to Malaysia and a one-month stay in Denmark in 1989 allowed for a more detailed study of all these sources. United Plantations provided full access to its rich set of company records. At the level of strategy and finance, the study is founded upon a full set of Directors' Reports and Accounts dating back to 1917, including most of the Chairman's Statements. By using techniques learnt at the London Business School, it was possible to extract details of cash flows from these sources.[17]

At the level of production, a full and fascinating picture emerged from the internal Annual Reports written by individual estate managers and engineers. These reports, again, go right back to the start of the palm oil adventure and are replete with detail on wage levels, housing and welfare schemes; production costs; major operational changes implemented during each year; and periodic crises which challenged the status quo. Further colour was added to the story by the letters preserved in the Chairman's Correspondence series and by the reminiscences of those who had lived through the events described. To supplement and balance the view obtained from internal documents and from interviews with United Plantations' staff, further interviews were conducted with industry colleagues and professional researchers. In England, extensive use has also been made of the publications of the Incorporated Society of Planters and of PORIM (now MPOB), which has an office in Hertford.[18]

The story that has emerged from all these sources still holds a fascination after 15 years of study. Its initial appeal came from the fact that it is so positive, unlike all the stories of Third World disasters which cram the pages of our newspapers in the West. Further interest has come from the detective work involved in uncovering the roots of successful strategic innovation and business survival, through a thicket of spectacular political events, social and economic transformations spanning a full century. Yet perhaps the most enduring charm has come from the culture and personalities that are revealed as the saga unfolds. For this reason, the organization of the chapters which follow has highlighted people, and not merely the drier divisions of theme and period.

The saga begins with Aage Westenholz's arrival in the East in 1885. The first chapter explores his family background, which has been of vital importance throughout United Plantations' history as family members have continued to be closely involved, both as investors and strategists, right into the twenty-first century. Westenholz's relationship with his wayward niece Karen Blixen is explored as a rich source of insights into his generous, compassionate but correct and hard-headed personality. His adventures with H.N. Andersen and other Scandinavians in Siam form the prelude to his decision to set up a rubber plantation in Lower Perak and to invite his brother-in-law Commander William Lennart Grut to join him in 1906. The orderly financial and administrative development of the new Malayan venture contrasts strongly with the anarchy which had prevailed in this frontier district before 1900 and with the tough daily lives of the early planting pioneers.

During the dramatic rubber slump of 1921–22 United Plantations came very close to bankruptcy, but as profits recovered Commander Grut began searching for opportunities to diversify the firm's output in order to spread future risks. Chapter 2 focuses on his decision to set up a new oil palm estate at Ulu Bernam, initially administered under a separate company name – Bernam Oil Palms – but which shared its managers and many board directors with the original firm. The sister companies finally merged under the name of United Plantations in 1966. From then on the two histories of the Malaysian palm oil industry in general, and the Perak estates in particular, are interwoven in each chapter. The story widens beyond Malaysia to include developments in Sumatra, where the palm oil plantation industry was pioneered. Later chapters include comparisons with smallholder production in Nigeria, and an account of technical break-throughs in the Belgian Congo, together with the story of how these innovations spread to Malaysia.

The timing of United Plantations' first investment in the palm oil industry was unfortunate; the trees matured and began producing fruit only in 1932, when the inter-war depression was reaching its worst stage. Aage Westenholz and Commander Grut faced a monumental battle to persuade the shareholders to carry on financing the planting programme at the expense of their own dividends. Conditions were equally difficult for the managers and workers on the estates, but they emerged from the crisis with a new sense of solidarity. This was reinforced both by Grut's fiery but loyalty-inspiring leadership style, and by Westenholz's philosophical ideals of co-operative working and profit-sharing. Bernam Oil Palms emerged from the slump as a well-run, cohesive company, poised to benefit from the new shipping and production technologies which were about to revolutionize the palm oil industry world-wide.

Chapter 3 explores the massive shock which then hit the system with the Second World War and the Japanese Occupation. These events are still vividly remembered by both managers and workers, and their life stories illuminate the general history of the era. The war devastated the palm oil trade but, thanks not least to the valiant efforts of the work-force in protecting the factory, European bungalows and furniture from post-war looters, the Danes were able to return in 1945 to estates that had been neglected but not destroyed. A new generation of managers set to work restoring them, led by Commander Grut's sons Olof and Rolf and by the extraordinary, instinctive engineer Axel Lindquist. Lindquist was an 'outsider' within the family firm, but he became essential to its recovery and to its future reform. He and his wife Ida worked together to obtain the essential spare parts needed to get the factory going, and he taught himself the necessary skills to begin making machinery on-site – thus beginning what has become a highly successful tradition of in-house engineering. Bernam Oil Palms got off to a flying start in the process of post-war reconstruction and made spectacular profits in the post-war boom.

The problem then arose of how to use these windfall gains, and Chapter 4 explores the strategy debates and experiments through which the directors attempted to resolve it. Set against the backdrop of the Malayan Emergency and the move towards independence (*Merdeka*) in 1957, the story has meaning not only for the debates on decolonization and development highlighted above but also for business strategists grappling anew with the issue of how best to invest plantation-sector profits today. Faced with political instability in tropical host countries, the temptation so often is to take the profits and invest elsewhere. However, United Plantations' experience suggests that this is by no means a safe option. Investing in agriculture in a new region simply adds unfamiliar environmental hazards to the known risks of local currency exchange rate movements, international commodity price fluctuations, war and revolution. Investing in a new sector, for example manufacturing, can add further risks. United Plantations has had some success with ventures in which it was able to apply managerial competences already developed in its core operations, but by 1960 its directors had taken the momentous decision to limit their exposure to fresh risks of this kind. Unlike the Agency Houses, which as Jones has shown were pursuing the path of geographic and sectoral diversification with increasing determination from the 1960s onwards, United Plantations turned back towards the plantations sector, towards the oil palm and towards Malaysia.[19]

Chapters 5, 6 and 7 show how this strategy was allied first with a continuing quest for quality linked with low cost in production, and second with a quest for integration. While Axel Linquist sought to integrate the production process right through the chain from seedlings to shipment, Olof Grut and Børge Bek-Nielsen strove to ensure that the quality gains were tailored to meet the changing needs of customers in the rapidly evolving world market. At the same time, Rolf Grut, aided and abetted by Bek and by the inspirational maverick Arne Bybjorg Pedersen, campaigned successfully to ensure that the firm kept abreast of the latest technical developments in the Congo and Sumatra. A complete cost revolution was achieved by the introduction to Malaysia of reliable breeding methods for the Tenera hybrid oil palm and the associated innovation of the screw press, which enabled mills to extract the oil efficiently from rich, pulpy Tenera fruit. United Plantations was quick to adopt both new techniques, and so by the 1970s was ideally placed to take full advantage of an unexpected explosion in world demand for palm oil. This arose in turn from separate technical developments in the West that had enabled refiners to process the red, strong-smelling and distinctively flavoured natural oil into a bland, white form that was ideal for use as an invisible ingredient in processed and convenience foods.

10

Not content with these achievements, Børge Bek-Nielsen rose to fame in the 1970s by developing an idea which Olof Grut had cherished for 40 years: that of making direct sales to Asia and Africa, and developing new products aimed specifically at end users within these markets. United Plantations' leaders thus anticipated, and then naturally found themselves in full agreement with, Mahathir's 'Look East' policy of the 1980s and 1990s. Marketing matters are notoriously ill-covered in company archives, as they represent a highly commercially sensitive area, and for United Plantations it has been possible to reconstruct only the origins and then the essential outline of the story. However, as shown in Chapter 8, United Plantations successfully led the way in the development of this branch of intra-Asian trade. As historians are beginning to argue with increasing conviction, the growth of intra-Asian trade in general is one of the great untold success stories of world economic history. Faced with the rise of American economic and political power even before the end of the cold war, and still more in the era of Internet-led globalization, it has been all too easy for Western historians to overlook the growing ability of Asian economies to derive strength from their links with one another.[20]

The story of the Malaysian palm oil industry since 1980 has been essentially the story of growth founded on intra-Asian trade, supported by the technical and marketing research of PORIM and by the development of a local refining and end-use manufacturing capacity within Malaysia itself. All these trends were strongly supported in their earliest stages by Børge Bek-Nielsen, who argued vigorously both at the industry level and within national policy-making circles for the establishment of PORIM in 1979 and before that for state support for the infant refining industry.

Ironically, United Plantations' own pioneering Unitata refinery, built inland and on a relatively small scale, has proved far better suited to the development of a specialty fats range aimed at high-value Asian and Western markets than to the bulk oil trade linked in with the more recent development of oleochemicals plants at Malaysia's major ports. With the development of the specialty fats trade has come an increasingly close relationship with the Danish firm of Aarhus Olie that eventually became the vehicle for the original shareholders' buyback of United Plantations shares in 1992. Hence, Chapter 9 concludes with the wheel turning full circle. United Plantations is once more a Danish as well as a Malaysian-owned company and once more selling high-quality products at a premium price to the European market. As shown in Chapter 10, this recent period has also seen a return to the earliest days of pioneering planting, with new jungle developments being made both by United Plantations and by the new Danish-Malaysian joint venture formed in 1987, United International Enterprises (Malaysia) Berhad. In developing and publishing new techniques for dealing with the ecological challenges encountered in the process of expansion, United Plantations' managers made a further contribution to the development of the industry as a whole.

Finally, Chapter 10 brings the story into the age of biotechnology and looks towards the future. So far, United Plantations has focused on orthodox plant breeding methods rather than on genetic engineering and has developed profitable lines of organic produce both in Malaysia and in its offshoot ventures abroad. However, the Malaysian palm oil industry in general is becoming increasingly interested in the idea of linking clonal plant breeding techniques to the more experimental gene technology. There is a very real possibility that the industry might be on the brink of yet another great leap forward, comparable to the sea-change of the 1950s – though, unlike the earlier advance, this new one may be seen to carry such high ethical and environmental costs that it simply cannot be allowed to happen.

Whatever the future may hold, the growth of the Malaysian palm oil industry has been a spectacular success story to date. Within this grander epic, the United Plantations saga is of special interest not only because of the company's strong contribution to the development process but also because of the culture and the charisma of the people involved. The enthusiasm shown by successive company chairmen and chief executives for employee welfare, national economic development and friendly collboration across both company and ethnic divides can only partly be explained by economic self-interest and political pressures. The culture created by the founders Westenholz and Grut, and before them by the pioneering community of Scandinavians in late nineteenth-century Siam, nourished by the Danish ideals of the Folk High School and co-operative movements, proved ideally suited to the new life of a late twentieth-century European business in an independent Asian state. Børge Bek-Nielsen could surely provide a template for the new generation of twenty-first-century foreign managers setting up fresh joint ventures in Malaysia in his easy embrace of the view that, after *Merdeka*, he was a guest in a sovereign Asian country, whose people had every right to a say in their own economic affairs.

The ease with which Bek-Nielsen accepted this view was not purely the result of his own culture and temperament; it also owes a great deal to the character of the people he was working with. Malaysia's national culture, emerging from the plural society of the colonial era, is not without its tensions but has been experienced by very many visitors as strikingly hospitable. Throughout a 50-year career, Bek-Nielsen and his fellow Europeans at United Plantations have found it congenial to work closely with a wide variety of local staff – whether Malay, Indian or Chinese in ethnic origin. Perhaps the key moment of truth came when Bek handed over the chairmanship of United Plantations to Dato' (now Tan Sri Dato' Seri) Haji Basir bin Ismail in 1982. Far from being a bitter pill to swallow, this proved to be the moment when a firm friendship was cemented. Two decades of further service as senior executive director have followed, throughout which Bek and his chairman have sustained a strong creative partnership which has brought new strength to the firm. In this way, as in so many others, the saga of United Plantations provides a beacon of hope for the future.

NOTES

1   Merrill Lynch quotation from Thomas Friedman, *The Lexus and the Olive Tree* (London: HarperCollins, 2000 edition), p. xvi; see also A.G. Hopkins, 'Back to the future: from national history to imperial history', *Past and Present*, vol. 164, 1999, pp. 198–243; and D.R. Headrick, *The Tentacles of Progress: Technology Transfer in the Age of Imperialism, 1850–1940* (New York: Oxford University Press, 1988).

2   On the concept of strategic innovation, see Charles Baden-Fuller and John M. Stopford, *Rejuvenating the Mature Business: the Competitive Challenge* (London: Routledge, 1992); Charles Baden-Fuller and Martyn Pitt (eds) *Strategic Innovation: an International Casebook on Strategic Management* (London: Routledge, 1996); and Constantinos C. Markides, *All the Right Moves: a Guide to Crafting Breakthrough Strategy* (Cambridge, MA: Harvard Business School Press, 2000).

3   More details on the history and culture of Danish businesses abroad may be found in Per Boje, *Danmark og de Multinationale Virksomheder før 1950* [Denmark and the multinational enterprises before 1950] (Odense: Syddansk Universitetsforlag, 2000).

4   On both trends, see J. Thomas Lindblad, *Foreign Investment in South-East Asia in the Twentieth Century* (Basingstoke: Macmillan, 1998); on business hostility to localization, see Nicholas J. White, *Business, Government and the End of Empire: Malaya, 1942–1957* (Kuala Lumpur: Oxford University Press, 1996).

5   J.J. Puthucheary, *Ownership and Control in the Malayan Economy* (Singapore: Donald Moore for Eastern Universities Press, 1960); Mohamed Amin and Malcolm Caldwell (eds) *Malaya: the Making of a Neo-Colony* (Nottingham: Spokesman Books, 1977).

6   A.J. Stockwell, 'Malaysia: the making of a Neo-Colony?' in P. Burroughs and A.J. Stockwell (eds) *Managing the Business of Empire: Essays in Honour of David Fieldhouse* (London: Frank Cass, 1998), pp. 138–156; and 'Introduction' in A.J. Stockwell (ed.) *Malaya: British Documents on the End of Empire* Series B, vol. 3, part I (London: HMSO, 1995), pp. xxxi–lxxxiv; P.J. Cain and A.G. Hopkins, *British Imperialism,* 2 vols. (London: Longman, 1993); Nicholas J. White, 'Gentlemanly capitalism and empire in the twentieth century: the forgotten case of Malaya, 1914–1965' in R.E. Dumett (ed.) *Gentlemanly Capitalism and British Imperialism: the New Debate on Empire* (London: Longman, 1999), pp. 175–196; and Nicholas J. White, 'The business and the politics of decolonization: the British experience in the twentieth century', *Economic History Review,* vol. LIII, no. 3, 2000, pp. 544–564.

7   White, *Business and Government* and *Decolonization: the British Experience since 1945* (London: Longman, 1999); D.J.M. Tate, *The RGA History of the Plantation Industry in the Malay Peninsula* (Kuala Lumpur: Oxford University Press, 1996). Contrast the positive view of British firms provided by G.C. Allen and A.G. Donnithorne, *Western Enterprise in Indonesia and Malaya: A Study in Economic Development* (London: Allen & Unwin, 1957), with the critiques provided in M. Havinden and D. Meredith, *Colonialism and Development: Britain and Its Tropical Colonies, 1850–1960* (London: Routledge, 1993); and I.G. Brown, *Economic Change in South-East Asia, c.1830–1980* (Kuala Lumpur: Oxford University Press, 1997), esp. Ch. 10.

8   The magisterial study by T.N. Harper, *The End of Empire and the Making of Malaya* (Cambridge: Cambridge University Press, 1999) is well complemented by the polemical approach of Frank Furedi, *Colonial Wars and the Politics of Third World Nationalism* (London: I.B. Tauris, 1994).

9   G. Krozewski, 'Sterling, the 'minor' territories, and the end of formal empire, 1939–1958', *Economic History Review,* vol. XLVI, no. 2, 1993, pp. 239–265 and *Money and the End of Empire: British Economic Policy and the Colonies, 1947–1958* (London: Palgrave, 2001); D.K. Fieldhouse, *Unilever Overseas: the Anatomy of a Multi-national, 1895–1965* (London: Croom Helm, 1978), and C. Wilson, *Unilever 1945–65* (London: Cassell, 1968); G. Jones, *Merchants to Multinationals: British Trading Companies in the Nineteenth and Twentieth Centuries* (Oxford: Oxford University Press, 2000). An instructive comparison is the case of Indonesia, most recently surveyed by Anne Booth, *The Indonesian Economy in the Nineteenth and Twentieth Centuries* (London: Macmillan, 1998).

10 On the problems of working with Agency House records, see Jones, *Merchants to Multinationals* and G. Jones and J. Wale, 'Diversification strategies of British trading companies: Harrisons & Crosfield, c. 1900–c. 1980', *Business History,* vol. 41, no. 2, 1999, pp. 69–101.

11 Edgar Graham and Ingrid Floering, *The Modern Plantation in the Third World* (London: Croom Helm, 1984) draws on Graham's personal experience of managing Malayan estates to argue that these benefits are characteristic of good plantation management and that Malaysian government planners have appreciated this to the extent of modelling their smallholder oil palm schemes upon the management structures of the estate sector.

12 C.W.S. Hartley, *The Oil Palm (Elaeis guineensis Jacq.)* 3rd edn (London: Longman, 1988), Table 1.6, p. 42; Malaysian Palm Oil Board (MPOB), *Malaysian Oil Palm Statistics 2001* (Kuala Lumpur: MPOB, 2002), Tables 6.5 and 6.9, also available via the website http://www.mpob.gov.my.

13 On palm oil, see for example J.H. Drabble, *An Economic History of Malaysia, c. 1800–1990: the Transition to Modern Economic Growth* (London: Macmillan, 2000); Jones, *Merchants to Multinationals*; and Lindblad, *Foreign Investment*. More detail on palm oil is provided in Tate, *RGA History*, Ch. 32. Classic publications on the rubber industry include Peter Bauer, *The Rubber Industry: a Study in Competition and Monopoly* (London: Longmans, Green & Co., 1948); J.H. Drabble, *Rubber in Malaya 1876–1922: the Genesis of the Industry* (Kuala Lumpur: Oxford University Press, 1973), and *Malayan Rubber: the Interwar Years* (London: Macmillan, 1991); C. Barlow, *The Natural Rubber Industry: Its Development, Technology and Economy in Malaysia* (Kuala Lumpur: Oxford University Press, 1978); C. Barlow, S. Jayasuriya and C. Suan Tan, *The World Rubber Industry* (London: Routledge, 1994); and A. Coates, *The Commerce in Rubber* (Kuala Lumpur: Oxford University Press, 1987). The view that rubber was unusually well suited to smallholders is supported by Headrick, *Tentacles of Progress*, p. 250.

14 The facts of expansion are detailed in Harcharan Singh Khera, *The Oil Palm Industry of Malaya: an Economic Study* (Kuala Lumpur: Penerbit Universiti Malaya, 1976) and H.A.J. Moll, *The Economics of the Oil Palm* (Wageningen Netherlands: PUDOC, 1987), but the interpretation in this paragraph is my own. For further details, see below, Chs 7 and 8; and K.G. Berger and S.M. Martin, 'Palm Oil', in K.F. Kiple and K. C. Ornelas (eds) *The Cambridge World History of Food*, vol. 1 (Cambridge: Cambridge University Press, 2000), pp. 397–411.

15 The 4th edition of Hartley, *Oil Palm*, revised by R.H.V. Corley and P.B.H. Tinker, is due to be published by Blackwell Science, Oxford, in 2003 and will provide further details on the world-wide picture. See also S.M. Martin, *Palm Oil and Protest: An Economic History of the Ngwa Region, South-Eastern Nigeria, 1800–1980* (Cambridge: Cambridge University Press, 1988).

16 Carrie Jørgensen, 'United Plantations and Bernam Oil Palms: highlights from a colourful past' (unpublished ms., 1984).

17   Claude Hitching and Derek Stone, *Understand Accounting!* (London: Pitman, 1984) is a good introduction to these techniques. Thanks are due to the School of Oriental and African Studies, University of London and to the Nuffield Foundation, which financed the fieldwork, and to United Plantations itself and its associated companies in Denmark, for providing hospitality, copies of the photographs and historical maps reproduced here and for sending regular updates on current events.

18   Dr B.A. Elias, Mohd Jaaffar Ahmad, and their staff in Hertford have also helped through informal discussions of the topics covered in this book. The responsibility for all the views expressed below, however, remains the author's alone.

19   Jones, *Merchants to Multinationals*, Chs 10–12.

20   The work of Japanese historians has been especially important in this field. See, for example, Kaoru Sugihara, 'Patterns of Asia's integration into the world economy, 1880–1913', in Wolfram Fischer, R. Marwin McInnis and Jurgen Schneider (eds) *The Emergence of a World Economy, 1500–1914. Beiträge zur Wirtschafts- und Sozialgeschichte*, Band 33–2 (Wiesbaden: Franz Steiner, 1986), and Shigeru Akita, 'British informal empire in East Asia, 1880–1939: a Japanese perspective', in Dumett (ed.), *Gentlemanly Capitalism*, pp. 141–156. Within Britain, John Latham has been the chief advocate of their point of view: see S.M. Miller, A.J.H. Latham and D.O. Flynn (eds) *Studies in the Economic History of the Pacific Rim* (London: Routledge, 1998); D.O. Flynn, L. Frost and A.J.H. Latham (eds) *Pacific Centuries: Pacific and Pacific Rim History since the Sixteenth Century* (London: Routledge, 1999); and A.J.H. Latham and H. Kawakatsu (eds) *Asia-Pacific Dynamism 1550–2000* (London: Routledge, 2000).

CHAPTER ONE

The Entrepreneur: Aage Westenholz

EARLY YEARS IN SIAM

*I*n 1885 a young Danish engineer arrived in the East, one of many Scandinavians who were attracted to Siam as naval volunteers or civil engineers, and who found themselves especially welcome there because of their status as citizens of neutral European states, posing no imperial threat. They were an enterprising and adventurous group; yet even within such a company, Aage Westenholz stood out. In partnership with his two equally energetic and forceful compatriots, Admiral Andreas de Richelieu and H.N. Andersen, he helped to transform Bangkok's infrastructure and made a fortune in the process. The capital which was later used to fund Karen Blixen's famous farm in Africa, and the first rubber trees at Jendarata, was therefore created in Siam, and had its roots in the three partners' rare combination of engineering skills, innovative flair and hard-headed business sense.[1]

Aage Westenholz came from a family rich in self-made men. His maternal grandfather was Andreas Nicolaj Hansen (1798–1873), who made his fortune in the shipping industry. In 1825 Andreas had married Emma Eliza Grut, the daughter of a vicar on Guernsey. The household was not altogether happy and, in reaction to this, the Grut rather than Hansen family name was later adopted by two of Andreas's and Emma's 12 children, Edmund and William. Their descendants in turn, under the family names Grut and Knudtzon, were later to play important roles in the UP saga. Aage's mother, on the other hand, remained her father's daughter. Mary Lucinde (1832–1915) kept the name Hansen until she married, and chose a husband some 17 years older than herself, cast in her father's entrepreneurial mould. The son of a town clerk from northern Jutland, Regnar Westenholz had grown wealthy through exporting Danish corn, especially during the profitable years following the repeal of the British Corn Laws in 1846. He retired in 1852 to the country estate of Matrup, near Horsens in central Jutland, and married Mary Lucinde the following year. Aage was the fourth of their six children, born on 18 April 1859.

This prosperous household was thrown into disarray in 1866 when Regnar died, leaving his widow to care for their children and to administer his estate on behalf of his elder son, Asker. The children were brought up in a strict and cloistered atmosphere. Aage's sister Ingeborg was to break out at the age of 25 by marrying the adventurous soldier and traveller Wilhelm Dinesen. The marriage ended abruptly with Wilhelm's suicide in March 1895, but not before it had produced a remarkable daughter, Karen Blixen (Isak Dinesen), who was to become a world-famous traveller and storyteller. Judith Thurman's outstanding biography of Blixen highlights the stifling effect of the upright bourgeois milieu within which the descendants of Andreas Hansen lived in Denmark and helps to explain the quest for adventure which animated so many of them. Aage Westenholz himself figures in the Blixen story as the stern uncle who financed her Kenyan coffee farm but who could not support it forever. In Karen Blixen's letters to her mother and brother, he appears from time to time in the guise of a hard-headed businessman with little sympathy for non-bourgeois values; but perhaps they had more in common than she realized, for in the very year of her birth, in 1885, Aage had launched forth on his own voyage of discovery and sailed for the East.[2]

When he first arrived in Bangkok as a newly qualified civil engineer, aged 26, Aage Westenholz began working for the Bangkok Brick and Tile Company. He then became manager of the Bangkok Tramways Co., Ltd., which was given a tax-free concession by King Chulalongkorn in May 1887. This company had an influential Danish chairman, Andreas du Plessis de Richelieu, chief naval aide to the king; but it suffered from a shortage of cash. The partners sought capital by public subscription from English shareholders, and in 1888 they opened their pioneer service, a car drawn by local ponies along a 4-mile track between the palace and the main wharf of the Bangkok Dock Company on the Chao Phraya River. Eventually this service expanded to use over 300 ponies, and in 1891 Westenholz travelled to America to study electric tramways and power generating systems there. On his return to Siam he electrified the existing Bangkok tramway, some ten years before an electric tramway system was constructed in Copenhagen. He also became involved in a new venture, the Paknam Railway,

Aage Westenholz

for which Richelieu had obtained a royal concession in 1891. Once again there were financial difficulties, eventually resolved by an investment of 172,000 baht from King Chulalongkorn. The 25-kilometre railway was eventually completed in 1893 and ran successfully as Siam's only private line until 1936, when it was taken over by the state.[3]

Despite Westenholz's technical successes in the field of railed transport, he was always reluctant to remain stuck in one groove. On 16 July 1893, in the face of a threatened French naval attack on Bangkok, he enlisted in the Siamese navy as a private. Almost immediately his bravery and his skills, not least his fluent command of the Thai language, were recognized and he was given the commissioned rank of captain. Naval and military matters were to remain important to Westenholz throughout his life; he attached great importance to the discipline and fortitude which a military training could produce. The sea captain and author Christmas Moller, who knew him in Siam, described him as being brisk and sure in his movements, on the move early and late, but hesitant in his speech because he wanted to choose exactly the right words to express his thoughts. Contemporary portraits bear out this impression of military precision, showing a slim, straight figure with a neat moustache, penetrating eyes and a firm chin. Moller also wrote that he was hospitable to a fault, a great arranger of games and dispenser of kindly advice, much liked and admired by all the young Danes who knew him. Nevertheless, even while at play he retained his dignity, as shown in a revealing photograph taken by Karen Blixen's brother Thomas in 1921. Sitting in the grass on a Kenyan hillside, his legs relaxed and his hands toying with a picnic mug, Westenholz's back remained straight, his shoulders well-thrown back and his jaw firm.[4]

Clearly, the mature Aage Westenholz was a man of great self-control and a man who respected this quality in others. He did his best to encourage its development in young Danes by a variety of means. In 1907 he wrote a stirring memorandum calling for improvements in the morale and training of Denmark's defence forces, and on his retirement from the East in 1911 he became involved in various projects, including a group of bicycle scouts and a motorcycle corps. His grandest adventure came during the years following the Russian Revolution of 1917, when he became caught up in the struggle of non-Bolshevik Baltic states against their strong eastern neighbour. Politicians in countries like Finland, Poland and Lithuania saw in the revolution an ideal opportunity to break free from Russian political domination, although there were profound divisions of opinion on whether this should be done in alliance with the Russian Bolsheviks, or in opposition to them. In the latter case it was vital to have outside support, as the Finnish White Guards found in appealing to both Sweden and Germany. Aage Westenholz's personal opposition to Bolshevism combined with the lure of such nationalist appeals to draw him into the Lithuanian campaign, in which the troops of independent Poland and Soviet Russia fought for control of the Lithuanian capital, Vilna, in January–April 1919. Westenholz raised and equipped a private army of about 3,000 men at his own expense. His family viewed the venture with mixed feelings, and Karen Blixen criticized her uncle vigorously for his involvement in what she saw as an anti-democratic struggle. In the event the expedition was not a military success, but it provided a good testing ground for potential managers. Several officers from the Westenholz Volunteer Corps became estate managers for United Plantations in the 1920s, including Major A. 'Fatty' Paulsen, who remained with the company from 1921 to 1934; Ivar Paulsson (1925–31); and V. Thorbjornsen (1925–30), the first general manager of Bernam Oil Palms.[5]

Back in the 1890s, however, Westenholz left the Siamese Navy once the French naval threat to Bangkok was at an end and returned to his earlier work on the city's newly electrified tramway. In 1895 he found a fresh challenge and joined the Siam Land, Canals and Irrigation Company, who were working on the Rangsit canal just north of Bangkok. Westenholz worked on the innovative lock gates which enabled the Rangsit system to retain water for cultivation. He also designed a huge wind-powered tricycle, with six-foot wheels and an enormous sail, which could be used to cross the paddy fields.[6]

Meanwhile, Andreas de Richelieu had gained the rank of admiral and commander-in-chief of the Siamese navy and had decided to join forces with H.N. Andersen of the East Asiatic Company in his most ambitious business venture to date: the creation of a new company to generate and supply electricity to Bangkok. Such a project could not fail to excite Westenholz, and he agreed to become manager of the new concern in 1898, a post which carried with it a seat on the board. The Siam Electricity Company quickly became profitable, taking over the Bangkolem and Samsen Tramway Companies by 1901 and moving all their generating equipment to a central electric light station at Wat Lieb, Bangkok. Westenholz's earlier experience with tramways helped him to manage the united concern with great efficiency, and by the time Andreas de Richelieu and his younger brother Louis retired from the East in 1902, Westenholz had become the dominant force in the firm's affairs. In 1903 he became chairman of the Board of Directors and remained at the helm until 1927. By 1906 he was actively promoting new business ventures of his own. One such venture was the Menam Motor Boat Co., Ltd., which ran steamers along the Chao Phraya River, and may be seen as a logical extension of Westenholz's earlier interest in transport innovations. The second was far more adventurous and marked a radical break with his earlier career. This was the Jendarata Rubber Company, set up to exploit the opportunities which had newly arisen under British colonial rule in Siam's southern neighbour, the Federated Malay States.[7]

No records survive of the early shareholders in the Jendarata Rubber Company, but the Siam Electricity Company was Jendarata's main promoter and it probably held a large proportion of the new shares. Certainly, the new company's seat was in Bangkok, although its nationality was Danish and it had an attorney in Copenhagen. Three out of the five original directors were also on the Board of Siam Electricity: Aage Westenholz, who was chairman of both companies; H. Dehlholm, who was vice-chairman of the new venture; and Captain T.A. Gottsche of the Siamese navy. The first estate manager at Jendarata, Captain Frederik von Zernichow, was a veteran of the Siamese provincial gendarmerie. Zernichow and one Vilhelm Gedde, who was based at Jendarata, formed the last two members of the board. It can thus be seen, not only that the Jendarata Rubber Company was very closely linked to Siam Electricity, but also that its board consisted solely of Eastern residents. This stood in contrast to the situation at Siam Electricity, where four out of the ten directors lived in Copenhagen. The Jendarata Rubber Company was essentially an Eastern spin-off venture from Siam Electricity, with an unknown contribution from private Bangkok investors and from the promoters' families back in Denmark.[8]

Aage Westenholz's motive for establishing the Jendarata Rubber Company was essentially financial. By 1906 the Siam Electricity Company's profits from tramways were levelling off, and he was seeking alternative outlets for the funds still flowing in from its power supply business. The rubber boom had just begun in Malaya, but Westenholz was reluctant to invest in rubber in the way which was becoming normal at the time – that is, indirectly, through one of the many small companies which were being floated on the London Stock Exchange under the auspices of large British trading houses like Guthrie's. Siam Electricity promoted the Jendarata venture itself, 'on the principle that this Company should avoid investing in concerns off which the cream has been taken by other promoters ("skimmed milk")'.[9]

22

RUBBER IN PERAK

Westenholz ventured into the Federated Malay States at a particularly auspicious moment. Thirty years earlier it would have been inconceivable to plant rubber in the Bernam region, in the far south of Perak. The crop itself was virtually unknown and the region was a thinly populated border zone, the lawless lair of pirates and smugglers. British officials were only just setting foot in it and took little interest in the land itself or in its agriculture. Their main concerns were to explore the rivers, control the tin and opium trades and identify the local leaders most likely to co-operate. Only slowly, and almost by accident, did they create the conditions under which, by 1906, rubber could be successfully planted at Jendarata.

Barbara Watson Andaya, the leading modern historian of Perak, paints a vivid picture of the Bernam region in the late eighteenth century as a 'canker area … underpopulated and undergoverned … low-lying, unhealthy and in-fertile.' Its main inhabitants were a group of rebellious junior royals from Kedah, who subsisted miserably on home-grown rice and piracy. By the late nineteenth century, little had changed. The Bernam region remained a thinly populated boundary area between the states of Perak and Selangor, with a few fishing villages near the Bernam River mouth and some rice cultivation further up-river. It does not even rate a mention in John Gullick's very thorough survey of contemporary Malay society and is treated only briefly in the writings of con-temporary travellers.[10]

Frank Swettenham was the first British official to visit this remote region, travelling there in a spirit of curiosity and adventure in 1875. His journey can be followed on Map 2.[11] Swettenham set off by steam launch on 7 February, travelling south from the British base at Bandar Bahru on the Perak River to the settlement then called Durien Sebatang (now known as Teluk Intan and in the colonial period as Telok Anson). Here the Perak River bends sharply westwards and is joined by the Bidor River, flowing in from the east. The Bidor River was too small for Swettenham's steam launch, and so he continued up it by oar, striking off after a further day's travel up the Songkei (now Sungkai) River, which flows further south and is smaller still. After some heavy poling the party reached Songkei, where they switched to a smaller boat, and after a further day's journey set off on foot to Trolah (now Terolak). One more day spent tramping up and down hills, past hot springs and through thickets of bamboo, and wading waist-deep through three rivers, brought Swettenham to Slim (now Selim). Tin

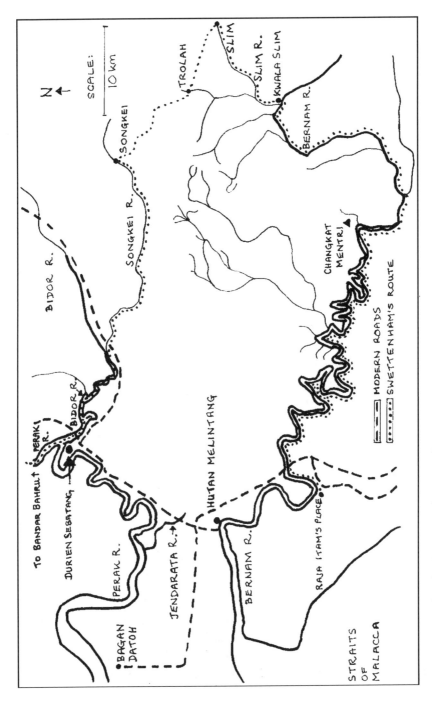

Map 2: Swettenham's visit to Southern Perak, 1875

mining had just begun in this region, which was well populated but very poor, and whose rulers were keen to assist Swettenham. He in turn was eager to explore the direct river route from Slim to the coast, not least because he had hurt his foot coming down the last hill and could no longer bear to wear socks and shoes. A five-man dug-out was brought from ten miles away, and on 13 February he set off down the Slim River, heading for the Bernam region.[12]

After two days of 'very exciting and enjoyable' adventures shooting rapids, and more tiresome manoeuvres dodging half-fallen trees and dragging the boat over fallen logs, Swettenham's party reached the Bernam River at 'Kwala Slim' and camped overnight on a deserted sand-spit. It took them a further three days to reach 'Raja Itam's place', where the steam launch had been sent to await their arrival. Raja Hitam, a Selangor royal, controlled the Sabak Bernam region. He was known to Swettenham because Sultan Abdullah had decided to grant Hitam temporary rights over the Perak side of the river too, at a meeting which Swettenham had attended. Raja Hitam's place thus represented a frontier post for the administration, a point to which they already knew that the Bernam River was navigable and where a launch could wait in safety. However, it was a long way from Kwala Slim, about 120 winding river-miles as estimated by Swettenham during his journey, and he soon began to wish fervently that he could summon the launch to meet him mid-way.[13]

On their first day on the Bernam River, Swettenham and his companions were plagued by wasps, terrified by crocodiles, confused by forks in the river and heard no sound save the shrieks of birds and the crashings of elephants in the jungle. They camped overnight near Changkat Mentri, now a landmark on United Plantations' upriver estates, where Swettenham noticed that the river was beginning to show the influence of the tides. He was sure that his steam launch could have penetrated that far upriver. The following day brought an encounter with a boat coming upriver from Raja Hitam's place, followed in the late afternoon by their first sighting of a house. Rowing through the night in torrential rain, they passed a further 50 or 60 houses, 'almost all new', before reaching Raja Hitam's kampong in the early afternoon of 17 February. From here to the sea the region was well populated, especially on the Selangor side, where fishing stakes extended well out into the river. Nevertheless, the people took care to live and bathe at a distance from the crocodile-infested banks.[14]

Swettenham concluded that the Bernam was 'a magnificent river', but it remained true that it was surrounded by a wild and forbidding region. The dense jungle was home to few if any people; its main inhabitants were barking deer, elephants, rhinoceros and black buffaloes, together with the occasional tiger. The area was very loosely controlled by Raja Hitam; it harboured at least one political fugitive, Raja Dolah of Klang in Selangor, and on the Perak side it was the location of a profitable opium trading route operated by one Raja Laxamana (also known as the Laksamana). This route ran through the jungle between Hutan Melintang on the Bernam River and the Jendarata River, which flows into the Perak River.[15]

The next British visitor to the region was Swettenham's superior, J.W.W. Birch, who had been appointed the first British resident to Perak in November 1874. He was drawn to the Bernam River in October 1875 by a rumour that Raja Dolah was about to become involved in a revolt against the sultan of his home state, Selangor. Once there, Birch decided to tighten up the system of tax collection in the riverside settlements, and he persuaded Raja Hitam to delegate this task to his brother, Raja Indut. Indut also promised Birch to cut a path through to the Jendarata River from Hutan Melintang, on the Bernam River. Birch hoped that once the road was cut, increased movement and settlement along it would halt Raja Laxamana's opium trade, which he viewed as smuggling.[16]

Birch was highly unpopular in Perak, and he was murdered just two weeks after his visit to the Bernam region. The Laksamana's smuggling career was brought to an unexpected close as a result: as one of the ten Perak chiefs implicated in the murder, he was arrested in September 1876 and exiled to the Seychelles. Raja Hitam, who had remained loyal to the British throughout, quietly took over his trade. By June 1877 the administration were well aware that he was growing rich by bringing opium surreptitiously from Selangor into Perak, exploiting the fact that the government import tax on opium was twice as high in the latter state. Yet Hugh Low, who served as resident in Perak from 1877 to 1889, preferred to avoid confrontations with the few remaining local leaders. He proved an extremely effective administrator, who persuaded the rajas and village penghulus to co-operate with his policies by generosity rather than through force. He established a political climate in which Europeans could feel safe; but he spent very little on path clearance, and it was not until Swettenham's residency in Perak, 1889–1895, that the region's rail and road infrastructure was put in place. A road along the route recommended by Birch was eventually cut and now forms part of the main trunk route from Kuala Lumpur to Teluk Intan. This road marks off the western boundary of Jendarata Estate, and the early planters could hardly have done without it. Together with the orderly administration established by Low, it enabled Aage Westenholz to move confidently in 1906 into territory which just 30 years before had been uncontrolled and virtually uninhabited.[17]

Westenholz was among the first plantation entrepreneurs to see the attractions of Lower Perak. During the nineteenth century, Chinese tapioca, gambier and pepper planters preferred to concentrate on Johore, Malacca and southern Selangor, which were closer to the lucrative Singapore market. Meanwhile, Europeans tended to leave the safe haven of the Straits Settlements (Penang, Malacca, Singapore and Province Wellesley) only in order to seek out the hilly land on which coffee could grow. The rise of a sugar industry in the mid-1880s attracted their attention to low-lying coastal areas, but within Perak the European sugar planters were slow to move south from their first base in Krian, just south of Province Wellesley. In 1898 John Turner made a pioneering investment in the Lower Perak region, planting sugar cane on the Rubana and Nova Scotia Estates. But this investment came just a few years before the sugar industry began to decline in 1905. Sugar exports from Perak had virtually ceased by 1914; most estates had been replanted with coconuts, though rubber had taken over on Rubana and Nova Scotia.[18]

One especially imaginative European planter, Thomas Heslop Hill, had begun planting rubber as a shade tree on his coffee estates as early as 1883. However, the crop did not catch on within the planting community as a whole until the mid-1890s, when H.N. Ridley began distributing rubber seedlings from the Singapore Botanical Gardens, and when coffee prices collapsed while rubber prices soared. Fungoid diseases and pest problems on coffee estates accelerated the growth of interest in rubber. Between 1895 and 1904 many hillside coffee estates were replanted with the new crop, and from 1897 the Federated Malay States were offering land concessions on fixed, low rents to rubber planters only. Selangor and central Perak were the most popular areas at first, but by 1905 the scramble for land was reaching all districts with reasonable river or rail transport facilities. By December 1906 there were 87 estates within Perak alone, with a total of 12,000 planted hectares, of which 60 per cent had been planted in 1906 itself.[19]

Aage Westenholz arrived in Perak at the height of the boom. In Lower Perak alone, a further 5,300 hectares of virgin jungle were applied for by would-be planters in 1906, including the 750 hectares applied for by the Jendarata Rubber

Company itself. The Jendarata Rubber Company was thus one of a crowd – but it was unusual in being promoted before the land was granted, and in the strong links outlined above between the owners, the promoters and the local managers. Most of the planters who were applying for land in Malaya at this time were adventurous individuals, who would form companies only at a later date, often once planting had already begun. Relatively little capital was needed to start up an estate, but heavy investment was required to extend planting across the full area of land granted and to sustain the venture through the five years of careful tending needed to prepare the trees for tapping.[20]

Most of the companies floated to finance the new rubber estates were London-based and were promoted through the 'agency house' system. A few were floated locally in Penang or Singapore, attracting investment from Europeans resident in Malaya or Shanghai, but even among these companies, several were later refloated in London, taking advantage of the much greater financial resources of the imperial capital. In either case, the newly created company would raise funds on the strength of its land assets. Within the 'agency house' system, the flotation would be arranged by one of the large merchant houses of Singapore, whose London office would act as guarantor of the new company's integrity for the British shareholders. The merchant house would also act as 'managing agent' to the new concern, supplying all its inputs, handling the sale of its produce and advising on its management. Often some kind of commercial or financial agreement had existed between the individuals concerned and their future agents, even before the advent of rubber. This was especially true of planters who were shifting from coffee to rubber in the late 1890s. For example, Thomas Heslop Hill had borrowed money from Tom Scott of Guthrie & Co. in 1877, at the start of his coffee-planting career. Hill later sold his main Perak estate, Kamuning, to a consortium including Tom Scott. Guthrie's acquired the agency for this estate in 1896, which marked the beginning of their plantations business.[21]

Clearly there was great scope for profit-taking by the Singapore/London merchant houses within this system – sometimes through their direct involvement in the sale and purchase of land, as well as through the commissions which they charged for their professional services. Westenholz therefore had every reason to be wary of buying shares in their 'skimmed milk' client companies. Yet his decision to make a direct investment had much wider implications than this simple one of concentrating the profit in fewer hands.

The concentration of profit sprang from a concentration of ownership and management control that in turn made for an unusual closeness of communication and of purpose that remains one of the hallmarks of United Plantations today. Local managers, board members and owners have remained closely linked – often by personal ties of friendship and family. Such links have continually renewed the company's distinctive culture, which over the decades has proved capable both of sustaining loyalty and of fostering innovation.

EARLY YEARS AT JENDARATA

Rubber cultivation began at Jendarata in 1907, when 255 hectares of jungle were cleared and planted up. Over the following four years a further 475 hectares were brought under cultivation, leaving just 20 hectares for houses, roads and factory buildings. These bare statistics are the only record which now remains of the first years at Jendarata, a time of toil and struggle both for the pioneering managers and for their indentured Tamil work-force. Not least among their difficulties must have been that of communication – Danes from Siam can have had little preparation for life in a society where the dominant languages were English, Tamil and Malay. Added to this difficulty were those of health, food and safety in the wild Bernam region, where elephants and other wild animals were slow to concede defeat. The jungle itself was difficult to clear; sometimes drainage was needed even before the first trees could be felled, because the low-lying ground was soft and marshy. The initial rounds of felling and burning had to be followed by more clearing of the lighter surface vegetation and then by repeated campaigns against lallang, the fast-growing grass which could strangle young rubber seedlings. No ground was cleared without a compelling reason, as can be seen in a rare surviving photograph of the first Jendarata Bungalow. Built in 1906, this was a simple wooden structure with a plain *atap* (palm-frond thatch) roof, fronted with a garden of rubber seedlings and backing straight on to the jungle. Home comforts were few and far between, and the isolation of the planters was great.[22]

Despite the difficulties of this pioneering life, the planters and their work-force managed to produce a healthy stand of rubber trees, and tapping began in 1911. A factory was erected, and 33,000 lbs of saleable rubber were produced. As the demands of this work grew, and as revenue began to flow in, the European staff of the estate grew to include an engineer, O.F.V. Busch (later to

Jendarata estate manager's bungalow, 1906

join the Westenholz Volunteer Corps) and five planting assistants, including Manager Zernichow's brother. The managers on the estate began to form a community and to become more involved in the affairs of the planting fraternity as a whole, especially when the Jendarata Rubber Company joined the Rubber Growers' Association in 1913. Finally, the shareholders began to see results when the company paid its maiden dividend, of 10 per cent for the year 1912.[23]

The question now arose of how the remaining profits should be reinvested. The rubber industry had already experienced a marked slump in 1907–08, followed by an equally marked boom in 1909–10. By 1912 prices were beginning to decline again and, as John Drabble has shown, this decline was to continue throughout the next decade. Hence the wisest course for an investor was clearly to diversify; and this is what Westenholz chose to do. Jendarata Estate was expanded through a fresh land concession of 200 hectares, which were planted up with coconuts between 1912 and 1914. The choice of coconuts was not accidental: Malay farmers had long appreciated the strength of this palm when grown on alluvial coastal soils, and it had been the first choice of Perak planters when they made their first switch away from sugar, on the eve of the rubber boom.[24]

Although his plantation venture was thriving, Westenholz himself was now in the process of retiring from the East to his family home, a small estate at Birkerød, now a suburb but then a rural area, near Copenhagen. In 1910 he had handed over control of Siam Electricity to his wife's brother, Commander William Lennart Grut (1881–1949). The family connection was extremely close, for Mrs Westenholz, nee Ellen Margrethe Grut (1875–1957) was the grand-daughter of A.N. Hansen. Her father, William Grut-Hansen, had served in the Danish army but became disillusioned following the loss of Schleswig-Holstein to Germany in 1864. He then decided to make a new life in Sweden and settled at Gammelstorp near Lake Vaenern. W.L. Grut had been brought up there and had begun his career in the Swedish navy, but following the marriage of Aage and Ellen in 1903 he became increasingly interested in the East. In 1906 he travelled out to join his brother-in-law and found himself committed to a permanent tie with Asia even before he had arrived. On the long sea journey he made the acquaintance of Helen Aiko Conder (1883–1974), the daughter of Professor Josiah Conder, the first English professor of architecture at Tokyo University, and his Japanese wife Kume Maeba. With typical decisiveness, Lennart became engaged to Helen before the voyage was out, and they were married in St Andrew's Church, Tokyo, on 8 November 1906. Returning to Bangkok, he resumed his training at Siam Electricity, and by 1910 he was sufficiently experienced to take over Aage's leading role there. He also became general manager of the Jendarata Rubber Company.[25]

Having handed over the management of his Eastern ventures, Aage Westenholz now became anxious to relinquish their ownership and to acquire fresh assets closer to home. In 1912 he sold a large stake in both Siam Electricity and Jendarata to the Belgian consortium of Jadot & Co., which agreed to retain all the staff employed at the time of the takeover. Jules Jadot himself was a Bangkok accountant, who had worked together with Lennart Grut in the Siam Electricity Company. However, the promised continuity was not so easily achieved in practice. By May 1913 Grut had withdrawn from the management of Siam Electricity and was becoming involved in an independent concern, the Siam Cement Company. Meanwhile, Westenholz had failed in an attempt to persuade another member of his family to take on the management of his Malayan venture. When Karen and Bror Blixen became engaged in December 1912, he had invited Bror to exchange his dairy farm at Stjarneholm in Skane, Sweden, for the rubber plantation. Bror was enthusiastic about this for a while

– until the more tempting project of Kenyan coffee farming was suggested by another uncle. In the event, Aage put up half the cash needed to buy the Kenyan farm, while retaining his interest in Jendarata. Meanwhile, three Brussels-based directors (Charles Charlier, Victor Dooms and William S. Hulze) had joined the Jendarata board, and plans began to be made for the establishment of a Brussels office for the company.[26]

These plans were thwarted only by the outbreak of the First World War in August 1914. Belgium became a major theatre of war and communications between Brussels and the British colonies in the East became impossible. Denmark's neutral status left her Jendarata board members in a far better position to maintain contact with their colleagues in Bangkok and their staff in Malaya; yet even in the Danish case, travel restrictions made it impossible for European-based board members to maintain a personal involvement in the company's affairs. Thus, although the Jendarata Rubber Company's head office had been moved to Copenhagen in 1914, the real architect of the firm's fate during the war years was Commander Lennart Grut, who was still residing in Bangkok and who made regular visits to the estates.[27]

Under Commander Grut's supervision a tight discipline was maintained on the estates. He had a well-known and passionate antipathy to lallang, the choking grass which was so quick to appear in the fields if weeding was neglected and would tour the estates on his bicycle looking for it. An assistant could be given 24 hours' notice if lallang was found in his fields. However, Commander Grut was warm in his support of those who passed muster. Two assistants from this period, Thorkild Dahl and a Swede, Sven Hallen Schwartz, eventually rose to become directors of United Plantations on their retirement from the East in the 1920s. During the war itself, their job involved plenty of challenge and excitement, with the opening up of fresh estates and the takeover of the formerly German-owned Rajah Una Company.[28]

The wider economic context of the Jendarata managers' activities was still dominated by the fluctuating fortunes of the rubber industry. During the early years of the war, Singapore rubber prices held up well, as the loss of German markets was offset by a tremendous growth in demand from the American automobile industry. Nevertheless, Commander Grut remained keen on developing Westenholz's policy of diversification into coconuts. This was an unusually far-sighted view, as most of his European contemporaries in Malaya were continuing to expand their rubber holdings, at least until the entry of the

United States into the war in 1917, which led to an abrupt shift of American industrial energies from automobiles to armaments. The wisdom of the Grut–Westenholz strategy became even more clear during the years which followed. Shipping shortages led to a large build-up of stocks in the East in late 1917, continuing throughout 1918. The depressing effect of these stocks on post-war prices had hardly begun to lift when the dramatic industrial slump of 1921 once again curtailed demand for rubber in the West. The new Malayan plantings of 1914–16 became an economic liability, and the voluntary output restriction schemes of the Rubber Growers' Association gave way to the government-sponsored Stevenson Scheme (1922–28).[29]

Within this turbulent context of war, boom and slump, the Jendarata Rubber Company continued to thrive and grow. Two hundred hectares were acquired in 1914 and planted up with coconuts by 1916. A further 800 hectares of peaty jungle land were then obtained, bringing the total Jendarata holding to almost 2,000 hectares – two and a half times its size in 1906. The rubber boom meant that a record profit was made in 1916, and a record dividend of 80 per cent was declared. Meanwhile, Westenholz had started a new venture, the Westenholz Brothers Estate, located on the south bank of the Bernam River just opposite Jendarata, and shown on Map 3. This was to become the heart of today's Sungei Bernam Estate. It contained 470 hectares of jungle land, of which 410 were cleared and planted up with coconuts in 1914–15. These stands were flanked on either side by the Erik and William Estates, both belonging to the Rajah Una Company, comprising 670 hectares which were cleared and planted with coconuts between 1913 and 1915. Aage Westenholz seized the opportunity to acquire these estates when they were expropriated from their former German owners after the outbreak of the First World War. At the same time he purchased the Corner Coconut Company from Straits Plantations Limited. The Corner estate consisted of 620 hectares of jungle land, which were planted up with coconuts between 1914 and 1917 under the supervision of the new Rajah Una manager, a former Jendarata assistant called Naested. From Straits Plantations' point of view the estate had been isolated, lying across the Bernam River from their main holdings on the Bagan Datoh peninsula. However, it made a useful addition to William, Erik and Westenholz Bros. Estates, neatly filling the gap between the northern boundary of William Estate and a sharp bend in the Bernam River. All four estates, low-lying and wetter than Jendarata, were plagued with malaria and cholera. Managers had to continue fighting these diseases for decades – not least

33

Map 3: United Plantations' estates, 1917

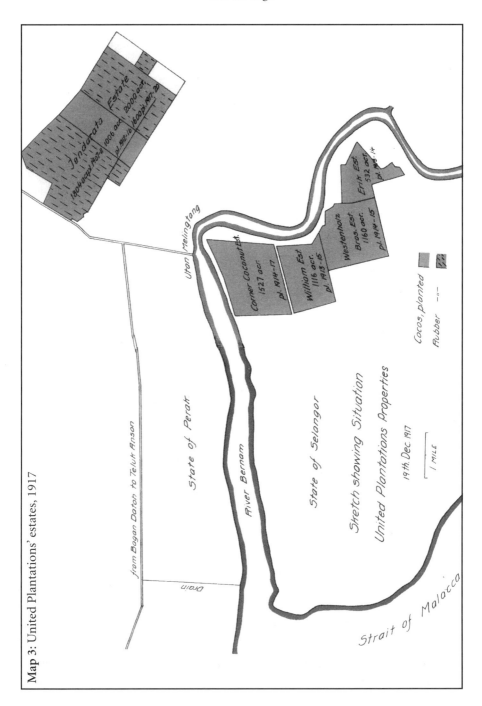

by constructing and maintaining an effective drainage system. However, the environment proved ideal for coconuts, which are still the major crop here and on the equally low-lying and swampy Bagan Datoh peninsula to the north.[30]

THE PLANTATIONS UNITE

Once the Corner, Westenholz Bros and Rajah Una Estates had been planted up and were almost ready to come into bearing, Westenholz's thoughts turned towards the legal framework surrounding their administration. It clearly made good practical sense to combine the neighbouring Corner, William, Westenholz and Erik Estates into a single managerial unit. The linking of this unit and Jendarata within a single corporate framework also seemed eminently sensible. The existing practice of moving managers between the various estates allowed the company to make flexible use of their skills and allowed individual planters much greater scope for career development and variety than would have been possible within a single estate. A further point in favour of union was that the 1,750 hectares of coconuts in the estates south of the river provided an admirable complement to the 750 hectares of rubber at Jendarata that Grut and Westenholz planned to expand to 1,150 hectares by the end of 1918. Fluctuations in the rubber market could be offset by revenue from coconuts to cushion the company against financial risks. Finally, the way in which the amalgamation was organized allowed the Belgian shareholders to withdraw gracefully from a venture which no longer attracted them in the way it had in the optimistic days before the war.[31]

On 19 December 1917 the formal amalgamation took place. The Belgian shareholders disappeared from the board, which now had eight members in Copenhagen, three in Bangkok and one in Malaya. Aage Westenholz was the first chairman, a post he held until his death on 23 December 1935. Commander Grut, the vice-chairman, was based in Bangkok, where he was supported by Herluf Elsoe and by a young adviser in the Ministry of the Interior, Richard Dudley Craig. Several of the Copenhagen directors were former associates of Westenholz's from the Siam Electricity Company: Captain Aage Jonsen, formerly of the Siamese navy; Commodore J. Tuxen; Lieutenant-Colonel Torben Grut; and Otto Benzon. The two last named, together with A.N. Hansen (later A.N. Grut) and the lawyer Thorkild Knudtzon, were also members of the extended Grut/Westenholz family. Finally, N. Stoltz completed the list of Copenhagen

35

members, while R.H. Phillips took over from Vilhelm Gedde as the only board member resident in Malaya. Phillips acted as the Copenhagen board's visiting agent from 1918 to 1923, a role which was well established in Agency House concerns but unprecedented in Westenholz's companies. He wrote annual reports on the state of each plantation that were displayed in the Copenhagen office and summarized with pride in the directors' Annual Reports. When he retired from the East, however, he was not replaced. Given Commander Grut's strong personal interest in the estates, it may be concluded that a second visiting board member was hardly needed – except, perhaps, to reassure new shareholders during the early years of the amalgamated company's operations.[32]

At the time of amalgamation the various estates were valued at a total of £397,000. Jendarata Estate was the most valuable (£282,000), reflecting the high profits which could still be earned from rubber despite the long-term price decline which had set in. In 1918, the gross profit margin on rubber sales amounted to 45 per cent of revenue, and although war taxes absorbed roughly half the resulting profit, it was still possible for the new shareholders to receive a dividend of 5.5 per cent on their investment. This investment included the £115,000 which was sunk into the coconut estates across the river, now amalgamated into one Sungei Bernam Estate and expected to begin bearing only in 1919.[33]

The previous owners of the various estates were reimbursed by being issued with shares in United Plantations that they could then sell if desired through the Copenhagen or Bangkok offices. A further £43,000 in shares was sold at par during 1918, to finance the further development of the estates. It is difficult to tell who the first shareholders were, or how quickly the Belgians sold their shares, since the earliest surviving list of shareholders dates only from 1929 and covers only the Copenhagen and London lists, omitting the Bangkok residents who still accounted for 21 per cent of United Plantations' shares. However, of the shareholders recorded, Belgians accounted for only £4,200 of shares. The overwhelming majority of shareholders were Scandinavians, with individual holdings rarely rising above £5,000 and often falling below £2,000. Aage Westenholz was the single largest shareholder, with a holding of £29,200; his wife and children owned a further £51,100.[34]

In the first three years after the merger, business continued much as before. The years 1918–20 were exceptionally good for rubber, and much profit was ploughed back into fresh planting on the virgin land acquired in 1916 at

Jendarata. By 1921 Jendarata's rubber land had expanded to a total area of 1,420 hectares – almost double its extent in 1916. Yet the policy of diversification had not been abandoned. The company retained 2,130 hectares of coconuts on both Sungei Bernam and Jendarata Estates and launched out into a new venture on Sungei Bernam, where indications of mineral oil were found in 1918. A Captain Rappoport was commissioned to direct experimental borings; the drilling rig arrived in 1920 and a test well was sunk to a depth of 120 metres. Straits $100,000 was spent in this way, before a renewed slump in the rubber market in 1921 forced the company to limit its efforts. Even then, a further Straits $40,000 was spent from company funds, and more raised by private subscription among the shareholders, to finance the drilling of two further wells in 1921–23. When the third well reached bedrock at 180 metres, still with no further sign of oil, the project was finally abandoned. The rig was sold to prospectors who planned to continue drilling on a sublease at Sungei Bernam, but nothing more was ever heard of them.[35]

Interesting though they seem now in the light of Malaysia's gains from the oil industry since the late 1970s, these oil prospecting efforts were only a very small part of United Plantations' activities at the time. Westenholz's first concern was to build up his rubber and coconut estates, with an investment of Straits $1,170,000 between 1918 and 1920. Most of the cash needed to finance this was raised by the issue of 100,000 ordinary £1 shares, which were sold at par and brought in Straits $860,000. Debentures, loans and an overdraft provided a further Straits $300,000. All the company's operating profits were absorbed in war taxes, dividend and interest payments, which together amounted to Straits $750,000 over the same three-year period. No fees were paid to the company's directors until 1925. During the early post-war years, therefore, United Plantations was by no means an established money-making machine. It was a growing company with one set of assets – the coconuts – which were only just beginning to yield cash income, and a second – the rubber – which had already proved to yield wildly fluctuating returns. The dividends payable for 1918 represented a 5.5 per cent return on investment, rising to 8 per cent in 1919, but falling to only 2 per cent in 1920, when a dramatic post-war slump in the rubber market had begun.

The coconuts planted at Jendarata in 1912 finally began yielding in 1919, and by 1921 some of the land at Sungei Bernam was also bearing fruit. This development came just in time to rescue the company from the terrible rubber slump of 1921, in which operating profits from rubber sank to Straits $8,000 and the European and Asian staff was cut by 40 per cent. Operating profits of Straits $72,000 from coconuts allowed the company to meet its Copenhagen overheads and interest charges, but nothing more; the payment of dividends was impossible.

The crisis of 1921 was felt throughout the rubber industry and led directly to the imposition of the Stevenson Scheme, by which Malayan output was limited from 1922 to 1928. The Rubber Growers' Association (RGA) had initiated an international voluntary restriction scheme in November 1920, which commanded the support of firms controlling 70 per cent of the estate-sector rubber lands. By March 1921 both the RGA and the Colonial Office had begun to feel that such a scheme was not enough, but they found it hard to agree on the terms of any official restriction scheme. In the event, the Stevenson Scheme limited acreage as well as output, for smallholders as well as estates, but did not apply to the Netherlands East Indies (NEI), which produced 26 per cent of world supply. Companies like Guthrie's considered it to be highly inequitable because NEI producers could gain from the higher prices it produced without cutting back their growth; and subsequent historians have also considered it unjust, because the smallholders had no voice in its administration.[36]

Under the Stevenson Scheme, Jendarata's rubber output was restricted to about two-thirds of capacity (500–700 lbs per hectare, rather than the 1,000 which was achieved without restriction in 1918–19 and in 1929–34). More seriously, for a company which had been characterized by growth, it became difficult to obtain new land, especially for rubber planting. Between 1921 and 1925 the company obtained government leases on an extra 500 hectares adjoining Jendarata, but on the condition that this land had to be used for coconuts rather than rubber. In the event, the land remained uncleared until 1930, when it was planted up with oil palms.[37]

However, the Stevenson Scheme had one great redeeming feature, from Aage Westenholz's point of view: it restored the profitability of United Plantations' existing rubber holdings and paved the way for yet more new ventures. During 1922 the company had come very close to bankruptcy and was saved only by a loan of Straits $100,000 raised by Commander Grut from his personal friends in Bangkok. However, by 1923 it had once more become possible to declare a dividend, this time of 5 per cent, and to pay off the overdraft of Straits $250,000 which had accumulated by the end of 1921. Virtually no new investment was undertaken in 1924–25, while the company concentrated on paying off its other loans and on restoring its shareholders' confidence through dividends (of 7 per cent in 1924 and 12 per cent in 1925). But by 1926 United Plantations was able not only to declare a dividend of 14 per cent but also to invest Straits $750,000 in two major new ventures: the purchase of Kuala Bernam Estate and the establishment of Bernam Oil Palms.

Of these two ventures, the purchase of Kuala Bernam fitted best with the existing pattern of United Plantations' business. Lying across the river from Sungei Bernam, on the main road towards Bagan Datoh, Kuala Bernam Estate consisted of 630 hectares of jungle, earmarked for coconuts, and 210 hectares which had already been planted up with these palms. In contrast, the Bernam Oil Palms' venture was something quite new. It continued the Westenholz tradition of seeking alternative investments to offset the unreliability of rubber profits, but it took the planters on an 8-hour boat journey down the winding Bernam River, and involved them with a completely new crop – one that was still highly experimental in Malayan conditions. This venture was the distinctive brainchild of Commander Grut and with its birth he moves decisively to the centre-stage of the United Plantations' drama.

NOTES

1   H.N. Andersen's life story has been well told by Ole Lange, in *Den hvide Elefant: H.N. Andersens Eventyr og ØK, 1852–1914* [The white elephant: H.N. Andersen's ventures and the East Asiatic Company, 1852–1914] (Copenhagen: Gyldendal, 1986), and *Jorden er Ikke Større ... H.N. Andersen, ØK og Storpolitikken, 1914–1937* [The earth is no bigger... H.N. Andersen, the East Asiatic Company and affairs of state, 1914–1937] (Copenhagen: Gyldendal, 1988). See also Erik Helmer Pedersen, *Pionererne* [Pioneers] (Copenhagen: Politikens Forlag A/S, 1986), and Per Boje, *Danmark og de multinationale virksomheder før 1950* [Denmark and the multinational enterprises before 1950] (Odense: Odense Universitetsforlag, 2000).

2   Interviews with R.L. Grut, nephew of Aage Westenholz, 19 and 21 April 1988; Grut and Hansen family trees by Erling Grut, interviewed on 3 September 1989; Judith Thurman, *Isak Dinesen: the Life of Karen Blixen* (London: Weidenfeld and Penguin, 1984), Chs 1–3; Karen Blixen, *Letters from Africa, 1914–1931*, edited by Frans Lasson (London: Weidenfeld and Picador, 1983), pp. 45, 61, 105–107, 110–111, 157 and 168 of Picador edn;   Mary Laugesen, Poul Westphall, and Robin Dannhorn, *Scandinavians in Siam* (Bangkok: Scandinavian Society of Thailand, 1980), p. 62.

3   Laugesen et al, *Scandinavians in Siam*, pp. 25–30, 56 and 62; The Royal Danish Ministry of Education, *Thai-Danish Relations: 30 Cycles of Friendship* (Copenhagen, 1980), pp. 59, 66–69, 140 and 149.

4   Blixen, *Letters from Africa*, plate facing p. 290; Laugesen et al, *Scandinavians in Siam*, pp. 58 and 62; recollections of Christmas Moller kindly translated for me from Hans Neerbek, *Ridder Uden Kors: Aage Westenholz og Danmarks Forsvar* [Knight without a cross: Aage Westenholz and Denmark's defence] (Odense: Odense Universitetsforlag, 1996) by Knud Sehested, a long-standing investor in and former vice-chairman of United Plantations.

5   Interviews, Grut, as note 1; Neerbek, *Ridder uden Kors*; A. Westenholz, 'Memorandum angaaende Danmarks forsvar' [Memorandum concerning Denmark's defence] (printed for private circulation, Holte, Denmark, 1907, and kindly translated for me by Bente Flensborg); Carrie Jørgensen, 'United Plantations and Bernam Oil Palms: highlights from a colourful past' (unpublished mss., 1984), pp. 134–140; D.G. Kirby, *Finland in the Twentieth Century* (London: Hurst, 1979), pp. 46–50; A.F. Upton, *The Finnish Revolution, 1917–1918* (Minneapolis: University of Minnesota Press, 1980), pp. 318–351; E.H. Carr, *The Bolshevik Revolution, 1917–1923*, Vol. I (London: Macmillan, 1950 and Pelican, 1966), Ch. 11(a); Blixen, *Letters from Africa*, p. 99.

6   Laugesen et al, *Scandinavians in Siam*, p. 62; Ian Brown, *The Elite and the Economy in Siam, c. 1890–1920* (Singapore: Oxford University Press, 1988), pp. 11–12.

7   Laugesen et al, *Scandinavians in Siam*, pp. 25–30, 56 and 62; Danish Education Ministry, *30 Cycles of Friendship*, pp. 67–69, 79 and 84; Siam Electricity Co., Ltd., 13th Directors' Report (on the 1906 Accounts).

8   Siam Electricity Co., 13th Directors' Report; Statutes of the Jendarata Rubber Co., Ltd., November 1907; Jørgensen, 'United Plantations', pp. 5 and 129; Danish Education Ministry, *30 Cycles of Friendship*, p. 102.

9   Siam Electricity Co. Ltd., 13th Directors' Report.

10 B.W. Andaya, *Perak, The Abode of Grace* (Kuala Lumpur: Oxford University Press, 1979), p. 335; J.M. Gullick, *Malay Society in the Late Nineteenth Century: the Beginnings of Change* (Singapore: Oxford University Press, 1987). The Bernam region was not visited, for instance, by Isabella Bird, *The Golden Chersonese and the Way Thither* (London: Murray, 1883, and reprinted Kuala Lumpur: Oxford University Press, 1967 and 1980).

11 F.A. Swettenham, 'From Perak to Slim, and Down the Slim and Bernam Rivers', *Journal of the Straits Branch of the Royal Asiatic Society*, 5 (1880), pp. 54–61. Map 2 is based on United Plantations Berhad's modern local map, onto which Swettenham's route has been plotted by the present author.

40

12 On the name Durien Sebatang, see also F. McNair, *Perak and the Malays: Sarong and Kris* (London: Tinsley Bros., 1878), p. 17 and S. Durai Raja Singam, *Port Weld to Kuantan: A Study of Malayan Place Names* (Singapore: Kwok Yoke Weng & Co., 3rd. edn 1957; 1st edn 1939), pp. 258–259. The miserable living conditions of government officials at Durian Sabatang (as it was called in the 1880s) are described vividly by Emily Innes, *The Chersonese with the Gilding Off*, Vol. II (London: Richard Bentley & Son, 1885, and reprinted Kuala Lumpur: Oxford University Press, 1974), Ch. IV.

13 Swettenham, 'From Perak to Slim', pp. 64–68; my account differs slightly from that of H.S. Barlow, *Swettenham* (Kuala Lumpur: Southdene Sdn. Bhd., 1995, also available from Dekalb, Illinois: Southeast Asia Publications, Northern Illinois University, 1997), pp. 103–111, but agrees with the original source, and with further details given in F.A. Swettenham, 'Journal Kept During a Journey Across the Malay Peninsula', *Journal of the Straits Branch Royal Asiatic Society*, vol. 15, 1885, pp. 1–2, and P.L. Burns and C.D. Cowan, eds, *Sir Frank Swettenham's Malayan Journals, 1874–1876* (Kuala Lumpur: Oxford University Press, 1975), pp. 255 and 59 (footnote 3).

14 Swettenham, 'From Perak to Slim', pp. 64–68a; see also H.W.C. Leech, 'About Slim and Bernam', *Journal of the Straits Branch Royal Asiatic Society*, vol. 4, 1879, p. 38.

15 Swettenham, 'From Perak to Slim', p. 68a; on wildlife and politics, see P.L. Burns (ed.), *The Journals of J.W.W. Birch, First British Resident to Perak, 1874–5* (Kuala Lumpur: Oxford University Press, 1976), pp. 361–367.

16 Burns (ed.), *Journals of Birch*, pp. 35–37 and 361–367.

17 Burns and Cowan (eds), *Swettenham's Journals,* Introduction; Barlow, *Swettenham*, pp. 65, 167–173 and 360–367; E. Sadka (ed.), 'The Journal of Sir Hugh Low, Perak, 1877', *Journal of the Malayan Branch Royal Asiatic Society*, vol. 27, no. 4, 1954, pp. 7, 28–31 and 90; E. Sadka, *The Protected Malay States 1874–1895* (Kuala Lumpur: University of Malaya Press, 1968), pp. 212 and 331–348; Amarjit Kaur, *Bridge and Barrier: Transport and Communications in Colonial Malaya, 1870–1957* (Singapore: Oxford University Press, 1985), Chs 2 and 3.

18 J.C. Jackson, *Planters and Speculators: Chinese and European Agricultural Enterprise in Malaya, 1786–1921* (Kuala Lumpur: University of Malaya Press, 1968), Chs 2–3, 5 and 8–9; D.J.M. Tate, *The RGA History of the Plantation Industry in the Malay Peninsula* (Kuala Lumpur: Oxford University Press for the Rubber Growers' Association (Malaysia) Berhad, 1996), Part I.

19 Jackson, *Planters and Speculators*, Ch. 10; Tate, *RGA History*, Chs 15 and 16; J.H. Drabble, *Rubber in Malaya, 1876–1922: the Genesis of the Industry* (Kuala Lumpur: Oxford University Press, 1973), Chs 1 and 2.

20 Drabble, *Rubber in Malaya*, Ch. 3; Jørgensen, 'United Plantations', p. 5; Eric and Violet MacFadyen, *Eric MacFadyen, 1879–1966* (Barnet, Herts.: The Stellar Press, 1968), pp. 3 and 132–133; Daniel Green, *A Plantation Family* (Ipswich: Boydell Press, 1979), pp. 146–154.

21 Jackson, *Planters and Speculators*, Chs 9 and 10; Tate, *RGA History*, Chs 18 and 19; S. Cunyngham–Brown, *The Traders: A Story of Britain's South-East Asian Commercial Adventure* (London: Newman Neame, 1971), p. 177; Drabble, *Rubber in Malaya*, pp. 78–86; debate between Drabble, P.J. Drake and R.T. Stillson, 'The financing of Malayan rubber, 1905–1923', *Economic History Review*, vol. XXIV, no. 4, 1971, pp. 589–598, and vol. XXVII, no. 1, 1974, pp. 108–123.

22 Picture from UPAR, 1967; information from original documents, since lost in a fire, summarized by Jørgensen, 'United Plantations', p. 5.

23 Jørgensen, 'United Plantations', pp. 5 and 130; *Fourth Annual Report of the Rubber Growers' Association, 1912–1913* (London: Rubber Growers' Association, 1913), p. 26.

24 Drabble, *Rubber in Malaya*, pp. 57–63 and Appendix I; Lim Chong-Yah, *Economic Development of Modern Malaya* (Kuala Lumpur: Oxford University Press, 1967), pp. 74–76.

25 Interviews with Rolf and Rothes Grut, 19 and 21 April 1988; Danish Education Ministry, *30 Cycles of Friendship*, pp, 68–69. Following Commander Grut's appointment as general manager, a number of Swedish planters were recruited to Jendarata, including Sven Hallen Schwartz (who served from 1912 to 1928, and was general manager from 1923 to 1928); Gusta Kylberg (1914 to 1916); Karl Nils Albin Bjorklund (1917 to 1930: general manager, 1928 to 1930); and Frederik Adelborg (who served from 1914 to 1919, and was manager of Jendarata, 1916–19, before being summarily fired when he and his aristocratic wife snubbed Helen Grut purely on the grounds of her Japanese ancestry). Adelborg later drew on his Malayan experiences to write a book of short stories, *Dichtung und Wahrheit* [Tales and truth], which became widely read in Sweden. Jørgensen, 'United Plantations', pp. 130–137, and personal communication from Knud Sehested, 15 December 1999.

26 Thurman, *Isak Dinesen*, pp. 116–117; Jørgensen, 'United Plantations', pp. 34–35.

27 Interview with Rolf and Rothes Grut, 19 April 1988; Jørgensen, 'United Plantations', p. 130.

28 Jørgensen, 'United Plantations', pp. 6 and 130–33; UPDR, 1924–28. The awe inspired by Commander Grut is still recalled by Tan Sri Dato' Seri Borge Bek-Nielsen, interview, 15 April 1989.

29 Tate, *RGA History*, Chs 20–26; Drabble, *Rubber in Malaya*, Chs 5 and 6, and Appendices II, IV and IX; Lim, *Economic Development*, pp. 75–76.

30 Jørgensen, 'United Plantations', pp. 5–7; UPDR, 1918. Source for Map 3: UPAR, 1967, commemorative supplement. Vigilance in monitoring disease and in combating it through water control is evident in UP's internal annual reports on Sungei Bernam Estate, 1930s–1950s; similar practices on other estates are documented in the *Bulletin of the RGA*, vol. I, 1919, pp. 9–10; vol. IV, 1922, pp. 373, 433 and 440; vol. V, 1923, pp. 355–357; vol. VII, 1925, pp. 230 and 289; and vol. XX, 1938, p. 414.

31 Jørgensen, 'United Plantations', pp. 34–35.

32 See note 7; also, A. Kann Rasmussen, *Danske i Siam, 1858–1942* [Danes in Siam, 1858–1942] (Copenhagen: Dansk Historisk Håndbogsforlag, 1984), pp. 175–176 and 313–314; and UPDR, 1918.

33 UPDR, 1918.

34 List of payees for the first interim dividend of 1929, payable 13 Sept 1929, in CB, 1928–33.

35 This, and the following two paragraphs, are based on UPDR, 1918–24.

36 *12th, 13th and 14th Annual Reports of the RGA, 1920–1922* (London: RGA, 1921–23); Tate, *RGA History*, Chs 25 and 26; Drabble, *Rubber in Malaya*, Ch. 6; Lim, *Economic Development*, pp. 76–78; Cunyngham-Brown, *The Traders*, Ch. 3; Lim Teck-Ghee, *Peasants and their Agricultural Economy in Colonial Malaya, 1874–1941* (Kuala Lumpur: Oxford University Press, 1977), Ch. 5.

37 Source for this and the following two paragraphs: UPDR, 1921–30.

Commander Lennart Grut

CHAPTER TWO

The Palm Oil Pioneer: Commander W.L. Grut

A NEW DEPARTURE

Ocean voyages provided Lennart Grut with some of the most important meetings of his life. In 1906 he had met his wife while sailing out to the East; and 20 years later, while on a steamer from Bangkok to Singapore, he encountered the Dutch planter Jaan Bloeminck of the Padang Halaban Estate, Sumatra. Bloeminck's estate specialized in oil palms, and his talk of the new crop and its great commercial potential inspired Grut to conceive a new business venture. The oil palm was being much discussed in Malaya at that time, but Bloeminck was unusual among Grut's acquaintances in having practical experience of the crop. Bloeminck invited Commander Grut to visit Sumatra, where he was especially encouraged to learn of the contemporary wisdom, which was that flat land was essential to get the best results from oil palms and that coastal alluvial soils would be ideal. Hence it seemed possible that a new oil palm venture could be started close by the existing United Plantations estates, taking advantage of the established tradition of moving UP managers between estates and enabling Commander Grut to continue supervising the whole group in reasonably brief trips from Bangkok.[1]

On his return to Perak, Commander Grut set out with some Danish soil scientists on an expedition up the Bernam River, searching for land which would be flat, fertile and available for cultivation. Much of the riverside land east of Jendarata was already designated as forest reserve, or occupied by smallholders growing coconuts and rubber. Small parcels of land were available in between the smallholdings, but the palm oil mills of the 1920s required supplies of fruit from at least 1,200 hectares of plantation, so that a large block of land was essential. Eventually the ideal site was found: a parcel of 3,300 hectares of flat, alluvial jungle land, located next door to the new Perak Oil Palms estate, Sungei Samak. The new Ulu Bernam Estate had only one drawback, namely its distance from Jendarata. As shown on Map 4, the two estates were separated by only 27 kilometres as the crow flies, but in the absence of a good road this meant 65 kilometres of slow, tedious travel along the tortuous and muddy Bernam River.[2]

The journey, which took 6–8 hours depending on the tides, became legendary among both managers and estate workers at Ulu Bernam. It was not only dull but also dangerous, because the river was infested with crocodiles – up to 7 metres long, and mean and sneaky by nature. These ugly creatures used to bump the river boats until people began falling out. Nowadays crocodiles are rare in Malaysian rivers and tend to attack children rather than adults; but Axel Lindquist, one of the first Danes to live at Ulu Bernam, saw grown men seized several times. On the day he arrived in Perak in 1929, he was horrified to learn that a body had just been recovered from the river; it belonged to a 12-year-old Indian boy who had been snatched by a crocodile a couple of days earlier. Axel immediately declared war on the crocodile kingdom and later told his children how he had managed to kill 155 of the beasts during the four years which followed. Mostly he shot them, but some he caught 'fishing'. A dead monkey would be tied to a very large, sharp hook, rather like an old-fashioned butcher's meat hook. This would be tied firmly to a tree, carefully chosen for its location in an eye-catching spot on the river bank. The hapless crocodile, in seizing its prey, would instantly find itself trapped. Guile was thus used to defeat guile, in a maneouvre which brought a touch of style to the grim business of survival on the jungle's edge.[3]

EARLIER PALM OIL PIONEERS IN MALAYA AND SUMATRA

Although Axel and his companions at Ulu Bernam were ingenious, daring and pioneering in spirit, they were not the pioneers of the plantation palm oil industry itself. This honour must go to the Belgian agricultural engineer Adrien Hallet and to the French author and planter Henri Fauconnier. Hallet had arrived in Sumatra in 1905 at the age of 38, having already made his fortune in the plantation industry of the Belgian Congo, where he had become familiar with palm oil as a minor, peasant-produced export. He quickly became interested in the

Axel Lindquist the crocodile hunter, 1934. Lindquist's foot is resting proudly on the crocodile's head

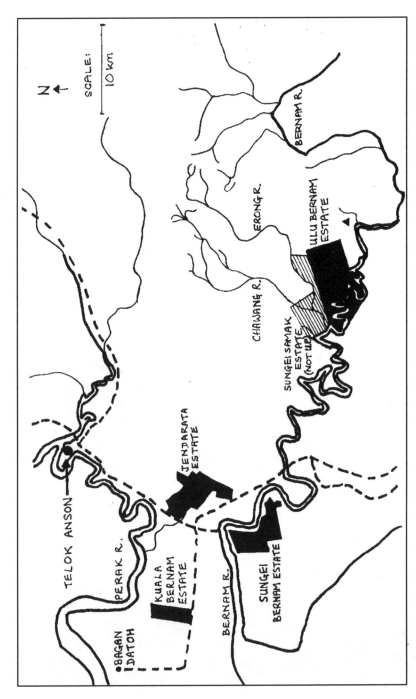

Map 4: United Plantations' and Bernam Oil Palms' estates, 1940

ornamental avenue palms then being grown on Sumatra's tobacco estates, noticing that these grew more rapidly and bore a richer fruit than their Congo counterparts. Hallet was busy setting up a range of planting and banking ventures which later grew into the Socfin Group. He decided to experiment with the oil palm among other things, making his first commercial planting in the Deli region of Sumatra in 1911. Meanwhile, he had become a close friend and business partner of the young Fauconnier, who had also arrived in the East in 1905, at the age of 27, having given up a rather dull teaching job at an English preparatory school. Fauconnier shared Hallet's spirit of adventure and enthusiasm for new experiments and, with the aid of Hallet's greater experience and financial acumen, he was able to set up a coconut estate at Rantau Panjang, deep in the jungle uplands of Selangor. In 1911 Fauconnier paid a visit to his friend in Sumatra, saw the oil palm at first hand and was inspired to begin his own trials of the new crop in Malaya.[4]

Botanists believe that all the palms grown before the Second World War in Malaya and Sumatra were descended from four seedlings which had been planted at the Buitenzorg (Bogor) Botanical Gardens in 1848. Two of the seedlings had been brought to Java from the Amsterdam Botanical Gardens and two imported more directly from Africa, via the French Indian Ocean islands of Reunion and Mauritius. A population descended from so few palms was bound to be highly uniform, which meant that the early Sumatran planters faced a relatively low risk of variable yields from their trees. [5]

By contrast, during the 1910s and 1920s the efforts of British agricultural officers to produce a West African equivalent of the Sumatran 'Deli Dura' oil palm were continually bedevilled by the failure of selected parent palms to breed true. In the early years of oil palm breeding, loose and very ineffective hoods were used to cover the female inflorescences before and after artificial pollination. In colonies like Nigeria where there was a dense population of wild palms near all research stations, insects could easily destroy the result of an artificial pollination experiment overnight. The problem was made worse because officials were trying to achieve Sumatran levels of productivity by breeding a new type of palm, the 'Lissombe' palm with a thin shell and a thick oil-yielding pericarp. This was later to be identified by scientists in the Belgian Congo as the Tenera palm, which is a cross between the thick-shelled Dura and shell-less Pisifera varieties. If Tenera pollen is used to fertilize a Tenera inflorescence, the resulting seeds will produce about 25 per cent Dura, 25 per cent Pisifera and 50 per cent

Tenera palms. Many of the Pisifera palms will be sterile, that is they will not produce fruit. Before all this was known, it seemed to the plant breeders that West African oil palms were simply subject to wild variations in their fertility, shell thickness and oil yields; planting became a 7-year gamble with genes.[6]

The Sumatran and Malayan palm oil pioneers were thus exceptionally lucky. Their palms were not only vigorously fruitful, but they also bred true and were free of the natural pests and diseases which afflicted the oil palm in its original habitat. Hallet's enthusiasm had a solid foundation, and the pioneering stands which he established at Sungei Liput and Pulau Radja in 1911 quickly attracted imitators. One of the first was a German called K. Schadt; another German company followed his example in 1915, planting 2,000 palms at Marihat Baris, which was later to become a major centre of plant breeding and research. Swiss planters also proved keen on the new crop: Bloeminck's estate, Padang Halaban, was Swiss-owned, and a second Swiss company, founded by a man called Ris, started planting oil palms on Gunung Melayu Estate in 1919. By this time the total extent of oil palm plantations on the east coast of Sumatra was just over 6,000 hectares.[7]

The planting community in Sumatra was remarkably cosmopolitan. It included Scots, Australians, Americans and even Hungarians, alongside the other Europeans who were leading pioneers of the oil palm industry. A few Dutch and American companies defended themselves against the softening effect of this cosmopolitanism by cultivating a tight and exclusive company culture, the claustrophobic effect of which is well captured in the novels of Ladislao Szekely and his wife, Madelon H. Lulofs. But in general, the planters were open to new ideas, and they exchanged views and pooled research efforts very effectively through AVROS, the powerful planters' association which Ris had helped to set up. The same willingness to communicate and to take an interest in fresh regions is shown in their relations with their Malayan counterparts.[8]

The oil palm arrived in Malaya by several routes. A few seedlings, probably from Kew Gardens, had been planted in the Singapore Botanical Gardens in 1875. However, the trees planted commercially in the twentieth century were descended not from these but from the Deli Duras of Sumatra. The pioneer planter of Deli Duras in Malaya was Henri Fauconnier, who is also well known for his novel, *The Soul of Malaya*. Fauconnier made his first trial planting of oil palms in 1911 around his own home, which he named the Maison des Palmes. The house, now rebuilt but still surrounded by some of the original palms, may still be seen at Socfin's Rantau Panjang Estate near Kuala Selangor. Meanwhile, by 1917 Fauconnier had become so impressed by the performance of his oil palms that he made an 80-hectare plantation of them on a former coconut estate nearby called Tennamaram. This estate, now owned by Sime Darby, still specializes in oil palms.[9]

Fauconnier's book provides some valuable insights into the world of the pioneers. It deals mainly with the drunkenness which beset the lonely planters and the tensions which could drive the Malays working for them to run amok. Yet it also contains some beautiful descriptions of the jungle, which he saw as a timeless and limitless oasis within which the newly cleared estates stood out like little deserts. Like Szekely and Lulofs, he was conscious of the violence which the Europeans were perpetrating on the landscape and aware of how little they understood the minds of the local people. Yet a speech which he made to the Paris Congress of Agriculture in 1918 reveals that he was also enthralled by the fecundity of exotic plants, like rubber and oil palms, when grown on the newly cleared Malayan soils. This combination of a sense of loss together with a sense of the grandeur of the planters' undertaking is also found in the work of Szekely and in the hearts of many older planters today. Their struggles in the heat and dirt, transforming an environment to create immense wealth, may be seen as an heroic endeavour. Yet many of them, including Commander Grut's son Olof, one of the pioneering managers of Bernam Oil Palms, loved the jungle which their labours cut away and would set off to explore it, or simply to find a hill from which they could look down across it in their leisure hours. Had they not felt this pull towards the jungle, they could hardly have survived the lonely and isolated life of those early years.[10]

After the First World War, as the world market for rubber entered a long period of restriction and uncertainty, an increasing number of companies in both Sumatra and Malaya began to take an interest in palm oil. In 1920 a number of Guthrie Group companies combined to found a new concern, called Elaeis, which purchased a small palm oil estate in Kluang, Johore. The Johore government allowed Elaeis to purchase a much larger area of virgin land around this nucleus, on which fresh plantings of palms began in 1924, using seeds obtained from Marihat Baris and from Tennamaram. One year later, Ris sold his Gunung Melayu Estate in Sumatra to Harrisons and Crosfield, joined them as a manager and went over to Bagan Datoh to advise on the prospects for oil palms in Perak. As a result a new company was formed, the Perak Oil Palms Ltd, which by the

1950s was to be absorbed into Harrisons' associated company, Straits Plantations. Perak Oil Palms Ltd benefited from the experience of oil palm planters in Malaya as well as Sumatra, for one of its directors was L.P. Jorgensen, who managed Tennamaram Estate from 1922 until his death in 1930. The new company quickly set up the Sungei Samak Estate, just west of what was to become Ulu Bernam Estate.[11]

By 1925 over 31,000 hectares had been planted up with oil palms in Sumatra, but only 3,400 in Malaya. Over the next five years the area planted in Malaya was to increase to 20,500 hectares, while the Sumatran area doubled. This rapid expansion was due not only to pessimism about rubber but also to a growing interest in palm oil as a potentially low-cost commodity with a buoyant market. The tree itself requires far less attention than rubber, although the cost of harvesting fruit from its leafy apex rises over its 25-year economic life, as the palm grows to its full height of 18 metres. In the early years of oil production many experiments were still being made with processing machinery, so that it was difficult to tell what the long-run costs were likely to be; but hopes ran high. Meanwhile, the oil which had first been exported from Sumatra in 1920 was finding a ready market in America. It was much cleaner and less acidic than the peasant-produced West African oils, and gave high yields of a valuable by-product, glycerine. These qualities made it ideal for use as a flux in tin-plate manufacture, as an ingredient in fine toilet soaps and as a substitute for cottonseed oil in the making of margarine.[12]

Planters in Malaya were able to get information about the oil palm not only through personal contacts, as in the case of Commander Grut and Jaan Bloeminck but also through the Malayan agricultural department, which had planted its own avenue of oil palms at its Central Experiment Station, Serdang, in 1922; and through the Incorporated Society of Planters (ISP). The ISP, founded in 1919 'to improve the position of planters; to raise the status of the planting profession; and generally to represent, secure, and promote the personal interests of planters', began publishing its own journal, *The Planter*, in 1921. By 1922 the ISP's membership had risen to 850, about 70 per cent of all eligible planters in Malaya, with an especially strong concentration in Lower Perak. When its first membership list was published in 1927, it included nine members of staff from Jendarata, Sungei Bernam and Ulu Bernam. Each of these men was entitled to subscribe to *The Planter*, and a full bound set of back issues is still to be seen in the manager's office at Ulu Bernam.[13]

The Planter began publishing articles on palm oil in June 1923, when it reprinted an article by Dr A.A.L. Rutgers, formerly of AVROS, from the journal *Inter-Ocean*. This piece emphasized that the Sumatran industry had passed its experimental stage and was growing fast. The planters were making substantial profits but were not resting on their laurels. Appreciating that the fast processing of fresh fruit was essential to achieve a high, edible quality of oil, they were aiming to integrate field and factory by means of a rail network, replacing the system of collecting sheds and bullock carts which had initially prevailed. Meanwhile, AVROS was organizing fresh imports of West African seed to see whether it was possible to improve on the Deli Dura. A subsequent article in 1925 summarized the results of further AVROS experiments on the ripening of oil palm fruits and the speed with which acidity built up after maturity; this research yielded some eminently practical conclusions regarding the ideal frequency of harvesting rounds on commercial estates.[14]

Alongside such serious pieces detailing the state of the art among producers, *The Planter* also found space for more lighthearted contributions. One Gold Coast veteran, 'B.O.W.K.', was inspired to set down his memories of 'Palm oil "chop": a delectable alternative to curry', following a 1925 visit to an oil palm estate near Kuala Lumpur. West African cooking methods were described in detail, from the boiling and pounding of the palm fruit itself, through to the blending of the oil with vegetables, chillies and a little fish or meat to create a rich soup. More recipes followed in further articles in 1929 and 1938, but few local cooks seem to have taken up the challenge – perhaps unsurprisingly as the Gold Coast pioneer described the end result as 'a very unappetising-looking mess'.[15]

As well as publishing *The Planter*, the ISP also ran courses and set examinations in Tamil and Telegu, and organized a series of public lectures and conferences. In April 1925 the Teluk Anson branch was favoured with a lecture on the oil palm from an Agricultural Department official, T.D. Marsh. Marsh spoke in great detail about all aspects of oil palm cultivation, from seed germination, planting and drainage through to pollination, harvesting and the choice of machinery for processing. He emphasized that palm oil produced from fresh fruit under factory conditions could be used as an edible fat, unlike the West African variety that was suitable only for low-grade soaps. This talk also gave Lower Perak planters direct access to information about Tennamaram Estate, where oil extraction had begun in 1922 under L.P. Jorgensen. On the advice of the Agricultural Department, Jorgensen had recently switched to a somewhat unorthodox processing plant. Contemporary estates in Sumatra preferred the hydraulic press developed by the German house of Krupp. But the Malayan Agricultural Department thought these machines expensive and inefficient and preferred the centrifuge which had been developed by the British firm of Manlove, Alliott & Co. for use in Nigeria, and which was exhibited at the British Empire Exhibition in 1924. This plant included a steam digester, which sterilized and mashed up the fruit before oil extraction and was thought to have a great impact on the final oil quality.[16]

By 1925, Tennamaram was running its factory on a daily basis and getting ready to pay its first dividend. Any investors who followed Fauconnier's pioneering example could thus expect not only to make a distributable profit within 8 years but also to benefit from the trials and errors of the early oil palm planters. Much had already been learnt about the keys to high quality in field and factory management, and new machinery was continually being brought on to the market by competing British, French and German firms – soon to be followed by Gebr. Stork & Co. of Amsterdam. Managers at Ulu Bernam had ready access to information about these developments, not only through personal contacts but also through lectures and journals. They were part of a community of innovators that gained much of its commercial strength, as well as its human warmth, from the ready exchange of views and experiences.

BERNAM OIL PALMS: FORMATION AND MANAGEMENT

Following Commander Grut's exploratory voyage up the Bernam River, land was applied for in 1926 and a prospectus was issued for the new company, Bernam Oil Palms Limited. Materials for a light railway were ordered as one of the first priorities, showing that Commander Grut had absorbed the Sumatran lesson about good field transport being vital to success. Work on the land itself began in February 1927, financed by United Plantations pending the in-corporation of Bernam Oil Palms later that year. On 9 June 1927 the ownership of the land was formally transferred to the new company, in exchange for 10,000 fully paid £1 shares. United Plantations also took up 100,000 con-tributing shares, for a down payment of 2 shillings per share, with a further 18 shillings payable by instalments which Bernam Oil Palms had the right to call in at its directors' discretion. A further 140,000 contributing shares were issued to individual shareholders, most of whom already had an interest in United Plantations itself. Each shareholder was also given one fully paid share for every ten contributing shares held. In total, shares with a fully paid value of £274,000 had been issued, out of an authorized capital of £500,000. However, the new company had received only £24,000 in cash. It spent £26,000 in planting and on equipment during 1927, the deficit being supplied by a loan from United Plantations.[17]

The first manager of Ulu Bernam Estate was V. Thorbjornsen, a veteran of the Westenholz Volunteer Corps who had joined United Plantations in 1925. A tough and independent man, he was well suited to the task of opening up a remote estate on virgin jungle territory. Once the planting of Ulu Bernam Estate was well under way, in February 1930, he resigned to set up his own oil palm plantation at Mentara, on the eastern railway line where it crossed the border between Pahang and Kelantan. This estate was even more remote than Ulu Bernam; it lay well to the east of the Cameron Highlands, on the fringe of a virtually uninhabited area which has since become Peninsular Malaysia's major national park.[18]

In his first two years at Ulu Bernam, Thorbjornsen was supported by just two European assistants: P.H. Hedenblad, who later transferred to Sungei Bernam Estate but died of leukaemia in 1933, and Sofren Ingemann, a Danish graduate in forestry who was specially recruited for the oil palm project. Carrie Jørgensen has recovered and translated Aage Westenholz's original letter offering the job to Ingemann that gives some interesting details of the terms on which assistants were employed. He was given a free passage to the plantation, with return passage after not less than three years. His first year's salary was £32 per month, rising to £44 by the end of his fourth year, plus free accommodation and medical treatment. He was also given £29 towards his furniture and other early household expenses. After 4 years he would be given free return passage on leave, by which time he would have accumulated 6 months' paid holiday entitlement; but if he resigned within his first year's service, he would have to refund the cost of his outward passage and would have no right to passage home.[19]

Having arrived in the East, a new assistant had every financial incentive to stay, and on travelling up to Ulu Bernam, many felt that money was indeed their only reason for not returning home forthwith. Axel Lindquist recalled that in 1929, as he chugged slowly up the muddy Bernam River and gazed for the first time at the crocodiles, his mind continually returned to Warsaw, where he had been offered a job just at the time he first met Commander Grut. Børge Bek-Nielsen experienced similar feelings as he travelled up to Ulu Bernam at the height of the Emergency, two decades later. Nevertheless, after living at Ulu Bernam for some months and getting used to the slow pace of life upriver, both came to appreciate the jungle, especially its birds, and the beauty of the skies over the gentle hills just east of the estate.[20]

Lindquist and Bek-Nielsen were to retain lifelong ties with Ulu Bernam, but the very first managers and assistants there moved on more quickly. Ingemann returned to Denmark at the end of his first tour, in 1929, but was hastily summoned back when Thorbjornsen resigned. He nobly held the fort until the end of August 1930, when Theodor Mayntz-Clausen arrived to take over. Mayntz-Clausen was an experienced planter, who had been in Malaya since 1923 and had joined United Plantations in 1927. However, within four years of his arrival at Ulu Bernam he had resigned and left the country. While on leave in the United States he had met and married an American, who spent a short time on the estate before returning home to have their baby. In late 1933 she came back out as far as Singapore with the child but could bring herself to go no further. She could not face the isolated upriver conditions, and especially the very limited medical facilities, awaiting her at Ulu Bernam. United Plantations' general manager, Poul Bent Heilmann, had some sympathy and was ultimately prepared to advance Mrs Mayntz-Clausen the S$1,500 needed to pay her fare back to America; but he urged her to take heart from his own wife Hedvig, who had already had firsthand experience of local medical facilities when her first baby, John, was born in Batu Gajah, near Ipoh, in June 1931. Both John and his brother, Flemming, who was born in Penang in April 1936, were brought up successfully at Jendarata until the family had to leave for Australia during the Second World War. However, it remained true that Jendarata was not as isolated as Ulu Bernam, and also that the Heilmanns had an especially deep commitment to plantation life. Both Hedvig and Poul Bent Heilmann were Danes from the Horsens area of Jutland who had family links to the board of United Plantations through Commander Grut, whose mother was born Valborg Heilmann. Poul Bent had first travelled out to work at Jendarata in 1925 and had been filling the role of general manager since 1930. He and Hedvig both found much to value in the life they were making in Malaya and urged Mrs Mayntz-Clausen to pay them a visit with her baby, sure that she would find friendly reassurance in doing so. However, their efforts were to no avail. Mrs Mayntz-Clausen refused to live at Ulu Bernam, and Theodor finally conceded defeat and followed her home. Olof Grut took over as acting general manager of Bernam Oil Palms, being confirmed in the post in 1935.[21]

The interconnections between United Plantations and Bernam Oil Palms, which are so clear at the levels of finance and local management, may also be seen at the level of the Boards of Directors. By 1927 the board of United Plantations had changed but little from the original group of 1917. Commodore Tuxen and Otto Benzon had died, and R.H. Phillips and Herluf Elsoe had resigned on retiring from the East. Meanwhile the former manager Thorkild Dahl, the Bangkok businessman L. Bisgaard and the Swedish architect Torben A. Grut had joined the board. Torben A. Grut was the brother of Commander Grut, and a great sporting enthusiast. He designed the stadium for the Swedish Olympic Games in 1912 and his son William won the Gold Medal in the modern pentathlon at the 1948 Olympics. However, his interests were mainly Scandinavian and he did not join the board of Bernam Oil Palms, which was much smaller than the United Plantations board and was composed of people with direct experience of the East.

When it was first set up in 1927, the Bernam Oil Palms board had just seven members, while United Plantations' had 13. Five out of the seven BOP directors were also members of the UP board: Commander Grut (the BOP chairman), Aage Westenholz, Major-General Torben Grut (who deputized for Westenholz as chairman of UP when he was ill), R.D. Craig (their trusted Bangkok ally) and Thorkild Dahl. Of the remaining two, Sven Hallen Schwartz was the general manager of United Plantations, who was to become a director of that company too when illness forced him to retire from the East in 1928; and Francis Harrison Grumitt was the representative of UP's auditors, Messrs McAuliffe, Davis and Hope, of Penang. Hence it can be seen that Bernam Oil Palms was effectively being run as a subsidiary of United Plantations. Its managers moved back and forth between the two companies, and its board comprised three men with a close working knowledge of UP's affairs at the local level, together with the four most powerful UP board members.[22]

EARLY YEARS AT ULU BERNAM

When he first went up the river on 14 February 1927, Thorbjornsen's first task was to put up shelters for himself and the four Chinese contractors he had brought with him. A temporary coolie line was erected, containing 20 rooms, each of 100 square feet, and a shop was built and opened by a Chinese operator. By the end of March 150 Chinese, Malay and Javanese labourers were living on the estate, and the construction of two permanent coolie lines and a further four temporary lines began. A few Tamil labourers had begun to arrive and set to work clearing the 15 acres needed for these buildings by hand; the frequent rains of that month ruled out any burning of the felled jungle trees. Meanwhile, Thorbjornsen himself was still waiting for his own small *atap* (thatched roof) bungalow to be put up and was living in a previously vacant manager's bungalow on Sungei Samak Estate, which by the slow river boat then in use was a full hour's journey downriver from Ulu Bernam.[23]

The heat and discomfort of these early days at Ulu Bernam can hardly be imagined. Living in the most basic of accommodation, labourers from many different backgrounds worked together to fell 400 hectares of virgin jungle between March and May. They were working on the parts of the estate closest to Jendarata, known as Tanjongs 1 and 2. These two small peninsulas, jutting out into the Bernam River, were riddled with small streams and marshy areas: a wet and unpleasant place in which to work. Epidemics of cholera and dysentery broke out in June and July but were quickly controlled. New latrines were built and the old dresser, a drunkard, was fired. An efficient replacement was hired at treble the salary – £18 per month.

Luckily, though, there were no swamps within the area, and virtually no malaria. The jungle itself turned out to be rather light by Malayan standards, with few really big trees. Thorbjornsen was also delighted to find that the soil survey had been accurate: the land was virtually all coastal clay with little or no peat. Established drainage and cultivation techniques could therefore be used with no need for costly experiments in new methods. This situation contrasted well with that on the neighbouring Sungei Samak Estate, which had much more peat. By 1927 only 90 hectares out of the 1,490 owned by Perak Oil Palms had been planted up, and many of the original workers had abandoned the estate. In despair, the management offered to sell out to Bernam Oil Palms but finally rejected their offer of just £8,000 in shares.

Meanwhile, at Ulu Bernam itself the construction of coolie lines had gone far enough by May 1927 to allow Thorbjornsen to arrange for an inspection by the Labour Department, following which the estate would be allowed to send its own recruiting agents (*kanganis*) to India. Tamil labourers were far cheaper to employ than Chinese contractors, but it was vital to have good accommodation and medical care for them. The tide of public opinion, especially in India, had already turned against the continuing outflow of labourers to Malaya, so that it was essential for fresh employers to show that they could offer new recruits the best possible living conditions. After 1927 this display became even more important, not merely to satisfy government officials and public opinion but also to attract labourers themselves as, having settled in Malaya, they began to move around from one estate employer to another. The settled Malayan Tamil population became the mainstay of the estate labour force as, from 1928 onwards, the flow of migrants diminished sharply. During the slump of 1931–33 this flow ceased altogether, resuming from 1934–38 as a mere trickle, until in 1938 the Indian government banned it altogether.[24]

By the end of 1927, 160 labourers had been recruited from India to work on Ulu Bernam Estate, at an average wage of Straits $10 (£1.3s.6d.) per month. However, most of the workforce, a further 370 people, were recruited locally, and Thorbjornsen found this increasingly easy as the recession in the rubber industry began to deepen. Many rubber estates began laying off workers or reducing wages, and once the coolie lines were completed in August, Ulu Bernam began to be increasingly attractive to Tamil labourers who had arrived in Lower Perak some years earlier. Meanwhile, the isolation of the estate was gradually being reduced as transport facilities were installed. Two jetties were built using old tram rails from Bangkok, and a steam launch was chartered locally for a round trip from Utan Melintang to Ulu Bernam three times a week. Late in 1927, this launch was replaced by two motor boats, bought from the Menam Motor Boat Company and each capable of carrying 5 tonnes of cargo and 80 passengers. Ulu Bernam now had daily communication with the outside world, and recruitment became much easier.

The next priority was to obtain enough seedlings to plant up the area that had been so painfully cleared during 1927. The aim was to plant 143 palms per hectare, neatly laid out in the standard triangular formation. For the first 400 hectares a total of 60,000 seedlings was therefore needed, of which 35,000 had already been grown in nurseries at Jendarata from Sumatran seed. Thorbjornsen made a trip to the heartland of the Malayan oil palm industry, the Kuala Selangor region, in search of more. He was given a friendly reception on the Sungei Tinggi and Raja Musa Estates, of which the former was owned by Adrien Hallet. The managers not only supplied him with the necessary seedlings but also gave him some useful tips on nursery practice and recommended that he follow their own rule of using only Sumatran seed. On his return to Ulu Bernam Thorbjornsen began to prepare for the following year's planting by ordering 200,000 seeds from Sumatra via McAuliffe, Davis & Hope. Only about 60 per cent of these seeds could be expected to germinate, given the rather rough-and-ready pollination, seed storage and sandbed germination techniques in use at the time.[25]

During 1927 about 250 hectares of oil palms were successfully planted, but at the end of the year a setback occurred. Rats fled out of the jungle and into the estate following the onset of the monsoon rains in November. They quickly started eating the young palms and had devoured 2,000 (equivalent to 14 hectares) within two months. This was just the beginning of a war of attrition, which raged for over 10 years. As soon as the palms began bearing fruit in 1930, the rats redoubled their efforts, eating the flowers and immature fruits as well as the growing tips of younger palms.

Early efforts to shelter the palms by placing wire netting or metal cones around their bases failed, as the rats simply relished the challenge of climbing over these obstacles. Traps were laid, catching 48,000 rats in 1930, and barium and other poisons were laid down on the fruits in the dry season. Poison was also added to rice, which was pressed into pellet form and scattered around the estate. Jaan Bloeminck suggested a variation on the same theme, the use of thallium torpedoes as practised in Sumatra. A less orthodox idea was the Ulu Bernam cat farm, which was started briefly in 1930, and revived in 1933 with the idea of breeding kittens to be let loose in the estate.

However, the most successful method of combating the rat menace proved to be systematic hunting by gangs of Tamil labourers. This method was hit on almost by chance, when there was a serious flood in May 1933. Work came to a standstill on two-fifths of the estate, and Axel Lindquist had the bright idea of asking the workers to hunt rats instead. Ten thousand were caught in the first two days of this campaign, as they swam about in the flood waters and scurried up the stems of taller palms. Three Highland Terriers were later imported to assist the campaign, and it was found that pruning the trees made it easier to spot the rats as they climbed up in a last attempt to evade the hunters. Labourers who caught rats were initially rewarded according to the number of tails they brought in; double was paid for a dead baby rat, with its eyes still unopened. But then it was found that large numbers of the rats still running around the estate had no tails, and it was suspected that a Chinese contractor who had been brought in to assist the hunt was actually breeding baby rats for sale. After that, the workers had to bring in whole adult corpses to qualify for payment, and within 18 months – by December 1937 – the pest had finally been contained.[26]

The young palms at Ulu Bernam fell prey to many other menaces: white ants, caterpillars and elephants being the most common. Hundreds of elephants were rumoured to live in the jungle to the north, south and east of Ulu Bernam, and every so often they would wander through a corner of the estate, absent-mindedly trampling down any palms which lay along their path and feasting on the young shoots of many others. The small part of the estate which lay south of the Bernam River was most vulnerable, because uninhabited at night; these Selangor Tanjongs were invaded repeatedly in 1931 and 1932, and over 200 palms were destroyed. The acting manager, Commander Grut's son Olof, ordered holes to be dug to catch the marauders, and reinforced these with boundary patrols. Unfortunately these pits were not quite deep enough. One elephant was trapped, but in the 20 minutes which elapsed between the guard seeing it and the arrival of Axel Lindquist, ready to shoot it with his Winchester, the elephant had managed to struggle out of the pit and had wandered back to the jungle, eating a few more palms on its way. The same intrepid beast was later seen inside the estate, and a moonlight patrol was set up to trap it – without success. It was later found that the most effective method of deterring the animals was simply to place a series of hurricane lamps along the estate boundary, backed up by a patrolling watchman. In 1940 these patrols were taken over by the professional rangers of the Game Department.

INVESTMENT, INCOME AND IDEALS

By 1930 it was clear that the young palms at Ulu Bernam were doing well, despite the rats and other pests, and that the planting programme had made 'wonderful progress – quick and cheap', as Aage Westenholz put it in an encouraging letter to Lennart Grut. It was characteristic of Westenholz that he should be warm in his praise, describing the progress of Bernam Oil Palms as 'a triumph to its management, but chiefly I think, to yourself'. The example of Ulu Bernam inspired Westenholz to believe that oil palms might even be a worthy substitute for rubber or coconuts on his own estates. In 1928 the Stevenson

Scheme had come to an end and rubber prices were falling. Many other European estate-owners were concentrating on plans for renewed rubber restriction schemes and devoting much time to the talks which finally resulted in the International Rubber Regulation Agreement of 1934. However, Westenholz preferred to search for a more creative solution to his company's economic problems. By January 1929 he was beginning to think seriously of planting oil palms at Jendarata, and in September 1929 an event occurred which forced his hand. A windstorm destroyed 250 hectares of mature rubber at Jendarata, underlining the fragility of the rubber tree by comparison with the palm, and clearing the way for a fresh start. Westenholz decided to plant 770 hectares with oil palms over the years 1930–1932, thus paving the way for a fresh wave of investment in the new crop by United Plantations' shareholders.[27]

Meanwhile, at Ulu Bernam the planting programme of 2,450 hectares was completed in January 1931. The next investment priority was to build a factory. One local example which could have been drawn on was Perak Oil Palms' centrifugal plant, which had been opened with a fanfare in March 1929 with several eminent visitors being conveyed upriver in a launch provided by Thorbjornsen. However, as shown above, Commander Grut and his managers had a low opinion of Perak Oil Palms' efficiency. Commander Grut's son Olof had graduated in engineering from Trinity Hall, Cambridge before joining the staff of Ulu Bernam Estate in 1930, and he and Lennart made a tour of factories in Europe, Sumatra and the Federated Malay States before choosing their own factory plant. They finally decided to follow the example of Guthries' Elaeis Estate in Johore, which had installed the new hydraulic press supplied by Stork of Amsterdam. Stork's factory allowed for an extension of the field rail network to carry the cages of fruit directly from the point of harvest into the steam sterilizers and incorporated digesters of the Manlove & Alliott type while giving the full extraction efficiency of the early Sumatran hydraulic presses.[28]

The factory was the best available, but it came at a high price. Its construction began in 1930 and extensions continued until 1937, by which time Olof was keen to begin modernizing the plant. Between 1930 and 1937 a total of Straits $700,000 (£82,000) had been spent on the building and machinery, including an electric power plant. Meanwhile, the same amount had been spent on the completion of the planting programme and the upkeep of immature areas. A further Straits $190,000 (£22,000) had been spent on the light railway network which ran throughout the estate.

All this spending had to be financed mainly by the shareholders, through a series of call-ups on their contributing shares: for no palm oil was produced until 1933, by which time the inter-war depression was reaching its worst stage. A working loss of £2,000 was made on palm oil and kernel production in 1933, and a profit of only £3,000 the following year. Between 1935 and 1937 a total working profit of £180,000 was made, but much of this was absorbed in repaying loans taken out in 1934–35 and in building up a cash float. Net (distributable) profit stood at only 8 per cent of shareholders' funds in 1935, rising to 14 per cent in 1936 and 22 per cent in 1937. Only in 1936, 10 years after the first investment was made in Ulu Bernam, did shareholders receive their first dividend – of just 5 per cent on the total book value of their investment in Bernam Oil Palms. Its payment coincided with the final call-up of 1 shilling per contributing share, so that no cash payment was actually made on the majority of shares held. The first effective dividend payment, of 12.5 per cent, was made only in 1937. This contrasted sadly with the 1926 Prospectus estimate of a return of 20–25 per cent to shareholders in 6–7 years.[29]

While Bernam Oil Palms survived the depression years by calling up the balance due on its contributing shares, United Plantations had more of a struggle. In 1927 the company had made a successful new issue of 19,576 £1 shares, which it was able to sell for 24 shillings each. The money was used to plant coconuts on the land acquired in 1926 at Jendarata and Kuala Bernam. Fresh planting in 1928–29 was financed by the issue of £79,400 in 7 per cent debentures. A further £10,000 of debentures was offered for sale in 1930, but only £4,100 found takers. In 1931 £200 more was obtained in this way. Meanwhile, the share-holders were becoming justifiably restless, as their dividends dwindled from a peak of 14 per cent relating to the 1926 financial year, to 5.5 per cent in 1929 and nothing at all in 1930–34. During the final five years, the company was continuing to make a modest operating profit in the region of Straits $200,000 (£23,000) per year; but these funds were earmarked for investment in its own estates and for paying the calls which continued to be made on its shares in Bernam Oil Palms.[30]

A deep division had thus developed between United Plantations' most dividend-conscious shareholders and its most powerful directors, the visionaries Westenholz and Grut, who believed firmly that it was worth continuing to invest even in the depths of the slump and who had faith that the capacity thus built up could be used profitably in the boom to follow. In 1930 a group of

Danish shareholders, led by Harald Grut, Harald Nielsen and Knud Dahl, sent round a circular to the rest, lobbying for an increase in the dividend proposed for 1929. Westenholz had some sympathy for their plight, declaring that 'I shall be loath to keep back, for the benefit of our children, an undue share of the dividends of old shareholders, who may never see the profits therefrom.' However, both he and Grut felt that the switch from rubber to coconuts and oil palms was essential because of the poor long-term profitability of rubber at Jendarata. Given the company's difficulty in raising funds from debentures, it was equally clearly foolish to pay out dividends if this would create a need to raise debt finance to pay for replanting.[31]

A further dissident circular followed in 1932, advocating the sale of United Plantations' shares in Bernam Oil Palms and the curtailment of UP's own planting programme, so that a dividend could be paid for 1932. The circular was sent while Lennart Grut was absent in the East and while Aage Westenholz was ill. Commander Grut eventually countered with a stinging reply, spelling out the case for self-restraint by the shareholders and appealing particularly to the Bangkok shareholders, who still held a 21 per cent stake in the company, to give him their proxies for the forthcoming Annual General Meeting in Copenhagen. He finally won the day, aided by a provision in the company's original Articles of Association, which prohibited the payment of dividends exceeding the amount recommended by the directors in their Annual Report. However, the battle resumed when the dissidents decided to challenge the Articles of Association. At an Extraordinary General Meeting held on 5 December 1932, two amendments were passed. The first removed the clause which had aided Commander Grut in June; and the second added a new clause, forbidding the acquisition of 100 acres or more of fresh land without the prior consent of a General Meeting. This clause was to prove a mighty thorn in the directors' sides after the Second World War, when there was an intense contest among established estate companies to buy out the smaller players and when decisions had to be made within weeks or even days.[32]

Emboldened by this success, Knud Dahl and his supporters mounted another attack on the Articles of Association in 1934, this time seeking to replace the British system by which three directors retired and offered themselves for re-election at each Annual General Meeting, by the d'Hondt system of proportionate voting to elect all directors every year. Once again Commander Grut rallied the Eastern Register shareholders to oppose the motion, and it was duly rejected by a majority of five to one. By 1935 it had become possible to begin declaring dividends again, with a modest 3 per cent on the face value of United Plantations' shares, and the revolt of the 'starving shareholders', as Aage Westenholz had dubbed them in 1933, was finally over. However, it had been a close-run thing, and but for the courage and conviction of Westenholz and, especially, Grut, it is possible that the oil palm projects at both Ulu Bernam and Jendarata would have been killed off by the slump.[33]

Throughout this period of struggle, Commander Grut had continued his regular visits to the estates, where Westenholz noted his extraordinary 'gift of infusing everybody with a fiery wish to do everything in his power at a super-human speed' – an enduring characteristic of the UP management style. His enthusiasm and drive were as badly needed in Perak as in Copenhagen, for the slump had brought cuts in salaries and postponements of plans to make estate life more comfortable. In 1931 salaries at Jendarata were cut by 20 per cent and at Ulu Bernam by 10 per cent for assistants earning Straits $300 or less per month, 15 per cent for assistants earning more than Straits $300 and 20 per cent for managers. Ulu Bernam staff were compelled to receive part of their salary in the form of BOP shares in every year from 1930 to 1935; while at both companies, the remainder of the salary cut was treated as a deposit kept by the company to be paid back with 7 per cent interest when the employee left. As for the Tamil work-force, an attempt made in 1932 to reduce daily wages from the established levels of 40 cents for men and 32 cents for women soon failed. The managers decided that their first priority must be to retain the best workers and to keep up the overall work-force numbers to sustain the replanting programme.[34]

Ironically, the salary restrictions adopted out of necessity during the slump provided a way of introducing some of Westenholz's cherished principles to his companies. As early as 1922 he had published an article on 'Co-Operation between capital and labour' in the magazine *Borups Højskole*, an organ of the Folk High School movement that had been founded by the nineteenth-century Lutheran pastor, Danish patriot and social reformer N.F.S. Grundtvig. Grundtvig's ideas have had a profound effect on twentieth-century Danish culture, not merely in education but also in the growth of the co-operative movement. The main form of co-operation in Denmark has been between independent farmers, but in the 1920s a debate sprang up about the chance of co-operation between the owners and employees of a capitalist enterprise, and it was to this debate that Westenholz sought to make a contribution.[35]

Westenholz felt strongly 'that capital and labour ought to co-operate as two hands on the same body, guided by one brain'. He felt that this was becoming increasingly difficult in manufacturing companies where ownership rested in the hands of numerous small shareholders, who 'have no feeling towards the workers they never see'. Meanwhile, workers who simply sold their time to the company, with no permanent interest in its loss or gain, could not be expected to feel responsible for its future. Therefore Westenholz suggested that co-operation should move beyond profit-sharing to make the workers shareholders, defining the workers as 'everyone doing a job by hand or spirit, from the directors to the delivery boy'. This would enable the workers not only to share in the company's fate but also to influence it through participation in the Annual General Meetings. Westenholz suggested that his idea could be implemented by giving workers free shares, in amounts proportional to their pay, which itself would be the full market rate for the job. When each worker left the company, his shares would be bought back at market value and reallocated. 'The ideal is that all workers will become capitalists, and all capitalists, according to their ability, workers'. The end result would be a cessation of industrial conflict, and a growth not only in productivity but also in human happiness.

Westenholz's ideas were inspiring, but it fell to Commander Grut to put them into action. The measures which he initiated to cushion the impact of pay cuts in the early 1930s were consolidated and built into the management structures of both Bernam Oil Palms and United Plantations once profits began to recover. In particular, an annual profit-related bonus was instituted for the managers and staff of both companies in 1937; and the funds held in trust for them as a result of the early 1930s pay cuts formed the basis for a pair of Provident Funds which were set up in 1938. The eligible members of the funds were all European staff, together with Asian assistants, office and hospital staff. The linking of pay to profit and the provision of company welfare benefits have remained among the hallmarks of United Plantations, and the system of welfare benefits in particular has been enlarged and extended to the work-force as a whole since the 1940s, thus going a long way towards realizing Westenholz's ideals. Sadly, Westenholz himself was unable to witness these developments, for after a long struggle with heart problems he died on 23 December 1935.[36]

On his brother-in-law's death, Commander Grut naturally succeeded to his position as chairman of United Plantations, with Major-General Torben Grut taking over as vice-chairman. At Bernam Oil Palms, where the position of vice-chairman had not previously existed, it was now created and Major-General Grut was elected to it. No further changes were made to the board of Bernam Oil Palms, but at United Plantations the vacancy left by Westenholz was filled by the pharmacist Niels Benzon, whose mother Emma Hansen was Aage's first cousin. Slightly earlier, in 1935, Sofren Ingemann had also joined the United Plantations board as a replacement for Mr Bisgaard, who had decided to retire. Ingemann was an interesting choice, for his original connection with the firm had come through Bernam Oil Palms, where his help in early staffing emergencies was well remembered. After leaving Malaya he had married into an extremely prosperous family from Dundee, and his new father-in-law had given the couple a large Danish forestry estate as a wedding present. Although well occupied in running the estate, Ingemann had kept up his connections with United Plantations and Bernam Oil Palms, both through shareholdings and through friendships with Mayntz-Clausen, Heilmann, Axel Lindquist and Svend Pontoppidan Møller. He was an ideal person to link the Copenhagen board with both shareholders and employees and to reinforce in an informal way the links between Bernam Oil Palms and its parent company. From 1945 he was able to play the last role in a more formal way, for he was appointed to the post-war boards of both companies. Ingemann continued to act as a director until ill-health struck him in 1951, when he was still in his early 50s. Like his father before him he died young, in November 1953.[37]

Only one further change affected the board of United Plantations before the Second World War: in 1937 one of the founder members, Captain Aage Jonsen, died and Aage Westenholz's eldest son Soren was elected to take his place. Meanwhile, at Bernam Oil Palms no further changes occurred at all. Having survived the shareholders' challenge of the early 1930s, the directors thus remained secure. Following Aage Westenholz's death, his family continued to have a strong say in United Plantations' affairs, and Bernam Oil Palms continued to be run as an extremely closely linked subsidiary.[38]

SURVIVAL AND GROWTH IN THE PALM OIL INDUSTRY

Following Commander Grut's victories in the boardroom battles of the 1930s, his oil palm ventures continued to grow and flourish. This was part of a more general trend within South-East Asia. By 1934 the Netherlands East Indies had replaced Nigeria as the world's major exporter of palm oil, and from 1934 to

1938 the NEI's annual exports averaged 171,000 tonnes, as compared with 137,000 for Nigeria. The Malayan industry was small by comparison, with an average annual export of 34,000 tonnes over the same period. Indeed, the Malayan industry was even smaller in relative terms than these figures suggest, for a substantial amount of Nigerian palm oil was consumed at home, whereas all of Malaya's palm oil was exported. However, Malayan palm oil production was growing rapidly: exports reached 60,000 tonnes in 1939. By this time, Bernam Oil Palms was exporting 7,500 tonnes of oil per year, with Jendarata shipping a further 2,600. The two Grut ventures thus held a 17 per cent share of Malaya's palm oil export trade.[39]

Further details of the Grut ventures' relative position within the Malayan palm oil industry may be seen in Table 1. Of special interest is the fact that, from 1934 onwards, their share of output was much higher than their share of the planted area. Commander Grut had chosen his location well; and with Lindquist and his hunters keeping the rats under control, the palms yielded plenty of fruit. Meanwhile, Olof's well-designed factory was making the most of its raw material, extracting a regular 17 tonnes of palm oil from every 100 tonnes of fresh fruit bunches delivered from the field.[40]

One of the key reasons why South-East Asian producers in general were able to continue expanding their exports of palm oil in the 1930s was the introduction of bulk shipments to Europe and North America. The expensive wooden barrels and metal drums used previously in West Africa were replaced by large tanks, which gave economies of scale and minimized losses from leakage. One early pioneer of this system was William Lever in his Congo operations. Railway tank wagons, heated by steam pipe coils to keep the oil liquid enough for pumping in and out, chugged back and forth from the hinterland upriver to the port of Matadi; ocean tankers then took the oil onwards. A similar system was developed in the 1920s by Socfin in Sumatra with a large bulking tank being built at the ocean port of Belawan. Socfin made its first bulk shipment of palm oil from Malaya in October 1931, taking it to Belawan in a specially adapted steamer belonging to the Straits Steamship Company.[41]

At this time the main market for high-quality palm oil was in the United States, and the ports there were well equipped to deal with bulk shipments. However, the Malayan agricultural department and companies like Guthries were keen to develop the British market and began pressing for the erection of the necessary plant in Liverpool. Meanwhile, Commander Grut and friends like Tom Barlow

Table 1: Planted area and output of palm oil, Bernam Oil Palms, United Plantations and Malaya, 1917–40

Year	Planted area of oil palms: BOP + UP (1,000 ha)	Planted area of oil palms: Malaya (1,000 ha)	Output of palm oil: BOP + UP (1,000 tonnes/yr)	Output of palm oil: Malaya (1,000 tonnes/yr)	Planted area: BOP + UP as % of all Malaya	Output: BOP + UP as % of all Malaya
1917	–	0.1	–	–	–	–
1918	–	0.2	–	–	–	–
1919	–	0.3	–	–	–	–
1920	–	0.5	–	–	–	–
1921	–	0.8	–	–	–	–
1922	–	0.9	–	–	–	–
1923	–	1.7	–	0.2	–	–
1924	–	2.4	–	0.3	–	–
1925	–	3.4	–	0.5	–	–
1926	–	5.1	–	0.8	–	–
1927	0.3	7.3	–	0.8	4	–
1928	0.9	9.6	–	1.3	9	–
1929	1.5	12.8	–	1.8	12	–
1930	3.0	20.5	–	3.4	15	–
1931	3.2	23.1	–	5.2	14	–
1932	3.2	24.7	–	8.5	13	–
1933	3.2	25.9	1.2	13.2	12	9
1934	3.2	26.3	3.6	17.8	12	20
1935	3.2	26.3	6.4	23.5	12	27
1936	3.2	26.3	8.5	32.4	12	26
1937	3.2	27.9	10.0	46.4	11	22
1938	3.3	29.5	9.9	51.9	11	19
1939	3.5	31.2	10.1	58.3	11	17
1940	3.7	31.6	10.2	58.9	12	17

Sources: UBAR and UPAR, 1933–65; Lim, *Economic Development*, Appendix 5.2, p. 337; Harcharan Singh Khera, *The Oil Palm Industry of Malaya: an Economic Study* (Kuala Lumpur: Penerbit Universiti Malaya, 1976), Appendix II.4, p. 305.

had begun planning for the erection of plant in Malaya itself to be funded jointly by producers on the same principles as the Danish co-operative dairies. Early negotiations fell through in 1930 – because Malayan production was still very small – but by 1932 it had become possible to set up the Malayan Palm Oil Bulking Company Ltd as a joint venture between producers. Bernam Oil Palms became a founder member, contributing £400 towards the cost of the new company's plant in Singapore that was leased from the Singapore Harbour Board and managed by Guthries. Transport from the estates to Singapore was to be handled by the Straits Steamship Company.[42]

Once the oil from Ulu Bernam or any other estate entered the bulking installation at Singapore, it inevitably became mixed with supplies from other producers. Hence a natural corollary of the bulking arrangement was the formation of a selling pool to handle the oil in Britain with revenues to be shared among Malayan producers in proportion to the volume of oil supplied. In 1936 the Malayan producers joined their Sumatran counterparts in an International Palm Oil Pool, which held together until 1940. Commander Grut was keen on the pooling idea from the outset; but difficulties soon arose in implementing it. A general problem arose because sales were usually made forward on the basis of pool members' estimates of production, and a bad year with floods or rat invasions could lead to quarrels among pool members about who should bear the costs of default. A more specific problem arose in relation to Bernam Oil Palms, because even at this early stage of the firm's history, the entrepreneurial spirit of managers like Olof Grut made them reluctant to develop just one type of oil for one market.[43]

Olof took an early interest in the possibility of fractionating palm oil to produce a liquid edible oil and a harder residue for non-edible uses. Several large-scale fractionation plants were eventually set up in West Malaysia during the 1970s, but in the 1930s Olof's experiments were considered highly avant-garde. He carried them out on a very small scale and produced only a few bottles of oil for trial by the estate cooks and by the visiting medical practitioner, Dr Watson. However, he had more success with an air-bleaching process which he had developed in order to compete with Sumatran bleached oil outside the European and North American markets; and it was this development which led to conflict between Bernam Oil Palms and the other pool members.

Ulu Bernam's bleached oil liquified at a lower temperature than the Sumatran equivalent, making it unpopular with established buyers of Sumatran oil in Penang and South Africa; but it proved well suited to the Indian and Middle

70

Eastern soap-makers' market. As the latter regions had no facilities for receiving bulk palm oil shipments, Ulu Bernam's exports there had to be sent in drums and negotiated outside the pool's framework. Indeed, when the Malayan producers joined the international pool, they did so on condition that Bernam Oil Palms be allowed to continue such independent sales. This seemed a reasonable request to the non-Malayan producers at the time, for the volume involved was small by world standards but important to Ulu Bernam; and they had no intention of competing in the Indian and Middle Eastern markets themselves. Ulu Bernam's sales of bleached oil were thus able to rise from 523 tonnes in 1933 to 1,202 tonnes (16 per cent of Ulu Bernam's total production) in 1939. However, the Sumatran pool members soon came to realize that these markets were very volatile: Ulu Bernam's sales to them swung from 285 tonnes in 1936 to 1,247 the following year. As a result, Ulu Bernam's supplies to the pool itself fluctuated even more from year to year than the vagaries of pests and climate would dictate. This intensified the pool's difficulties in forecasting supplies and fulfilling forward contracts and caused increasing ill-feeling in the remaining years of the pool's brief life.[44]

During the 1930s the Malayan and Sumatran palm oil industries had thus grown steadily. Costs were cut through bulk shipment, and the concerted sales policies which developed among producers who shared the same transport also enabled them to make the most of the world-wide economic revival which began in 1935. Meanwhile, the management of Bernam Oil Palms was already displaying many of the key qualities which were to set it apart from the general run of palm oil producers after 1945. Not content with developing an integrated field-to-factory operation to produce high-quality, unrefined red palm oil for bulk sale to established Western markets, Olof Grut was experimenting with further processing and refining methods. Within the Asian and African markets, his team was not content to follow the Sumatran bulk shippers of bleached oil but developed their own markets in India and the Middle East and fought for the right to do so irrespective of pool priorities. Olof Grut was emerging within the firm as an inspired developer of his father's grand vision; and Bernam Oil Palms was becoming well known within the industry as an innovative *enfant terrible*.

NOTES

1   Personal communication from R.L. Grut, 21 April 1988; interview with Tan Sri Dato' Seri B. Bek-Nielsen, 2 April 1989.

2   Interview with Axel Lindquist, 6 April 1989; UPDR, 1925 and BOPDR, 1927. Sources for Map 4: UPAR, 1967; UBAR, 1940 and JAR, 1940.

3   Interview with Axel Lindquist, 6 April 1989; and personal communication including the photograph reproduced here, from his son Valdemar, born in the late 1930s and now living in Colorado, 15 August 1997. Crocodiles are now rare along the western rivers of Peninsular Malaysia, not just because of hunting but also because of the high volume of traffic and its attendant noise, which disturbs their breeding: personal communication from Knud Sehested, 15 December 1999.

4   L. Anciaux, *La Participation des Belges à l'Oeuvre Coloniale des Hollandais aux Indes Orientales* (Brussels: Académie Royale des Sciences d'Outre-Mer, 1955); E. Leplae, *Le palmier à huile en Afrique: son exploitation au Congo Belge et en Extrême-Orient*, Mémoires Tome VII (Brussels: Institut Royal Colonial Belge, Section des Sciences Naturelles et Médicales, 1939), pp. 25–27; D.J.M. Tate, *The RGA History of the Plantation Industry in the Malay Peninsula* (Kuala Lumpur: Oxford University Press for the Rubber Growers' Association (Malaya) Berhad, 1996), pp. 452–453, and p. 464 note 6, which details other early Malayan oil palm trials of less significance than Fauconnier's.

5   E. Rosenquist, 'The genetic base of oil palm breeding populations', *Proceedings of International Workshop on Oil Palm Germplasm and Utilisation, 26–27 March 1985* (Kuala Lumpur: ISOPB/PORIM, 1986), pp. 27–56; C.W.S. Hartley, *The Oil Palm (Elaeis guineensis Jacq.)* 3rd edn. (London: Longman, 1988), p. 21.

6   Interview with Eric Rosenquist, formerly of the Malayan agricultural department and of Guthries' Chemara Research Station, 11 August 1988; A. Beirnaert and R. Vanderweyen, 'Contribution a l'étude génétique et biométrique des variétés d'Elaeis guinéensis Jacquin', *Série Scientifique*, no. 27 (Brussels: Publications de l'Institut National pour l'Etude Agronomique du Congo Belge, 1941); Nigerian research efforts are outlined in the Agricultural Department's *Annual Reports* for 1916, 1923 and 1940, available in the UK PRO, series CO 657.

7   P. Creutzberg (ed.), *Changing Economy in Indonesia*, vol. I, *Indonesia's Export Crops, 1816–1940* (Amsterdam: Royal Tropical Institute, 1975), Table 11.

8   Interview with Thomas Fleming, based in Sumatra 1939–64 with Harrisons and Crosfield, 4 October 1988; L. Szekely, *Tropic Fever: the Adventures of a Planter in Sumatra* (Kuala Lumpur: Oxford University Press, 1979); M.H. Lulofs, *Rubber* (Kuala Lumpur: Oxford University Press, 1987).

9   Hartley, *Oil Palm*, p. 21; Tate, *RGA History*, pp. 453–454 and 464–465, note 12. I would also like to thank Jeremy Diamond of Socfin for inviting me to visit the Maison des Palmes, by then his home, on 30 August 1987.

10 H. Fauconnier, *The Soul of Malaya* (London: Penguin, 1948), p. 33 and Ch. 2; Leplae, *Le palmier à huile*, pp. 25–27.

11 S. Cunyngham-Brown, *The Traders* (London: Newman Neame, 1971), p. 252 and Appendix C; Peter Pugh *et al.*, edited by Guy Nickalls, *Great Enterprise: a History of Harrisons & Crosfield* (London: Harrisons & Crosfield, 1990), pp. 94–96 and 156; interview with Mr Thomas Fleming, 4 October 1988; *The Planter*, vol. X, nos. 9–11, 1930, pp. 242 and 321.

12 Creutzberg (ed.),*Changing Economy in Indonesia*, vol. I, Table 11; Lim Chong-Yah, *Economic Development of Modern Malaya* (Kuala Lumpur: Oxford University Press, 1967), Appendix 5.2, p. 337; Hartley, *Oil Palm*, p. 61; B. Bunting, C.D.V. Georgi and J.N. Milsum, *The Oil Palm in Malaya* (Kuala Lumpur: Agricultural Department, 1934), pp. 235–238.

13 *Bulletin of the Rubber Growers' Association*, vol. I, no. 3, 1919, p.33; Hartley, *Oil Palm*, p. 196; *The Planter*, vol. II, nos. 6–7, 1922, pp. 10 and 60, and vol. VII, no. 12, 1927, p. x of Appendix following p. 352.

14 A.A.L. Rutgers, 'African oil palm: developments in Sumatra', *The Planter*, vol. III, no. 11, 1923, pp. 595–596; H.N. Blommendahl, 'A preliminary paper on the ripening of oil-palm fruits', *The Planter*, vol. VI, no. 4, 1925, pp. 101–102; Bunting et al., *Oil Palm in Malaya*, pp. 125–129.

15 *The Planter*, vol. V, no. 8, 1925, p. 219; vol. X, no. 3, 1929, pp. 80–81; and vol. XIX, no. 11, 1938, p. 572.

16 *The Planter*, vol. V, no. 11, 1925, pp. 313–315; vol. XVIII, no. 11, 1937, pp. 510–513; Bunting et al., *Oil Palm in Malaya*, pp. 136–149; Hartley, *Oil Palm*, pp. 704–705.

17 UPDR, 1926–27; BOPDR, 1927.

18 C. Jørgensen, 'United Plantations and Bernam Oil Palms: highlights from a colourful past' (unpublished mss., 1984), pp.137–138.

19 Jørgensen, 'United Plantations', letter to Mrs Ida Ingemann from Aage Westenholz, 19 April 1925, in Appendix 4A, following p. 50.

20 Interviews with Axel Lindquist, 6 April 1989, and Tan Sri Dato' Seri B. Bek-Nielsen, 15 April 1989.

21 Jørgensen, 'United Plantations', Ch. 4 and pp. 134–145; personal communications from Christian Flemming Heilmann, 7 January 1999, and from John Heilmann, 8 February 1999; interview with Marianne Mayntz-Clausen, Theodor's daughter from his second marriage, 11 June 1998. Sadly, despite Theodor's willingness to follow his first wife and baby son back to America, the marriage did not last.

22 Interview with Mr and Mrs R.L. Grut, 19 April 1988; UPDR and BOPDR, 1927–28; insights into personal relationships from surviving 1930s correspondence.

23 This section relies essentially on material collected by Carrie Jørgensen in 1983–84, written up and partially reproduced in her 'United Plantations', Chs 2–5. This material was later destroyed in a fire at Ulu Bernam.

24 K.S. Sandhu, *Indians in Malaya: Some Aspects of their Immigration and Settlement, 1786–1957* (Cambridge: University Press, 1969), esp. Appendix 2.

25 Hartley, *Oil Palm*, Ch. 6.

26 Jørgensen, 'United Plantations', Ch. 8; interview with Mr and Mrs R.L. Grut, 19 April 1988; UBAR, 1927 and 1930–37. The rat menace remains a live issue on Malaysia's many oil palm plantations today, especially since pollinating weevils were introduced in the 1980s. Weevil larvae provide a source of protein, which the rats would otherwise lack in palm estates: Mohd. Basri Wahid and Hj. Abdul Halim bin Hj. Hassan, 'The effects of *Elaeidobius kamerunicus* Faust on rat control programmes of oil palm estates in Malaysia', *PORIM Occasional Papers,* 14 (June 1985), pp. 29–30.

27 Tate, *RGA History*, Ch. 27; UPDR, 1929–32; Westenholz to Hjartved, 22 January 1929 and Westenholz to Grut, 29 April 1930, CB, 1928–33.

28 Jørgensen, 'United Plantations', Ch. 9; 'Oil palms in Malaya: first factory opened in Perak', *The Planter*, vol. IX, no. 9, 1929, p. 265; 'Stork palm oil digester and press', *The Planter*, vol. XII, no. 12, 1932, p. ix.

29 Westenholz to Craig, 6 August 1929, CB, 1928–33; BOPDR, 1930–37.

30 UPDR, 1927–34.

31 Westenholz to Grut, 25 February, 8 and 22 April 1930, CB, 1928–33.

32 Jørgensen, 'United Plantations', Ch. 3; summary of changes to Articles of Association, in CB, 1928–33.

33 Westenholz to Grut, 11 April 1933, CB, 1928–33; Helvard to Grut, 10 March 1934, CB, 1934–39; UPCA, 1934; UPDR, 1935.

34 Westenholz to Grut, 22 March 1931, CB, 1928–33; Jørgensen, 'United Plantations', Ch. 3.

35 Aage Westenholz, 'Samarbejde mellem kapital og arbejdere' [Co-operation between capital and labour], *Borups Højskole 1922*, pp. 20–22 (kindly translated for me by Bente Flensborg; the ideas behind the Folk High School movement were first explained to me by Poul K. Vestergaard, who had personal experience of it); W.G. Jones, *Denmark: A Modern History* (London: Croom Helm, 1986), pp. 55–57 and 82–85; Henning Ravnholt, *The Danish Co-Operative Movement* (Copenhagen: Det Danske Selskab, 1947), pp. 12–16.

36 UPDR and BOPDR, 1937–38; Jørgensen, 'United Plantations', pp. 41 and 47.

37 Share Registers for Bernam Oil Palms, 1927–39 and 1947, and United Plantations, 1947, held in the Copenhagen office; lists of directors in UPDR and BOPDR, 1935–54; correspondence with Mrs Inge Asboe Mitchell, who was attached to the Ingemann household from 1945 to 1952, 8–9 October 1998.

38 UPDR and BOPDR, 1935–40.

39 Lim, *Economic Development*, Appendix 5.1, p. 336; Creutzberg (ed.),*Changing Economy*, Table 11, p. 98; S.M. Martin, *Palm Oil and Protest: an Economic History of the Ngwa Region, South-Eastern Nigeria, 1800–1980* (Cambridge: Cambridge University Press, 1988), Table 5, p. 149; UPDR and BOPDR, 1939.

40 Extraction rate figures from UBAR, 1937–41.

41 'Shipment of palm oil in bulk', *The Planter*, vol. XI, no. 12, 1931, pp. 353–354; C.D.V. Georgi, 'Bulk shipment of Malayan palm oil', *The Planter*, vol. XII, no. 6, 1932, pp. 167–168.

42 Jørgensen, 'United Plantations', Ch. 10; BOPDR, 1932.

43 Jørgensen, 'United Plantations', Ch. 10; BOPCA, 1935.

44 BOPCA, 1935; BOPDR, 1933–39; Olof Grut to Benzon, 10 June 1950, and Mann (Guthries) to Benzon, 1 August 1950, CC, 1948–51; an even earlier experiment with palm oil fractionation is described by K.G. Berger in 'Dr Lewkowitsch and early palm oil technology', *Chemistry and Industry*, 17 April 1989.

Jendarata estate's Hindu temple, 1919

Jendarata estate hospital, 1928

CHAPTER 3

War, Survival and Revival

LIFE AT ULU BERNAM IN 1939

The Second World War was to prove a great watershed in the history of United Plantations and Bernam Oil Palms, but its outbreak in September 1939 had little immediate impact on estate managers and workers in Malaya. The theatres of war seemed far away; and while all the European staff of United Plantations and Bernam Oil Palms had been members of the Federated Malay States Volunteer Force since 1936, the outbreak of war made little difference to their settled routine of monthly exercises. Meanwhile, there continued to be a strong overseas demand for plantation produce. Trading patterns within Europe itself soon began to change, but this had only a small effect on the prices paid in Malaya. In October 1939 the British Ministry of Food began to requisition all supplies of palm oil from the Malayan pool at a fixed price. Singapore prices fell as a result from the 1938 average of £14 per tonne to a 1939 average of £11 before rising again to £13 in 1940. This meant a slight dip in Bernam Oil Palms' gross profit margin, from 54 per cent of sales revenue in 1938 and 1940 to 50 per cent in 1939; but it in no way threatened the survival of the firm, and at Ulu Bernam itself, palm oil production continued unabated.[1]

Perhaps the greatest initial impact of the war was on the movements of Indian estate workers. The total work-force at Ulu Bernam had grown from 1,003 in 1933 to a peak of 1,855 in 1937, partly as a result of improvements in living conditions which had done much to compensate for Ulu Bernam's isolation. But following the end of immigration from India in 1938, other estates began to compete for the available workers with increasing vigour. The war brought increased tin and rubber export quotas and higher wages in all sectors. Meanwhile, some workers began to be uneasy at the long distances separating them from their

Sungei Bernam estate railway and field workers, 1928

relatives in India during wartime, and they began to move back to India in increasing numbers. As a result, the total work-force at Ulu Bernam had fallen to 1,366 by 1941. This was especially depressing for the Danish managers, since they had only just completed a long campaign to improve work-force living standards in the hope of encouraging Tamil workers to regard the estate as their permanent home.[2]

The campaign to improve Tamil workers' living conditions had begun as soon as Bernam Oil Palms began to make substantial profits in 1935. Two Hindu temples and a hospital had already been built as early as 1930. In the case of the temples, construction almost certainly took place on the workers' own initiative and at their expense. At Jendarata, where the first Hindu temple was built in 1916, the estate management had been willing to supply the land but it was the workers who organized and controlled the project. The historians of Jendarata's temple, Mr Munusamy and Mr Ramulu, emphasize the key role played by the temple in the Tamil people's cultural lives, its recognized ability to settle disputes and the people's eagerness to work overtime and donate income in order to raise the building and sustain its administration. Such eagerness was vital at a time when the European managers were preoccupied with getting the estate itself cleared and planted.[3]

Company funds for welfare projects were just as scarce at Ulu Bernam as at Jendarata during the 1920s and became even scarcer during the worst phase of the depression, 1930–34. Nevertheless, the management was proud to record that three schools surrounded by vegetable gardens had been established at Ulu Bernam by 1935. A Tamil recruiting pamphlet dating from that year emphasizes the estate's natural advantages of a good river water supply and freedom from malaria, together with its entertainment facilities – a drama hall with visiting Tamil actors and musicians, paid for by the management. This was a fairly modest start, but from 1935 onwards, more systematic improvements were made. The workers' houses were repaired, and the lines provided with piped, filtered and chlorinated water and bored-hole latrines. All these facilities were provided in line with government directives, but the company also provided further amenities on its own initiative. Two recreation grounds were made, and a co-operative savings society was formed, with the funds administered by Olof Grut. The

Jendarata estate workers' bathing place, 1919

river boat service was extended to run twice daily in each direction between Ulu Bernam and Hutan Melintang; and the central shopping area along 'Broadway', the main street next to the palm oil factory, was enlarged to provide a choice of 20 shops run by Chinese, Muslim and Tamil tradesmen – including a post office from which remittances could be sent directly to India. The hospital was expanded and put in the charge of a 'special grade assistant' under the visiting medical practitioner, Dr L.A. Watson. A nurse was also hired to develop antenatal and child welfare services. Finally, in 1938 a grazing ground was created for the workers' cattle, and space was allocated for vegetable gardens.[4]

By 1937, it had become possible for General Manager Olof Grut to report that 'conditions on Ulu Bernam have improved considerably during the last few years from a Tamil point of view'. Wages had also been kept a few cents higher than on the rubber estates downriver, not counting the extra pay available to workers who hunted rats or reared puppies in their spare time. From 1936 to 1939 the standard wages remained steady at 35–55 cents per day, depending on the tasks involved and the sex of the worker. The rates paid to male harvesters were the highest, averaging 55 cents per day but depending on the quantity of fruit harvested. This was about 10 per cent higher than the top wage paid to

Jendarata estate workers' housing, 1919

Jendarata estate assistant's bungalow, 1928

male rubber tappers on other Malayan estates. As most workers at Ulu Bernam turned out to the field on about 22 days per month, their average earnings per worker may be estimated at Straits $120 (£14) per year. For a household in which husband and wife worked, and one older child earned a little in the afternoons, annual earnings were in the region of £30–35. Food had to be bought out of these wages, but housing, schooling and medical care were free.

One interesting comparison is between these wages and the average incomes of smallholders in Nigeria's oil palm belt at the same period. Colonial officials had found these incomes extremely hard to assess when making their first survey for tax purposes in 1927, because much of the local farm produce was consumed by the people who had grown it and never passed through the market. But £16–18 per household was held to be a reasonable annual estimate in the Aba District of south-eastern Nigeria, where both food and palm oil were produced by most farmers. In the neighbouring Ikot Ekpene District, where farmers concentrated more heavily on producing palm oil for export, average household incomes were estimated at £19–24 per year. In 1938–39 the anthropologist Jack Harris conducted a more accurate and detailed budget study of just 16 individuals in the Igbo village of Ozuitem, north of Aba District. Here, farmers devoted most of their efforts to food production and earned cash from the sale of cassava as well as palm oil and kernels. Six of the people surveyed were women, earning £1–6 per annum; ten were men, earning £3–19. Only two of the men had annual cash incomes greater than £14, though some of those with low cash incomes may well have been producing large quantities of food for household consumption, and this food did not enter into Harris's evaluation.[5]

While the Nigerian evidence is very patchy, it does have enough substance to indicate that the field workers at Ulu Bernam were not badly off in comparison to their smallholder counterparts in the palm oil industry. Even where the small-holders' cash incomes had been adjusted to include the cash value of their own food production, they remained lower than the Ulu Bernam earnings; and Ulu Bernam workers had free access to medical services, a crèche and schools, all of which were either unobtainable or extremely expensive in rural Nigeria. It is clear that by the late 1930s, this plantation – and probably many others in Malaya – differed sharply from the nineteenth-century stereotype of a rapacious enterprise which relied for its profits on the misery of its work-force.

By modern standards, however, work-force living conditions were still far from ideal. A typical family home in the lines contained one room and a loft; children would sleep in the loft and parents in the downstairs room, which was also used for cooking during the day. The women in a household would rise at 4 a.m. to heat up the curry which they had made the night before and to cook rice, which would be taken to the fields to provide their lunch. Work began with the roll call in the lines at 6.30 a.m., after which the workers would get into the locomotive cars to travel to the fields for the day. A half-hour break for lunch would be taken at 11 a.m., after which they returned to work until 3.30 p.m., when they were able to leave the fields. However, for women the working day did not end then. When they returned in the evening, they had not only to cook but also to collect firewood from the jungle. They occasionally brought back scattered over-ripe palm fruits from the estate, which could be used to ignite the house-hold fire. Their final task, water collection, was perhaps the most time-consuming of all, because there was only one tap for every three rows of lines, or 36 homes – very similar to the conditions prevailing in eastern Nigerian villages today. Low water pressure meant that each bucket took a long time to fill, and there was plenty of scope for quarrels to break out in the queue. For bathing and washing clothes, the Bernam River remained essential, despite the risk of crocodiles.[6]

Managers and their wives also considered their facilities at Ulu Bernam by 1940 to be fairly basic. Their houses were well built, to Axel Lindquist's designs, and roofed with shingles or corrugated iron rather than *atap* thatch; and a Club House was built in 1936, next to an open strip which later became a combined airfield and recreation ground. However, there were very few white women to join the men in the Club House; only Olof Grut and Axel Lindquist had their wives with them by this time. Axel had only just got married to Ida Youngs, a British nurse from the hospital at Batu Gajah. Ida had helped Axel to recover from malaria and a bad leg injury the year before, and had seen through the bad temper brought on by his illness to the wit, resourcefulness and courage which lay beyond. Ida herself was both resourceful and brave, qualities which she needed in full measure in order to cope with her isolated life on the estate. There was little opportunity at Ulu Bernam for the entertaining which enlivened the life of Hedvig Heilmann at Jendarata during the 1930s: no wide circle of European wives to invite for bridge or Mah Jong parties on weekdays, or with whom to exchange family visits for curry tiffin on Sundays. Ida soon found a useful role for herself, obtaining medical supplies for the estate workers and giving first-aid and antenatal classes. The birth of two young sons followed, keeping her fully occupied. Nevertheless, it was a lonely life, as Rolf Grut's wife Rothes, who arrived from New Zealand shortly after the Second World War, and Andal Krishnan, who arrived in the 1970s, also recall.[7]

Rothes's most enduring memory is of being surrounded by tall trees, in both the jungle and the palm plantations; walking her babies felt like swimming underwater in a green sea. Andal remembers long, tedious journeys up and down the Bernam River. Even when the company began to use speedboats, the journey time was still 1 1/2 hours, and breakdowns were not unknown. Both Andal and her husband Krish often tell the story of how they set off on the speedboat one evening in the early 1970s with their daughter Hema, who was then just 2 months old. The boat broke down and Krish and the driver had to set off through the jungle by torchlight in search of a kampong where milk could be found – and boiled – to feed the crying baby. By the end of the 1980s, when I visited Ulu Bernam, it was readily accessible by road and such occurrences were a thing of the past. However, back in the 1930s the estate was deeply isolated. Even the men who managed it, who by that time formed a sizeable group, felt their isolation. They could make no use of the motorbikes and small Morris, Austin or Hillman cars that helped their counterparts at Jendarata to get out and make friends at the Telok Anson Club, which by the late 1930s boasted a swimming pool, golf course, tennis courts, dance floor and library as well as the all-important bar and dining room. If the young Europeans at Ulu Bernam wanted to taste such delights, their best option was to take up flying, which now became their most popular sport. Even the more fortunate managers at Jendarata found flying attractive, offering as it did a rapid route to the city lights of Kuala Lumpur and Singapore.[8]

Ulu Bernam's first pilot was L.K. Pay, a Danish aristocrat who was well known among the Tamils for his determination and his hot temper; the 'Tiger' of Ulu Bernam was renowned for his ability to control even the 'bad fellows'. With characteristic energy, Pay used to motorcycle down to Kuala Lumpur at the weekends in order to take flying lessons at the club there. Having graduated, he bought his own, aptly named Tigermoth in 1932 and used to fly it down to Singapore, taking with him his butler Mathalamuthu, suitably dressed in a white uniform complete with cap. His example inspired others, and when the Ipoh Flying Club was formed in the mid-1930s, it agreed to carry out weekly flying instruction from the Jendarata air field. Peter Milson, a veteran of the Royal Flying Corps, would fly over in his Avro Cadet biplane every Saturday morning, and the rest of the day would be spent with various keen pupils practising their 'circuits and bumps'. Olof and his younger brother Rolf Grut, Poul Bent Heilmann, P. Bedey and S.A.R. Jacobsen all became pilots before 1939, and the company bought its first aircraft, a Hornet which had been rebuilt after hitting a coconut palm near Penang, in 1937.[9]

Flying continued to be a vital part of the managers' experiences during the war years. During 1941, as the war drew closer to Malaya, Pay joined the Royal Malayan Volunteer Air Force together with P.B. Heilmann, H.C. Madsen, T. Lunoe and A. Laursen. In the event, they had little opportunity to join in the short-lived defence of Malaya against the Japanese, and Laursen, Madsen and Lunoe became prisoners of war. Together with Dr Watson, Madsen and Lunoe were sent to the notorious 'Death Railway' in Siam, while Laursen was held in Java. However, Pay managed to escape to America where he joined the Air Force. P. Bedey escaped to England where he too joined the Air Force. Finally, Rolf and Olof Grut made an extremely dramatic escape, initially to Singapore by plane, and used their flying skills to serve the Allied cause in Australia: Rolf Grut flew supplies to American troops with Australian Airways, and Olof Grut joined the Royal Australian Air Force. Their adventures will be told more fully in the third section of this chapter.[10]

MANAGEMENT IN WARTIME

On 9 April 1940 Germany occupied Denmark. This invasion was bitterly resented by the Danes, but they could offer little defence. Their official policy of neutrality and of maintaining a minimal defence force, which Westenholz had criticized in 1907, had been maintained throughout the 1910s, 1920s and 1930s. Furthermore, as a flat country with a small population of three million, Denmark was poorly equipped to resist an overland invasion such as that mounted by Germany in 1940. Her main hope lay in support from Britain, which had taken the bulk of her 1930s food exports and was reluctant to see this food diverted to German use. However, after some internal debate, Britain had decided in 1939 not to include Denmark in her list of small neutral countries which the Allies would commit themselves to defend. Hence, when the Germans invaded in 1940, they met little armed resistance. The Danish government felt that it would be pointless to declare war on the invaders and maintained a neutral stance in the hope of preserving its control over internal affairs. Meanwhile the Germans proceeded to expel the British legation and halt Danish trade with Britain.[11]

The Danish government's appeasement policy was extremely unpopular at grassroots level, where it led to a great resurgence of Grundtvig's patriotic Christian ideals. The farmers resisted wartime pressures to supply eggs, bacon and butter to Germany; and the general population successfully thwarted a German plan to arrest the 8,000 Danish Jews in October 1943 by taking them into hiding, later smuggling 7,200 out to Sweden. Westenholz's niece Karen Blixen was among those who gave shelter to the Jews, an action of which her uncle would have been proud.[12]

Despite the opposition of many Danes to the German occupation, and their government's neutral stance, the possessions of Danish individuals in British colonies after 9 April 1940 were declared to be 'enemy property'. United Plantations and Bernam Oil Palms were both incorporated in the Federated Malay States, but because the majority of their capital was owned by Danes, it thus fell into the hands of Malaya's Custodian of Enemy Property. The Custodian promptly withheld the payment of dividends to Danish residents and appointed a new Board of Directors for each company.

The new boards of United Plantations and Bernam Oil Palms were identical. They included just two members of the pre-war United Plantations board, namely Commander Grut, who had escaped to Sweden, and the British citizen

R.D. Craig. The pre-war Bernam Oil Palms board supplied a further two members: the Penang auditor F.H. Grumitt and the general manager of United Plantations, Poul Bent Heilmann, who was Commander Grut's cousin. Olof Grut was appointed a board member for the first time; and the custodian appointed two further members, Lieutenant-Colonel G.D.A. Fletcher and the Honourable Mr E.D. Shearn. Fletcher became the new vice-chairman, while Commander Grut remained chairman.[13]

Although the pre-war Copenhagen directors lost a great deal of power through these changes, they had drawn up contingency plans to cover just such an event. As Poul Bent Heilmann later explained to his sons, he did his best to carry out the management strategy which they had previously agreed. Even after direct communications with Denmark were cut off, he did his best to maintain some form of contact through Henrik Kaufmann, the Danish ambassador to Washington. The overall impact of the custodian's intervention, therefore, was by no means to transform the Danish culture of United Plantations and Bernam Oil Palms but rather to bring the two companies still more closely together than before and to reinforce the control of the Grut family over them. During the brief time before the Japanese occupation, the companies were not only incorporated in Malaya but also controlled in Malaya by a small group which included the key serving managers, and within which there was a close personal relationship between the chairman and these managers. This made for an even sharper distinction than had existed in the days of Aage Westenholz between the United Plantations' style of management and control and the more bureaucratic, arm's length style of the British Agency Houses. After the war this distinction continued and was reinforced; it remains strong today.[14]

Meanwhile, at the local level, business continued as before during 1940 and much of 1941. High palm oil yields of 1.3 tonnes per acre continued to be a source of pride, and Olof Grut introduced a new continuous purification system at Ulu Bernam that had been developed to his own design and patented in 1939. New storage tanks were ordered for both Ulu Bernam and Jendarata palm oil factories. Both companies continued to be profitable, and large sums of money built up in the hands of the Public Trustee and in the companies' bank accounts. At the end of 1941, the two companies had a total of Straits $111,000 in their Malayan bank, $208,000 in New York, $406,000 in London and $115,000 in Scandinavia. The public trustee held a further $420,000 in Kuala Lumpur, in trust for the companies' shareholders. All this cash was to be vitally important in enabling managers to rehabilitate the estates quickly after the Japanese occupation; for between December 1941 and October 1945 much was destroyed.[15]

INVASION AND FLIGHT

Olof Grut himself, being determined not to let valuable stocks and food stores fall into Japanese hands, began the process of destruction in December 1941. He, Poul Bent Heilmann and the other senior managers had decided to stay on the estates until the last possible moment, flying on reconnaissance missions for the Volunteer Force in the meantime. On the last of these missions Olof was forced to make an emergency landing on Kuantan beach, and soon after his return, on 23 December, the final evacuation order was given by the district officer. Olof and Poul Bent stayed just long enough to distribute all the rice, sugar and money left on the estate to the Tamil work-force and office staff, giving them each two months' food rations. They then drove down to Kuala Lumpur, a dangerous and slow journey owing to the absence of lighting. But no sooner had they arrived safely than Olof began to worry about the palm oil left on the estate, which the Japanese might find useful, and about the company records left in the office. Leaving Poul Bent to continue on to Singapore, Olof made his way back overland on Christmas Day, borrowing a motorcycle on which he rode along the irrigation embankment between the Tengi River and Torkington Estate on the Bernam River. Here he found a small boat in a kampong which took him up to Ulu Bernam. By this time the Japanese had already arrived at Hutan Melintang. Olof discharged 150 tonnes of palm oil into the river, seized the vital documents and left on 27 December. He then travelled with all speed to Singapore, pausing only to leave the rescued records in Kuala Lumpur with Harrisons, Barker & Co., the company secretaries who had been appointed in 1940 by the custodian.[16]

Once in Singapore, Olof rejoined his wife Annette and two sons, the youngest a baby of only a few months, who had left Lower Perak with the other European women on 15 December. With some difficulty a berth was found for Annette and the children on a steamer leaving for Perth, but Olof and his brother Rolf had to stay behind. The Volunteer Force had by now been disbanded, so they were free to leave, but in contrast to the luckier members of the regular military and government services, no official transportation was available to evacuate them.

Like Poul Bent Heilmann, who had arrived a couple of days earlier, they had to fend for themselves. Poul Bent managed to squeeze in as a deck passenger on a crowded, flat-bottomed coastal freighter bound for Batavia (now Jakarta) in Java. Meanwhile, the Grut brothers fell in with an old friend from the Forestry Department and joined the team which he had formed to repair an old boat; but just as they had rigged it out with water, fuel and sails and were setting the day to sail, fellow Ipoh flying club members alerted them that a Japanese strike against Singapore was imminent. Luckily, the Gruts' fellow aviators had obtained some old planes which they were keen to have flown over to Sumatra, and Olof and Rolf flew out of Singapore in one of these the very day before Singapore fell. They skimmed over the water to Medan at an altitude of little more than 6 metres, landing in between the craters which Japanese aircraft had already made on the airfield there. Together they fled by road to the southern tip of Sumatra, dodging Japanese parachutists en route, and took a boat to Java.

The journey on from Java to Australia, where their wives and families were waiting anxiously, proved equally hazardous, both for Poul Bent Heilmann and for the Grut brothers. Poul Bent never liked to recall his passage on a flat-bottomed river freighter, shared with 20 other desperate European refugees and a skeleton Chinese crew, which made its way precariously through the Indonesian archipelago from Java to Timor, and thence across the open sea to north-western Australia. Despite grave shortages of food, and especially of water, the boat continued on southwards along the coast until it finally reached the port of Fremantle, near Perth, in March 1942. Hedvig, who had been settled since January 1941 in the seaside town of Barwon Heads, near Melbourne, never forgot the moment when she opened his telegram: 'Arrived by the grace of God. Will see you soon. Love Poul.' Meanwhile, the Grut brothers had been travelling overland through Java to the southern port of Cilacap, where they had to take their chance on separate ships. Rolf found a berth on a small ship destined for Australia and survived a hazardous journey in which the ship was attacked by Japanese bombers. Its size, combined with the quick thinking of its captain, helped to save it from a direct hit. Rolf and his fellow passengers lay on the deck and shot at the aircraft with Bren guns and rifles, forcing it to gain height and lose accuracy, while the captain himself lay on the deck with binoculars, shouting directions to the crew for swerving evasive action. Meanwhile, Olof had boarded a convoy destined for Sri Lanka. It suffered a similar bombardment and half its ships were sunk off Sumatra in the Bangka Strait. Olof was lucky enough to escape and made his way on from Sri Lanka to South Africa, eventually getting a passage back to Australia. Annette, believing herself a widow, was astonished to receive his telegram saying, simply, 'Meet me in Melbourne'.[17]

Meanwhile, back in Malaya, several managers from United Plantations and Bernam Oil Palms had been interned by the Japanese. A number of fellow Danes had been caught in Singapore but, because they were not members of the Royal Air Force, were allowed to claim neutral status and remain free. O.C. Dalsgaard and M. Alsing returned to Sungei Bernam Estate, and Svend Pontoppidan Møller to Jendarata, where he became inspector for estates, Lower Perak, under the Japanese. Møller had joined United Plantations in 1925 and had been sub-manager at Jendarata since 1936; Dalsgaard had been sub-manager at Sungei Bernam since 1935. Thus there was some continuity of management during the early years of the Japanese occupation, although there were no European assistants other than Alsing and no Europeans at all at Ulu Bernam.[18]

However, by 1943 the three Danes had fallen out with the Japanese, who had become increasingly sceptical of their claims to non-enemy status and had set them to work as labourers in the fields, greatly to the surprise of the Tamil workers who still remember seeing Møller toiling in the sun without his shirt. Møller eventually fled to the Cameron Highlands, while Dalsgaard and Alsing were imprisoned at Pudu Jail. Axel Paulsen, a former United Plantations manager and by 1943 the inspector for coconut estates, Selangor, brought food and medicine to the imprisoned Danes and campaigned vigorously for their release, which came after 8 months. Dalsgaard and Alsing then fled to the Cameron Highlands to join Møller.

In 1936 United Plantations had bought a small plot of land near the highest point of the Highlands, just below the newly opened, Danish-owned Sungei Palas tea estate. Axel Lindquist had designed a bungalow for the site that was built and furnished just before the war. A more modern 'Jendarata Bungalow' still marks the spot. However, when Møller and his fellow refugees reached it in 1943 they found the original building had been wrecked by the Japanese – only the roof remained. The Sungei Palas Estate had also shut down, and the Danes remaining in the area had taken refuge in a bungalow still further up the Brinchang mountain that had luckily escaped Japanese notice at the beginning of the occupation. Here they were helped with food and other supplies by the jungle-based resistance movement until the occupation ended and they were able to return to Jendarata in October 1945.

89

ESTATE LIFE UNDER THE JAPANESE

For the estate workers, the occupation meant a rapid change in the nature of their work and a more gradual fall in their living standards. Both changes resulted from the distinctive economic aims of the Japanese in South-East Asia. The Japanese were keen to block the supply to Britain and her allies of vital raw materials like rubber, tin, iron ore and mineral oil, all of which were urgently needed by industry and by the armed forces. However, Japan itself could absorb only a small proportion of the exports which had previously gone from Malaya to Europe and the United States, especially after the Americans won the Battle of Midway Island in June 1942. This turned the tide of warfare in the Pacific against the Japanese, and Allied submarines began to make the shipping lanes decidedly unsafe for their freighters. Later on, Allied aircraft reinforced this trend, and the Japanese had to begin making tough decisions about which goods to ship back home from the South. Rubber lost out in favour of rice, which had previously been traded extensively within South-East Asia and imported in bulk by Malayan estates but which the Japanese now required to feed their own armies and home population. This shift in Japanese trading priorities had a strong impact on the lives of plantation workers in Malaya, who now came under pressure to feed themselves, and who therefore had to switch their energies away from rubber and towards starchy food crops which could substitute for imported rice. At the same time, imported cloth, medicines and luxuries like sugar and tobacco became increasingly scarce in Malaya, because of the shortage of export revenue with which to pay for them. By the beginning of 1944 the situation was desperate.[19]

Retired estate workers at Jendarata and Ulu Bernam recall that living conditions were slightly better in the oil palm areas than in the rubber areas, because palm oil was valued by the Japanese as a foodstuff. Crude palm oil is rich in Vitamins A and E and, as the author of 'Palm oil "chop" ' had observed in *The Planter* in the 1920s, it can add a delicious and savoury flavour to soups and stews. Building on these characteristics, Japanese nutritional chemists set to work in March 1942 and within 8 months had developed a new brand of palm oil for local sale. 'Refined Medicinal Red Palm Oil' was marketed as 'a crystal-clear oil of port-wine colour', rich in Vitamin A and 'free from injurious substances of any kind', not unlike United Plantations' own Nutrolein brand, which was launched some 50 years later. Back in 1942, the high nutritional value of palm oil may explain why the Japanese assigned five resident officers to oversee Ulu Bernam, while Jendarata was covered simply by four visiting agents, who lived in a house at Hutan Melintang and paid daily visits to the estate. The visiting officials took far harsher disciplinary measures to ensure their authority than those which were used by the resident managers. On Division I of Jendarata Estate, which specialized in rubber, the officer in charge used to raid the houses of absent workers, confiscate their food and take it to his office, where he would leave it publicly to rot. Although no one was killed, beatings were common; and several hundred workers were sent to Siam to labour on the 'Death Railway', of whom only about half came back.[20]

One early result of the occupation at Jendarata was that wages ceased to be paid in cash, and supplies of rice were no longer available from the estate management. Instead, the workers were paid in tapioca (manioc), of which each received 2 katis (1.2 kilograms) per day. Later on they were ordered to plant tapioca, sorghum and sweet potatoes on former rubber land. Although they had never eaten tapioca before, they grew to accept it because there was no alternative. They were hungry, and the sour-tasting flour could be made more palatable by baking it into cakes and eating it with stews made with fresh fish from the river and edible leaves from the jungle. Salt and vegetables could be bought from the *kampongs* (villages) nearby, but the only means which most people had of earning cash was to go secretly and work for the Chinese smallholders, planting tapioca and sweet potatoes. They used to go before dawn and return after dusk, thus escaping notice from the visiting Japanese.

Moonlighting was the most effective way of keeping up living standards during the occupation, but its extent was limited by the harsh penalties which the Japanese imposed on anyone who was found out. At Jendarata, women and children suffered most of all from the resulting shortages of sugar, vegetables and milk. By 1944 many were reduced to holding the few remaining cubes of sugar in their hands, looking at them and imagining the taste while they took their coffee without it. Young children had to be given coffee instead of milk, tapioca instead of cereal, and poor nutrition combined with the closing of the estate hospital meant that many died. Meanwhile, their mothers were increasingly distressed by shortages of clothing. During the last two years of the war some women found themselves with nothing at all to wear; they were too ashamed to go to the field, to fetch firewood or even to collect water. One of the first priorities of the returning Danes in 1945 was to get supplies of cloth to distribute to the desperate women.[21]

At Ulu Bernam, the estate had become even more isolated than it had been before the war, since most of the boats had been destroyed by the British military forces during their withdrawal in December 1941. The workers had even fewer opportunities of outside work than there were at Jendarata, as their neighbour-hood was still very sparsely populated and uncommercialized; but payment in the form of sugar, rice, dried fish and cigarettes was available from the Japanese. The work-force was more kindly treated and felt that their labour on the estate was more highly valued than at Jendarata, but the task of the harvesters became increasingly dangerous as the trees grew taller. At the end of 1944 the danger was intensified, as the harvesters were asked to stop pruning the trees in order to leave more time for tapioca and sorghum planting. The half-cut or rotten fronds at the top of unpruned palm trees could easily give way when the harvester grasped hold of them for support, sending him off balance and possibly hurtling to the ground.[22]

One person who managed to escape the more depressing and dangerous results of the Japanese occupation was Mathalamuthu, who had come to Jendarata in 1926 and was eventually to serve Tan Sri Dato' Seri B. Bek-Nielsen for 42 years as his chef and friend. Muthu was only 12 years old when he came to Jendarata with his father and stepmother. They had been recruited through the *kangani* system from Hadmai in Southern India, by Muthu's uncle who had been working for United Plantations since 1917. The family initially settled at Jendarata, where Muthu worked as a grass-cutter along with 65 other children. He was very dis-tinctive in appearance, with long hair tied back to reveal earrings, and because of this he was noticed in 1928 by the aviator L.K. Pay. Pay cut Muthu's hair, gave him a job cleaning his bicycle and running errands and eventually trained him as a cook and butler to accompany him on his air journeys to Kuala Lumpur. By 1938 Muthu had become settled and prosperous and was able to travel to India to find a bride. When his eldest son was born in 1939 Pay presented the family with an excellent Australian cow, which saw them through the worst milk shortages of the war years.[23]

When Pay left and the Japanese came, a clerk at Ulu Bernam told the Japanese that Muthu was a good cook and they sent for him to come and serve them. Muthu did not like this at all; he feared that working for the Japanese would be as tough as working for one of the notorious European 'Mems'. So he and his family quickly slipped away to the small United Plantations coconut estate of Kuala Bernam, where they stayed with his stepmother. The Bagan Datoh delta was full of smallholdings and of small coconut estates like Kuala Bernam, and so was a backwater from the Japanese point of view, not unlike the Dindings region further north in Perak, where Dato' Malcolm E. Mathieu spent a fascinating war hunting wild game, first for sport and then for survival. Strangely enough, though coconuts were a staple food item and source of oil for Malay cooking, the Japanese did not take nearly as much interest in this crop as they did in palm oil. Hence there was a thriving private-sector trade in coconut oil, and Muthu was fortunate in having a Raleigh bicycle which he could use to join in this trade. He had hidden this bicycle in his loft during the early months of the occupation, when Tamil workers and Japanese military officers had looted many other valuables at Ulu Bernam, including L.K. Pay's treasured silverware.[24]

There was a great demand for coconut oil in the inland villages of Bidor and Langkap, but Muthu soon found that other traders from the coast were unwilling to travel so far and to pass the military encampment at Cicely Estate, just east of Teluk Intan. Muthu began making the journey regularly, and moved from Kuala Bernam to a house on the main road to Teluk Intan, just opposite Jendarata Estate. He discovered that the tobacco grown in Langkap made an even more profitable trading commodity. Muthu himself made the leaves into cigars, which fetched a good price in Japanese currency at Kuala Bernam, Sabak Bernam and Ulu Bernam.

The trade was not without its dangers, especially because the Japanese had outlawed all private commerce between Perak and Selangor, and Sabak Bernam was on the Selangor side of the Bernam River. One day Muthu was caught by the military police while carrying 10,000 cigars across the river in a sampan. Luckily this was seen by an Indian Muslim friend of his who owned a restaurant which was a favourite with the Japanese. The friend ran out and pleaded with the police, who eventually let Muthu go with a warning. On another night, Muthu was cycling towards Teluk Intan without lights when all of a sudden he ran into a Japanese sentry post. He greeted the Japanese with a bow, murmuring polite words in their own language and improvising a story about his wife being gravely ill in the hospital nearby. Two Chinese travellers then appeared, causing much more excitement among the sentries; while the newcomers were being beaten up and thrown into a lorry, Muthu was left alone and seized the opportunity to escape.

Through braving such dangers, Muthu was able to carry on an extremely profitable trade and accumulated a great deal of Japanese currency. He ploughed much of this capital back into the business but spent some on vegetables for his family. He was fortunate in having a good pre-war stock of clothes, some of which he gave away as the war progressed and the shortage became acute. After the war, Muthu continued for a while with his bicycle trade until one day he met Olof Grut, who was also cycling along near Hutan Melintang. Olof recognized him straight away and asked him to return to Ulu Bernam as his cook. While being very fond of the Danes whom he had known before the war, Muthu was reluctant to abandon his career as an entrepreneur and a compromise was eventually reached. Muthu resumed his duties as a cook but also became the business manager of the company bus service, employing a driver and taking a share of the profits. He was able to continue saving money and to provide for the education of his children. His daughter, Mary Rose, went to teacher training college and now teaches in Teluk Intan; one son, Jesudass, became a lawyer and the other, Louis, graduated in mechanical engineering from Singapore University and now works in a palm oil mill in Johore. Muthu's is a remarkable success story; his only regret was that so much work left little time for anything else.

THE END OF THE WAR

Far from ending the sufferings of the work-force at Jendarata and Ulu Bernam, the Japanese capitulation initially brought nothing but chaos. The Japanese who had been administering Lower Perak and its plantations left the region just one week after their nation's surrender in August 1945, but it was not until October that the first European estate managers arrived to replace them. In the intervening months the work-force had been harassed by armed bandits, who came to their homes at night demanding sugar and cigarettes and led off their bullocks. They received no rations and no pay and had to live off the tapioca and sweet potatoes which they had planted under the Japanese. Yet despite these trials, few deserted the estates, partly because of the valiant morale-boosting efforts of the Asian office staff, especially the chief clerk at Ulu Bernam, K. Thomas.[25]

Asger Laursen was the first Dane to return to the estates, after being released from his internment in Java at the end of September. When he arrived at Ulu Bernam early in October, he found 70 per cent of the pre-war work-force still living on the estate, ready to set to work again with a will. He was especially impressed by their efforts in protecting the factory, European bungalows and furniture from the looters and recommended that they be paid in full and in cash for the work done between August and October. Luckily, the money left in local bank accounts at the end of 1941 was still available, and cash could be ordered from Singapore. This was of great importance to the workers in enabling them to settle their debts and get fresh supplies of goods from Ulu Bernam's shopkeepers. Laursen also saw that malnutrition and illness were rife on the estate, and one of his first priorities was to reopen the hospital under the pre-war dresser, Appadurai. Finally, he held a constructive meeting with the local 'Three-Star men', Chinese communist leaders, who agreed on a policy of mutual tolerance. At this stage it was still unclear what position the Chinese would take under the re-established British administration; the Emergency had not yet begun, and it was still possible to hope for a peaceful resolution of its underlying political issues.[26]

Meanwhile, Møller and Alsing had returned from the Cameron Highlands to Jendarata and Sungei Bernam Estates, respectively. Both estates were in a far worse condition than Ulu Bernam; Sungei Bernam had been thoroughly neglected and most of its work-force lost during the occupation, while 350 acres of rubber had been lost at Jendarata because of neglected drainage on the low-lying alluvial clay soil. Nevertheless, being nearer to Teluk Intan, both managers found it easier to obtain the necessary supplies than did Asger Laursen, who was reduced to sending Møller imploring letters begging for rice, petrol, clothing, saucepans, drinking mugs, ladder-bamboos and cash.[27]

Despite these shortages, and helped by a willing work-force, Laursen managed to organize further food cultivation and palm fruit harvesting and to get the palm oil factory machinery going, helped by the fact that the Japanese had carried on using it up to the time of their withdrawal. He also obtained enough drums to hold the 500 tonnes of oil in stock by the end of October. However, he had only three cargo boats, each of just 45 tonnes' capacity, in which the oil could be shipped downriver and only one small Japanese-made launch in which he could travel out from the isolated estate. To make matters even worse, there was a severe shortage of petrol and kerosene oil for starting the engines and diesel oil for keeping them going. Laursen was forced to follow the Japanese practice of running machinery and boats on low-grade 'rubber-petrol' and palm oil that led to frequent cloggings and breakdowns. He found all this depressing, and the sufferings of the ill-nourished people in his hospital continued to be heart-rending. He had come straight from his prisoner-of-war camp to a tough and lonely life at Ulu Bernam, and by the end of December his strength was giving out:

> I am about to collapse half the time and at the point of despair the other
> half and am not even allowed to curse loudly for fear of harming the

general morale. It is nothing but "Mud and sweat and tears" but I suppose it will come right sometime.[28]

Fortunately for Laursen, matters began to improve very soon after he wrote this desperate letter. During the Japanese occupation, R.D. Craig had been able to arrange for United Plantations and Bernam Oil Palms to be temporarily registered in London under the Companies Registration (Emergency) Act. As a result, Olof Grut was eligible for appointment to the British Palm Oil Inspection Committee which arrived in Malaya at the end of October, 1945. Meanwhile, Poul Bent Heilmann had been summoned at the end of 1944 to join the Brisbane branch of the newly formed United Nations Reconstruction and Rehabilitation Agency, which was drawing up plans for the economic recovery of South-East Asia following the anticipated Allied victory in the Pacific War. In June 1945 he and his family were sent over to London on a British troop ship, so that he could join the team which was preparing to set out for Malaya as soon as hostilities ended. Once in Malaya, Poul Bent swiftly obtained permission to concentrate his efforts on the rehabilitation of his own estates, which he visited together with Olof early in November, returning to live there the following month.[29]

Poul Bent Heilmann's special task was to ensure the recovery of Jendarata's devastated rubber stands, while Olof Grut concentrated on the oil palm operations at Ulu Bernam, where he arrived just a week after Laursen wrote his letter. With the help of Axel Lindquist, who placed orders for essential spare parts supplies in Australia, together with his own official contacts, through whom he arranged local supplies of diesel and kerosene oil, Olof was soon able to relieve Laursen's situation. Meanwhile, Laursen himself had managed to salvage one of Ulu Bernam's pre-war launches, and another had been found sunk in a drain near Jendarata. By the beginning of 1946 it had become possible to start a twice-weekly service between Ulu Bernam and Hutan Melintang. With their vital lines of supply and communication now re-established, Bernam Oil Palms' managers were finally able to begin the task of reconstruction.[30]

RECONSTRUCTION AND INNOVATION

At the end of 1946 Poul Bent Heilmann retired as general manager of United Plantations, although he continued to play an advisory role as a member of the board of directors until 1951, and returned as acting general manager in 1948, when Olof Grut undertook a lengthy foreign tour in search of fresh machines. His retirement marked an important departure in the history of United Plantations and Bernam Oil Palms, for from now on they had the same general manager – Olof Grut – who took overall responsibility for all the estates, whether planted with coconut, oil palm or rubber. From December 1946 Olof was assisted by Benny Olsen, the first joint secretary of the two companies, who ran their central office at Jendarata. By June 1947 Olof had been appointed vice-chairman of both companies, a post he held jointly with his father's old friend and cousin, Niels Benzon, who lived in Denmark. Commander Grut was now 66 years old, ailing in health and eager to ensure a smooth succession. Olof was still too young to take over as chairman, but his new position ensured that his views would be heard with respect by the rest of the board. Meanwhile, his energy and enthusiasm proved an inspiration to his staff throughout the period 1946–1952, when he continued to live at Jendarata and made frequent visits to Ulu Bernam.[31]

During 1946 and 1947 the day-to-day management of Jendarata was carried out by Rolf Grut and of Ulu Bernam by S.P. Møller. Asger Laursen continued to work as a field manager at Ulu Bernam, taking a well-earned long leave in 1948 and returning to manage Jendarata from 1949 to 1954, when he retired. But Laursen's main contribution to the work of post-war reconstruction had been made in 1945, and during the three years which followed he played a less strenuous role. During these years the most active contributor to the work of reconstruction was Axel Lindquist, the newly appointed chief engineer of both companies, who arrived back at Ulu Bernam from Australia in February 1946 and remained there until he retired 11 years later.[32]

Axel Lindquist, the planter, engineer and crocodile hunter, had few formal educational qualifications but had a great flair for making things work. After a typical Danish general education to the age of 16, he had spent two years studying mechanical engineering at a vocational or trade school before joining General Motors in Copenhagen as an apprentice mechanic and engine tuner. His talents were soon noticed, and Commander William Grut was among the regular clients who insisted that Axel alone should retune their cherished cars. General Motors was on the point of appointing Axel to a senior post in Poland when he was lured away by Commander Grut to run the transport facilities at Ulu Bernam. With typical firmness, Axel insisted that he be given a wider training as a planter, and this later stood him in good stead when developing systems of integrated quality management at all stages of palm oil production, from seedlings to shipment (see Chapter 6). However, even before the Second World War it had become obvious that Axel's distinctive flair was still for engineering. During his first decade in Malaya he had set up the railway lines on the oil palm estates, built several motor boats for Ulu Bernam, designed the Cameron Highlands bungalow and several staff bungalows at Jendarata and Ulu Bernam, and trained as a palm oil factory manager under Olof Grut. From 1934 to 1941 he had run the Jendarata palm oil mill, achieving a consistently high extraction rate of 16 per cent while reducing the percentage of free fatty acids in the palm oil from 4 per cent to 3 per cent.[33]

A dogged perfectionist, Axel Lindquist contrasted sharply in character with the more impressionistic thinker, Olof Grut. Olof was full of inspirational ideas but relied on good practical men to make them work. He had great faith in Lindquist, and the two were strong personal friends. They enjoyed sailing together down the Bernam River and along the coast to Penang; and they used to hold snipe-shooting contests on the hill just above the little gravel pit which was opened up on the jungle fringes of Ulu Bernam after the war. Beaters would go down into the jungle around the gravel pit to startle the birds, while Lindquist and Grut stayed on the hilltop watching for the birds to come up. These expeditions were not undertaken only, or maybe even mainly, for the sake of 'sport'; fresh food was in desperately short supply at the time, and much of the available tinned food had 'blown' and was unfit to eat. Axel, ever the keen hunter, went on after dark to shoot wild boar and spear freshwater prawns by torchlight, luring them from their hiding places with palm fruit and rice and drifting silently down the Bernam River in a flat-bottomed sampan, aiming to catch them unawares. For Olof, by contrast, hunting was a daylight affair. A good half of its attraction was the excuse it offered to walk and sit quietly in the jungle, and after a shooting session with Axel he would often stay on the hill alone, simply looking around. He could talk for hours about the different butterflies and birds he had seen on these occasions.[34]

Although Olof had given Axel some warning of the conditions to be expected at Ulu Bernam after the war, he still received an unpleasant shock when he arrived there from Australia in February 1946. Having turned down a comfortable job and a partnership in the 'Green Star' bus line serving the seaside community of Barwon Heads, near Melbourne, Axel found himself back on the edge of the jungle, coping with chaos. Ida, who stayed on in Australia for a further three months to settle their sons in boarding school, soon found herself bombarded with telegrams requesting medicines and equipment which were urgently needed but quite unobtainable in Perak. Dr Watson had returned after a harrowing ordeal on the Burma–Siam railway to find a work-force badly weakened by hookworm and other intestinal parasites, and Ida's medical knowledge and understanding of hospital organization proved invaluable in getting hold of appropriate treatments. She faced a still greater challenge when asked to track down machines and spare parts but was amazed by the generous response she encountered in Australia. Many friends and neighbours went out of their way to help her and, through her, Axel. The value of this help can hardly be overstated, for after several years spent running on rubber petrol and palm oil, the factory at Ulu Bernam needed a complete overhaul. A small workshop had been set up there before the war, but it had no capacity for making spare parts. Given Ida's heroic efforts at obtaining equipment in Australia, it was especially frustrating when some of her consignments were lost in chaotic conditions in Singapore Harbour, and many more were urgently needed. In particular, parts were needed for an almost complete rebuilding of the boilers, digesters (stirring kettles) and centrifugal oil purifiers at Ulu Bernam; and for the steam engine, digesters and depericarpers at Jendarata. New conveyors and kernel baths were needed at both factories.[35]

The greatest difficulty was in getting fresh internal shells for the digesters. A reliable pre-war supplier, United Engineers of Ipoh, undertook to make some but had extremely limited capacity. Efforts to speed up the supply by ordering extra shells from Singapore failed because of endemic strikes there. In desperation, Lindquist set off for Ipoh to see if steel plate or channel iron could be obtained, with the idea of using these to make casings and simple parts in the Ulu Bernam workshop. He found that only pig iron and cast iron were available, and even for these the prices were exorbitant and there was a three-month waiting list.[36]

Outraged, Lindquist bought a book on foundry operation and brought it back to Ulu Bernam. Olof Grut was somewhat surprised, but gave his usual firm support to Lindquist, who then set about building and running the firm's own foundry. He bought up obsolete and worn-out machinery of all kinds and melted it down to get iron, thus starting an operation which ran successfully for 25 years; only in 1972 did cheaper iron and brass castings become available locally. Meanwhile, the workshop buildings were extended, using a hangar-style shed which had previously been built by the Japanese to house a currency printing works in Kuala Lumpur.[37]

Olof Grut became intensely interested in these developments, and thought that if the workshop was going to begin producing spare parts which could not be bought on the market, there was no reason to limit its efforts to straightforward casings and shells. He managed to obtain two small lathe machines, a drilling machine, a shaping machine, and a grinding machine from the custodian of enemy property. With these it became possible to manufacture more complicated replacement parts. At this time Olof also got involved in negotiations with Werkspoor NV of Amsterdam about the possibility of developing an improved machine for the continuous centrifugal purification of palm oil. Lehmann Nielsen had developed this process at Ulu Bernam before the war, using a Titan Rotojector, but this machine had been expensive to maintain even in peacetime, and Olof's experience in trying to get it running smoothly again after the war led him to take a keen interest in alternative suppliers.[38]

In this way, out of desperation rather than through careful planning, the United Plantations' tradition of in-house engineering was born. It involved two characteristic traits: trying out experimental machinery and perfecting it in co-operation with a wide range of specialist suppliers; and making as well as maintaining some standard machines in the firm's own workshops, so that the experience of running and maintaining the original models could be built into the design of the next generation. These propensities have often been identified by Western observers as key reasons for the success of Japanese operations, but clearly they are not uniquely Japanese. Instead, as the Ulu Bernam example shows, they are actions fostered by trying to build an efficient factory quickly, in an economy which is desperately short of the necessary equipment – but not of technical skills and ingenuity.[39]

Thanks to Lindquist's energy and determination, the factory at Ulu Bernam was rapidly overhauled and began palm oil production again in March 1946. The mechanics in Ulu Bernam's workshop then turned their attention to Jendarata's needs, and this factory too was producing palm oil again by the end of May. Repairs to the kernel-cracking equipment took longer but were completed by the end of November. United Plantations and Bernam Oil Palms thus gained about 6 months' lead over their rivals in Malaya, who had been much slower to begin the task of reconstruction after the Japanese occupation. Lindquist's initiative was probably the key reason for this achievement, but it is also possible that the Copenhagen directors were more willing than their British rivals to finance such an initiative from the firm's own funds, without waiting for the outcome of official policy debates over war damage compensation and rehabilitation financing. As White has shown, the British debates ground on slowly from May to November 1946, with the Ministry of Food pressing for cash grants to speed the resumption of edible oil imports to Britain, and the Colonial Office and the Treasury resisting. In the event, a rather weak scheme of soft bank loans backed by the Malayan Union was introduced in December 1946, well after Lindquist's factories had swung back into action. The total 1946 production of palm oil at Ulu Bernam was 3,300 tonnes and at Jendarata, 1,400. This was about 27 per cent of the total Malayan production for 1946, a doubling of the two estates' output share in comparison with 1939. Lindquist's achievement was soon noticed elsewhere, and he found himself in demand as a consultant to help other estate managers to get their factories going again. His first assignment was for the neighbouring Sungei Samak Estate, and this was quickly followed by others for Highlands & Lowlands and Harrisons & Crosfield.[40]

By 1947, production was reviving throughout the Malayan oil palm industry, but the Grut estates never lost the advantage they had gained from their early recovery. At 8,200 tonnes, the combined production of Jendarata and Ulu Bernam Estates still accounted for 21 per cent of total Malayan output in 1947. Between 1948 and 1953, the colony's palm oil production stayed just under pre-war levels at an average of 49,000 tonnes per annum, and the Grut estates' share of this trade stayed roughly constant at 18 per cent. Meanwhile, it was becoming clear that in Sumatra, the pre-war giant of the palm oil plantation industry, political instability was making the task of economic reconstruction far more difficult. Indonesian exports of palm oil in 1947 totalled just 2,000 tonnes as compared with Malaya's 43,000. Even by 1949, when Indonesian exports once again overtook those from Malaya, their total volume was only half that of 1939. Between 1949 and 1953 Indonesian exports of palm oil averaged just 110,000 tonnes per annum, compared with 200,000 between 1936 and 1940.[41]

While production levels recovered slowly in the East, demand was growing rapidly in the West. The United States, which had been Sumatra's main market before the war, had given up using palm oil in its soap and compound lard industries, but demand was growing fast in Britain. The acute post-war shortage of butter in that country led to a search for other edible oils and a growing interest in the use of groundnut oil, palm kernel oil and palm oil for making compound lard and margarine. The Colonial Office sent representatives to West Africa to investigate means of boosting supplies, and the Labour government formed an Overseas Food Corporation, with a budget of £41 million, to manage a tractor-based groundnut farming scheme in Tanganyika. Malayan planters were still not considered worthy recipients of grants from Treasury funds, even after – or maybe because of – the costly failure of the Tanganyikan scheme, which had been proposed and run in its early stages by the United Africa Company and was closed down ignominiously in 1949. However, the Malayan planters were considered to be useful suppliers, and the British Ministry of Food moved swiftly to corner the market in their produce. It contracted to buy the whole Malayan output of palm oil from July 1946 to December 1952.[42]

The prices paid by the Ministry of Food were quite extraordinary by pre-war standards. In the late 1930s Ulu Bernam palm oil fetched between £12 and £13 per tonne, ex-estate; in 1946 it fetched £46, or Straits $400. The main Malayan producers had reunited into a Palm Oil Committee in December 1945 and negotiated successfully with the ministry to achieve further price increases in the years which followed. The 1947 contract gave Ulu Bernam a price of Straits $600 per tonne ex-estate, rising to Straits $660 in 1948. Production costs had risen too, from between £5 and £7 per tonne in the late 1930s to £17 per tonne in 1946; but this was a very gentle rise in comparison with that in sales revenues. The results of all these cost and price changes can be seen quite clearly in the gross profit margins for palm oil. At Jendarata and Ulu Bernam, these margins averaged 73 per cent between 1946 and 1949, compared with 57 per cent during the post-depression years of 1936–39.[43]

From the directors' point of view, the rapid start-up of production in 1946, and the high prices paid by the Ministry of Food thereafter, meant that ample cash was available to fund the work of reconstruction at both United Plantations and Bernam Oil Palms. Straits $1,100,000 was spent on the rehabilitation of Ulu Bernam alone between 1946 and 1948, but enough extra funds were generated for Bernam Oil Palms to accumulate bank deposits of over Straits $2 million and to pay dividends of Straits $850,000 and staff bonuses of Straits $220,000 over the same period.[44]

The money spent on reconstruction funded not only the overhaul of the factory and expansion of the workshop and foundry but also the rehabilitation of the fields themselves. Trees had to be pruned, undergrowth cleared and drains, railways and roads reconditioned. Shortages of gravel led to the opening of the quarry where Axel and Olof used to shoot snipe and to the purchase of expensive stone-crushing equipment. Fresh rolling stock also had to be bought for the railway, and new river boats had to be built. Shortages of steel plate and marine engines made such construction impossible in 1946, but Axel Lindquist had an unexpected stroke of luck when he found a Japanese semi-diesel landing craft in the hands of the Penang harbourmaster, an old friend who let him have it for Straits $500. This made an excellent cargo vessel and was still in use 40 years later, ferrying cars and passengers across the Bernam River from the newly built main road nearby. More good fortune with supplies enabled Lindquist to build three new launches for Ulu Bernam in 1947 and a further three for sale; at last it became possible to resume the daily river service between Hutan Melintang and Ulu Bernam.[45]

Once the fields and transport networks had been restored to their pre-war condition, managers turned their attention to the fresh problems that had arisen with both harvesting and fruit collection. As the Tamil harvesters had already found during the last years of the war, climbing had become very hazardous as the older palms lost the leaf bases which had provided footholds; and the bamboo ladders used in the 1930s were no longer tall enough to reach the fruit bunches on the older palms. Harvesting became an extremely unpopular job, and while the work-force in general kept up in numbers during and after the occupation, the number of harvesters at Ulu Bernam fell dramatically from 270 in the late 1930s to 150 in May 1946. Attempts were made to reduce the dangers of tree-climbing by issuing harvesters with spiked shoes, and a short-lived experiment was made with long aluminium ladders. But the shoes proved to be too clumsy and the ladders too fragile. Olof Grut then had the idea of using a crane to lift the harvester up to the crown of each palm. He ordered two Neals Harvesting Machines, of which the first arrived at Ulu Bernam in 1949. However, by the time Børge Bek-Nielsen arrived at the estate in 1951 the machines had already fallen out of favour. Not only were they expensive to operate; they also had a most unfortunate effect on the harvester, who was suspended from a high boom in a big bucket. As Bek was told, 'the slightest uneven ground caused the bucket to swing in all directions with the result that the harvester, instead of cutting the fresh fruit bunches, delivered his morning meal to the fruit collectors at the ground'.[46]

Some years later the harvesting problem was at least partly resolved by applying the method used on United Plantations' coconut holdings. A knife attached to a long pole was used to slash down the fruit bunch, in a technique widely used within Malaysia today. Even this method had its limitations, however. It required

103

*Harvesting tall oil palms by
ladder, Ulu Bernam, 1963*

highly skilled workers, and the task became more tricky – and more risky – the taller the palms involved. In the long run the only effective solution was to replant the tallest palms with young seedlings, preferably of a variety that gave early yields while the tree was still short. The circumstances of the late 1940s militated against this solution for, as Poul Bent Heilmann pointed out, the absence of planting during the Japanese occupation meant that no new areas were then coming into bearing. To fell old palms at such a time would lead to a sudden drop in output, especially costly when palm oil was fetching its best ever price on the export market. Hence the decision was taken to clear and plant up new land before beginning to replant the old, tall stands. Oil palms were thus planted on 400 hectares of pre-war reserve land on the eastern fringes of Ulu Bernam Estate between 1946 and 1948 and on 160 hectares of rubber land at Jendarata which had been damaged in the 1929 windstorm.[47]

Harvesting tall oil palms with pole, Ulu Bernam, 1963

Dura seedlings bred from local palms were used for these projects, but Rolf and Olof Grut saw this as no more than a short-term stopgap measure. Rolf took an especially strong interest in planting matters and was excited by news of the new, high-yielding Tenera variety which had been developed in the Belgian Congo. Tenera field trials had been laid down in Sumatra before the war, and these had survived the Japanese occupation and were giving good results by 1946. Rolf was keen to make similar trials in Malayan conditions as soon as possible and to investigate a second variety, the Malayan Agricultural Department's 'Dumpy palm'. Slow-growing and squat, this palm held the promise of substantial harvest-labour savings in the long run. As will be shown in Chapters 5 and 9, Rolf's interest was no mere eccentricity. The use of new planting materials was one of the most important innovations through which the Malaysian palm oil industry was eventually to rise to a leading position world-wide.[48]

A similar development from short-term measures to long-term investment proposals occurred when managers began to tackle their second labour-supply bottleneck, that of fruit collection. This task, which involved carrying heavy baskets from the trees to the railway lines, had become extremely unpopular even before the Second World War. Bullock carts and trailers had been introduced at Ulu Bernam in the early 1940s, but these had completely vanished during the occupation, as had the bullocks themselves. More bullocks, mules and carts were bought in 1946, but in 1947 Major A.C. Smith, a consultant from Straits Plantations, recommended the replacement of this 'circus' by a fleet of tractors and trailers. By this time Olof Grut had also developed a great enthusiasm for field mechanization. He went on a 5-week tour of the United States in April–May 1948, looking for possible suppliers of equipment. By the end of the year he had obtained a total of six Fordson tractors and trailers, and four second-hand American 'Caterpillar' track trailers, for use at Ulu Bernam. These were tried out in land clearance, drain-making, mulching and weeding, as well as in harvesting. However, they were clumsy machines which easily churned up the ground in stiff clay areas and disturbed the roots of the oil palms when used for weeding along the avenues. They were also expensive to buy and maintain, and even when fully used on all conceivable tasks, they could not compete on costs with manual or bullock-cart operations.[49]

Pierre Boulle, who worked for Socfin, has written a hilarious fictional account of a similar experiment in post-war mechanization. Having been assigned three ex-American army bulldozers, which were only cost-effective if they could be kept running 10 hours a day, Boulle's hapless hero was forced to invent a series of increasingly meaningless tasks for them, culminating in moving two mountains. Things never reached this stage at United Plantations or Bernam Oil Palms, but it quickly became obvious that mechanization was a sure way to spend money, not to save it. The main question which then arose was whether the use of tractors improved results, for example by allowing useful but previously impossible jobs to be done. In this case mechanization would become a profitable investment for the future, like crop research, fresh plantings and experimental factory improvements.[50]

In all three of the areas outlined above – field operations, replanting and factory design – the experience of post-war reconstruction had led managers rapidly into a more radical process of innovation. By 1948 Axel Lindquist, Rolf and Olof Grut were firmly convinced that great financial gains could be made from systematic, long-term investment in field mechanization, experimental factory machinery, workshop development, seed selection and expanded oil palm acreage. In Chapters 5 to 8 it will be shown that their views finally won the day and were to prove the foundation of United Plantations' success from the 1960s to the 1990s. But in the short run, as will be shown in Chapter 4, they had difficulty making their voices heard in Copenhagen, where changes in the Board of Directors were soon to usher in an era of radical experimentation in company strategy.

NOTES

1   This and the following paragraph are based on C. Jørgensen, 'United Plantations and Bernam Oil Palms: Highlights from a Colourful Past' (unpublished mss., 1984), Ch. 11; and BOPDR, 1938–40. For an excellent general survey of the period, see Paul H. Kratoska, *The Japanese Occupation of Malaya 1941–1945: a Social and Economic History* (London: Hurst and Company, 1998).

2   On labour migration, see also P.H. Kratoska, 'Imperial unity versus local autonomy: British Malaya and the depression of the 1930s', in P. Boomgaard and I. Brown (eds.), *Weathering the Storm: the Economies of Southeast Asia in the 1930s Depression* (Leiden and Singapore: KITLV Press and ISEAS, 2000), pp. 284–289.

3   UBAR, 1930–35; and, on Jendarata's temple, the history contained in the Souvenir Programme for the opening of the new temple building, 25 November 1987, pp. 29–44; written in Tamil, it was kindly translated for me by Andal Krishnan.

4   This and the following paragraph are based on Jørgensen, 'United Plantations', Chs 5 and 6, and UBAR, 1935–40. Government legislation on health, housing and

education is described in J.N. Parmer, *Colonial Labor Policy and Administration: a History of Labor in the Rubber Plantation Industry in Malaya, c. 1910–1941* (Association for Asian Studies: New York, 1960), Ch. IV; rubber tappers' wages are also given, p. 277. Subsequent health and welfare developments within Malaya are well covered in T.N. Harper, *The End of Empire and the Making of Malaya* (Cambridge: Cambridge University Press, 1999), Ch. 2.

5   1920s Tax Assessment Reports held in the Nigerian National Archives and listed in S.M. Martin, *Palm Oil and Protest: an Economic History of the Ngwa Region, South-Eastern Nigeria, 1800–1980* (Cambridge: University Press, 1988), p. 193; J.S. Harris, 'Some aspects of the economics of sixteen Ibo individuals', *Africa*, vol. 24, no. 6, 1944, pp. 302–335.

6   Interviews with Mme Renganayagi Ganapathy, aged 64, on 24 February 1989, who came to Ulu Bernam to join her brother and sister-in-law in 1940; and with Muthama, Vallathi, Amirtham, Pasupathu, Rajamma, Pakiam and Muniamna at the Jendarata Old Folks' Home, 5 April 1989. The labourers' housing and working hours were similar at Jendarata, where Poul Bent Heilmann's sons recall a $5^{1}/_2$-day working week: Saturday afternoons and Sundays were free. Personal communication from John Heilmann, 29 January 1999, with comments by Flemming, 3 February 1999.

7   UBAR, 1930–40; personal communications from Axel's son Dr Valdemar Lindquist, 15 August 1997, and from the Heilmann brothers, as note 6; informal conversations with Andal Krishnan and interview with S. Krishnan, then of Unitata Berhad, 16 April 1989; interview with Rothes Grut, 19 April 1988.

8   As previous note.

9   Jørgensen, 'United Plantations', Ch. 4; interviews with R.L. Grut, 19 April 1988 and with Mathalamuthu, aged *c.* 74, 8 April 1989; personal communication from John Heilmann, 29 January 1999, with comments by Flemming, 3 February 1999.

10   Jørgensen, 'United Plantations', Ch. 11 and p. 145.

11   S. Seymour, *Anglo-Danish Relations and Germany, 1933–45* (Odense: University Press, 1982), Chs 1, 3 and 5; Brinley Thomas, 'The changing pattern of Anglo-Danish trade, 1913–63', in Brinley Thomas and B.N. Thomsen, *Anglo-Danish Trade, 1661–1963: a Historical Survey* (Aarhus: University Press, 1966), Ch. V.

12   Thomas, 'Anglo-Danish Trade', p. 386; W.G. Jones, *Denmark: a Modern History* (London: Croom Helm, 1986), Ch. 8; R. Petrow, *The Bitter Years: the Invasion and Occupation of Denmark and Norway, April 1940–May 1945* (London: Hodder and Stoughton, 1974), Ch. 15; J. Thurman, *Isak Dinesen: the Life of Karen Blixen* (London: Penguin, 1984), pp. 335–338.

13 UPDR and BOPDR, 1940.

14 Personal communications from John Heilmann, 29 January1999, and Flemming Heilmann, 3 February 1999.

15 UPDR and BOPDR, 1940, and UP and BOP Balance Sheets, 1941.

16 BOPDR, 1940; interview with Mathalamuthu, aged *c.* 74, 8 April 1989. This and the following two paragraphs are also based on an interview with Tan Sri Dato' Seri B. Bek-Nielsen, 15 April 1989; Jørgensen, 'United Plantations', Ch. 11; and personal communications from John and Flemming Heilmann, 29 January and 3 February 1999.

17 Also living in the Melbourne district from 1941 onwards, like the Heilmanns in Barwon Heads, were Axel and Ida Lindquist with their young family. They had already been in Australia on leave when the Japanese invasion of Malaya began. After Poul Bent's arrival, the Heilmanns moved to Bendigo, an inland agricultural settlement about 100 miles north of Melbourne, where he felt they would be safer in the much-feared event of the war spreading to Australia. After a long struggle to remove the 'Enemy Alien' label which prevented him, and others with a similar background, from finding professional work, Poul Bent found a job in the State of Victoria's Forestry Department and settled his family in the Melbourne suburb of North Balwyn. The Grut brothers also settled in the Melbourne area, while the Lindquists chose to stay in Barwon Heads, where they found themselves in the congenial company of several other refugees from British Malaya. Sources as previous note, and personal communication from Axel's son, Dr Valdemar Lindquist, 15 August 1997.

18 This and the following two paragraphs are based on Jørgensen, 'United Plantations', Ch. 11; interviews with Axel Lindquist, 20 February 1989 and H.V. Speldewinde, 9 April 1989; and interview with a group of 20 residents of the Jendarata Old Folks' Home, 22 March 1989.

19 Kratoska, *Japanese Occupation*, Chs 6, 8 and 9; W.G. Beasley, *Japanese Imperialism, 1894–1945* (Oxford: Clarendon Press, 1987), Chs 14 and 15; D.J.M. Tate, *The RGA History of the Plantation Industry in the Malay Peninsula* (Kuala Lumpur: Oxford University Press for the Rubber Growers' Association (Malaya) Berhad, 1996), Ch. 35; Junko Tomaru, *The Postwar Rapprochement of Malaya and Japan, 1945–61: the Roles of Britain and Japan in South-East Asia* (Basingstoke: Macmillan, 2000), Ch. 2.

20 Kratoska, *Japanese Occupation*, p. 235 and picture facing p. 278; K.G. Berger, 'Palm Oil', in H.T. Chan (ed.), *Handbook of Tropical Foods* (New York and Basel: Marcel Dekker, Inc., 1983), pp. 433–468; 'B.O.W.K.', 'Palm oil "chop": a delectable alternative to curry', *The Planter*, vol. V, no. 8, 1925, p. 219; BOPDR and UPDR, 1945; this and the following three paragraphs also draw on an interview with a group of 20 residents, Jendarata Old Folks' Home, 22 March 1989.

21 UPDR, 1945; interview with Muthama, Vallathi, Amirtham, Pasupathu, Rajamma, Pakiam and Muniamna at the Jendarata Old Folks' Home, 5 April 1989.

22 Interviews with Mme Renganayagi Ganapathy, aged 64, 24 February 1989, and Mr Tamaya, aged *c.* 90, in Jendarata Hospital, 22 March 1989; Jørgensen, 'United Plantations', p. 101.

23 This and the following four paragraphs are based on an interview with Mathala-muthu, 8 April 1989. See also Seelen Sakran, 'A planter at heart', *Malaysian Business*, 16 August 2001.

24 Dato' Malcolm E. Mathieu, *I Lived By The Spear: an Autobiography, 1941–1945* (Ipoh: Rajan & Co., 1987). The story of Muthu's flight from Ulu Bernam is also told in Jørgensen, 'United Plantations', Appendix 4B.

25 Jørgensen, 'United Plantations', Ch. 13.

26 Jørgensen, 'United Plantations', Ch. 13, and BOPDR, 1945.

27 Laursen to Møller, 20 October, 5 November, and 13 November 1945, BOPMC, 1945–46.

28 Laursen to Møller, 11 December 1945, BOPMC, 1945–46. His experience was shared by many other Europeans returning to Malaya's rubber and tin enterprises after the war: Nicholas J. White, *Business, Government and the End of Empire: Malaya, 1942–1957* (Kuala Lumpur: Oxford University Press, 1996), pp. 74–76.

29 Møller to Grut, 21 November 1945 and telegram, Grut to Lindquist, 29 December 1945; personal communication from John Heilmann, 8 February 1999.

30 As previous note and BOPMC, 1945–46.

31 BOPDR and UPDR, 1946–52.

32 JAR, 1946–54; UBAR, 1946–57; Jørgensen, 'United Plantations', pp. 146–156.

33 JAR, 1938–40; interviews with Axel Lindquist, 20 February 1989, and Tan Sri Dato' Seri B. Bek-Nielsen, 15 April 1989; personal communication from Axel's son, Dr Valdemar Lindquist, 15 August 1997. The extraction rate is calculated by dividing the weight of palm oil extracted by the weight of the fresh fruit bunches used in the process.

34 As previous note.

35 Personal communication from Valdemar Lindquist, as previous note; Møller to Senior Malay Agricultural Officer, Ipoh, 7 November 1945, BOPMC, 1945–46; JAR and UBAR, 1946.

36 Olof to Com. Grut, 26 February 1946, CC, 1946–47.

37 UBAR, 1946–72; interview with Lindquist, 20 February 1989.

38 Grut to Werkspoor, 6 August 1946, BOPMC, 1945–46.

39 R.H. Hayes, 'Why Japanese factories work', *Harvard Business Review*, vol. 59, no. 4, 1981, pp. 64–65.

40 JAR and UBAR, 1946; Lim Chong-Yah, *Economic Development of Modern Malaya* (Kuala Lumpur: Oxford University Press, 1967), Appendix 5.2, p. 337; Kratoska, *Japanese Occupation*, pp. 336–339; White, *Business and Government*, pp. 72–73; interview with Lindquist, 15 April 1989.

41 Lim, *Economic Development*, Appendix 5.1, p. 336.

42 Lim, *Economic Development*, pp. 130–132; White, *Business and Government*, pp. 7–8 and 274–275; Colonial Office, Colonial No. 211, *Report of the Mission Appointed to Enquire into the Production and Transport of Vegetable Oils and Seeds Produced in the West African Colonies* (London: HMSO, 1947); J. Hogendorn, 'The East African groundnut scheme: lessons of a large-scale agricultural failure', *African Economic History*, vol.10, 1981, pp. 81–115; Heilmann to Com. Grut, 18 May 1946, CC, 1946–47; BOPCA, 1952.

43 BOPDR, 1936–40 and BOPCA, 1946–49.

44 BOPDR, 1946–48.

45 Interview with Lindquist, 20 February 1989; UBAR, 1946.

46 Report by Major A.C. Smith on a visit to Bernam Oil Palms, 11–14 July 1947; Jørgensen, 'United Plantations', Chs 14 and 16; UBAR, 1946–49; personal communication from Tan Sri Dato' Seri B. Bek-Nielsen, 11 October 1988.

47 Sources as previous note and Heilmann to Com. Grut, 13 June 1946, CC, 1946–47.

48 UBAR, 1946–49; General manager's summary of UP and BOP's internal annual reports, 1949.

49 Report by Major A.C. Smith on visit to Bernam Oil Palms, 11–14 July 1947; Olof to Com. Grut, 14 August and 28 October 1947, CC, 1946–47; UBAR, 1946–48; General manager's summary of UP and BOP's internal annual reports, 1949.

50 Pierre Boulle, *Sacrilege in Malaya* (Kuala Lumpur: Oxford University Press, 1983; first edn 1958), pp. 282–298.

The Grut brothers, Olof (left) and Rolf

CHAPTER 4

Wealth Creation and Strategic Choice

SUCCESS AND STRATEGY

*I*mmense profits were to be made from palm oil in the post-war world for anyone who could start up production quickly enough. Thanks to their pre-war plantings and to the efforts of men like Asger Laursen, Olof Grut and Axel Lindquist, United Plantations and Bernam Oil Palms had moved swiftly ahead in the race to exploit new market opportunities; and for the first time since the oil palm adventure began, the two companies started to earn more money than their directors knew what to do with. The boards were finally able to reward the faith of their long-suffering shareholders and employees and to consider a wide range of fresh investment opportunities. The oil palm was at last proving itself to be a golden crop.

Although expensive, the work of reconstruction on the estates had soaked up only a small fraction of the post-war profits, and a vigorous debate now began among the companies' directors about the best use of the rest. Essentially this was a debate about the future structure and strategic direction of the companies themselves. The three main options considered were: first, to expand by acquiring new land, whether in Malaya or elsewhere; second, to intensify the use of existing land by replanting rubber areas to oil palms and by investing in oil palm crop research, field mechanization and factory development; and finally to diversify into new crops or business activities.

The first and the third of these options were the ones which had most appeal in the 1950s, and this chapter will show why and how they were tried out in practice. New men in Copenhagen led the drive for expansion and for diversification away from Malaya that had to be accepted even by the Grut brothers in a context of increasing political risk. But the results of this drive show clearly why the directors eventually turned back to Malaya and chose the course of intensification, through which United Plantations achieved a leading position in the palm oil industry. The story of their adventures also shows some of the pitfalls which lie in wait for companies facing similar strategic investment decisions. In particular, it exposes some of the difficulties involved in applying agricultural skills to fresh environments and fresh crops. It also reveals the problems that can arise in applying plantation-based managerial skills to fresh businesses. The classic issues of defining and building on a 'core business' are most often discussed in the case of Western industrial or service-sector conglomerates, but they are no less relevant to the case of a tropical agricultural enterprise like United Plantations.

NEW MEN IN COPENHAGEN

By December 1946 the shares of United Plantations and Bernam Oil Palms had been divested from the Custodian of Enemy Property, and the way was clear for a reorganization of the boards of both companies. Commander Grut's first instincts were conservative, and he brought back the pre-war Copenhagen directors, Major-General Torben Grut, A.N. Grut, Thorkild Dahl, S. Ingemann, J. Jadot and R.W.S. Westenholz, to reinforce the wartime stalwarts – himself, Olof Grut, P.B. Heilmann and R.D. Craig. The only new member of the board was the pharmacist Niels Benzon, the son of Commander Grut's first cousin Emma Hansen. However, the retirements of Major-General Grut and J. Jadot in 1947, the death of R.D. Craig in the same year, followed swiftly by the retirement of Aage Westenholz's son Regnar and the deaths of A.N. Grut and of Commander Grut himself in 1949 all forced the pace of change.

Commander Grut died on 24 March 1949, having already overseen the appointment of many new directors. By 1950, the changes were complete. United Plantations and Bernam Oil Palms had identical boards in which the key figures were Niels Benzon as chairman, and Olof Grut as vice-chairman. Heilmann, Dahl and Ingemann retained their seats on the boards, but were joined by seven newcomers: the scientist Professor O. Winge, the British oilseeds trader G.M. Smyth and five close relatives of the previous board members. The two who were to have the greatest influence on the companies were Sven Torben ('Bubba') Westenholz, the younger son of Aage Westenholz and a successful entrepreneur in his own right as the founder of Nordisk Ventilator; and Major Edmund Grut, the son of General Torben Grut and his wife, Lennart's sister Mary. Edmund

114

Grut had started his business career in Bangkok with Siam Electricity in 1924 but returned to Sweden after the war and took up a successful second career with the Scandinavian Airlines System. He was joined on the boards by the British lawyer G.D. Craig, Richard Craig's son; Corey Grumitt, of Grumitt, Reid & Co., Penang, whose brother had been the main business adviser to both companies before the war; and Jorgen Knudtzon, who had been the Bangkok secretary of Siam Electricity before it was nationalized in 1949, and whose uncle Thorkil, the nephew of General Grut, had been United Plantations' valued legal adviser.[1]

Although the new board members were almost all directly related to the old, their career backgrounds were quite different. Whereas most of the pre-war board members had direct experience of living and working in the East, only a few of their post-war successors had; and among those few, Edmund Grut and Jorgen Knudtzon had experienced Thailand very differently from their predecessors. The traumas of war and nationalization were fresh in their minds, in contrast to the memories of youthful innovation with which the East had been associated for Aage Westenholz and Commander Grut. Meanwhile, the new chairman, Niels Benzon, was very strongly Western in his business interests and personal background. Having trained in Copenhagen as a pharmacist, Benzon gained his business experience in the United States before returning to take over the family firm. He owned a string of pharmacies and a chemicals manufacturing plant in Denmark and could afford the time to become president of the Royal Danish Yacht Club and the Danish Golf Association. Several of his business letters were dictated by telephone from his yacht *Safari*, on which he took frequent summer cruises. While he enjoyed visits to Malaya, he could display little knowledge of estate management and was apt to conclude a rapid motor tour of the plantations with the comment that 'it all looked very nice'. A greater contrast to the irascible and keen-eyed Commander Grut could hardly be imagined.[2]

The new chairman was thus closer, both geographically and in his personal interests, to the Danish shareholders than to the managers in Malaya; and he was supported by several board members of like mind. Indeed, Professor Winge had actually been nominated to the board by a small group of shareholders, led by a man outside the close-knit Grut–Westenholz family group, the broker H.B. Moller. The character of the shareholders themselves was beginning to change, as investment trusts started to take a closer interest in the companies and as Westerners resident in the East began to return home, or to transmit their shares to relatives in Europe. The holders of only 12 per cent of Bernam Oil Palms'

Niels Benzon

shares were resident in the East in 1948, as opposed to the holders of 21 per cent in 1938. Although the vast majority of shareholders were still individuals with family ties to the Gruts or to Thai royalty, many were now second-generation holders who saw the companies as a potential source of dividend income rather than as a pair of innovative ventures offering future capital gains. Their concerns were shared by investment trusts like TIF Ltd of Guernsey and the Malayan Securities Trust Ltd of Penang, which appeared on the share registers for the first time in 1948.[3]

EXPERIMENTATION AND FRUSTRATION IN MALAYA

The shareholders' concern for safe and substantial dividends was well understood by the Copenhagen directors, and it inclined their strategic thinking towards expansion outside Malaya, linked with diversification into new crops and businesses, rather than towards the intensification recommended by the managers on the spot at Jendarata and Ulu Bernam. Olof Grut lobbied to maintain investment in Malaya, but he met with numerous frustrations in his attempts to develop new local outlets for the funds being generated there. These frustrations combined with his own enthusiasm for new crops and new ideas, so that by the autumn of 1948 he was ready to support the Copenhagen directors in their move towards overseas expansion.

Even before the war, Olof Grut had begun to share his father's interest in agricultural diversification. He had visited the Cameron Highlands when the first bungalows and tea estates were being set up there in the early 1930s and had been especially impressed by the Sungei Palas tea estate which was owned and run by Danes. A small hilly area in the south-eastern corner of Ulu Bernam was cleared and planted with tea in 1939, and between 1946 and 1956 this area was gradually extended to encircle the newly made quarry, finally covering 156 hectares. In 1950 a factory was built to make black tea, and until tea prices slumped in 1964–65 the enterprise made a modest operating profit. However, tea was always a rather marginal crop at Ulu Bernam because of the estate's relatively low rainfall compared to the Highlands and because of the sandy soil of the hilly corner in which the tea bushes had to be planted. The tea enterprise made operating losses for 6 consecutive years after 1963 and for a further three years before operations were finally halted in 1975.[4]

Olof's enthusiasm for tea may well have been as much aesthetic as economic – well-pruned tea bushes give an attractive carpeting effect to a hillside, a welcome change in texture from the rippling fronds of the oil palm. Olof's favourite place on Ulu Bernam was the hill above the quarry, from which views of the jungle on one side were complemented by the tea slopes on the other, stretching down to the vast expanse of oil palms below. His sister-in-law Rothes Grut, a New Zealander who lived at Ulu Bernam when her husband Rolf was manager there between 1949 and 1954, also recalls the welcome relief she felt when escaping from the sea of tall palms into the open space of the tea plantation. The slopes have since been covered with oil palms, but the hilltop is still clear, and Olof is buried there. The jungle bordering it to the east has been made into a permanent forest reserve in his memory.[5]

Although Olof's tea venture was not solely a business enterprise, it was nevertheless linked to a fundamental business philosophy. United Plantations and Bernam Oil Palms were doing extremely well from palm oil and coconuts, but this rendered them dependent on the world market for oils and fats, and in Olof's view such dependence was as dangerous in the late 1940s as Jendarata's dependence on rubber had been in the 1910s. Hence he was eager to replant some of Jendarata's old rubber stands with high-yielding clones and to extend Ulu Bernam's tea area. In 1947 trials began of yet another idea, the intercropping of rubber, coconuts and cocoa at Ulu Bernam, and some five years later the first underplantings of cocoa were made on the coconut stands at Kuala Bernam Estate. By the late 1960s the novel cocoa–coconut combination was seen to have succeeded and was extended to Sungei Bernam Estate in 1969. Experimental plantings of cocoa under oil palms at Jendarata began in 1975, with large-scale field trials from 1979. By 1986 United Plantations had 1,600 hectares of oil palms and 2,400 of coconuts underplanted with cocoa. However, the high labour costs of cocoa production, and the low world market prices of the late 1980s and 1990s, combined to make the venture ultimately unprofitable, and the last cocoa stands were cut down and replanted with high-yielding coconuts in 1999. Even in 1947 the cocoa experiment had been seen as a long shot, and little publicity had been given to it. Far more attention was focused on Olof's final cropping initiative: the planting of pineapples at Jendarata.[6]

Pineapples had first been established as an export crop in Malaya by Chinese smallholders, and the industry had enjoyed rapid growth during the 1930s, when Malaya and Hawaii were the world's two major exporters of the fruit, packaged in tins ready for eating. However, the idea for planting pineapples at Jendarata owed little to this local source but came from the travels of Poul Bent

Heilmann. As soon as he saw the new pineapple estates being formed in Southern Africa in the 1940s, Heilmann was struck by the quick returns to be gained from the crop. To Olof it seemed that such short-term gains would be an ideal compensation for the lost income from the older oil palm and rubber areas, as these were gradually replanted. Pineapple processing and canning operations also seemed to offer an ideal opportunity to apply the engineering skills of Jendarata's managers. Niels Benzon was sceptical of these arguments but was won over by the Malayan government's willingness to grant virgin land for the project. The land would initially be held on a Temporary Occupation Licence, renewable annually, but Benzon hoped that this could eventually be converted to a long-term lease enabling the company to plant oil palms instead.[7]

In 1950 Olof obtained 130 hectares of land adjoining the south-eastern oil palm area of Jendarata Estate. This area was rapidly planted up, and in 1953 a further 100 hectares of young oil palms was underplanted with pineapples as a catch crop. In 1955 the venture made its first operating profit, a modest Straits $41,500, and in the following year a further 350 hectares of neighbouring jungle reserve was purchased from Straits Plantations. By 1957 the pineapple monocrop plantation had reached its maximum extent of 390 hectares, but the enterprise was once more making an operating loss and never again succeeded in breaking even. Prices were being driven down by competition from large-scale producers abroad and fell from Straits $21 to $12 per case between 1957 and 1960. Meanwhile, the peaty soils on which United Plantations' pineapples were planted subsided too rapidly for sustained fruit cultivation. In 1960 the whole area was cleared and replanted with oil palms, thus bringing to a close a venture which had cost United Plantations a total of Straits $920,000 in start-up costs and operating losses.[8]

Although both the tea and pineapple ventures failed, they gave evidence of Olof Grut's openness to new ideas and of his eagerness to avoid over-specialization. These qualities enabled him to encourage other, ultimately successful innovations like the planting of cocoa under coconuts and to appreciate the concern of the shareholders about over-dependence on a single country as the source of their dividend income. His willingness to accept moves to invest outside Malaya was further strengthened by the difficulties he experienced in pursuing the local investment strategy which he preferred, namely the purchase of neighbouring rubber estates and the development of fresh jungle land adjoining Jendarata and Ulu Bernam.

As early as February 1947 Olof had begun pressing for expansion by acquisition, making enquiries about Sungei Samak Estate in particular. This estate, adjoining Ulu Bernam, had been founded by Perak Oil Palms Ltd and sold to Straits Plantations in 1937, but it fitted rather awkwardly with its new owners' other estates, which all specialized in copra production and were located on the Bagan Datoh peninsula north of the Perak River. Olof had high hopes of acquiring Sungei Samak until he found that Straits Plantations were planning to expand the property on their own behalf. The secretaries and agents for Straits Plantations, Harrisons & Crosfield, had extensive oil palm interests in Sumatra and were just becoming interested in the growth possibilities of the same industry in Malaya. Eric MacFadyen, who had planted rubber and coconuts in Malaya before the First World War and was now director of Harrisons' Estates Department in London, championed the idea of replanting old rubber estates with oil palms. He saw Sungei Samak as a useful source of knowledge about the crop, and even as a possible base for a research station. Brian Gray, who joined Harrisons in 1953 and was appointed as their first oil palm research officer in 1955, spent a few lonely months at Sungei Samak before managing to convince his superiors that the site was too isolated.[9]

Thwarted at Sungei Samak, Olof Grut turned his attention to the Kampong Rimau district to the south of Hutan Melintang Forest Reserve, which lay to the west of Ulu Bernam. The district was enclosed by a long, undulating stretch of the Bernam River and by the two sections of Sungei Samak Estate. During 1948 the land was surveyed and an application made to the government for 1,600 hectares. However, by September it was already becoming clear that, in general, applications by expatriate companies for new Malayan jungle land were meeting an unsympathetic government response. Partly as a result of heightened Malay political activity within the deeply unpopular Malayan Union, 1946–48, officials were showing a growing concern about the problems of Malay rural poverty and of national supplies of food (especially rice). Since 1913 it had been possible for State Councils to designate areas of uncleared land as Malay Reservations, which could then be alienated only to Malays and used only for kampong settlements, padi or coconut cultivation. After a wave of such designations in 1914, little more had happened during the 1920s and 1930s, but now the issue was coming alive again. Kampong Rimau was just one of many areas in Perak which were soon to be designated Malay Reservations and to be prepared for rice cultivation by the government's Drainage and Irrigation Department. A similar fate had already befallen a much larger area on the Selangor side of the Bernam River, Sungei Panjang, which Olof had tried unsuccessfully to acquire in 1947.[10]

Olof remained keen on Malayan investment, but in view of these setbacks he was forced to concede that it might be necessary to seek an outlet for the companies' surplus funds elsewhere. Such views provided a powerful reinforcement to the Copenhagen directors' own inclinations, which in turn were decisively influenced by the outbreak of the Malayan Emergency in June 1948. Isolated European settlements like those of the planters at Jendarata and Ulu Bernam proved to be prime targets for the jungle-based guerrillas. Poul Bent Heilmann and his family bore the brunt of their initial attacks, which took place while Olof Grut was away on his combined long leave and machinery-buying tour. Poul Bent's son Flemming, who was then just 12 years old and staying at Jendarata in between spells at boarding schools in Denmark and England, recalls several midnight attacks which were so severe that police or military intervention was needed to repel the terrorists. In July 1948 the Bernam Oil Palms Directors' Committee approved the purchase of machine guns for use by estate managers and of light aircraft for transporting cash to the estates. They also began discussing the question of the investment of 'surplus cash'. It was surely no coincidence that the first investment outlets examined after this meeting were in London rather than in Malaya.[11]

This shift in geographical focus was reinforced when Olof's fruitless attempts to obtain extra land in Malaya were reported to the committee in September. Sven Torben Westenholz and Poul Bent Heilmann argued powerfully that it was time for geographic diversification, not only of financial holdings but also of plantation operations. They were supported by Heilmann's old friend, the experienced and trusted board member Sofren Ingemann, who had been settled since 1947 in Cape Town, where he had become the Danish government's agricultural attaché. Olof accepted the strength of their arguments, so that the committee was united in asking Heilmann and Ingemann to conduct a systematic search for opportunities in Africa. From this time onwards considerations of political risk took the centre stage in Copenhagen strategy debates.[12]

EXPERIENCING THE EMERGENCY

The political risk which loomed so large in the minds of the Copenhagen directors was by no means an abstract, bloodless affair. Since May 1948 the Chinese-run

Malayan Communist Party had been mounting a campaign of arson, tree-slashing and machine-wrecking on European-owned tin mines and rubber estates, and this escalated swiftly into a campaign of death. As the Emergency progressed, attacks on individuals gave way to more ambitious ambushes on buses, trucks and trains, and it became especially difficult and dangerous to transport cash to meet routine payroll needs; hence the need felt by the Ulu Bernam managers for machine guns and air transport. Led by jungle-based guerrillas, the campaign built on the widespread hostility felt by the rural Chinese population to the government's increasingly pro-Malay stance, and its extensive popular support made it extremely difficult to suppress. By the end of 1952 a total of 81 planters had been killed and a further 2,712 civilians had either been killed or gone missing. Even those Europeans who had yet to experience guerrilla action lived in fear.[13]

Until the appointment of General Sir Harold Briggs to co-ordinate the efforts of civilian officials, the army and the police from April 1950, government attempts to contain the uprising had little effect. Briggs tackled the situation by resettling over 400,000 Chinese squatters into New Villages, a coercive policy which was rendered acceptable to the squatters by giving them land, schools and dispensaries within their wired and defended perimeters. His successor from February 1952, General Sir Gerald Templer, built on this achievement through a concentrated military campaign against the jungle-based guerrillas, bringing the annual toll of civilians killed or missing down to 128 by 1953. However, numerous pockets of guerrilla activity remained, especially in Perak and Johore. A further 362 civilians were killed or went missing before the Emergency finally ended on 31 July 1960. Over the whole period 1947–60, 99 planters had lost their lives.[14]

Those planters who survived the Emergency never forgot the fear which spread through their community at the time. Nor have they forgotten their fallen friends: for example, Tan Sri Dato' Seri B. Bek-Nielsen still recalls J.W. Barrell, A.F. Nightingale and Major Sutton more than 50 years after they helped him through his first year in the 'Ulu' of Lower Perak. Since 1980, he has been a keen supporter of the 'God's Little Acre' programme, through which an annual Remembrance Day ceremony has been held at Batu Gajah, commemorating the lives of all those who died, whether planters or miners, policemen or soldiers, combatants or civilians. He also became a patron of the Perak branch of the Veteran Security Association of Malaysia, which was founded in 1956 to help all those – mainly smallholders and farmers – who had served, whether in the armed forces, the police force or as volunteers, during the long period stretch-ing from the outbreak of the Second World War to the end of the Emergency. Several veterans or their family members were given jobs at Jendarata and Ulu Bernam, and they, together with others who were already employed by United Plantations, were encouraged to join the association.[15]

After the initial period of intense danger, which had made such a strong impression on Bek-Nielsen and on the Heilmann family, United Plantations and Bernam Oil Palms were relatively lightly affected by the Emergency. As Harper has recently argued for Malaya as a whole, the social and ecological tensions underpinning the uprising were strongest within the rainforest frontier region along the central mountain ranges. Here, colonial roads, mines and rubber estates competed with Chinese squatter settlements for access to an increasingly fragile set of natural resources. Located by contrast in the coastal lowlands, Jendarata and Ulu Bernam were relatively far removed from the flashpoints of conflict. In Lower Perak the struggle reached its peak in 1952, and even then Ulu Bernam remained free of serious trouble, although managers there and at Jendarata were deeply shocked by the murder of two white planters at Selaba Estate near Teluk Intan. The victims were especially well known to the Jendarata managers, because Selaba was in the process of converting from rubber to oil palms. Fruit from Selaba was processed at the Jendarata mill from 1953 to 1958, while Axel Lindquist acted as a consultant to the estate's owners, Harrisons & Crosfield, in their own mill-building plans. Hence the Jendarata managers felt a sense of personal loss after the killings. They were also touched more directly by the wave of guerrilla activity which swept the district in 1952, when one of the Jendarata labourers was abducted and possibly killed by the 'bandits'. Financial losses followed, as 2,000 rubber trees along the north-eastern boundary of the estate were killed by being slashed and when the 'bandits' sabotaged the burning and clearing of 140 acres of felled jungle land further south. The estate workers became understandably nervous at working anywhere near the bound-aries, and armed escorts had to be laid on to protect them. The government supported this effort with a force of 50 special constables, commanded by four non-commissioned officers, who were stationed on the estate until 1957. Finally, a curfew was imposed throughout the hours of darkness.[16]

Meanwhile, strong measures had been taken to prevent similar outbreaks at Ulu Bernam. As soon as the Emergency had begun, Poul Bent Heilmann had become concerned about the upriver estate's isolated position, flanked to the north-east only by a Sakai (Orang Asli) settlement which he believed 'would offer excellent opportunities for the bandits to take refuge'. The government shared his view, and by the end of July 1948 a permanent guard of two British sergeants and 40 Malay special constables, armed with .303 rifles, had been stationed on the estate. This guard remained at Ulu Bernam until June 1959; and from August to December 1948 it was reinforced at monthly intervals by visits from the regular troops of the Malay Regiment, the Seaforth Highlanders and the Coldstream Guards. Also in 1948, all European members of staff were enrolled as auxiliary police constables, armed with automatic pistols at the company's expense. One brave assistant lived alone in a hilltop bungalow on the south-eastern boundary of the estate, surrounded by sandbags and clasping his gun for reassurance. By 1954, however, the police had come to believe that this bungalow's attractions as a guerrilla target outweighed its usefulness as a deterrent, and it was dismantled and moved to Ulu Bernam's centrally located airstrip, where it still stands and serves as a clubhouse for the executive staff.[17]

Although very little guerrilla action was taken against Ulu Bernam or Jendarata Estates, 'bandits' were frequently seen in the neighbourhood and even within the boundaries of the two plantations. Constant vigilance was needed to protect lives and property. Both managers and workers learnt to live with barbed wire fencing, shots in the night and numerous petty restraints on their freedom. The twice-daily Bernam Oil Palms launch service was maintained to Hutan Melintang, but travel further afield was severely restricted. The Chrislea Super Ace aircraft which the company had bought in 1949 fell prey to numerous mechanical problems; and the Cameron Highlands bungalow was given up because of its remote and dangerous location. Rice rationing was imposed throughout Malaya in a government attempt to limit food supplies to the Communists and was lifted in Lower Perak only in November 1958, after the district had been declared a 'White', or guerrilla-free, area. For managers at Ulu Bernam a life which had always been hard and lonely became increasingly restricted and insecure.[18]

Living in such conditions, the younger European staff in particular became restless and began using their pistols and sub-machine guns in ways which greatly alarmed their seniors. Tan Sri Dato' Seri B. Bek-Nielsen, now a respected senior executive in his turn, recalls two especially reckless episodes from his first year at Ulu Bernam. Soon after his arrival in September 1951, he was called out of the shower by his gardener, who was shouting excitedly in Malay. Assuming that the 'bandits' had arrived, he rushed out with his sub-machine gun towards the creek by the airfield, where he found the gardener gesticulating wildly towards the opposite bank. At first he could see nothing and thought the gardener had gone mad, but all of a sudden what he had thought was a log of wood started blinking its eyes, and he realized it was a crocodile. Swiftly raising his gun, Bek aimed at its head and rattled off a round of ammunition – only to be startled yet again by the tail lashing up out of the mud. A crocodile's tail has its own nerve centre and so has to be dealt with separately. Eventually, after several more shots, the beast was dead and Bek, shaken but proud, was able to report his achievement to Axel Lindquist. The veteran hunter was not impressed:

> 'You shot a crocodile. With what, if I may ask?'
> Bek replied: 'With my sub-machine gun.'
> 'O-o-oh', came the response, 'You mean you have murdered it!'

Undeterred, Bek continued to explore the possibilities of the local guns and ammunition. One night after curfew he tossed a kerosene tin out from his bungalow into mid-river, and asked the night guard to hit it with his rifle. After several attempts the guard had no success, so Bek seized the rifle and took aim. Two more unsuccessful shots later, Bek examined the curious ammunition – consisting of spherical balls, quite unlike the pellets he was used to. 'This is useless ammunition – how can you ever protect me with things like this?' he exclaimed in disgust, and handing the weapon back he thought no more of it. But half an hour later, all of a sudden, somebody shouted and all the special constables rushed off towards the sound, while Bek searched for his sub-machine gun. Once again, however, his fears of CTs (communist terrorists) proved unfounded. The voice belonged to Rolf Grut, who had heard the earlier shots from his bungalow downriver and had driven out into the night to bring help. Impressed by Rolf's selfless courage and shamed by Axel Lindquist's stern lecture on the following morning, Bek now began to settle down. But he has never forgotten the atmosphere of fear and claustrophobia which characterized the years 1951–52 at Jendarata and Ulu Bernam and which made it easy for young recruits to become trigger-happy.[19]

FROM ASIA TO AFRICA AND LATIN AMERICA

Against this background of frustration, tension and uncertainty the Copenhagen directors began planning fresh investments outside Malaya. Africa was the continent which first attracted their attention, partly because Sofren Ingemann was living in Cape Town, and partly because of the Tanganyikan Groundnut Scheme, which was then being sponsored amid fanfares of publicity by the British Overseas Food Corporation. In the early days after the Second World War, before African nationalism had emerged as a major political force and before agricultural schemes like that in Tanganyika had proved to be costly failures, it seemed possible that Africa contained vast natural resources which enterprising and well-capitalized planters could exploit at minimal political risk.[20]

Having won their fellow directors' enthusiasm for the idea of investing in Africa, Sofren Ingemann and Poul Bent Heilmann set off to explore the practical possibilities in the spring of 1949. Starting off on his own in Nairobi, Heilmann conducted an eight-week tour of Kenya, Uganda, Tanganyika, Nyasaland and Southern Rhodesia, before meeting up with Ingemann to survey South Africa and Swaziland. The two men rapidly concluded that the political and ecological conditions for planting operations were best in the last two territories. Heilmann returned there before the end of the year, hoping to find specific investment opportunities in coniferous forestry, citrus and other agricultural developments.[21]

The directors' decision to back this venture is entirely understandable given the context of the Malayan Emergency and shortage of land for fresh planting in Perak. Men like Poul Bent Heilmann were careful and experienced strategists who believed that their actions would reduce the risks to which their firms' shareholders were exposed while offering a good opportunity of using their funds profitably. However, with hindsight it can be seen that the Southern African option was just as risky as the plans being put forward at the same time by Axel Linquist and Rolf Grut, the managers in Malaya who wanted to invest more in the local palm oil industry and to raise returns through more intensive land use, better planting materials and innovative processing and marketing techniques. While the Malayan investment option was more risky in political terms, the Southern African option was more risky in the practical sense, because it took United Plantations' and Bernam Oil Palms' people into a completely new ecological and commercial environment. In putting their money into agricultural or tree-planting ventures in Africa, the directors were placing a great deal of faith in their managers' ability to work effectively in an alien setting. This faith was not without foundation, as they were able to draw both on the extensive tree-planting expertise which had been built up within their Malayan estates before the war by a generation of managers which was still a long way

126

from retirement and on the long-standing tradition of forestry which continues to flourish within Denmark itself. However, they had no means of predicting whether the expertise gained from planting timber in temperate Denmark, or rubber trees, coconut and oil palms in tropical Malaya, could profitably be transferred to pine and citrus planting operations in the much drier environment of another continent. As will be shown below, in the event the transfer process proved slow and fraught with difficulty. Expertise could not simply be flown in; it had to be modified and developed further within the local setting before the new ventures could succeed.

United Plantations South Africa Limited (UPSA) was founded in 1950 as a proprietary company, going public in 1957. The parent companies, United Plantations and Bernam Oil Palms, had invested £600,000 in its shares by 1951, and a five-member board had been appointed of which Niels Benzon was chairman and Poul Bent Heilmann managing director. Heilmann's first action was to purchase a stake of £200,000 in Peak Timbers Ltd of Pretoria, which had recently been formed by Captain D.B. Fitzgerald of London to develop a 22,000-hectare pine estate in Swaziland and which was co-financed by a consortium of banks including Baring Bros, Robert Fleming & Co., and Barclays Bank. Peak Timbers absorbed a further £120,000 of UPSA's capital between 1952 and 1955, but its plans to construct a boxmill and a coreboard manufacturing plant were slow to materialize. Further industrial plans made in 1957 attracted the attention of Sir Ernest Oppenheimer's Anglo American Corporation, and UPSA took the opportunity to sell its stake for a profit of £200,000.[22]

The investment in Peak Timbers proved to be a reasonably successful speculation, but UPSA's attempts to set up its own operations were less profitable. The first of these attempts was made in 1951, when the company acquired Hebron farm, consisting of 1,400 hectares of grassland in the Eastern Transvaal. The property was swiftly converted to a pine plantation, but equally swiftly proved to be too small for economic working and was sold in 1954. Meanwhile, following a study tour by Heilmann of the successful citrus industries of California and Florida, UPSA had decided to diversify away from the timber industry. Three further properties were bought, this time in Swaziland: the Ngonini and Mkiwane Estates, both of which required substantial investment in irrigation facilities before citrus farming could begin, and the Gollel property on which UPSA planned to build a rice mill. These investments absorbed the remainder of UPSA's starting capital, together with a further £300,000 which was lent to the company by United Plantations and Bernam Oil Palms before being converted into shares in 1957. However, by 1957 it was becoming obvious that little return could be expected from these outlays. The Gollel rice mill proved unable to compete for local paddy supplies against Indian merchants, and the Mkiwane property proved unsuitable for citrus cultivation. The mill was shut down and the equipment sold at a loss in 1959, while the Mkiwane estate was sold to a Natal entrepreneur who replanted it with sugar cane.

By 1957 the only estate which showed any sign of repaying UPSA's initial investment was Ngonini, which in 1954 had been placed under the control of a wholly owned subsidiary registered in Swaziland, United Plantations (Swaziland) Limited. Numerous problems had been met in making irrigation canals and constructing a hydro-electric system on this rocky estate and in maintaining the trucks and tractors which were essential for field work. Nevertheless, a plantation of pineapples and bananas had been successfully established by 1955. The pineapples proved no more profitable in Southern Africa than they had been in Malaya, but the bananas found a good market in the South African Republic. Income from this source underpinned a long series of experiments with different varieties of oranges, limes and grapefruit, which eventually enabled the company to enter the export market. From 1960 onwards these citrus experiments were extended to the newly purchased estate of Tambuti, also in Swaziland; and by 1968 the two estates were making enough profit to support dividend payments. Before then, the only dividend payments made had been in 1958–1960, as a distribution of the profits from the sale of UPSA's Peak Timbers shares.

After 1968 the citrus estates continued to prosper, and the company was able to fund the development of a third estate, the Tekwane lemon and tobacco estate, while continuing to make regular dividend payments. Ultimately the venture had been successful; but the shareholders had been forced to wait almost 20 years for its first sustainable cash returns. When they finally came, these regular dividends were founded not on the application of a distinctively Malayan or Danish expertise to the new challenges, but on a new kind of expertise, in citrus production, which had been built up painfully slowly in Southern Africa. Although the idea of entering the citrus industry had come from one of United Plantations' old Malaya hands, Poul Bent Heilmann, he had depended for its execution on fresh recruits and in particular on Hans Noddeboe, who had been recruited just after completing his agricultural college training and military service in Denmark.

Noddeboe was one of five such recruits who joined UPSA in the early 1950s, and the only one who remained with the company in the long term. He was appointed general manager in 1963 and a director in 1976, eventually becoming the honorary consul for Denmark in Swaziland. In his career pattern he clearly carried on the United Plantations' tradition of long service and continuing attachment to Denmark; but in his personal background and experience he had little connection with the parent companies. His early mentors were Alexander Matthew, a South African citrus farmer who joined UPSA's board in 1952, and Dr Roy Impey, who served UPSA as a technical consultant from 1969 onwards. From 1974 onwards further vital support was provided by Ken Stimpson, then working mainly in Malaysia as United Plantations' planting director, who began visiting the UPSA estates regularly as a new board member. Stimpson and Noddeboe worked well together and, after his retirement from the East in September 1983, Stimpson became still more heavily involved as chairman of UPSA, or United Plantations Africa Ltd as it became in May 1987. During the 13 years of his chairmanship, to the end of 1996, Stimpson worked effectively to integrate his Malayan with Noddeboe's Southern African expertise. From January 1990 Noddeboe received further support from Peter Cowling, Stimpson's successor as United Plantations' executive director (planting), who served in this capacity in Malaysia from 1984 to 1994, and was a board member of UP Africa until December 1998. However, this injection of planting expertise from South-East Asia came relatively late in the day and certainly could not have provided UPSA with a short cut to profits in the early years.[23]

United Plantations' experience in Southern Africa clearly demonstrates the pitfalls of geographical diversification for an agricultural enterprise. Managers accustomed to judging the potential of freshly surveyed land in the tropical rainforests of Malaya could not automatically make accurate judgements about the potential of South African farms; still less could they ensure the efficient running of irrigation-dependent enterprises on the basis of experience in water-logged Perak. Given that United Plantations' shareholders wanted to place a growing share of their investment outside Malaya, they might well have made faster and more reliable profits had they taken the necessary funds into their own hands and invested directly in locally formed agricultural enterprises run by experienced South African managers. In short, this case illustrates the classic conclusion of finance theory, that diversification by a firm is only in the share-holder's interest if its management can add distinctive value to the new enter-

129

prises it takes over. If not, the shareholder would do better to build a diversified portfolio of shares in separately managed enterprises.[24]

However, such an argument assumes the existence of well-developed financial markets through which investors can gain accurate information about a wide range of international investment possibilities; and it assumes that there are no tax or legal obstacles to the transfer of funds. Neither assumption was true in the world of the late 1940s. At this time, Danish income taxes were rising rapidly and provision had not yet been made to eliminate 'double taxation' between Denmark and the Sterling Area, so that post-tax Malayan earnings simply attracted fresh income taxes when distributed to shareholders in Denmark. Meanwhile, many of United Plantations' shareholders, the widows and children of its founding families, had too little information about South African affairs to be able to make a sound choice of investments there. In effect, then, Poul Bent Heilmann and Niels Benzon performed a valuable brokerage service for their shareholders, and made a tax-efficient transfer of funds between nations. However, this strategy made only limited use of United Plantations' distinctive managerial and technical strengths. By 1951 Olof Grut had begun to have doubts about it, arguing that the Southern African venture carried a very high cost in terms of lost investment opportunities in Malaya, where other estates were beginning to come up for sale and where exciting technical developments offered fresh chances to raise yields from the existing properties.[25]

Despite the high cost and high risks involved in investments outside Malaya, the Copenhagen directors continued to prefer this way of using the profits from palm oil. Meanwhile, Lindquist and the other managers in Malaya lost a powerful champion of innovation when Olof Grut retired from the East in 1952, starting a new career as an arable farmer in Norfolk the following year. Olof continued to serve as vice-chairman of both United Plantations and Bernam Oil Palms and to pay annual visits to the estates. But his views on future Malayan investments had swung back in favour of caution: he now shared the other Copenhagen directors' fears about political risks in Malaya, as the turmoil of the Emergency gave way to fresh uncertainties about the stability of Tunku Abdul Rahman's Alliance regime. Secessionist movements in Penang, Johore and Kelantan marred the negotiations which preceded Malaya's *Merdeka* (Independence) on 1 September 1957. By the time the Federation of Malaysia was formed in September 1963 such internal tensions had been overcome, only to be succeeded by a fresh wave of disputes between Singapore's People's Action Party and Malaya's Alliance, culminating in the renewed separation of Singapore from the Federation in 1965. Communal tensions continued to simmer within West Malaysia, finally coming to the boil in the riots of 13 May 1969. Meanwhile, the country endured three years of confrontation with Indonesia, which bitterly opposed the inclusion of Sabah and Sarawak in the federation.[26]

Looking back on this period, and viewing events in Malaysia in the context of the civil wars, coups and revolutions which plagued so many other African and Asian states at the time, what seems most remarkable about the Malaysian case is not the existence of social and international tensions but the great skill shown by the Tunku and his administration in containing them. Tragic though they were, the events of 13 May 1969 were small in scale and short in duration, not least because the government responded rapidly in developing new policies to deal with their underlying causes. On the estates of United Plantations and Bernam Oil Palms, life continued to be peaceful, and a gross profit margin of over 50 per cent continued to be made throughout the 1950s and 1960s. Nevertheless, the very existence of political tensions raised the spectre of nationalization in the minds of the Copenhagen directors: not without cause, as had been demonstrated by the fate of the Thai Electric Corporation and the Dutch plantation companies in Indonesia.[27]

In 1953, S.T. Westenholz began urging that UPSA's assets should be separated from those of United Plantations and Bernam Oil Palms to safeguard their control by the Danish shareholders. By December 1954 a scheme had been worked out whereby the UPSA shares could be distributed to individual United Plantations and Bernam Oil Palms shareholders and the nominal value of the two companies' capital written down by a corresponding amount. During 1955 and 1956 a series of Extraordinary General Meetings were held in Denmark and Malaya, at which shareholders discussed and finally approved the details of the scheme. Following approval from the Malayan High Court, almost 600,000 £1 shares in UPSA were finally distributed in 1957, leaving just over 300,000 shares in the ownership of the parent companies.[28]

Meanwhile, both United Plantations and Bernam Oil Palms had built up substantial holdings of British bonds and Treasury bills, amounting to just over £1 million by December 1956. In 1955 Major Edmund Grut began a wide-ranging discussion about the best use of these funds, arguing forcefully that they should be invested in profitable going concerns outside Malaya. Grut was eager to spread the geographical range of such investments, not only because of the risk of nationalization, but also because shareholders were likely to suffer interruptions to their dividend flows if remittance and exchange controls should be tightened in any one country. After almost a year of debate it was decided to act on his advice, and Dudley Craig was asked to draw up a list of suitable investments. By September 1956 a wide range of possibilities had emerged, including further investment in forestry and sugar production in Southern Africa, tea and banana plantations in Tropical Africa, forestry in Ireland and Canada, and investment in a tankship – the last being Edmund Grut's own favourite option. Meanwhile, Peat, Marwick, Mitchell & Co. had been called in to advise on the choice of location for a holding company. In December 1956 it was decided to base the new company in the Bahamas, one of the few countries in the Sterling Area where no income tax was levied and to organize its formation in such a way that at least 75 per cent of voting shares would be directly in the hands of the parent companies' shareholders.[29]

International Plantations & Finance Ltd (IPF) was duly established in 1957, with assets of approximately £1,300,000 including the parent companies' residual holdings of UPSA shares. Most of the capital continued to be owned by the parent companies in the form of non-voting preference shares, but 260,000 1-shilling ordinary (voting) shares were distributed to United Plantations' and Bernam Oil Palms' shareholders as part of their final dividend for 1956. This ensured that the Danish shareholders had direct control over the management and dividend policy of the new company, at least in theory. In practice, the policy of the new company was determined by the same directors who controlled its parents, especially Niels Benzon, S.T. Westenholz and G.D. Craig. Their decisions set a general direction for IPF's initial investment strategy, which was then worked out in detail by Benny Olsen. Having risen from the post of secretary to become assistant general manager of United Plantations and Bernam Oil Palms in 1956, Olsen retired from Malaya just three years later to become the managing director of IPF. For the next 13 years, his was to be the decisive influence on the company's development.[30]

The initial aim of IPF's directors was to obtain a yield of at least 8.5 per cent per year on 'reasonably prudent' investment in financial assets. Undeterred by early reports from investment consultants in New York, Toronto and Nassau that indicated that such a yield could only be gained from shares in real estate and risky commercial ventures, they placed the bulk of their funds in government securities and the shares of well-known British and North American companies.

By 1960 this strategy was clearly giving poor returns, and Olsen initiated a search for agricultural investment openings in Latin America. From now on he and his fellow directors abandoned Major Grut's quest for going concerns which could yield quick profits, located in a wide spread of countries or on the high seas. They began to repeat the UPSA experiment, starting a new plantation venture which had only the most tenuous of links with its Malayan counterparts.[31]

Olsen was initially attracted to Latin America by the possibility of growing oil palms in countries like Colombia and Ecuador, where plantations had been established on a trial basis earlier in the 1950s and where a substantial local market for vegetable oils existed. Ecuador was especially attractive because of its government's enthusiasm for foreign investors, its stable currency and minimal exchange controls, and its flourishing international trade. Its maximum corporation tax rate was 27 per cent, in contrast with the 40 per cent levied in Malaya from 1958, and there was a generous system of capital allowances. Olsen's choice of Ecuador was finally settled when he made contact with two well-established Danish residents there, Olaf Holm and Henning Jørgensen. Holm lived in the leading commercial city of Guayaquil, where he had many personal contacts with local politicians and businessmen; he seemed an ideal local agent to handle the legal side of IPF's affairs. Jørgensen worked on a nearby coffee estate, Rockefeller's Hacienda Coffee Robusta, but was eager to gain independence and to experiment with other crops. From April 1960 he was employed as a part-time adviser to help IPF identify and acquire suitable plantation land; his position became full time once a few promising estates had been identified in February 1961.[32]

As Olsen's knowledge of Ecuador increased, he realized that bananas and cocoa were likely to be safer crops than oil palms. The banana was Ecuador's main agricultural export in the late 1950s, while cocoa had been dominant there until fungal disease problems and low-cost African exports undermined the industry in the 1920s. By the late 1950s fungal-disease-resistant strains of cocoa were being developed in Trinidad, while the distinctive West African virus diseases of swollen shoot were devastating the rival industry. It thus seemed possible that the Ecuadorean cocoa industry might revive; and Olsen's knowledge of the cocoa experiments carried out at Ulu Bernam and Kuala Bernam since 1947 gave him a special interest in this possibility.[33]

After a few false starts, IPF finally acquired its first Ecuadorean estate in December 1961. The Machala properties, the farms of Santa Irene, San Juan and

La Beatriz, were located in El Oro Province, a dry region to the south of Guayaquil. They had been partly developed as banana plantations during the mid-1950s, when generous government incentives encouraged the clearing of virgin land for this purpose. It was quickly discovered that poor planting materials had been used, and further plantings were made with better corms. However, by December 1963 nearly all the young plants had been destroyed by Panama disease, a virulent fungus which had already devastated the Caribbean banana industry in the early 1930s. Poul Bent Heilmann paid an inspection visit to the farms and helped to convince Holm and Jørgensen to abandon the failing crop. On the grounds that El Oro, with its poor soils and cold, dry weather, was never likely to provide the ideal environment for banana production even if the Panama fungus were eliminated, the managers recommended a switch to cocoa planting at Machala and the purchase of fresh estates in the more attractive Guayas Province.[34]

In July 1964 IPF created a new subsidiary, the Sociedad Anonima San Antonio, of which Benny Olsen became the president, Olaf Holm the general manager and Henning Jørgensen the field manager. The new company bought a partly planted cocoa estate about 80 kilometres east of Guayaquil. By 1967 this cocoa area had been extended and trial plantings of oil palms and bananas had begun, under the direct supervision of Henning Jørgensen. Meanwhile, the Machala estate had been placed in the hands of a new recruit from Denmark, Jespersen, who soon married a local girl and settled down to become a reliable planter. In 1967 Olof Grut visited both Machala and San Antonio and was well pleased with the progress being made. It was decided to unite both estates under the ownership of Sociedad Anonima San Antonio, and early profits were confidently expected: by July 1966 the first modest harvest of cocoa beans had already been made.[35]

Despite the promising estate developments of the years 1964–67, doubts were beginning to be felt in Copenhagen about the long-term merits of the Ecuadorean venture. During the early 1960s Ecuador was controlled by a military junta, under which the fiscal deficit and local inflation levels had begun to soar. In 1966 the junta handed over power to a civilian regime, which began to attempt the task of fiscal reform. New measures were introduced to eliminate tax concessions for foreign creditors, and although these were quickly withdrawn they threatened the viability of SA San Antonio's financing arrangements. Meanwhile, the regime itself proved unstable and was defeated in the 1968 elections by Velasco Ibarra, a populist leader who had already been president on four occasions since 1933 and who had been deposed by military coups in 1947 and 1961. Ibarra had no clear vision of Ecuador's economic future, and mounting fiscal problems finally led him to assume dictatorial powers, devalue the Ecuadorean sucre and briefly ban all US$ remittances and foreign travel in June 1970. New financial decrees were issued almost daily, but the economic situation continued to deteriorate and the military seized power again in February 1972. The political risks of Malaysia paled by comparison.[36]

As the political and economic situation in Ecuador went from bad to worse, so too did the situation on the San Antonio estates. Jørgensen was taken ill with a stomach ulcer in November 1967 and from then on took a less active role in the management of San Antonio. Jespersen moved to San Antonio from Machala, leaving behind an estate which continued to be plagued by water shortages. At San Antonio, Jespersen developed a keen interest in cattle-raising but found the problems of cocoa cultivation quite intractable. He struggled to make the best of stands which had been haphazardly planted and poorly maintained, but this best was not good enough. During February 1971 Olsen visited the estates and noticed that the two main fungal diseases of Latin American cocoa, *Crinipellis perniciosa* (Witches' Broom) and *Moniliophthora roreri* (Monilia), had both made their appearance at San Antonio. Witches' Broom shrivelled the young shoots and pods to give the appearance of dry sticks and wizened apples, while Monilia simply rotted the pods. Highly labour intensive, and hence expensive, measures of field sanitation were required to check the spread of these diseases, but even then cure was not guaranteed. Olsen and others had hoped to avoid the fungal scourge by using the new resistant cocoa clones of the 1950s, but it was later found that the fungi which caused the disease of Witches' Broom in Ecuador belonged to a different species from those which caused the same disease in Trinidad, where the resistant cocoa clones had been developed. Hence the Trinidad clones were not resistant to Witches' Broom when planted in Ecuador.[37]

A combination of bad luck and poor management had brought the San Antonio estates to the point of no return. Three senior United Plantations experts visited them late in 1972 and recommended that not more than a year should be spent on a final salvage operation, including a six-week period of training for Jespersen on the Malaysian estates. In October 1973 a follow-up visit to Ecuador, made by a team led by Olof Grut himself, confirmed that the infestation with Witches' Broom was irreversible. The bulk of IPF's starting capital had been irretrievably lost. In March 1974 the Sociedad Anonima San Antonio was sold for US$400,000, and IPF embarked on a period of retrenchment and reform. Between 1974 and 1978 it functioned essentially as a holding company for UPSA shares and sterling-area securities; and when it finally embarked on a new role in 1978, this was as a result of developments in Malaysia, rather than in Africa or Latin America. The Copenhagen directors, now under the leadership of Olof Grut, had learnt a valuable lesson from the Ecuadorean debacle: from now on, investments outside Asia were designed to strengthen the core palm oil business rather than to provide an escape route from it.[38]

MALAYSIAN COMMITMENTS RENEWED

After 1960 the Copenhagen directors began to take more interest in the Malaysian core business, though at first this change was hardly noticeable. During the period 1958–65 both United Plantations and Bernam Oil Palms continued to accumulate liquid reserves, initially in the form of Treasury bills, and later in the form of fixed-term bank deposits, reaching a total of £700,000 by 1965. They also accumulated shares in quoted companies, to a total value of £1,200,000. A lengthy debate went on over the best location for long-term investment of these funds: there was a consensus that fresh oil palm estates would be the ideal choice but possible locations ranged from North Borneo through Costa Rica to Ecuador itself. The only sign that attitudes towards Malaysia were changing came through a gradual increase, quiet and undiscussed, in the sums reinvested in the original estates. Between 1958 and 1960 such investment averaged just 24 per cent of the total funds generated by Malaysian operations, after tax, dividend and interest payments had been made and changes in working capital accounted for. Between 1963 and 1965, in contrast, this proportion averaged 58 per cent. Over the whole period 1958–65, a cumulative total of £1,600,000 was invested in Malaysia, allowing not only for replanting and factory innovations but also for the purchase of an additional 1,500 hectares of jungle, rubber and coconut land from various estates adjoining Jendarata.[39]

At the same time, the two Malaysian companies were moving towards unification under their new chairman, Olof Grut, who took over from Niels Benzon in 1963. Once formally merged under the name of United Plantations on 1 October 1966, the companies embarked on a phase of rapid expansion which has continued to this day. Many fresh subsidiaries were formed but most were based in Malaysia and all bore a clear relation to the core business.

Meanwhile, the innovative ideas which had been developed by Axel Lindquist, Rolf and Olof Grut during the late 1940s could finally be acted upon. United Plantations could make a full-scale switch to the Tenera palm and could at last move towards a leading position, if not in terms of volume then certainly in terms of engineering and marketing skills, in what was fast becoming the world's leading palm oil industry.

NOTES

1   Family information supplied by Mette Bjerglund-Andersen, granddaughter of Thorkil Knudtzon; Preben Sten Petersen, son-in-law of Sven Torben Westenholz; Erling Grut, the family historian, brother of Major Edmund Grut; and Mogens Jensen, until January 2003 the general manager of International Plantation Services Ltd, which runs the Copenhagen office. Lists of board members from UPDR and BOPDR, 1946–50.

2   Obituary of Edmund Grut in *Berlingske Tidende*, 9 April 1958; biography celebrating Benzon's 60th birthday in *Berlingske Tidende*, 22 April 1953; personal reminiscence from numerous sources. Photograph of Benzon supplied by Mogens Jensen, and of Olof Grut with his brother Rolf in the early 1940s, by Dr Valdemar Lindquist.

3   Com. Grut to R.D. Craig, 12 June 1947, CC, 1945–47; BOP share registers, 1938 and 1948; and United Plantations share register, 1948. United Plantations held 41 per cent of Bernam Oil Palms' shares in both 1938 and 1948.

4   UBAR, 1946, account of visit by E. Anker of Sungei Palas Tea Estate; BOPDR, 1946–65; UPAR, 1966–76.

5   Interview with Rolf and Rothes Grut, 19 April 1988; visit to Olof's grave with Axel Lindquist and Tan Sri Dato' Seri B. Bek-Nielsen, 20 February 1989.

6   Olof Grut to Benzon, 29 June 1950, CC, 1947–51; BOPDR, 1947; UPDR, 1959–65; UPAR, 1966–99.

7   D.J.M. Tate, *The RGA History of the Plantation Industry in the Malay Peninsula* (Kuala Lumpur: Oxford University Press for the Rubber Growers' Association (Malaysia) Berhad, 1996), pp. 439–446; Olof Grut to Benzon, 19 May 1950 and 24 April 1951; and Benzon to O. Grut, 20 March 1951; CC, 1947–51.

8   UPDR, 1950–60; Carrie Jørgensen, 'United Plantations and Bernam Oil Palms: highlights from a colourful past' (unpublished mss., 1984), pp. 17–19; interview with Rolf Grut, general manager UP/BOP 1956–63, 21 April 1988.

9   Olof Grut to General T. Grut, 17 February 1947 and to Com. Grut, 25 August 1947, CC, 1946–47; Rolf Grut to Benzon, 23 September 1960, CC, 1959–60; V.S. MacFadyen (ed.), *Eric MacFadyen, 1879–1966* (Barnet, Herts: The Stellar Press, 1968), pp. 3–5

and 132–141; Peter Pugh *et al.*, edited by Guy Nickalls, *Great Enterprise: a History of Harrisons & Crosfield* (London: Harrisons & Crosfield, 1990), pp. 157 and 182–184; interviews with former Harrisons' staff: Douglas Gold, 9 August 1988; Thomas Fleming, 4 October 1988; and Brian Gray, 6 June 1989.

10 Lim Teck Ghee, *Peasants and their Agricultural Economy in Colonial Malaya, 1874–1941* (Kuala Lumpur: Oxford University Press, 1977), pp. 106–116 and 209–216; A.J. Stockwell, *British Policy and Malay Politics during the Malayan Union Experiment, 1942–1948* (Kuala Lumpur: Malaysian Branch of the Royal Asiatic Society, 1979), Chs 4 and 5; Lim Chong-Yah, *Economic Development*, Chs 6 and 7; David Lim, *Economic Growth and Development in West Malaysia, 1947–1970* (Kuala Lumpur: Oxford University Press, 1973), Chs 4 and 5; J.M. Gullick, *Malaysia: Economic Expansion and National Unity* (London: Ernest Benn, 1981), pp. 83–85; Olof Grut to Com. Grut, 8 December 1947 and 8 January 1948, CC, 1947–51; BOPCA, 1948; Rolf Grut to Benzon, 6 July 1957, CC, 1952–58.

11 Olof Grut to Benzon, 11 July 1949, CC, 1948–51; personal communication from Flemming Heilmann, 10 March 1999; BOPCM, 5 July 1948.

12 Sources as previous note, and BOPCM, 2 September1948; personal communication, 8 October 1998, from Mrs Inge Asboe Mitchell, who was attached to the Ingemann household from 1945 to 1952.

13 R. Clutterbuck, *Conflict and Violence in Singapore and Malaysia, 1945–1983* (Singapore: Graham Brash, 1984), Ch. 9; Cheah Boon Kheng, *Red Star Over Malaya: Resistance and Social Conflict During and After the Japanese Occupation of Malaya, 1941–1946* (Singapore: University Press, 1983), Part I; Tate, *RGA History*, Ch. 37; 'Roll of honour: planters killed in the Emergency', *The Planter*, vol. XXXIX, no. 9, 1963, p. 407; interviews with Peter Cowling, 4 September1987, and with Axel Lindquist and Tan Sri Dato' Seri B. Bek-Nielsen, 15 April 1989.

14 Clutterbuck, *Conflict and Violence*, Chs 9–14; Gullick, *Malaysia*, pp. 85–93; Kernial Singh Sandhu, *Indians in Malaya: Some Aspects of their Immigration and Settlement, 1786–1957* (Cambridge: Cambridge University Press, 1969), pp. 214–217 and 231; 'Roll of honour', *The Planter*, vol. XXXIX, no. 9, 1963, p. 407.

15 Interview with Bek-Nielsen, 'A planter at heart', *Malaysian Business*, 16 August 2001; R. Thambipillay, *God's Little Acre 1948–1960* (Batu Gajah: Perak Planters' Association, 1998); Souvenir Booklet produced by the Veteran Security Association of Malaysia when Bek-Nielsen received the title of Darjah Seri Paduka Mahkota Perak, 8 July 1989; contributions by Thambipillay and H.V. Speldewinde, president, Penang Veterans' Association, to *Messages of Congratulation to Y.Bhg. Tan Sri Dato' Seri B. Bek-Nielsen on the Occasion of his Golden Anniversary with United Plantations Berhad, 15th September 2001* (Jendarata: United Plantations Berhad, 2001), pp. 14–16 and 44–45.

16 T.N. Harper, *The End of Empire and the Making of Malaya* (Cambridge: Cambridge University Press, 1999), Ch. 3; interview with Muthama, Vallathi, Amirtham, Pasupathu, Rajamma, Pakiam and Muniamna at the Jendarata Old Folks' Home, 5 April 1989; interviews with Tan Sri Dato' Seri B. Bek-Nielsen and Axel Lindquist, 15 April 1989; JAR, 1952–58; UPAR and BOPAR, 1952.

17 Heilmann to Lennart Grut, 20 July 1948; UBAR, 1948–54; interview with Axel Lindquist, 20 February 1989. Knud Sehested recalls that the 'brave assistant' was, from 1951 to 1954, Ole Schwensen, who was recruited to Bernam Oil Palms in 1951 and rose to become general manager (UP and BOP) 1963–71; personal communication from Sehested, 18 December 1999, and Jørgensen, 'United Plantations', pp. 150–170 and 185.

18 A. Short, *The Communist Insurrection in Malaya, 1948–1960* (London: Muller, 1975), Ch. 19; JAR and UBAR, 1948–58.

19 Interview with Tan Sri Dato' Seri B. Bek-Nielsen, 15 April 1989.

20 J.S. Hogendorn, 'The East African Groundnut Scheme: lessons of a large-scale agricultural failure', *African Economic History*, vol. 10, 1981, pp. 81–115.

21 BOPCM, 2 September 1948; Heilmann and Olof Grut, Memorandum for BOPCM, 19 October 1949; UPCA, 1950; P.B. Heilmann, 'An outline of the history of United Plantations South Africa Limited and United Plantations (Swaziland) Limited, 1950–1971' (unpublished mss., 15 March 1972); personal communication from Flemming Heilmann, 10 March 1999.

22 This and the following two paragraphs are based on Heilmann's 1972 'Outline history' and on UPCA, 1950–55. Further details were kindly supplied by Flemming Heilmann, personal communication, 10 March 1999.

23 Heilmann, 'Outline history', and United Plantations Africa Ltd, 'Introduction to the stock exchange', 28 May 1987; UPAR, 1974–94; UP Africa AR, 1987–98. It should also be noted that the vagaries of climate, international commodity markets and local currency exchange rates combined to make the 1990s difficult years for UP Africa.

24 R. Brealey and S. Myers, *Principles of Corporate Finance* (Singapore: McGraw-Hill, 1984), Ch. 7.

25 W.G. Jones, *Denmark: A Modern History* (London: Croom Helm, 1986), Ch. 9; UPCA, 1950–55; Olof Grut to Benzon, 28 September 1951, CC, 1948–51.

26 BOP board meetings, 27 August 1952 and 17 December 1953; Mohamed N. Sopiee, *From Malayan Union to Singapore Separation: Political Unification in the Malaysia Region, 1945–65* (Kuala Lumpur: Penerbit Universiti Malaya, 1974), Chs 4–7; B.W. and L.Y. Andaya, *A History of Malaysia* (Basingstoke: Macmillan, 1982), Ch. 7.

27 A. Coates, *The Commerce in Rubber: The First 250 Years* (Singapore: Oxford University Press, 1987), Ch. 39; General manager, Thai Electric Corporation, to

Messrs UP/BOP, 19 September 1949, CC, 1948–51; Olof Grut to Benzon, 12 August 1959, CC, 1959–60; BOPCA and UPCA, by Olof Grut, 1964–66.

28 BOP board meetings, 19 May 1953 and 25 May 1955; BOPCM, 15 December 1954; UP Extraordinary General Meetings, 8 December 1955, 17 May 1956, 15 June 1956 and 18 January 1957; UPDR and BOPDR, 1956.

29 BOP board meetings, 25 May 1955, 8 March 1956, 16 May 1956, 6 September 1956 and 6 December 1956; report by Peat, Marwick, Mitchell & Co., Newcastle, 30 August 1956.

30 BOP Board Meetings, 22 May 1957 and 24 September 1958; UPDR and BOPDR, 1956–57.

31 UP Copenhagen office files: 'IPF: memoranda on formation', 1956–57 and correspondence with the Boston investment consultant John P. Chase, 1961–64.

32 C.W.S. Hartley, *The Oil Palm (Elaeis Guineensis Jacq.)* 3rd edn (London: Longmans, 1988), pp. 33–36; UP Copenhagen office file, 'Ecuador, 1960–61', especially Benzon to Rubber Culture Maatschappij, Amsterdam, 6 January 1960; Empresa Electrica del Ecuador Inc., 'Investing in Ecuador' (October 1959); and Olsen to Jørgensen, 27 February 1961.

33 D.H. Urquhart, *Cocoa* (London: Longmans, 1956), Chs II, XI and XII.

34 C.D. Kepner, *Social Aspects of the Banana Industry* (New York: Columbia University Press, 1936), Ch. 1; D.W. Schodt, *Ecuador: An Andean Enigma* (Boulder and London: Westview Press, 1987), Ch. 3; UP Copenhagen office file 'Ecuador, 1963–65', especially Report by B. Olsen to the board of directors, 11 December 1963; personal communication from Flemming Heilmann, 10 March 1999.

35 UP Copenhagen office file, 'Ecuador, 1967', esp. Olof Grut to Holm, 18 April 1967.

36 Schodt, *Ecuador*, Ch. 4; UP Copenhagen office files, 'Ecuador, 1966–70', regular bulletins from Holm to Olsen.

37 R.A. Lass and G.A.R. Wood (eds), *Cocoa Production: Present Constraints and Priorities for Research*, Technical Paper No. 39 (Washington: World Bank, 1985), Ch. VI; UP Copenhagen office files, 'Ecuador, 1967–72', especially Holm to Olsen, 26 November 1967; Olsen to Jørgensen, 8 February 1971; reports by Rolf Grut, Ken Stimpson and Ng Siew Kee on visits to Ecuador, 15 November – 2 December 1972.

38 IPFAR, 1972–8; UP Copenhagen office files, 'Ecuador, 1972–74', especially reports by Rolf Grut, Ken Stimpson and Ng Siew Kee on visits to Ecuador, 15 November – 2 December 1972; report by Olof Grut on visit to Ecuador, 23–28 October 1973; Olof Grut to Jespersen, 22 March 1974.

39 UPDR and BOPDR, 1958–65; UPBM and BOPBM, 1958–65.

CHAPTER 5

The Tenera Palm

INVENTION AND INNOVATION

*U*nited Plantations was not alone in moving into a new era of high profits and innovation after the Second World War. From the 1950s to the 1980s, as Malaysia's oil palm acreage expanded, so too did the country's role as a world centre of research and development. Few of the new ideas, plant breeding methods and machines that were now developed or put into use in Malaysia had actually been invented there. Yet with its increasingly evident political stability and economic prosperity, the country provided an ideal environment for the application and diffusion of inventions and for the investment which was vital for their transformation into practical and effective innovations.

The first technique to be taken up and developed by oil palm planters in post-war Malaysia, and the one which proved the vital cornerstone for all the rest, was the plant breeding method which produced the Tenera variety of oil palm, distinguished by its thin-shelled, pulpy fruit. Until the 1930s the Tenera palm had been found only in West Africa, where it grew rarely and unpredictably in the wild. It was valued for its high content of oil-rich mesocarp, especially striking in West Africa where the local Dura varieties were very thick shelled. Observers realized as early as 1902, when the Tenera variety was first identified, that Tenera plantations would make it possible not only to achieve high oil yields per hectare but also to experiment with powerful pressing machinery without fear of producing a messy mix of crushed shells, kernels and pulp. However, subsequent attempts to breed from Tenera parents produced wildly varying results, and it was clear that expensive research would be needed to find out why. It was not until the Second World War that researchers in the Belgian Congo identified the Tenera as a hybrid of the Dura and yet another variety, the shell-

141

less Pisifera, the rarest of all African oil palms because it was often sterile. Being a hybrid, the Tenera if crossed with itself would produce a varied progeny: 25 per cent Dura, 25 per cent Pisifera and only 50 per cent Tenera. Once this was known, it became a relatively simple task to develop breeding programmes using Dura and Pisifera parents, but until then, planters viewed any investment in the Tenera variety as a highly speculative venture.[1]

In South-East Asia, where the Deli Dura variety already offered planters a relatively pulp-rich fruit, sceptical attitudes towards Tenera breeding programmes lingered on for 20 years. Yet by the time Malaysia's first large-scale Tenera plantings came into full bearing in the 1970s, it could be seen that the speculation had been a dazzling success. Not only was the fruit easier to process mechanically, but the yields had risen dramatically. On Ulu Bernam Estate for example, yields of fresh fruit bunches per annum from 10-year-old palms rose from 17 tonnes per hectare for the pre-War Deli Dura plantings to 24 tonnes for the Tenera plantings of the late 1960s.[2]

Many plant breeders in both the public and private sectors, in the Belgian Congo as well as in Sumatra and Malaysia, were involved in the Tenera success story. United Plantations was involved at an early stage in the Malaysian breeding programme, but it could never have achieved success alone. The switch to Tenera at Ulu Bernam, like the renewal and growth of Malaysia's oil palm industry as a whole, was founded on the willingness of planters to exchange research results and to sell or even give away their vital supplies of pollen and seedlings. Within United Plantations, Rolf Grut played a key role, not only because he was committed to the new variety from the start but also because of his warmth of character and wide range of friendships within the planting community. In this chapter his achievements will be set within the context of Malaysia's remarkable history of co-operative oil palm research and development.

EARLY EXPERIMENTS WITH THE TENERA PALM

Although there were extensive selection programmes for the oil palm in Malaya and Sumatra before the Second World War, it was only in Africa that the Tenera palm was singled out. In his magisterial study of the subject, C.W.S. Hartley has suggested that this was because of the low quality of African Dura fruit that naturally stimulated crop breeders to look for a radical alternative. It may be added that the whole enterprise of crop breeding had more radical motives in

Africa than in Asia. The officials who sponsored it in Africa were aiming not simply to serve an established plantation industry but to create a new form of permanent agriculture to replace local systems of hunting, gathering and shifting cultivation. Belgian officials in the Congo held an especially strong ideological belief in the virtues of modern intensive agriculture. As early as 1913 the agricultural engineer M. Laurent was urging the state to invest in seed selection and plant breeding so as to lay the foundations of a plantation oil palm industry. By the 1920s it had become clear that such state-led research was vital not only in theory but also in practice. The main private investor in the Congo's oil palm industry, Lever Brothers' subsidiary Huileries du Congo Belge, was unwilling to venture beyond its original processing business to establish plantations, unless a radically improved strain of oil palm was available to give them a competitive edge against producers using wild trees. Hence there was every reason for officials in the Congo to sponsor oil palm experiments which went beyond the selection of good Dura palms and sought out ways of breeding the rare but valuable Tenera palm.[3]

The first experimental plantation of Tenera palms was made by M. Ringoet at the Yangambi research station of the Institut National pour l'Etude Agronomique du Congo Belge (INEAC) in 1922. At the same time, Tenera seed was sent from the Eala Botanic Gardens in the Congo to Sumatra, where the Dutch planters' association AVROS was establishing an experimental plot at Sungei Pantjur. Some experiments were made by AVROS and on private estates in Sumatra to measure the yields of imported Tenera palms and their progeny, but no systematic attempt was made to discover methods of breeding the Tenera true. In Malaya, the Department of Agriculture decided in 1925 that experiments with Tenera were worth making, and imported a variety of seeds from West Africa which were planted at Serdang in 1926 and 1927. However, interested planters were warned that the Tenera type 'probably requires years of selection to make it safe for plantations'; and little attempt at such selection was made in Malaya before the Second World War.[4]

Only in the Belgian Congo was any systematic attempt made to discover how to breed reliably from the Tenera palm; and here the key discoveries were essentially the work of one man, M. Beirnaert, who tragically died just before his pathbreaking findings were published. In the early 1930s Beirnaert carried out a painstaking 3-year programme of yield recording and further tests on the palms planted earlier by Ringoet at Yangambi. He found a number of palms which were rich in both pulp and kernels, with a very small percentage of shell. Using these as mother palms, Beirnaert embarked on a further series of experiments which clearly demonstrated the hybrid nature of the Tenera. Hartley has described Beirnaert's research methods and findings in detail, and they are also recorded in the seminal paper by Beirnaert and his colleague M. Vanderweyen which was published shortly after Beirnaert's death in 1941. Briefly, the key finding was that a Tenera palm which had been self-pollinated or crossed with another Tenera would yield the following mix of progeny: Tenera 50 per cent, Dura 25 per cent and Pisifera 25 per cent. A Tenera crossed with a Dura would yield 50 per cent Dura and 50 per cent Tenera progeny. The implication was that a Dura fertilized with Pisifera pollen would yield 100 per cent Tenera.[5]

The shell-less Pisifera palm thus acquired a new value for plant breeders. Previously it had been seen as a mere curiosity, rarely found in the wild and of little interest to planters because it was frequently sterile: that is, it usually produced a large number of female inflorescences, many of which failed to develop into fruit bunches. Now the very rarity of Pisiferas with sufficient male, pollen-bearing inflorescences heightened the value of those which could be found. Pisiferas were especially rare in South-East Asia, where the great majority of seeds produced and imported before the Second World War had been of the Dura type. After the war, planters soon began scrambling to obtain Pisifera pollen and to build it into their oil palm breeding programmes.[6]

INNOVATION ON A SHOESTRING

Deli Dura seed selection had begun at Ulu Bernam in 1935, at about the same time as the Malayan Agricultural Department and the Guthrie Corporation began similar work at Elmina Estate and at Ulu Remis (Chemara) respectively. Socfin also carried out seed selection in both Malaya and Sumatra. All these efforts were brought to a halt by the Second World War and the Japanese Occupation, following which the main priority on the estates was simply to reclaim fields left poorly tended under the Japanese. Nevertheless, the Sumatran planters quickly began experimenting with Deli/Pisifera crosses, using pre-war imported material. In Malaya, H.M. Gray of the Guthrie Corporation arranged an import of Pisifera pollen from Yangambi to Chemara in 1947; and in 1949 Eric Rosenquist began experimenting with the African palms planted before the war at Serdang. By the early 1950s, the news of Beirnaert's discovery was spreading throughout the Malayan planting community and local supplies of Tenera seed were becoming available.[7]

Meanwhile, as shown in Chapter 3, problems in harvesting tall palms at Jendarata and Ulu Bernam had already stimulated Rolf and Olof Grut to consider more systematic seed trials and to take an interest in new oil palm varieties. By 1949 Asger Laursen had been commissioned to visit estates in Nigeria and the Belgian Congo on his return journey from leave in Denmark and had brought back promising news of the Tenera palm. Belgian researchers were also experimenting with crosses between *Elaeis guineensis* and the Latin American species *Elaeis melanococca* (now known as *Elaeis oleifera*), which was of special interest because its trunk grew along the ground and so the fruit could easily be reached for harvesting. United Plantations had obtained several consignments of *Elaeis melanococca* seed, but these failed to germinate. Meanwhile, Olof Grut was following with interest the Malayan Agricultural Department's experiments with the 'Dumpy palm'. In an attempt to improve United Plantations' ability to replicate such experiments, he engaged two new graduate assistants, one Danish and one Indian; however, there is no record of their actually arriving in Malaya. In June 1952 Jendarata's first recorded research officer, Ben Skaarup, did arrive, but he stayed only two years and the trials which he laid down on Division II of the estate were abandoned immediately after his departure. It was left to Rolf Grut, then the manager of Bernam Oil Palms, to ensure that United Plantations was not left behind in the post-war rush to breed better palms.[8]

Rolf Grut had arrived in Malaya in 1933 at the age of 24. Like his brother Olof he had an early training in engineering, but unlike Olof he had little enthusiasm for it. He did enjoy flying and was such an expert pilot that his passengers felt he was at one with his machine, but his main love was tennis, a game at which he excelled. He once partnered a Danish Davis Cup player against the Swedish champion and King Gustav V and twice became a finalist in the Malayan national championships. Through his tennis he made many friendships which were to prove vital to United Plantations. In the early years of oil palm breeding in Malaysia, government research scientists played a key role and their most fruitful contacts with planters in the private sector were often made informally, through sport and the social round of Sunday tiffin. Hence it was the sociable and sporting Rolf Grut who made contact with two men whose help was later to prove vital in developing the United Plantations breeding programme: Charles Hartley and Eric Rosenquist.[9]

Charles Hartley, who was later to become one of the world's leading authorities on the oil palm, happened to serve as the agricultural officer for Teluk Anson in the mid-1930s. His wife Marie soon became Rolf's mixed-doubles partner and, 50 years later, still remembered vividly how he used to fly to their matches, always arriving at the very last minute with a dashing and independent air. After the war her husband became the senior agronomist at the Malayan Agricultural Department. Back trouble was soon to interrupt his career, which he later resumed outside Malaysia, so that his links with United Plantations took on the much looser form of occasional consultancy visits. Before this happened, however, Hartley had been able to direct the early work of Eric Rosenquist, who was appointed to the department as oil palm botanist in January 1949. Rosenquist was the son of a Dane who had moved to England in the service of the Danish Bacon Company. His Cambridge University education in the natural sciences was interrupted by the war, during which he volunteered for Secret Scientific Service in India and, in 1945, for service with the Department of Agriculture in the British Military Administration of Malaya. This experience left him determined to join the Colonial Agricultural Service, and after two further years of Cambridge training in agricultural science and plant breeding, he was posted back to Malaya. He travelled out with his wife, whom he had met in Singapore and who had also learned to love Malaya, and their small daughter. Mrs Rosenquist, like Mrs Hartley, was a keen tennis player and so the Rosenquists soon became friendly in their turn with Rolf and Rothes Grut.[10]

At this time the Agricultural Department's Experiment Station at Serdang was supplying palm oil to the Prison Department, and one of Eric Rosenquist's first tasks was to find a way of increasing the carotene and Vitamin A content of the oil, in order to improve the prisoners' diet. A quick survey revealed that the carotene content of palm oil varied widely from tree to tree and that the West African palms planted in the mid-1920s had a markedly higher content than the rest of the Serdang palms. Later scientific studies carried out in Africa confirmed this general difference between Deli Dura and African palms which was of special interest in the 1990s when consumers were highly sensitive to the nutritional content of competing fats. In the late 1940s, however, the finding was of fleeting concern. Its main practical result was that Eric Rosenquist's attention was directed towards the African palms growing at Serdang. Several of the high-carotene palms also happened to be Teneras, and Rosenquist quickly realized that they could be used in a breeding programme to follow through the implications of Beirnaert and Vanderweyen's 1941 paper. By 1950 he had begun to organize imports of seed and of Pisifera pollen from Nigeria, French West Africa and the Belgian Congo, followed in 1956 by imports from Sumatra, which paved the way for an extensive programme of experimental crosses between imported Pisiferas and Teneras on the one hand and the Deli Dura and 'Dumpy' palms on the other.[11]

The main problem faced by the Agricultural Department in carrying out this breeding programme was to find enough land. Quite apart from the need to test the merits of different crosses, there was also a need to develop more effective techniques for controlled pollination and so to plant additional experimental plots in order to raise seedlings produced by competing methods. Finally, many estate managers were keenly interested in the 'Dumpy palm', which Robert Jagoe had identified when carrying out seed selection work for the Agricultural Department at Elmina Estate in the 1930s. Short and squat, the 'Dumpy' seemed to offer the ideal answer to post-war harvesting problems. Trial plantings soon revealed that the pure 'Dumpy' had low fruit and oil yields, but Rosenquist hoped that experimental crosses between it and taller, high-yielding Deli palms would yield an ideal tree. All this activity required land, and the best offer the Malayan Administration was finally able to make was of a second research station at Jerangau in Trengganu, 13 ferries and an appalling road journey away from Serdang.[12]

In the face of these difficulties Rosenquist decided to revive the pre-war tradition of active co-operation between the Agricultural Department and Malaya's oil palm planters. Instead of collecting planting material from the estates, however, the department began distributing experimental seedlings to them. The seedlings had to be planted out in clearly marked trial areas and their growth monitored closely if the experiments were to have scientific value, but it was not always easy for the department to persuade estate managers to invest the necessary land, time and money. As the director of agriculture lamented in a letter published in *The Planter* in 1950, 'Planters...would like to take part in experiments but feel that their Boards would not support actions which might detract from the estate's main objectives and would be reluctant to authorize expenditure the results of which would be problematic.' This was especially true at a time when Malaya's Emergency was causing many European directors to rethink their commitment to the country, as seen in Chapter 4.[13]

Personal contacts between Agricultural Department officers and individual planters were vital if enough enthusiasm was to be generated to counteract such corporate pressures. Eric Rosenquist's friendship with Rolf Grut was just the kind of contact needed; and it was helpful that Rolf was in a sufficiently strong position within his company to authorize experiments confidently. Although United Plantations and Bernam Oil Palms were becoming more bureaucratic and conservative at this time, with proliferating statistics in the annual estate reports and new men in Copenhagen, they still retained much of the 'family firm' ethos developed in the days of Aage Westenholz and Commander Grut. This is not to suggest that either company was characterized by unbridled nepotism: both planters and non-executive board members were recruited from outside the extended family descended from Andreas Hansen to which both Westenholz and Grut had belonged. Meanwhile, the Hansen family itself was so large by the 1940s that it could provide a very wide range of talent. Rolf and Olof Grut could not afford to rest on their laurels, especially because Commander Grut died while they were still young, leaving them to compete with men not only from their own generation but also from the generation above. Finally, they suffered a social handicap which may be hard for twenty-first century readers to understand but which became especially burdensome in the decade following the Second World War: that is, the Japanese family connection on their mother's side. Rolf, the younger son, felt this handicap more keenly, yet retained loving and protective memories of his mother till the end of his life. He did not become a member of the board until 1954, but Olof had been on it since 1940 and remained a staunch advocate of innovation. The cause of Rolf's plant-breeding experiments was a relatively easy one to champion since the investment needed was small, even in comparison with Olof's own tea and pineapple schemes.[14]

In 1952 Eric Rosenquist took two boatloads of oil palm seedlings up to Ulu Bernam. He travelled in the estate's own cargo vessel, the *M.V. Kertang*, which picked him up at Port Swettenham for the 18-hour overnight trip along the coast and up the Bernam River. The boat, an old 50-ton *tongkang* (sea-going barge) that had been rebuilt in the yard at Ulu Bernam in 1949, had no radio and Rosenquist found the experience hair-raising – even more so in retrospect, as soon after his last trip the *Kertang* hit a submerged fish trap off the Perak coast and sank with the loss of one life.[15]

The seedlings which Rosenquist carried up to Ulu Bernam included some Tenera x Tenera crosses and 'dumpy' Duras, as well as some material from Serdang's Field 19, which had been planted in 1927 with open-pollinated West

African seed. This was the first Tenera material to arrive at either Jendarata or Ulu Bernam, and it was to be of vital importance in the estates' later plant-breeding programmes. Initially, however, the Agricultural Department material was kept apart from the Deli Dura seedlings which were being grown under Ulu Bernam's own seed selection programme. Rosenquist planted out the Department's seedlings himself and made periodic visits in Rolf Grut's plane to check on their progress. However, by 1954 he had become so frustrated with the administration's failure to provide more land for the Agricultural Department itself that he resigned to join Guthrie and Company. The seedlings at Ulu Bernam remained accessible in theory to the department's researchers, but shortages of staff seem to have prevented Rosenquist's successor Arthur Haddon from following the experiment through. Haddon initially concentrated on the department's own plots at Serdang and Jerangau, and when he revived the idea of co-operative experiments in 1956 he decided to make a fresh set of arrangements and to plant new plots.[16]

By 1956 Ulu Bernam, like many other estates, already had its own Tenera breeding scheme. The Agricultural Department's researchers could no longer hope to play a leading role in the process of innovation; the most they could do was to facilitate and share in it. Haddon's new Co-operative Breeding Scheme involved four Host Estates, including Jendarata but not Ulu Bernam, who agreed to provide not only land, as before, but also skilled research staff and some Tenera or Pisifera planting material for fresh experiments. Under this scheme 57 hectares were planted at Jendarata between 1957 and 1960, but the private sector remained the key source of the Tenera seedlings used there and at Ulu Bernam. In 1959, for example, only 120 germinated Tenera seeds were received by Jendarata under the department's scheme, but 35,000 were bought from Guthries' Ulu Remis Estate and 27,000 were produced by Jendarata and Ulu Bernam themselves, using Pisifera pollen obtained from Nigeria, the Belgian Congo and Sumatra.[17]

At the same time as Haddon set up the Co-operative Breeding Scheme, he also decided to resume imports of Tenera and Pisifera planting material to Malaya. Here again the department's new reliance on the private sector can be shown clearly. Haddon and his colleague Van Thean Kee organized their first expedition to Sumatra in collaboration with Brian Gray, who had studied with them for the Cambridge University Diploma in Agricultural Science before joining Harrisons and Crosfield in 1955 as their first oil palm research officer in Malaya.

Harrisons' Sumatran oil palm industry contacts were far better than those of the Malayan Agricultural Department; but the department's involvement in the trip provided the vital government contacts which were needed for the open export of Pisifera and Tenera material from Sumatra. When Rolf Grut had first drawn on pre-war friendships to obtain Pisifera pollen from Medan in 1954, he lacked official contacts and so the pollen had to be smuggled out of Sumatra in the guise of face powder. The whole operation was so secret that not even Rolf's friend Eric Rosenquist knew of it; and in the internal estate reports for that year, it was barely alluded to – much greater prominence was given to the pollen supplies obtained at the same time from West Africa through official channels. In contrast, the joint expedition mounted by Gray, Haddon and Van in 1956 was highly public. Indeed, Brian Gray was astonished at the level of protocol surrounding it. When he stepped off the DC3 in his ordinary shorts, he found himself being formally received by the governor of North Sumatra. The vital supplies of Tenera x Pisifera seeds were duly obtained from AVROS and exported with the government's blessing; but the Agricultural Department's staff had relatively little to do with them thereafter. Owing to the shortage of land at Serdang, the seeds were entrusted to Gray for planting at his new research station at Banting. Fruit from the resulting trees was later supplied to the Agricultural Department as needed, but the care of the trees was carried out by Gray and his staff, who were also free to use the remaining fruit and pollen in their own research and plant breeding schemes.[18]

While the Agricultural Department struggled to maintain its involvement in the process of innovation, the private sector was becoming increasingly willing to fund research. In part this was because research could sometimes be made to fund itself. This was especially true in the case of Guthries' Chemara Research Organization at Ulu Remis, where seed selection had begun before the war and where genetic blocks of known parentage had been laid down in the mid-1930s. In 1947 H.M. Gray arranged to import Pisifera pollen to Chemara from the Yangambi Research Station in the Belgian Congo, and two further genetic blocks were planted with crosses between this material and the best Chemara Deli Duras. Guthries' directors were by no means convinced that Tenera was the palm of the future, fearing that the use of African genetic material would lower the quality of the palm oil produced. However, Eric Rosenquist managed to persuade them to make small commercial plantings of the new material once he joined the company in 1954. He obtained further supplies of Pisifera pollen from Nigeria through the Pamol Estates at Kluang that had been acquired in 1947 by Unilever's United Africa Company and which used Chemara's consultancy services. By 1957 Chemara was able to produce ample amounts of Tenera seedlings, not only for Guthries' own use but also for sale, and became an important supplier to companies like Harrisons and United Plantations. The profit from these sales was ploughed directly back into oil palm research, in particular the creation of a pure Pisifera block at Ulu Remis which eventually provided enough pollen for a self-sufficient Tenera breeding programme. Meanwhile, it was becoming clear that the Tenera palm offered increased yields with no loss of quality in the resulting palm oil.[19]

In 1964 Rosenquist moved on to a post as agricultural adviser with the Cameroun Development Corporation, but his achievements had convinced the Guthries directors of the value of further crop research and removed the doubts they had originally held about using African genetic material in their plant breeding programmes. Hence they were keen to participate in a scheme put forward by Unilever to widen the genetic range of Malaysia's oil palm stock and to employ the latest scientific techniques to select the highest-yielding Tenera palms. In 1965 they set up the Oil Palm Genetics Laboratory in collaboration with Harrisons and Dunlop, employing the geneticist Dr Jaap Hardon to make the initial collections of planting material and later the plant physiologist Dr Hereward Corley to identify the most productive palms, which could then be subjected to genetic analysis and breeding. All this work was funded by the four companies without government assistance until 1973, when the laboratory was taken over by the Malaysian Agricultural Research and Development Institution.[20]

Meanwhile, Rolf Grut continued to champion the cause of the Tenera palm at United Plantations and Bernam Oil Palms, where he had become general manager in 1956. He faced an increasingly uphill task in persuading the Copenhagen directors to fund further experiments, or even to sanction the purchase of Tenera seedlings once these became available from Ulu Remis. In part the directors' conservatism reflected their doubts about Malaya's political future, together with the personal tensions that inevitably accompanied the Grut brothers' rise to power within the firms. However, it was also true that like Guthries' directors, the Copenhagen board found it hard to believe that Tenera palms could really increase yields without decreasing quality. In particular they were concerned about the increased extraction rate predicted for the thin-shelled Tenera fruit, yielding an oil:FFB ratio of 23 per cent instead of the 18 per cent achieved with Dura. They doubted that this could be achieved without crushing the kernels and so adulterating the palm oil itself. Such doubts could hardly be answered until enough fruit had been produced for factory testing, that is, until about four years had passed since the first substantial planting experiments had been made. In 1957 Rolf applied for permission to purchase 10,000 Tenera seedlings from Ulu Remis, marshalling supporting evidence from Professor Vincent Schmidt of AVROS, Dr Larter of the Malayan Agricultural Department and Eric Rosenquist. But he had to concede that the evidence about Tenera's factory viability was inconclusive, since all these experts' experiments were still at a relatively early stage. It was also rumoured that Socfin had decided to concentrate its plant breeding efforts on Dura rather than Tenera, and this rumour strengthened the hand of conservatives elsewhere. In the event Rolf had to wait until 1959 before his first purchase of Ulu Remis seedlings was allowed.[21]

Shortages of staff provided a further obstacle, especially to the development of an independent Tenera breeding programme at Ulu Bernam or Jendarata. Following the departure of Ben Skaarup in 1954, no further attempt had been made to establish a Research Department, and although Olof Grut strongly favoured the idea he was unable to implement it until 1963, when he became chairman of United Plantations and Bernam Oil Palms. In the meantime experiments on the Tenera palm depended solely on the enthusiasm of individuals, in particular Arne Bybjerg Pedersen, a bright young planting assistant based at Jendarata. Pedersen had joined United Plantations in 1953, and soon made his mark as a fiery and independent character, capable of learning about plant breeding from a manual and of picking up news about the Tenera palm from Dutch journals. He was keen to make a name for himself within the wider planting community, for example by writing a series of articles for *The Planter* on oil palm nursery techniques and on plant breeding advances in Sumatra and the Belgian Congo. After the secret Sumatran venture of 1954 he began cultivating more public contacts at the West African Institute for Oil Palm Research (WAIFOR) in Nigeria. These efforts ensured a regular annual supply of Pisifera pollen for Jendarata and Ulu Bernam's nurseries from 1958 onwards. But they got him into trouble with the Jendarata estate manager, Alsing, a correct and conscientious person who was outraged at Pedersen's decision to print letterheads with the legend 'Research Department' in order to impress scientific correspondents.[22]

In the cautious company climate of the 1950s, innovation could hardly have taken place without the initiative of people like Pedersen, yet this very caution made it difficult for the company to retain and motivate young entrepreneurs. By 1960 Pedersen was convinced that he could find more scope for his un-orthodox talents elsewhere. He resigned, learnt to fly and left for Denmark. There he developed an electrical repair business and began experimenting with ideas for new equipment in his garage. One such idea, an electrically heated roller to help his wife curl her obstinately straight hair, was eventually to make him a fortune. Pedersen had little success when he first tried to market the invention in Denmark in 1964, but a chance meeting with a British saleswoman for Rootes cars, Mrs Jackie Pressman, soon led to a winning campaign. Sold as 'The Carmen', with a distinctive red rose symbol designed by Mrs Pressman, the curler caught the imagination of women throughout Europe. Pedersen's factory at Kalundborg expanded rapidly and continued to act as sole supplier to Mrs Pressman's marketing and distribution company, as well as to the American Clairol Company which sold the curlers under the name of 'Kindness'. By 1970 Pedersen was able to retire from the business, selling his Danish company to Clairol's parent, Bristol Myers, while retaining his right to royalties on the patented curler design. The owner of three private planes and three homes in Switzerland, Denmark and Spain, he could well have felt that his decision to leave the plantation was fully justified; yet, for United Plantations, the loss of his entrepreneurial talent and inventive spirit had been a serious blow.[23]

Despite all these difficulties, Rolf Grut persevered with his Tenera breeding programme. Taking a leaf out of Eric Rosenquist's book, he began to sell Dura seedlings to the East Asiatic Company and to the Eastern Region Development Corporation, Nigeria, as a means of raising further funds for his experiments; and from 1957 he was able to make small experimental plantings of Tenera palms at Ulu Bernam, totalling 30 hectares by the end of 1959. These plantings relied heavily on seeds produced internally, supplemented in 1958 by 2,000 Tenera x Tenera seeds from the Highlands Estate, Klang. Personal contacts had once again proved useful in obtaining the Klang seeds: Rolf Grut had just begun to act as a visiting agent for Highlands and Lowlands, whose chairman, Tom Barlow, had long been friendly with his brother Olof.[24]

After 1959, when Rolf was first allowed to buy germinated Tenera seeds from Ulu Remis, his planting programme began to gather speed. Thanks to Pedersen's efforts in obtaining Pisifera pollen from WAIFOR, the breeding programmes at Ulu Bernam and Jendarata were beginning to produce significant quantities of seed; and the Ulu Remis purchases roughly doubled the number of seedlings available for planting. From 1960 onwards, Tenera seedlings were used for all the replanting carried out at Ulu Bernam, renewing 160 hectares of pre-war plantation each year. About twice as much land was being replanted to oil palm at Jendarata, replacing rubber and pineapple stands as well as pre-war oil palms, so that it took a little longer before sufficient Tenera seedlings were available for the entire programme. However, from 1961 all replanting at Jendarata was also using Tenera material, supplied by Socfin as well as Ulu Remis and Jendarata itself. By 1962 it was possible to carry out the first factory tests on Tenera fruit from Ulu Bernam, and an oil:FFB ratio of 21 per cent was achieved. While this was not quite as much as the 23 per cent predicted by earlier experts, it was still much better than the 18 per cent which was typically achieved by the Ulu Bernam factory using Dura fruit in the early 1960s; and it proved possible to sustain the 21 per cent figure once Tenera fruit was being routinely processed at Ulu Bernam in the late 1970s. When this improvement in extraction efficiency was combined with the higher yields of FFB per hectare offered by the Tenera palm – 24 as opposed to 17 tonnes – it could be seen clearly that the Tenera palm was superior. It yielded 65 per cent more oil per hectare than the Dura palm, a tremendous jump in productivity which was to have profound implications, not just for United Plantations but for the Malaysian oil palm industry as a whole.[25]

GROWTH AND RENEWAL

For United Plantations and Bernam Oil Palms, the proof of the Tenera palm's merits came at just the right time. The Copenhagen directors, disillusioned by their South African and Ecuadorean adventures, were beginning to adopt a more sympathetic attitude towards Malaysian investments, led with enthusiasm from 1963 by their new chairman, Olof Grut. Olof's Board included the old stalwarts S.T. Westenholz, who now became vice-chairman; G.D. Craig, the son of Aage Westenholz's British friend and ally from Bangkok days; J.H. Reid, the business associate of C. Grumitt, the brother of another early British ally based in Penang; and Rolf Grut, who now retired as general manager of United Plantations and Bernam Oil Palms but retained a keen interest in their affairs. The former company secretary Benny Olsen, and the lawyer W.J. Huntsman, who had joined the Board in 1958 and 1960 respectively, stayed on. Two further seats had been vacated by the retirement of the London trader G.M. Smyth in 1962 and of

Niels Benzon the year following. These were now filled by the former chairman's son, Eggert Benzon, and by Poul Bent Heilmann, who had resigned from the board in 1951 to focus on United Plantations South Africa Ltd, but who now felt he could leave that venture in the safe hands of his newly appointed general manager, Hans Noddeboe. Finally, in 1965 Olof appointed an extra director, Ole Traugott Schwensen, bringing the total number of board members up to ten. Schwensen had joined Bernam Oil Palms as a planting assistant in 1951, while Rolf Grut was still serving there as manager. The two had developed an excellent working relationship, together with their chief engineer, Axel Lindquist, who was deeply impressed with Schwensen's intelligence and efficiency. Schwensen went with Rolf to Jendarata as his senior assistant (oil palms) in 1955, and was appointed to succeed him as general manager in 1963. He proved a great success in the role, being both a skilled planter and an excellent manager of people; and he shared Rolf's excitement about the Tenera palm.[26]

The new board was therefore heavily weighted towards people with direct experience of the East and contained no fewer than four planters: the two Grut brothers, O.T. Schwensen and P.B. Heilmann. The stage was set for a renewed commitment to planting in general and to the Tenera palm in particular. As Table 2 illustrates, the pace of new oil palm planting had slowed dramatically in the 1950s, especially once the Ulu Bernam land frontier had been reached in 1954, but it picked up swiftly in the early 1960s.

The focus of oil palm expansion within the United Plantations' group was now shifting towards Jendarata Estate, where the replanting of pre-war rubber stands to oil palms had been proceeding off and on since 1953. The estate itself began to grow again through the purchase of adjoining rubber plantations from 1961 to 1966, and the board swiftly decided that the best use for the new land would be to convert it to oil palms. The logic behind this decision was clear: not only was the land at Jendarata and neighbouring estates relatively ill-suited to rubber, but following the development of the synthetic rubber industry in the 1940s and 1950s, the market prospects for natural rubber were looking increasingly gloomy. Despite the development of new high-yielding rubber clones with similar cost implications to the Tenera palm, the expected returns from planting rubber in the 1960s were considerably lower than they had been before the Second World War. At United Plantations, the contribution made by rubber growing to company profits had already dropped from 55 per cent of rubber sales revenues in the years 1935–1939, to 31 per cent in the years 1955–59.

Table 2: Area planted with oil palms at Ulu Bernam and Jendarata Estates, 1945–65

Year	Area planted with oil palms at Ulu Bernam (1,000 ha)	Area planted with oil palms at Jendarata (1,000 ha)	Total area planted with oil palms at both estates (1,000 ha)
1945	2.6	1.1	3.7
1946	2.7	1.1	3.8
1947	2.9	1.1	4.0
1948	3.1	1.2	4.3
1949	3.2	1.4	4.6
1950	3.3	1.4	4.7
1951	3.3	1.4	4.7
1952	3.3	1.5	4.8
1953	3.3	1.7	5.0
1954	3.4	1.7	5.1
1955	3.4	1.8	5.2
1956	3.3	1.9	5.3
1957	3.3	1.9	5.2
1958	3.4	1.9	5.3
1959	3.4	2.1	5.5
1960	3.4	2.2	5.6
1961	3.4	2.6	5.9
1962	3.4	2.8	6.2
1963	3.4	3.0	6.4
1964	3.4	3.1	6.5
1965	3.4	3.3	6.7

Sources: UPDR and BOPDR, 1945–65.

Meanwhile, the corresponding margin for palm oil and kernels had fallen only slightly, from 54 per cent to 48 per cent, and was soon to recover again through the combined impact of the Tenera palm on costs and developments in processing and marketing on prices. By 1965–69 the oil palm contribution margin had reached 53 per cent and maintained an average of 54 per cent throughout the 1970s. By contrast, the rubber contribution margin continued to fall, averaging 27 per cent in the years 1965–69, and the crop had been phased out altogether at United Plantations by 1975.[27]

United Plantations' strategy of switching from rubber to palm oil during the period 1953–75 may also have been influenced by the fact that rubber was a labour-intensive crop compared with the oil palm. Following the formation of the National Union of Plantation Workers in 1954, employers were constantly aware of the risk that labour costs would be forced up. In the event, throughout the 1960s the union proved willing to fit into a consensual relationship of what Jain has described as 'welfare paternalism', whereby a minimum wage was maintained with increases tied firmly to rubber prices. At a time of declining natural rubber prices, this meant that wages remained fairly stable and estate managers could concentrate on improving the workers' housing and other non-wage benefits. Yet the threat of wildcat strikes remained at the local level, and even non-wage benefits could prove costly for employers to provide.[28]

The pressure to improve workers' housing, schools, medical and social facilities increased throughout the 1960s and 1970s, coming not only from the union and the politicians, but also from the employers themselves as they competed fiercely for a shrinking pool of labour. The new system of Employment Permits introduced in October 1969 was especially important, as it gradually reduced the number of Indians able to work on estates. For example, of the 984 Indians employed at Ulu Bernam in 1969, only 346 were Malaysian citizens. Some 70 per cent of the rest were eligible to apply for citizenship, but despite company assistance with the paperwork, over a hundred of these were still waiting for a decision in 1975. Many more Indian workers had been forced to leave the estate in the meantime, following citizenship refusals and the expiry of their work permits. As similar tales unfolded on other estates, employers began to compete keenly, not only with one another but also with Malaysia's growing industrial sector, to attract young Malays to take the Indians' place. In the case of United Plantations, a final source of pressure to spend more on work-force facilities came from the company's own philosophy as laid down by Aage Westenholz in the 1920s and developed by Lennart and Olof Grut in the 1930s. As shown in Chapters 2 and 3, these pioneers hoped that company welfare benefits would be of value not just to the workers themselves but also to the company by improving motivation and productivity. A necessary corollary of such a policy on workers' welfare was a commitment from management to use the workers' time as productively as possible and so to concentrate on crops that gave the best possible returns per man-hour. Hence, concerns about the cost, availability and welfare of the work-force reinforced Olof Grut's decision to phase out rubber in favour of oil palms.[29]

United Plantations and Bernam Oil Palms were not the only companies to phase out rubber in favour of oil palms at the same time as adopting the Tenera palm. Nor were they alone in their decision to expand. Throughout the 1960s and the 1970s companies like Guthries, Harrisons and Crosfield, Dunlop and Sime Darby were busy taking over smaller rubber producers and replanting at least part of their rubber stands to oil palms. A small increase in the estate sector's total planted area was also taking place: in 1975 this amounted to 920,000 hectares as compared with 890,000 in 1940. Thus, through a combination of replanting rubber stands and making fresh plantations, the estate sector was able to increase its oil palm holdings more than ten-fold between 1960 and 1980 from 50,000 to 550,000 hectares. Meanwhile, the total area planted to tree crops within Malaysia was expanding at a tremendous rate through the smallholder schemes run by the Federal Land Development Authority (FELDA) and by individual Malaysian states including Sabah and Sarawak. By 1980 FELDA alone had developed 170,000 hectares of new rubber stands and 300,000 hectares of oil palms. Such dramatic developments brought Malaysia swiftly to a leading position within the oil palm industry world-wide. By 1966 Malaysian palm oil exports had overtaken those of the three countries which had formerly dominated the industry: Nigeria, Indonesia and Zaire (the former Belgian Congo, known since July 1997 as Congo once again). The gap between Malaysia and these three major rivals continued to widen throughout the 1970s until by 1982 Malaysia accounted for 56 per cent of world production and 85 per cent of world exports of palm oil.[30]

Malaysia's world dominance in the palm oil industry was not simply a matter of scale. By the end of the 1960s the country's producers had gained a reputation for quality-enhancing innovations in mill technology that made new end uses possible and so expanded the market for palm oil. They were also building on the productivity gains made from adopting the Tenera palm and containing production costs through a whole series of improvements in field practice. Such changes, which will be surveyed in depth in the following chapters, were vital to ensure that individual growers could still make a profit given the rapid expansion of production overall. Between 1960–64 and 1970–74 world exports of palm oil doubled in volume, rising from about 0.5 to 1 million tonnes per annum. In the following decade the rise was more than threefold, and the pace of growth scarcely slowed thereafter. Between 1980 and 1984 world palm oil exports averaged over 3, and from 1990 to 1994 over 8 million tonnes per annum.[31]

In the wake of such an enormous expansion of supply, it is remarkable that the nominal prices paid for palm oil at European ports (c.i.f. prices) actually rose: from an average of US$ 220 per tonne in 1960–64, to US$ 360 per tonne in 1970–74 and US$ 570 per tonne in 1980–84. Only in 1985 did nominal prices begin to fall, averaging US$ 390 per tonne in 1990–94. In real terms, that is when deflated by the industrial countries' wholesale price index, the prices paid for Malaysian palm oil in Europe rose from a base level of 100 per cent in 1960–64 to 118 per cent in 1970–74. Only after this time did real prices begin to fall, a movement triggered initially by the petroleum 'oil shocks' which upset the pattern of relative costs and prices within the world commodity trade as a whole. In 1980–84 the real prices paid for Malaysian palm oil in Europe averaged 77 per cent of the early 1960s level, and for 1990–94 the corresponding figure is 42 per cent. It can thus be seen that palm oil prices proved buoyant for some time despite the massive increase in supplies; and over the whole period from the 1960s to the 1990s, while supplies rose 16-fold, real prices fell by little more than half. The resilience of palm oil prices is a testament to the success of producers in developing new markets. Yet it is also clear that they could not afford to sit back on their laurels. Supply increases exerted a continuous downward pressure on prices, and Malaysian planters had to innovate in order to survive.[32]

UNITED PLANTATIONS TRANSFORMED

Within this context of industry-wide expansion and increasingly tough competitive conditions, United Plantations' position began to change completely. From being a relatively large-scale producer, distinctive for its culture rather than its technology, it became a relatively small-scale and inventive operator. Its dynamism and efficiency now made it a source of inspiration to others. To some extent this transformation was forced upon the firm. As the number of Malaysian oil palm

Table 3: Planted area of oil palms and output of palm oil, Bernam Oil Palms, United Plantations and Malaya, 1945–65

Year	Planted area (1,000 ha)		Output of palm oil (1,000 tonnes/yr)		BOP and UP as % of Malayan Total	
	BOP + UP	Malaya	BOP + UP	Malaya	Area	Output
1945	4	n.a.	n.a.	n.a.	n.a.	n.a.
1946	4	n.a.	5	n.a.	n.a.	n.a.
1947	4	32	8	40	13	20
1948	4	34	9	46	12	20
1949	5	37	9	51	14	18
1950	5	39	8	54	13	15
1951	5	39	9	49	13	18
1952	5	41	8	46	12	17
1953	5	44	9	50	11	18
1954	5	44	10	55	11	18
1955	5	45	10	57	11	18
1956	5	47	9	57	11	16
1957	5	47	10	59	11	17
1958	5	48	10	71	10	14
1959	5	51	10	73	10	14
1960	6	55	12	92	11	13
1961	6	57	12	95	11	13
1962	6	62	11	108	10	10
1963	6	71	14	126	8	11
1964	7	76	13	122	9	11
1965	7	84	15	149	8	10

Sources: UPDR and BOPDR, 1945–65; Lim C.-Y., *Economic Development*, Appendix 5.2, p. 337; D. Lim, *Economic Growth*, Table 11.7, p. 229; and Khera, *Oil Palm Industry*, Appendix II.4, p. 305.

plantations soared in the 1960s and 1970s, United Plantations fell sharply behind in the race to grow more palms. Tables 3 and 4 illustrate this point. In the period 1945–65, while United Plantations and Bernam Oil Palms were still two separate companies, and while the growth of oil palm planting was still largely taking place on estates, the two firms' combined acreage fell from 13 per cent to 8 per cent of the Malayan total. In the following period, 1966–85, the two firms were

Table 4: Planted area of oil palms and output of palm oil, United Plantations and Malaysia, 1966–80

Year	Planted area (1,000 ha)		Output of palm oil (1,000 tonnes/yr)		UP as % of Malaysian Total	
	UP	Malaysia	UP	Malaysia	Area	Output
1966	7	120	18	190	6	9
1967	7	160	18	230	4	8
1968	8	200	20	280	4	7
1969	8	240	21	350	3	6
1970	8	320	22	430	3	5
1971	8	340	26	590	2	4
1972	8	400	25	730	2	3
1973	9	470	25	810	2	3
1974	11	570	29	1,040	2	3
1975	12	640	33	1,260	2	3
1976	12	710	35	1,390	2	3
1977	12	780	42	1,610	2	3
1978	12	850	44	1,790	1	2
1979	12	940	48	2,190	1	2
1980	13	1,020	49	2,570	1	2

Sources: UPAR, 1966–80; Malek bin Mansoor and Colin Barlow, 'The production structure of the Malaysian oil palm industry with special reference to the smallholder subsector', *PORIM Occasional Papers*, 24 (1988), Appendix Table 1.1, p. 53; and *PORLA Palm Oil Statistics* (Kuala Lumpur: PORLA, 1994 edn), Tables 1.1 and 3.1.

fully united, and rapid oil-palm developments were taking place on FELDA and similar schemes, and in Sabah and Sarawak. At this time United Plantations' share of Malaysia's oil palm acreage fell from 6 per cent to 1 per cent.

Throughout the 1960s and 1970s, United Plantations was prevented from making major additions to its planted area by two main factors: government land policy, which it could not influence, and its own directors' cautious approach to acquisitions. During the mid-1960s Olof was concentrating on three main projects: the replanting of existing pre-war stands to the Tenera palm; the formal merger between Bernam Oil Palms and United Plantations, which took place in 1966; and the new IPF venture in Ecuador that took up increasing amounts of his attention until it was finally wound up in 1974. The other nine members of the Copenhagen board at this time, who stayed in place until the end of the 1960s, were composed of lawyers and traders (Craig, Reid and Huntsman); prominent Danish businessmen who also represented the main shareholding families (Westenholz and Benzon); men with a strong personal involvement in the South African and Ecuadorean ventures (Olsen and Heilmann); and just two, Rolf Grut and Ole Schwensen, who had up-to-date experience of planting palms in Malaysia and, growing out of this, a strong conviction that, out of all the industries in which their firm was then interested, this was the one which had the brightest future. Within this complicated context of company politics, it is hardly surprising that Olof settled for a Malaysian palm oil policy of innovation without acquisition.

The results of this policy could easily have been catastrophic. As United Plantations' share of the total area planted to oil palms within Malaysia shrank from 10 per cent to 1 per cent, the company could have been laid wide open to takeover bids from its European rivals, or might simply have entered upon a demoralized spiral of long-term stagnation and decline. Yet in the event, United Plantations was able not only to remain an independent player within Malaysia's palm oil industry but also to move well beyond its previous position of technical soundness and to operate at the cutting-edge of innovation. As the company grew smaller in relative terms, so its managers grew sharper, and its share of Malaysian palm oil output proved highly resilient. As shown in Table 4, United Plantations' share of national output remained between 50 per cent and 100 per cent higher than its share of the oil palm planted area, throughout the period 1966–80. This ability to maintain a leading edge contrasts strongly with the earlier trends shown in Table 3. When the first post-war national statistics had been collected, in 1947–49, United Plantations and Bernam Oil Palms were indeed achieving an output per hectare almost 50 per cent above the national average. In the mid-1950s this productivity lead reached a peak of 65 per cent, but it had dipped sharply in the early 1950s and fell again continuously from 1957 to 1962. In this final year, the two firms reached an all-time low, when their share of output only just matched their 10 per cent share of Malaya's palm oil acreage, and their long-prized productivity lead had vanished altogether.[33]

United Plantations' ability to bounce back and regain its leading edge in the late 1960s, and then to sustain it through the following decades, was due in large part to its success in making the transition from the Dura to the Tenera palm. This underpinned a strong growth in productivity, not only in relative but also in absolute terms. In 1980–84 the firm's average annual output stood at 3.6 tonnes of palm oil per hectare of oil palm plantation, an increase of 80 per cent over the 1960–64 average of 2 tonnes. This impressive leap in land productivity was achieved while keeping labour and materials costs firmly under control. Over the same period United Plantations' contribution margin for palm oil shrank only slightly, from 56 per cent to 52 per cent – and this was at a time when, as shown above, palm oil prices were failing to keep pace with general wage and price inflation. In other words, the firm was making real efficiency gains and was becoming an increasingly strong player in economic as well as technical terms.[34]

Vital though the Tenera innovation was, however, it was only one part of United Plantations' remarkable post-war success story. Of equal importance were the changes in mill technology which underpinned a rise in the extraction rate of oil from the fresh palm fruit bunches (FFB). In the period 1946–49 the mill at Ulu Bernam had been able to get just 16 tonnes of oil from every 100 tonnes of FFB, an extraction rate of 16 per cent. As will be shown in the chapter which follows, Axel Lindquist's patient work in rehabilitating and reorganizing the mills both at Jendarata and at Ulu Bernam during the early 1950s brought a worthwhile improvement to a rate of 18 per cent in the period 1956–59. During the 1960s Børge Bek-Nielsen faced an uphill struggle in finding and refining fresh types of machinery to cope with the distinctive physical characteristics of the Tenera fruit, but by the early 1970s these problems had been resolved triumphantly. The extraction rate had risen once again, averaging 19 per cent from 1970 to 1974 and then rising gradually to a fresh peak of 21 per cent in 1977–80. At this point it becomes impossible to disentangle the value of the oil-rich Tenera fruit from the value of the new screw press technology which enabled the planters to make the most of it. Beyond this, as will be explored in Chapters 7 and 8, lay a whole series of further innovations in product design and sales strategy, without which the ever-more-abundant supplies of Malaysian palm oil could hardly have been absorbed by the world market. The era of the planter as master of the plantation industry was coming to an end; the era of the engineer and the marketing man was just beginning.[35]

NOTES

1   C.W.S. Hartley, *The Oil Palm (Elaeis guineensis Jacq.)* 3rd edn (London: Longman, 1988), pp. 50 and 82. It should be noted that the Tenera, Dura and Pisifera palms are all varieties of the same species, that is the African oil palm, *Elaeis guineensis Jacq.*, which is in turn closely related to the species *Elaeis oleifera* (formerly called *Elaeis melanococca*), the American oil palm. Attempts to produce an *oleifera–guineensis* hybrid are currently bearing fruit in Malaysia: UPAR, 1998, discussed in Ch. 9 below.

2   UBAR, 1936–85. Through the series of small incremental changes detailed in Chapter 6, which improved both the Tenera planting materials and the growing techniques used by United Plantations, yields per hectare continued to rise after the initial Tenera breakthrough. In 1995, 7-year-old oil palms at Jendarata Estate were yielding 33 tonnes of fresh fruit bunches per hectare per annum: UPAR, 1995.

3   Hartley, *Oil Palm*, p. 190; B. Jewsiewicki, 'Rural society and the Belgian colonial economy', in D. Birmingham and P.M. Martin (eds), *History of Central Africa*, Vol. II (London: Longman, 1983), pp. 99–101; M. Laurent, 'Notes sur l'Elaeis au Congo Belge', *Bulletin Agricole du Congo Belge*, vol. IV, 1913, pp. 700–701; F.M. Dyke (a Lever Brothers employee), *Report on the Oil Palm Industry in British West Africa* (Lagos: Government Printer, 1927), p. 6; W.J. Reader, *Unilever Plantations* (London: Unilever, 1961), p. 12; D.K. Fieldhouse, *Unilever Overseas: the Anatomy of a Multinational, 1895–1965* (London: Croom Helm, 1978), Ch. 9.

4   Hartley, *Oil Palm*, pp. 21–23 and Ch. 5; E.A. Rosenquist, 'The genetic base of oil palm breeding populations', in *Proceedings of International Workshop on Oil Palm Germplasm and Utilisation, 26–27 March 1985* (Kuala Lumpur: ISOPB/PORIM, 1986), pp. 27–56; Department of Agriculture, Straits Settlements and Federated Malay States, *Guide to the Experimental Station, Serdang* (Serdang: Government Printer, 1931), pp. 17–29; quotation from T.D. Marsh, 'The oil palm (Elaeis guineensis)', *The Planter*, vol. V, no. 11, 1925, p. 313.

5   Hartley, *Oil Palm*, pp. 202–210; A. Beirnaert and R. Vanderweyen, 'Contribution à l'étude génétique et biométrique des variétés d'Elaeis guineensis Jacquin', *Publications de l'INEAC, Série Scientifique No. 27* (Brussels, 1941).

6   Rosenquist, 'Genetic base'; Hartley, *Oil Palm*, p. 82.

7   UBAR, 1936 and 1940; E.A. Rosenquist, 'Post war food and cash crop production in former colonial territories', Rhodes House, Oxford, Mss. British Empire s. 476, Box IV, pp. 8–10; Rosenquist, 'Genetic base'; Hartley, *Oil Palm*, pp. 192–202 and 270–272.

8   General manager's summary of UP and BOP's internal annual reports, 1949; JAR and UBAR, 1949–54; on *Elaeis melanococca*, P.J.S. Cramer, 'A comparison between oilpalms and coconuts', *The Planter*, vol. XXVI, no. 10, 1950, pp. 433–434; Hartley, *Oil Palm*, pp. 85–89.

9   Interviews with R.L. Grut, 19 and 21 April 1988; personal communication from Knud Sehested, 19 December 1999.

10 Interviews with Mr and Mrs C.W.S. Hartley, 10 August 1988, and with E.A. Rosenquist, 11 July 1988; Rosenquist, 'Post-war production', pp. 4–5; C.W.S. Hartley, 'Reflections on a career in tropical agriculture', Rhodes House, Oxford, Mss. British Empire s. 476, Box III, p. 10.

11 Rosenquist, 'Post-war production', p. 9; Hartley, *Oil Palm*, pp. 677–679; A.V. Haddon and Y.L. Tong, 'Oil palm selection and breeding: a progress report', *Malayan Agricultural Journal*, vol. 42, 1959, pp. 124–156.

12 R.B. Jagoe, ' "Deli" oil palms and early introductions of Elaeis guineensis to Malaya', *The Planter*, vol. XXVIII, no. 6, 1952, pp. 249–255; Hartley, *Oil Palm*, p. 199; Haddon and Tong, 'Oil palm selection', pp. 124–126; Rosenquist, 'Post-war production', pp. 8–9; interview with E.A. Rosenquist, 11 July 1988.

13 Director of Agriculture to general secretary, Incorporated Society of Planters, 22 July 1950, *The Planter*, vol. XXVI, no. 9, 1950, pp. 399–400.

14 BOPDR and UPDR, 1950–55; interview with Rolf Grut, 19 April 1988 and personal communication from Knud Sehested, 19 December 1999.

15 Interview with E.A. Rosenquist, 11 July 1988; UBAR, 1949 and 1952.

16 Interview with E.A. Rosenquist, 11 July 1988; Haddon and Tong, 'Oil palm selection', p. 133.

17 Haddon and Tong, 'Oil palm selection', p. 133; JAR, 1957–60; UBAR, 1959; Alsing to Benzon, 27 November 1959, CC, 1959–60.

18 Haddon and Tong, 'Oil palm selection', pp. 143 and 147; interview with Dr Brian Gray, 6 June 1989; interview with Tan Sri Dato' Seri B. Bek-Nielsen, 31 March 1989; UBAR, 1954; UP and BOP, *Annual Reports Summary*, 1954. The face powder story

is told in the *Far Eastern Economic Review*, 8 October 1987, p. 91; and in the *Review's* letters' column of 4 February 1988. The fact that Pisifera pollen reached Malaya by many routes is stressed in a further letter to the *Review* by Ng Siew Kee, published 17 March 1988; the role of Guthries and the Agricultural Department was given further emphasis by E.A. Rosenquist, whose memorandum on the subject was sent to the *Review* by Dr R.H.V. Corley of Unilever PLC on 28 July 1988. The present account is based on this correspondence, but several dates and details have been corrected and others added as a result of cross-checking with contemporary sources.

19 Interview with E.A. Rosenquist, 11 July 1988; Rosenquist, 'Post-war production', pp. 9–11; Hartley, *Oil Palm*, pp. 200–201 and 271–272; S. Cunyngham-Brown, *The Traders: a Story of Britain's South-East Asian Commercial Adventure* (Newman Neame, for Guthrie & Co., London, 1971), pp. 319–323; Fieldhouse, *Unilever*, p. 546; B.S. Gray, 'A study of the influence of genetic, agronomic and environmental factors on the growth, flowering and bunch production of the oil palm on the West Coast of West Malaysia' (unpublished PhD thesis, University of Aberdeen, 1969), p. 181.

20 Rosenquist, 'Post-war production', p. 6; Hartley, *Oil Palm*, p. 273; interview with Leslie Davidson, then Chairman, Unilever Plantations Group, 7 July 1988; interview with Dr Hereward Corley, 11 July 1988.

21 BOPCA, 1964; UBAR, 1957–59; Benzon to Rolf Grut, 27 May 1957 and Grut to Benzon, 5 and 12 June 1957, CC, 1952–58.

22 A. Bybjerg Pedersen, 'The young oil palm', *The Planter*, vol. XXXIII, no. 2, 1957, pp. 134–5, 'Notes on the factors governing the straight growth of the oil palm (Elaeis Guineensis)', vol. XXXIII, no. 10, 1957, pp. 626–627, 'Some notes on oil palm selection', vol. XXXIV, no. 3, 1958, pp. 151–154 and 'Some notes on oil palms', vol. XXXIV, no. 7, 1958, pp. 389–392; JAR, 1953–60; UBAR, 1954–65; interview with Tan Sri Dato' Seri B. Bek-Nielsen, 31 March 1989.

23 This paragraph relies on information from the following papers, kindly supplied by Mrs Shirley Young, formerly of the Carmen Curler Company: *Electrical and Electronic Trader*, 22 September 1967; *Electrical and Radio Trading*, 28 September 1967; *Daily Telegraph*, 2 January 1970; *Marketing*, January 1970.

24 UBAR, 1956–60; BOP board meeting, 4 December 1958; interview with Tom Barlow's son Henry, 18 April 1989.

25 UBAR, 1959–80; JAR, 1959–62; Alsing to Benzon, 27 November 1959 and 7 May 1960, CC, 1959–60.

26 Interview with Rolf Grut, 21 April 1988; personal communication from Knud Sehested, 19 December 1999; UPDR and BOPDR, 1958–65.

27 JAR, 1949–61; UPDR, 1960–65; UPAR, 1966–72; Lim Chong-Yah, *Economic Development of Modern Malaya* (Kuala Lumpur: Oxford University Press, 1967), Ch. 3; D. Lim, *Economic Growth and Development in West Malaysia, 1947–1970* (Kuala Lumpur: Oxford University Press, 1973), Ch. 2. Contribution margins have been calculated from company records by subtracting direct and indirect production costs from sales revenue for each crop in each financial year and expressing the resulting figure as a percentage of the relevant sales revenue figure.

28 J.T. Thoburn, *Primary Commodity Exports and Economic Development: Theory, Evidence and a Study of Malaysia* (London: Wiley, 1977), Ch. 6.5; R. Ampalavanar, *The Indian Minority and Political Change in Malaya, 1945–57* (Kuala Lumpur: Oxford University Press, 1981), Ch. 3; R.K. Jain, *South Indians on the Plantation Frontier in Malaya* (New Haven: Yale University Press, 1970), p. 327; D. Lim, *Economic Growth*, p. 21; stable wage rates are documented in UBAR, 1950–70.

29 UBAR, 1969–75.

30 E. Graham with I. Floering, *The Modern Plantation in the Third World* (London: Croom Helm, 1984), p. 123; P.P. Courtenay, 'The plantation in Malaysian economic development', *Journal of Southeast Asian Studies*, vol. XII, no. 2, 1981, p. 333; Harcharan Singh Khera, *The Oil Palm Industry of Malaya: an Economic Study* (Kuala Lumpur: Penerbit Universiti Malaya, 1976), p. 183; H.A.J. Moll, *The Economics of the Oil Palm* (Wageningen, Netherlands: PUDOC, 1987), pp. 140 and 162.

31 Moll, *Economics*, pp. 53, 159 and 162; Khera, *Oil Palm Industry*, pp. 169 and 185; S. Mielke (ed.), *Oil World 1958–2007* (Hamburg: ISTA Mielke GMBH, 1988), Commodities – Past Section, p. 77; T. Mielke (ed.), *Oil World 1963–2012* (Hamburg: ISTA Mielke GMBH, 1994), Commodities – Past Section, pp. 81–82; T. Mielke (ed.), *Oil World Annual 1996* (Hamburg: ISTA Mielke GMBH, 1996), World Summary Tables Section, p. 7. The original *Oil World* figures for world exports include re-exports and so have been deflated by excluding the component of exports from 'other countries' (non-producers). Exports from Zaire (known since July 1997 as Congo once again), the only major producer included by *Oil World* in the 'other countries' category, have been added back in. For figures on Zaire, see Hartley, *Oil Palm*, p. 24.

32 Since the European nominal prices quoted here for palm oil are wholesale prices, the wholesale rather than consumer price index has been used when calculating real palm oil prices. If the consumer price index had been used, the real price of palm oil would have appeared as follows: 1960–64 100 per cent; 1970–74 108 per cent; 1980–84 70 per cent; 1990–94 31 per cent. Sources for both sets of calculations: Mielke (ed.), *Oil World 1958–2007*, Commodities – Past Section, pp. 120–121; *International Financial Statistics Yearbook 1987* (Washington, DC:

International Monetary Fund, 1987), pp. 110–113 and 180–181; *International Financial Statistics Yearbook 1996* (Washington, DC: International Monetary Fund, 1996), pp. 108–111 and 162–163.

33 UPDR and BOPDR, 1960–65; UPAR, 1966–84; Khera, *Oil Palm Industry,* pp. 28, 183 and 189; H.A.J. Moll, *The Economics of the Oil Palm* (Wageningen, Netherlands: PUDOC, 1987), pp. 140 and 159.

34 UPDR and BOPDR, 1960–65; UPAR, 1966–84; the contribution margin is a measure of the profit made by the company from palm oil production and is calculated by subtracting direct and indirect production costs (excluding depreciation) from sales revenue and expressing the resulting figure as a percentage of sales revenue. In other words, it is a measure of palm oil profits relative to palm oil sales, and not of palm oil's share relative to rubber etc. in total company profits.

35 UBAR, 1946–80.

CHAPTER 6

Quality at Low Cost:
Axel Lindquist and Børge Bek-Nielsen

ENTREPRENEURSHIP RENEWED

*I*n the mid-1950s it could hardly have been predicted that United Plantations would soon rise to fame as an oil palm innovator. The company was
a mature player in the Malaysian industry, and the Copenhagen directors'
more experimental investments lay elsewhere. Yet United Plantations'
oil palm holdings were completely rejuvenated in the 1960s and have continued
being renewed ever since. Alongside the Tenera replanting programme came a
long series of innovative engineering and marketing developments, bringing the
firm a leading-edge reputation world-wide. Olof Grut backed these developments to the hilt, but their practical success was largely due to one man: Børge
Bek-Nielsen, who joined the company as an assistant engineer in 1951.

Born in modest circumstances in Denmark in 1925 and elevated to the rank
of Tan Sri by the King of Malaysia seven decades later, Børge Bek-Nielsen has
been far more than a successful engineer. From his earliest years at Ulu Bernam
he showed a distinctively entrepreneurial flair and verve. A man of tremendous
energy and enthusiasm, he also had the gift of integration: allying the quest for
technical progress to the search for market breakthroughs and linking a concern
for staff and workers to an awareness of shareholders' needs. His clarity of
vision, backed when necessary by forthright and forceful speech, enabled him
both to inspire and to control all those who worked for him. As his team's track
record grew ever more impressive he became a powerful contender in boardroom
battles, for which he quickly developed a healthy appetite. By the early 1970s he
was well on the way to fulfilling his vision of United Plantations as a 'state-of-

169

the-art' producer of high-quality palm oil at low cost, and in 1978 he succeeded Olof Grut as chairman.

Bek was the first United Plantations chairman to have no family link with the founders, and his first mentor in Malaysia was another outsider: Axel Lindquist, the hero of the post-war reconstruction saga, who continued to visit the estates and advise on factory projects until his death in 1990. Despite being outsiders, these two men did not see themselves as challengers to an outmoded oligarchy. Rather, they felt a strong sense of kinship in temperament with Rolf, Olof and the early pioneers. Long after he had become an established industry leader in his own right, Bek continued to speak often of the business vision and wealth-sharing ideals of Aage Westenholz, the determination and practicality of Commander Grut and the Renaissance versatility of the commander's son, Olof. After Olof died in December 1980, Bek was keen to carry out his wish to be laid to rest close to the people with whom he had worked and in the land he loved. A burial ground was created in one of Olof's favourite places, the old tea hill at Ulu Bernam, which has since been named the Margrethe Hill. Over the years the hill has become a permanent memorial both to the Grut brothers and to their comrades and successors. At Axel Lindquist's request, a part of his ashes was taken there to be placed under a memorial stone in 1990, the remainder joining those of Ida in the family grave at Vestre Kirkegaard in Denmark. A garden was created, with a little church, named after Bek's mother Petra-Andrea. Rolf Grut was laid to rest in this garden in 1997. Only a few months earlier Rolf and his wife Rothes had penned a touching tribute for the memorial service held for Puan Sri Datin Seri Gladys Bek-Nielsen at the Petra-Andrea Church.

Gladys, who died of cancer in December 1996, was a woman of great warmth, serenity and charm. Since marrying Bek some 25 years earlier she had quietly done much to strengthen the distinctive 'family firm' ethos of United Plantations, adapting it to meet the transition not just from one family of Danish entrepreneurs to their successors but later from mainly Danish to mainly Malaysian management. For many years entertaining was a central part of Bek and Gladys's life, creating a strong web of informal contacts within the top management team and between staff and visitors. After 1980, visitors would usually be taken up to Margrethe Hill to be regaled with tales of Bek's early years at Ulu Bernam. Over lunches and dinners at his home, Bek would also tell stories about this time, illustrating both the dramatic appeal of life at the edge of the jungle during the Emergency and the way in which his own character had been influenced by seeing and admiring certain qualities in his mentors under pressure, especially the warmth and compassion of Rolf Grut and Axel's ingenuity and fire. Bek's stories of this time, and of United Plantations' leaders in the more distant past, have entered into the modern company's folklore and culture, providing a set of standards to which the present and future managers are expected to measure up. The emphasis throughout is on entrepreneurship and innovation. Bek believes that he is one of a long series of entrepreneurs who first created and then revitalized United Plantations and that this series can and should continue.

LINDQUIST'S LEGACY

The biggest single influence on the young Bek-Nielsen was undoubtedly that of Axel Lindquist, 'the old Viking' who had done so much to restore Ulu Bernam's factory and river fleet after the war. When Bek first arrived in Malaysia he was assigned to work closely with Axel, and they survived some memorable early clashes to become lifelong friends. Axel was a strict disciplinarian with 'a very short fuse' and he did not hesitate to tell the new recruits what he thought of them, especially after reckless shooting incidents like those described in Chapter 4. However, Bek had an equally combative spirit and was well able to hold his own in such encounters. The relationship quickly improved as he came to respect Axel's ability to get things done and to share his ambition to make strategic engineering innovations, not simply to achieve expensive quality gains, or to cut costs by cutting corners, but to reach the far more elusive goal of higher quality output at lower cost. After a struggle, he also accepted Axel's help with his English. As a young engineer, keen to make a practical impact, Bek found it frustrating to have to sit down with a dictionary at his side, composing a monthly report. Yet the discipline was to pay off handsomely later on, when as a rising executive he began to win an international reputation through well-phrased speeches and conference papers.[1]

On a more personal level, Bek also came to see the value of the discipline which Axel applied not only to himself and his assistants but also to the workforce. Coming from a deeply religious home, initially Bek felt that compassion should be the only keynote of his dealings with the labourers, but he soon came to accept Axel's view that even fair rules had to be enforced firmly if they were to have any effect. Over the course of a 50-year career with United Plantations, Bek too became known as 'a hell of a fiery bloke', with a fighting spirit equal to

171

that of his great hero from history, the Emperor Napoleon. Yet he also acquired the knack of 'disagreeing without being disagreeable'. He never turned a fight into a vendetta, and in being firm, he never forgot to be fair. His employees appreciated his compassion and his care for their needs in sickness and in old age, in housing and in schooling for their children. He was known for his energy and dedication, regularly putting in 15-hour days. He preferred to manage by walking around, flying around – or, in recent years, driving around. The company's many visitors would be invited to go along for the ride, travelling at a startling speed along the dusty estate roads and frequently pulling to a halt. Bek would leap in and out of his bright red Mercedes four-wheel drive, inspecting points of interest and chatting to the work-force, while his visitors looked on in awe. By such means Bek gained a solid reputation among the estate staff for being hard-working as well as vocal and for treating each case on its merits without fear or favour. Meanwhile, his opponents in boardroom battles soon came to appreciate that, while by no means infallible, he always acted in good faith. Like Napoleon, he did not fight just for the sake of it: his battles were always undertaken with a clear sense of purpose and a keen eye for strategy.[2]

Despite their early clashes, Bek and Axel had much in common. Not only were they both outsiders in relation to the founding families of United Plantations, but they shared a history of childhood adversity and an educational background which was practical rather than academic. Axel's father had died just two years after Axel was born, leaving a widow with four young children and little money. Bek spent his first six years in relative prosperity as the son of a master butcher and cattle exporter from Baekmarksbro near Holstebro in Jutland, but his father's death in 1931 led to the sale of the family business and a long struggle for the widow to educate her young family. Both Bek and Axel took up paper rounds to relieve the family finances, and both served engineering apprenticeships, although Bek's formal education continued for longer than Axel's. He eventually graduated in mechanical engineering from the Copenhagen Engineering School in 1951. Finally, although neither had family links to United Plantations or Bernam Oil Palms, both were recruited through personal contacts. As shown in Chapter 3, Axel had been lured away from General Motors in 1929 by Commander William Grut. Some 20 years later, Bek responded to a newspaper advertisement for assistant engineers, taking this action on the advice of his tutor at engineering school who knew one of United Plantations' directors.[3]

On his arrival in Perak Bek found a man to whom engineering was no static set of skills, to be learnt and then applied, but the basis of a lifelong quest to find new ways of working. As shown in Chapter 3, Axel's quest was given fresh impetus by the buoyant markets and chaotic estate conditions of the late 1940s. However, Commander Grut had discovered his great natural aptitude for tinkering long before. The Commander's son Olof, who came out to Malaya in 1930 to set up the Ulu Bernam palm oil factory, soon found that Axel shared his own love of experimentation. When Olof became general manager of Bernam Oil Palms in 1935 he continued to keep a close eye on the running of Ulu Bernam's factory, where he was assisted by A. Lehmann Nielsen, but he knew that Axel was capable of running Jendarata's mill, opened in 1934, with little or no supervision.[4]

Axel soon set up a workshop at Jendarata and, although he did not join in Olof Grut's more ambitious experiments with palm oil bleaching and fractionation processes, he played a full role in the fundamental factory trials which were going on at the same time. These trials were designed to compare the merits and find ways of improving the two main press systems available in Malaya at the time, the hydraulic version installed at Ulu Bernam and the centrifugal tried out at Jendarata. Experiments carried out by the Agricultural Department in the early 1930s had shown that hydraulic presses extracted a high proportion of oil from the fruit fibre, but that this oil was cloudy and required much clarification before it was fit for shipment. The standard way of clarifying oil was to let it settle in tanks; the process could be speeded up using centrifuges but much skilled labour was still required to load and unload the batches. Olof was extremely dissatisfied with this situation and decided to attack the problem on two fronts. At Ulu Bernam, he encouraged Lehmann Nielsen to develop a pioneering system of continuous clarification through which oil could flow automatically through the settling tank. Patent rights were applied for in 1939. Meanwhile the factory at Jendarata was equipped with centrifugal palm oil presses, which produced a relatively clean oil requiring less clarification, and Axel set to work adjusting these to improve their extraction efficiency.[5]

In his first trials, made in 1935, Axel confirmed the Agricultural Department's finding that centrifugal pressing left a high residual oil content in the waste palm fruit fibre, of 25 per cent in the case of Jendarata. By continual tinkering over the next four years he managed to bring this down to 16 per cent. A final comparison could then be made between the centrifugal system at its best and the hydraulic system assisted by continuous clarification. Axel found that the hydraulic press still gave lower wastage, leaving a residual oil content of just 13 per cent in the dry fruit fibre. Any researcher who has laboured long and hard, only to disprove the theory which had initially inspired him, will be able to appreciate Axel's feelings on completing this comparison. His findings, together with the fact that Lehmann Nielsen's invention had greatly reduced the total cost of hydraulic pressing, led directly to Olof Grut's decision to abandon the centrifugal system. By now, however, the world was in the throes of war. The decision could not be implemented until the 1950s, and in the meantime the expertise Axel had gained during his years of careful tinkering was to prove invaluable.[6]

After the Japanese invasion of Malaya Lehmann Nielsen found his way to South Africa, while Axel settled in Australia along with Rolf and Olof Grut. As shown in Chapter 3, Axel was among the first to return to Lower Perak in 1946. Not content merely to use his previous knowledge to get the factories going again, he also built a foundry from scratch at Ulu Bernam, which from then on became his permanent base. He trained a new generation of assistant engineers, who typically began work under him at Ulu Bernam and then progressed to running the Jendarata mill. Many stayed only a couple of years in Perak, suffering from loneliness and fear during the Emergency and finding it hard to cope with the basic living conditions. Two of the more resilient were C. Bjoljahn and E. Valbak, who stayed for five and 12 years respectively. Valbak, who had arrived in 1947, succeeded Axel as chief engineer ten years later but stayed only two years in the post. Against this background Bek-Nielsen's qualities of endurance appear all the more exceptional, matched only by those of his mentor Lindquist. Both were survivors, braving the terrors of crocodiles, jungle fighters and amoebic dysentery to build careers spanning decades. Bek was initially held at Ulu Bernam more by his dislike of the drab, heavily taxed society of post-war Denmark than by any instant attraction to the planter's life. Gradually he began to enjoy the peace of the long evenings, sitting on the verandah of the manager's bungalow and listening to the elephants crashing about in the undergrowth across the river. At the same time he also came to appreciate the vast potential for making money from a well-run estate and to see from Axel's example how vital an engineer's skills could be within the enterprise.[7]

Axel's skills were well appreciated both within Bernam Oil Palms and among its neighbours. After he had performed the remarkable feat of getting the Ulu Bernam factory going within three months of his return in 1946, he was called in to help with the recovery of the neighbouring estate, Sungei Samak. The success of this project brought Axel a steady stream of consultancy assignments, especially from Sungei Samak's managing agents, Harrisons & Crosfield. The work was done mainly in the evenings, after hard days spent trying to improve factory operations at Ulu Bernam itself.[8]

The main obstacle Axel faced in trying to restore the factory to its pre-war condition was the continuing shortage of materials and spare parts. The Dutch company Stork was still the main supplier of machinery, but it had long lead times. In the late 1940s orders for relatively small parts like press indicators could take over a year to be met, and even in the 1950s there could be a two-year wait for a major item like a sterilizer. Other companies, like the Danish firm Titan, proved equally unreliable. A few, like the local supplier of special firebricks which had allowed the boilers to run smoothly on bunch waste and kernel-shell fuel before the war, had simply vanished. In this context Axel's ingenuity and determination proved invaluable. Working in conjunction with the locally based engineering consultants Steen Sehested and the local workshop of United Engineers Ltd, he improvised solutions to the boiler problem and produced good working substitutes for the missing spare parts. Equipment like sterilizer cages and conveyors began to be made in the estate workshop on a regular basis, using iron from the foundry and proving cheaper than the imported equivalents even when these became available again.[9]

Axel's skills were vital not only for the recovery of Ulu Bernam but also for the transformation of Jendarata's oil mill, where shortages of equipment threatened to postpone indefinitely the planned move from centrifugal to hydraulic presses. Two hydraulic presses were bought from the Dutch firm Werkspoor in 1949, but these were inferior to the standard Stork model, of which new units were impossible to obtain. One Stork unit was obtained secondhand from Guthries' Ulu Remis Estate in 1950, but it remained out of commission for over a year while the vital spare parts were being made. A second was bought in working order from Ulu Bernam in 1952. Meanwhile, Axel was conducting trials of new machinery for Lehmann-Nielsen's patented continuous purification process. Werkspoor and the Swedish firm Alfa-Laval produced two effective alternatives to Titan's centrifugal sludge separator, and Axel took an active part in perfecting their designs. Finally, before making the new conveyors and elevators which were needed to take the basic raw materials of fruit, nuts and oil from one piece of processing machinery to the next, Axel undertook a fundamental review of the factory layouts at both Jendarata and Ulu Bernam.[10]

175

In 1953 the factory at Jendarata was shut down for 124 days and completely overhauled. The building was extended to make space for the continuous purification unit and to provide for future expansion, as the replanting of old rubber stands to oil palm began. New cement floors, platforms, ladders, drains and roofing were provided and the two remaining centrifugal presses were dismantled. A new oil collecting arrangement and an energy-saving back pressure system were set up. All the other equipment was overhauled and its corroded metal parts replaced. These changes brought dramatic savings in labour, energy and other manufacturing costs, which fell from Straits $58 per tonne of oil extracted in 1952 to Straits $27 in 1954. Axel's ingenuity and his ability to design a factory as a whole, rather than as a collection of disparate machines, had thus realized to the full the cost-saving potential of Lehmann Nielsen's pre-war invention.[11]

This achievement came at just the right time, as the post-war boom in palm oil prices was ending. Supplies of butter, lard and alternative vegetable oils had revived in Britain, and the Ministry of Food decided that it could safely stop buying up Malayan palm oil. On 1 January 1953 its final bulk-buying contract expired. In contrast to the price for 1952, which had been set in October 1951 at a fixed rate of Straits $950 per tonne of palm oil, the Malayan export prices for 1953 were determined by the market and averaged Straits $610 for the year. At a time of general stability in Malayan retail prices, such an enormous fall for palm oil put great pressure on producers to cut costs. Axel's achievement provided a heartening illustration of what could be done; and it also showed that reduced costs did not have to be pursued at the expense of quality. Through the 1953 overhaul, and while keeping the extraction rate of oil from the fresh fruit bunches (FFB) roughly constant at an average of 16 per cent by weight in 1948–52 and in 1954–58 alike, Axel managed to reduce the level of free fatty acids (FFA) present in the fresh palm oil from 3.7 per cent to 2.6 per cent. Although the level of FFA in the oil tended to increase during storage and shipment, such a low level on leaving the factory meant that Jendarata's output now came well within the key international limit of a 5 per cent FFA content for edible oil on delivery to the customer. This quality gain was especially vital at a time when market developments in Europe seemed likely to produce higher price premiums for low-acidity oil in the future. The soap industry, a traditional user of the fatty acids that emerged as a by-product from margarine manufacture, was under threat from recently invented synthetic detergents, and fatty acid prices were falling fast.[12]

In 1954 a similar overhaul was carried out at Ulu Bernam. The task had seemed less urgent there than at Jendarata, as Ulu Bernam already had a full system of hydraulic presses and the prototype continuous clarification plant. New boilers had been installed in 1952, bringing an immediate drop in factory running costs, from Straits $30 per tonne of oil extracted in 1951 to Straits $21 in 1953. Yet the factory was showing signs of age, and the FFA content of its palm oil was as high as at Jendarata, averaging 3.7 per cent in the five years before the overhaul. Fluctuating dirt and moisture levels may also have occurred, for in some years the FFA level in Ulu Bernam's oil had been found to rise sharply while it was awaiting shipment out of the estate. In 1949 and 1952 a standard level of 3.7 per cent in the oil leaving the factory had been transformed into the high level of 4.2 per cent by the time it was loaded onto the tanker for export, a rise in FFA of about five times the normal rate. High levels of dirt and moisture were known to increase the rate at which FFA formed in oil during storage, and after the overhaul these indices of quality began to be carefully monitored. During the 1954 renovation itself, Axel paid most attention to the oil purification plant, which was completely rebuilt to his own design, using tanks and supporting structures made in Ulu Bernam's workshop. An immediate improvement in oil quality resulted, with ex-factory FFA levels averaging 2.8 per cent in the five years following the overhaul, and ex-estate levels averaging just 2.9 per cent. The low level of factory running costs was also maintained, averaging Straits $19 per tonne of oil extracted over the same period. Most impressively of all, these gains were achieved alongside an increase in the extraction rate of oil from the FFB from an average of 16 per cent in 1949–53 to 18 per cent in the five years following the overhaul. As there was normally a direct tradeoff through which a higher extraction rate brought a higher level of FFA, Axel's achievement was extraordinary.[13]

High extraction rates were especially welcome at Ulu Bernam because of the labour shortages which continued to make harvesting difficult. Field managers were exploring ways of easing the labour problem, especially at the stage of fruit collection where mules and bullock carts were brought in to supplement women workers, accounting for almost half of all fruit collected by 1951. Yet labour scarcity remained an acute problem in the male tasks of tree-climbing and harvesting, only gradually eased by the replanting of Ulu Bernam's tall pre-war palms. Replanting began in 1952 but did not affect harvesting patterns until the new palms began yielding at the end of the decade. Meanwhile estate managers were tempted to encourage the collection of riper fruit so as to increase the yield of oil from each hard-won bunch. But such fruit bruised easily, encouraging a rapid build-up of free fatty acids during its journey to the mill. Since high levels of FFA would be reflected in lower oil prices, estate managers were caught in a double bind which could be eased only by transport improvements – reducing the risk of bruising – or by innovation at the mill. In transforming the FFA/extraction rate tradeoff, Axel's overhaul thus relaxed a keenly felt constraint on the profitability of the estate as a whole.[14]

Not content with these factory achievements, Axel also sought to improve the rail and river transport facilities serving the estates. He fully understood the importance of smoothness and speed in keeping FFA levels low and the value of good passenger services in keeping morale high at Ulu Bernam. Despite his passionate interest in mill machinery, he never saw the factory as a stand-alone unit, but as one link in an integrated chain stretching from seedlings to shipment. This vision, inherited from Commander Grut and his sons, and passed on to Bek-Nielsen in his turn, has been the hallmark of United Plantations' quality culture.

Good field transport had characterized the Ulu Bernam Estate from its earliest days. When Commander Grut began his quest for oil palm land in 1926 he sought out flat terrain and ordered materials for a light railway as one of his first priorities. By choosing to have the fruit loaded directly into sterilizer cages in the field, and then brought by rail right into the factory, he ensured minimal bruising and gave little time for FFA to build up within the pulp before processing. As the estate expanded after the war, the railway network expanded with it, as shown on Map 5. By the 1960s United Plantations was widely recognized as the leading Malaysian practitioner of this system, and Rolf Grut was invited to write the chapter on field transport for the Agricultural Department's new handbook of best practice. In 1976, Harcharan Singh Khera used a map of Ulu Bernam to illustrate a discussion of the topic in his classic study of Malaysia's oil palm industry.[15]

Axel Lindquist had set up the railway lines and built several motor boats for Ulu Bernam in the pre-war years, and after the war he set to work with a will, restoring and extending the railway system, buying and adapting the Japanese landing craft for cargo use and building new passenger launches. In 1947 he began making new sterilizer trolley frames in the factory workshop, and in 1949 he established a separate workshop for tractor and locomotive repairs. In the

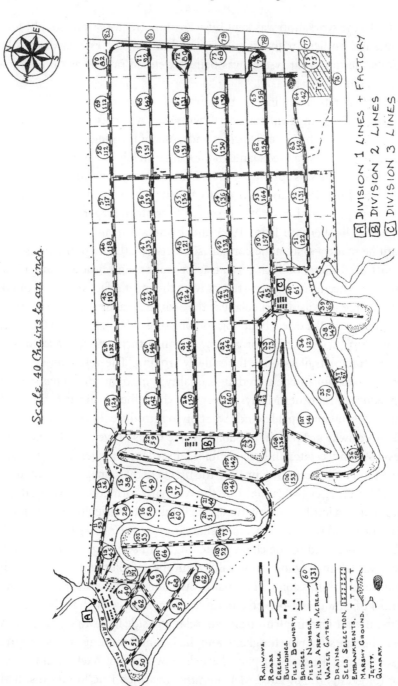

Scale 40 Chains to an inch.

A DIVISION 1 LINES + FACTORY
B DIVISION 2 LINES
C DIVISION 3 LINES

1 RAILWAYS.
2 ROADS.
3 CREEKS.
4 BUILDINGS.
5 FIELD BOUNDRY.
6 BRIDGES.
7 FIELD NUMBER.
8 FIELD AREA IN ACRES.
9 WATER GATES.
10 DRAINS.
11 SEED SELECTION.
12 EMBANKMENTS.
13 MARSHY GROUND.
14 JETTY.
15 QUARRY.

Map 5: Bernam Oil Palms, Ulu Bernam Estate, 1955

early 1950s the workshop was kept busy as more tractors were bought for Ulu Bernam, and bodies for their trailers were built on the estate. Meanwhile, at Jendarata the monorail system was being extended rapidly as oil palms were planted in old rubber areas.[16]

After Axel's retirement in 1957 the impetus for reform in field transport began to come more from the field managers themselves. A particularly important contribution was made by Harold Speldewinde, one of the jungle resistance fighters who had helped the stranded Danes in the Cameron Highlands during the Japanese occupation. He was appointed to be United Plantations' first Asian planting assistant in June 1946 and proved to be an effective yet relaxed manager, extremely popular with his staff. He served as estate manager at Sungei Bernam from 1956, Ulu Bernam from 1963 and Jendarata from 1966. While at Ulu Bernam he made a systematic comparison between the three methods of field transport used there: bullock carts, tractor-trailers and headloading. He soon became convinced that tractor-trailers were the most effective means of taking fruit from tree to railside, especially if they could be adapted to carry sterilizer cages to minimize the direct handling and bruising of fruit. He asked Bek-Nielsen to design a special machine, or gantry, to winch the sterilizer cages smoothly from the tractor-trailers onto the railway trolleys. The resulting system was quick, cheap to run and delivered high-quality fruit to the mill. It has since been widely adopted on other Malaysian estates where the terrain is flat enough to permit it. Meanwhile, Speldewinde went on to introduce the bullock cart system to the more awkward terrain of Sabah, where it has proved invaluable both on Unilever's Pamol estates and on smallholder settlement schemes. Eventually he returned to Perak, becoming in 1987 the first general manager of United International Enterprises (Malaysia) Ltd, the company formed to develop the Gula Perak Estate as a joint venture between the Perak State Agricultural Development Corporation and the former Danish shareholders of United Plantations.[17]

At the other end of the chain stretching from seedlings to shipment, Bek-Nielsen was the man who finally realized another of Olof and Axel's ambitions: to design and commission Ulu Bernam's own tanker. The estate had long owned a number of slow diesel-powered barges, or tongkangs, which in the 1930s were used mainly for ferrying fruit from the Selangor-side fields to the factory. After the war the sole surviving tongkang and the Japanese landing craft were pressed into service to take sacks of palm kernels downstream. Axel rebuilt a second motor tongkang, the ill-fated *M.V. Kertang* on which Eric Rosenquist had his

The bullock-cart system of field transport, 1965

hair-raising journey bearing Tenera seedlings in 1952, and it spent most of its short life taking 50-tonne cargoes of palm kernels to Port Swettenham and Penang. After it sank a new wooden cargo boat was completed in Ulu Bernam's boatyard, and launched in 1953 under the name *M.V. Kertang II*. The new *Kertang* had a capacity of 100 tonnes and was used to carry pineapples as well as palm kernels; but for the bulk transport of palm oil both Ulu Bernam and Jendarata remained dependent on the Straits Steamship Company and its smaller rival, the Malayan Stevedoring Company. These shipping firms gave such poor service that in 1951 Olof Grut began to consider building his own motor tank vessel.[18]

Finance was a major problem, especially as the firm was investing heavily at the time in building a bulk palm oil installation at Penang. Olof tried and failed to get a commitment to co-financing from Straits Plantations Ltd., the owners of Ulu Bernam's neighbouring estate Sungei Samak. He then began planning to

The tractor-trailer and gantry system of field transport, 1966

convert the steel hull of an old Z-craft which he and Axel had bought for its engines in 1947 from an owner 'whose smuggling activities in Indian waters had come to an end'.[19]

These plans never progressed far beyond the drawing board, but the keen sailor Niels Benzon and his fellow Copenhagen directors continued to take an

Palm fruit arriving at the Jendarata mill by rail, 1972

interest in the idea. In 1956 Major Edmund Grut suggested a more ambitious investment in a custom-built tankship. Sadly he died in 1958, too soon to see the idea become reality. One year later, in one of his first actions as chief engineer, Bek presented a detailed and fully costed plan to the board. With Olof's support the spending was finally sanctioned. The Japanese firm of Kure Shipbuilding and Engineering was commissioned to build a tanker with additional cargo space, designed by Bek to meet Ulu Bernam's special requirements at a cost of Straits $730,000. The large scale of this investment can be seen when it is compared with Ulu Bernam's total spending on new planting and replanting, new buildings, boats and factory equipment, which averaged Straits $300,000 a year in the five years before the tanker was paid for. In February 1961 the *MS Ulu Bernam* was launched by Niels Benzon at Kure Shipyard, and by the end of April it was

Palm oil mill at Ulu Bernam, showing the river launch and tanker, 1963

carrying regular shipments of palm oil to Penang at a running cost of Straits $16 per ton, just two-thirds of the rate charged by the Straits Steamship Company. The total savings amounted to Straits $170,000 a year before depreciation, giving a very healthy return on the initial investment. Bek hoped to make further gains by selling the *Kertang*, but it proved 'too slow to be useful for the Chinese trading between Penang and Sumatra' and failed to find a buyer.[20]

In choosing the tanker scheme as his first major investment project, Børge Bek-Nielsen identified himself firmly with Lindquist's belief that an engineer's brief stretched well beyond the factory floor. Yet with his next project Bek showed that, again like Lindquist, he saw the mill as being at the centre of his mission. In switching from hydraulic to screw presses, and then designing a distinctive single-screw press offering heightened energy savings, he and his engineering team made the first of many contributions to the palm oil industry's development nation-wide. As will be shown below, Bek became well known not only for adopting major innovations quickly but also for his continuous experimentation and refinement of the basic technology. In his eagerness to follow through, to make innovation a continuous process and to reject turnkey solutions, he showed himself to be the true heir of Axel Lindquist. In developing the second part of Lindquist's legacy, the quest for perfect integration of the whole sequence of operations from seed selection to shipment, Bek later showed himself to be an outstanding general manager. At the end of his life, Lindquist was the first to admit that it was Bek who had achieved the dream of the previous generation: to make United Plantations an extremely efficient and profitable producer, consistently achieving high quality at low cost.

THE SCREW PRESS

The screw press, or expeller, was likened memorably by Charles Wilson to 'a vast mincing machine, in which the prepared seed was forced along the barrel by a rotating screw'. Originally developed for use in the wine industry, it gained favour among European animal-feed producers in the late 1930s because it yielded a fine broken meal, easy to bag up and use, rather than the heavy slabs which emerged from the battering-ram of the hydraulic press. Unilever's oil millers were quick to spot the expeller's potential for reducing the dirt and heavy labour demands of their own operations and began using it in Britain in 1942. It was then only a matter of time before the new technology was tried out in the Belgian Congo, where it was to prove a perfect match to the Tenera palm.[21]

The first trials of the screw press in the oil palm industry were carried out some ten years after Beirnaert and Vanderweyen completed their pathbreaking work on the Tenera palm. Pilot plants were set up in 1952 using presses supplied by the French firm of Colin (now Pressoir Speichim Colin) and by Usine de Wecker in Luxembourg, and the results were carefully monitored until 1955. The plants were set up in two locations: at the Mongana research station by the Congo's government-sponsored Institute for the advancement of Scientific Research in Industry and Agriculture (IRSIA) and at the Yaligimba plantation by Unilever's subsidiary, Huileries du Congo Belge (HCB).[22]

Yaligimba was a flagship plantation, founded in 1938 following a major policy shift within HCB. In 1933 the company had commissioned a detailed cost analysis of its operations compared with those of the United Africa Company's plantations in the Cameroons and Hallett's estates in Sumatra. The results showed that wild fruit in the Congo had relatively low oil yields, and that the labour costs of obtaining and processing it were startlingly high by comparison with the estate system. With Beirnaert's research on Tenera breeding methods now well under way, Unilever decided in 1935 that the time was ripe to move away from its costly dependence on wild fruit and to begin constructing fully integrated mill-and-plantation units. An ideal site was found at Yaligimba, close to Beirnaert's Yangambi research station, which supplied all the Tenera x Tenera seeds needed to complete the new estate's planting programme.[23]

Through its links with both Yangambi and Mongana, the Yaligimba estate brought together two streams of botanical and mechanical innovation. The union between the two was vital for the commercial success of each. On the one hand, Tenera fruit was hard to process with the standard HCB presses, while on the other, the application of labour- and energy-saving screw press technology to the palm oil industry could not have been done with thick-shelled Dura fruit. The thicker its shell and the thinner its oily outer pulp, the more likely palm fruit was to collapse under pressure, forming an unwieldy mass of cracked shell, kernels and fibre. Indeed, HCB had been unable even to follow the Sumatran Deli Dura growers into using the hydraulic press during the inter-war period. HCB's reliance on the exceptionally thick-shelled Congo Dura fruit had forced it to stick with the gentler centrifugal press. The screw press in its turn was far more powerful than the hydraulic press, so that despite its clear advantages of a low energy requirement and of continuous operation rather than labour-intensive batch production, its use was unthinkable even in South-East Asia before the 1950s. This situation changed overnight following the first experiments with processing the thin-shelled, pulp-rich Congo Tenera fruit in centrifugals. The adoption of screw presses no longer seemed a remote, desirable possibility; instead, it had become an immediate necessity. When spun round in a low-pressure centrifuge, the abundant fibres found in the pulp of Tenera fruit quickly compacted into a dense cake. Very little oil could then be squeezed out of the mass, and even if some did emerge it tended to form into a visible 'oil wall' around the cake, rather than flowing away for collection.[24]

The difficulty of processing Tenera fruit in centrifugal presses may help to explain why oil palm planting at Yaligimba stopped between 1947 and 1953, when oil prices were high and while HCB retained a strong commitment in principle to extending the planted area. Between 1939 and 1947 nearly 7,000 hectares of oil palms had been planted at Yaligimba, and planting swiftly resumed following the start of screw press trials in 1952, taking the total cultivated area up to 9,800 hectares by 1959. A second possible explanation for the pause is that managers may have been waiting for the next generation of planting materials to become available. From 1953 Yaligimba relied on pure Tenera (Dura x Pisifera) material, rather than the Tenera x Tenera seeds of which only 50 per cent could be expected to yield Tenera trees, the other 50 per cent yielding equal shares of Dura and Pisifera palms. Having waited so long to begin making plantations, HCB were now keen to get their technology exactly right.[25]

By the late 1950s it was becoming clear that the Tenera palms and experimental screw presses established at Yaligimba would indeed prove a winning combination. The Mongana Report, written for the exclusive use of members of the CONGOPALM society, showed that the screw press achieved extraction rates (oil:FFB) of 22–24 per cent on pure Tenera fruit. This compares extremely well with the rates of 16–18 per cent achieved with Deli Dura fruit and hydraulic presses at Jendarata and Ulu Bernam following Axel's overhauls. Extraction rates for palm grove fruit using centrifuges were not given in the Mongana Report, but it may safely be assumed that they were lower still, both because palm grove Congo Dura fruit contained less oily pulp than Deli Dura fruit, and because the percentage of available oil extracted by the centrifugal press from grove fruit peaked at 90 per cent, as compared with 96 per cent for Tenera fruit processed in a screw press.[26]

Unfortunately for HCB, very little time elapsed between the publication of the Mongana Report and the eruption of the 'Congo crisis' in 1960. Hardly had it been established that the screw press and the Tenera variety formed a winning combination, than the whole future of HCB's plantation operations was thrown into doubt. The root of the problem was that the Belgians were unprepared for decolonization. Only in 1956 did they allow a public debate to begin within the Congo about the possibility of independence. Surprised by the strength of feeling which the debate revealed, and particularly by the popular passion behind the Leopoldville riots of 4 January 1959, the administration quickly moved to meet the ABAKO party's demand for 'immediate independence'. Power was transferred to ABAKO's leader, Joseph Kasavubu, and to the charismatic Patrice Lumumba on 30 June 1960; but the upper echelons of the army and the civil administration continued to be staffed almost entirely by Europeans. Africans in the lower echelons quickly rejected this situation, their sometimes violent protests prompting a rapid exodus of Belgians from the country. Disarray in the army and administration was swiftly followed by fragmentation of the country itself, with secessions in the mining regions of Katanga and Kasai, and a bitter power struggle between the followers of Lumumba, based at Stanleyville (near Yaligimba) and the followers of Kasavubu, based at the capital Leopoldville (now Kinshasa). The crisis quickly became internationalized through the involvement, first of Belgian and then of United Nations troops, and through the supply of Soviet equipment and advisers to the Lumumba forces. The situation remained highly unstable until the coup which brought General Mobutu to power in November 1965.[27]

While daily life and work in the Congo's private sector were able to continue throughout the crisis, bold new investments were clearly out of the question. On decolonization HCB was renamed Plantations Lever au Congo (PLC). The new concern continued to produce increasing amounts of palm oil until 1963 but made a succession of losses on its post-tax accounts owing to falling European prices for the product and soaring inflation which pushed up costs in the Congo itself. The plantations proved vulnerable to terrorist attack and their managers had difficulty in obtaining vital imported components to maintain the mills and machinery. In the circumstances it is remarkable that Unilever continued to support its Congo subsidiary, and its loyalty was later praised by President Mobutu and rewarded with a relatively brief period of nationalization, from 1975 to 1977, during which Unilever staff continued to run the estates. Nevertheless the size of PLC's plantations shrank during the 1960s, and Unilever took steps to reduce its exposure to political risk in the palm oil industry. For example, the focus of research and development work shifted away from engineering, and hence from fixed-site factories, towards the production of clonal planting materials, which were portable and could be sold to a wide range of producers world-wide. Research on cloning the oil palm by tissue culture began at Unilever's Colworth laboratory in Britain in 1967.[28]

Meanwhile, the focus of Unilever's applied plantation work began to shift towards Malaysia. In 1947 the company had used its war damages' windfall to buy a small estate in Johore, which it gradually enlarged by buying adjacent plots until by 1960 its planted area covered 4,600 hectares. In the same year a new palm oil estate was founded by Unilever in Sabah. Both ventures were intended to make profitable use of Unilever's existing technologies, rather than to be sites for fresh experiments. Hence the engineers brought in to design Pamol (Malaya)'s new mill at Kluang, Johore in 1960 were men like Jack Maycock, who had worked for HCB throughout the 1950s. They replaced Kluang's existing centrifugal presses with an all-electric screw-press system, which created great interest among the other planters. In 1963 *The Planter* carried a three-part article by the Belgian engineer Alex Wolversperges expounding the merits of the screw press, in particular the Colin press which had been tried out at Yaligimba.

Many firms became interested in the new technology but shied away because of its high capital cost.[29]

One man who did not shy away was Børge Bek-Nielsen. Following his first factory trial of the oily pulp-rich Tenera fruit in 1962, he quickly saw that it required the most powerful press available. He made contact with Usine de Wecker, the Luxembourg wine-press manufacturer whose equipment had been tried out along with the Colin press at Mongana, and in July 1964 he began operating one of their screw presses at Ulu Bernam. At first the press gave disappointing results, producing an oil with an exceptionally high sludge content and discharging large quantities of broken kernels along with the residual fibre. Bek needed to invest plenty of his own time in working out improvements to the design. De Wecker then carried out some of the necessary changes free of charge. Others were made in Bek's own workshop at Ulu Bernam, including the introduction of steam injections to aid the separation of sludge from the crude oil.[30]

It took two years of collaborative work on the press 'to get it really good; but when it was in, it was a winner'. The maximum oil:FFB extraction rate which could be attained using the hydraulic press and Tenera fruit was 21 per cent, and this was feasible only in small-scale trials, not in industrial production. The screw press made this rate feasible for regular large-scale processing and kept the accompanying FFA level reasonably low at 2.9 per cent. Extraction rates as high as 25 per cent (with a corresponding FFA level of 3.2 per cent) were obtained in the small-scale trials of Bek's modified de Wecker press in 1966, bettering even the results reported from Mongana. Additional benefits, as valuable in Malaysia as they had been in the Congo, were the high capacity, continuous operation and low energy costs of the screw press.[31]

Bek quickly decided to convert the Ulu Bernam mill to the new technology, and in 1966 he began transferring its old hydraulic presses to Jendarata as the new screw presses were phased in. In 1967 he began experimenting with alternative screw press designs, buying new units from Krupp in Germany and Speichim in France; but by 1969 it had become clear that the de Wecker press led the field. Not only was it an efficient extractor of oil, but its distinctive straight screw also gave it very low rates of wear and tear, so that only one-third as much iron was absorbed into the palm oil from this screw press as from the standard hydraulic press.[32]

A quality gain of this kind was especially useful because buyers were beginning to find new edible uses for palm oil and developing fresh quality standards to match, going well beyond the traditional criterion of less than 5 per cent FFA on arrival in the West. Bleachability became a key criterion of quality for those consignments of palm oil destined to be transformed from their red, strong-flavoured crude form into pale, flavour-free cooking oils and shortenings. As Bek and other speakers explained at the Incorporated Society of Planters' 1969 quality symposium, bleachability was influenced by a wide range of factors including bruised fruit and exposure of the oil to air while heating, but one of the most important causes of poor bleachability was contamination of the oil by copper and iron. J.J. Olie of the Dutch firm Gebr. Stork & Co., leading designers of turnkey factories using the hydraulic press, had long maintained that a switch to the screw press would increase the amount of iron absorbed into the crude palm oil; and Bek took great pleasure in refuting this view in Olie's presence at the symposium. Privately, Bek could take equal pleasure in the knowledge that, in his work on the screw press, he had upheld the Lindquist tradition of pursuing higher quality and not just lower cost.[33]

BEK'S REPUTATION GROWS

By 1969 Bek was becoming well known within Malaysia's oil palm industry, not only because of his work on the screw press but also because of his concern to get all aspects of factory operation right. Like Axel, he saw that it was vital to ensure a smooth flow of raw materials from one stage of processing to the next and to look beyond an apparently self-contained innovation like the screw press to consider its knock-on effects. This approach was to take him beyond the world of conferences into those of consultancy and wholescale factory construction; and it gave him much in common with the engineers of Pamol (Malaya) and their colleagues who had written the Mongana Report.

Much of the Mongana Report had been devoted to operations other than pressing, and the authors emphasized that the switch from centrifugals to screw presses would entail a switch in managers' attention from some of these ancillary operations to others. Whereas the processes of sterilization and digestion had to be managed with military precision in order to get the best results from centrifugals, variations in these processes had little effect on the efficiency of the screw press. In contrast, the processes of oil clarification and kernel extraction, which were relatively simple with centrifugals, posed tough challenges to the managers of factories using screw presses. In nut cracking, further complications arose from the switch to Tenera fruit, which had smaller nuts and thinner shells than the Dura variety.[34]

The Unilever managers who arrived in Malaysia in the 1960s, fresh from the lessons of Mongana, quickly recognized the value of the expertise which Bek had accumulated at United Plantations. Bek shared their scorn for turnkey solutions and their enthusiasm for in-house engineering; and he had the advantage of being able to build on a long tradition of experimentation with oil clarification at Ulu Bernam. By 1963 it had already become clear that Bernam Oil Palms' patented continuous separation tanks had been well designed. Stork brought out their own, 'very bulky' version which Bek inspected with interest, reporting it to have, greatly to his satisfaction, a much smaller volume relative to the separating surface than the Bernam version. Meanwhile, he had been investing in new Stork nut crackers and designing his own kernel separator to go with them. In 1966, immediately following his decision to switch to screw presses, Bek began designing and manufacturing a special kind of machine to recover the crushed nuts from the press cake. Here was a man whose thinking was right in line with that of the Mongana engineers and who had the energy, patience and company resources needed to put such thinking into practice.[35]

Unilever's managers were not the only ones to appreciate Bek's qualities in the mid-1960s. Throughout the period 1957–64 he had kept up the consultancy work begun by Axel and developed close collaborative friendships with engineers elsewhere. Then, in 1965 he shifted into a higher gear. Within United Plantations he was made acting general manager, running both that firm and Bernam Oil Palms when Ole Traugott Schwensen was abroad. This role was to be made permanent with Bek's promotion to deputy general manager in 1967. By this time he was clearly being groomed for his eventual succession to Schwensen with the new title of senior executive director in 1971. Meanwhile, one of Bek's first actions on being earmarked for promotion in 1965 had been to establish consultancy as a mainstream company activity. Previously each consultancy assignment had been seen as an individual initiative, a spare-time money-spinner for which special permission had to be granted by the board of directors. Consultancy was seen in a negative light as a potential drain on company resources, rather than in a positive way as a valuable source of corporate income and goodwill. In 1965, however, Bernam Oil Palms launched a new technical advisory and consultative service, whose achievements immediately joined the regular roll of honour in the annual Chairman's Statement to shareholders.[36]

191

The new service went well beyond pure consultancy to include the design and construction of factories for other firms. Much of the necessary machinery was bought in from suppliers like Stork, but some was made in the Ulu Bernam workshop using distinctive United Plantations and Bernam Oil Palms designs. Between 1965 and 1987 16 palm oil mills were built for organizations outside the United Plantations group. Of these, the vast majority were commissioned by private planters; Bek's trenchant criticisms of the early FELDA operations may well have influenced the pattern of demand. About half the mills were in Perak, and the rest equally divided between the states of Selangor, Sabah, Trengganu and Johore. Thirteen were built by 1981, in which year United Plantations claimed the credit for designing, constructing or rehabilitating some 15 per cent of all Malaysia's palm oil mills. This last tally included the group's own mills, which by 1981 numbered three. In addition to the mills at Jendarata and Ulu Bernam, a third had been built about ten miles to the north-east of Jendarata in 1977 to serve a new estate run by Syarikat Seri Pelangi Sdn. Bhd., a wholly owned subsidiary of United Plantations.[37]

Bernam Advisory Services, as it had been known since its formation as a separate subsidiary company in 1971, spent two long periods fully engaged on work for United Plantations and closely related enterprises. The first was from 1971 to 1975, during the construction of the joint-venture Unitata palm oil refinery, whose history will be discussed in more depth in Chapters 8 and 9. The second is from 1988 onwards, when Bernam Advisory Services has been involved in three main projects. First, its engineers built a new bridge across the Bernam River, a complete estate railway network and an enormous palm oil mill at Ulu Basir, all serving United Plantations' new jungle development to the north and east of Ulu Bernam. Axel Lindquist returned from retirement to help with this work, which proved to be the last project he was able to undertake before his death in February 1990. The mill at Ulu Basir was completed later that year, with a capacity of 100 tonnes of FFB per hour. Meanwhile, the engineers began work on designing new end products for United Plantations and Unitata, of which the first to be launched on the market was a vitamin-rich red palm oil, unveiled under the brand name 'Nutrolein' in 1993. The third and final project, which was Bernam Advisory Services' major priority in the early 1990s, was to assist chief engineer Poul K. Vestergaard of the Danish-Malaysian joint venture, United International Enterprises (Malaysia) Sdn Bhd, with the construction of a new palm oil mill at Gula Perak. Poul Vestergaard, who was tragically killed in a car accident in Selangor in June 1999, was himself a remarkable man. Like Axel Lindquist, he was an engineer from a humble Danish background, who had continued to educate himself and to develop his chosen skills throughout his life; and like Aage Westenholz, he was an adventurer who managed to combine a pioneering spirit with great personal kindness and warmth. He and Bek-Nielsen formed a firm friendship and worked effectively together to create a state of the art palm oil mill complex, opened in February 1992 with the same capacity as Ulu Basir's, and designed to handle the fruit from yet another large jungle development. Børge Bek-Nielsen's close personal involvement with both ventures has ensured that his machines and methods will continue to play an important role in developing Malaysia's oil palm industry.[38]

Through Bernam Advisory Services, Bek's innovations influenced the technical development of Malaysia's palm oil industry in one further way: the sale of specific machines. In 1972 a lucrative trade began in palm fruit digesters, horizontal nut crackers and vacuum driers, all made to Bek's designs in the workshop at Ulu Bernam. Over the years, four more designs became popular with buyers: the single-screw press, the empty bunch press, pneumatic palm kernel extraction plant and palm oil mill effluent plant. Some of these were the work less of Bek himself than of Hans Kristian Jørgensen, who had joined the engineering staff at Ulu Bernam in 1963 and who rose to become chief engineer in 1978, and executive director (technical) from 1981 until his retirement in 1984. Jørgensen's most notable contribution was the decanter–drier system for effluent plants, developed in association with the equipment manufacturers Alfa-Laval and Humboldt between 1977 and 1979. This system anticipated the impact of laws passed in Malaysia from 1981 to 1984 that progressively restricted the discharge of palm oil mill waste into rivers and streams. In response to these laws various plantation enterprises developed new ways of treating their effluent, one very popular means being the use of anaerobic ponds. However, Jørgensen's alternative method was compact, effective and lucrative, yielding as a byproduct a dry palm oil meal which could be sold for use as a fertilizer or an animal feed. By 1992 50 units were in operation in Malaysia and Indonesia. Meanwhile the Jendarata group engineer, Toh Tai San, was beginning to work with United Plantations' deputy director of research, Dr Gurmit Singh, on an improved design which, by 1996, was allowing the company to produce a granulated fertilizer in three grades, the finest of which could be used even on golf course greens.[39]

Of the other machines sold through Bernam Advisory Services, the most influential was the single-shaft, stainless steel screw press. Jørgensen perfected the final design of this press, of which the prototype was built in 1976 and which first went on sale in 1979 under the brand name 'Unipress'. But the drive behind its development came from Bek, who had become widely known as a leading authority on the screw press following his work with Usine de Wecker in 1964–1966. The Usine de Wecker press, as modified by Bek, had proved a great commercial success: 500 units were in operation throughout Malaysia by 1981. Nevertheless, Bek was always unwilling to rest on his laurels. Between 1967 and 1971 he tried out presses made by Krupp and Speichim and encouraged these manufacturers to modify their designs too. Between 1971 and 1975 Bek and his engineering staff were preoccupied with Unitata, but continued to monitor the performance of the various presses in routine operations at the mill. It gradually became evident that the de Wecker press was by far the most reliable and easy to maintain. Many mill owners would have been happy to cease research at that point and simply purchase all future presses from de Wecker, but Bek was still not satisfied. He urged Jørgensen to try his hand at designing an in-house alternative. As described in the Ulu Bernam Annual Report for 1977, 'the aim of the design was to produce an inexpensive piece of equipment which would be easy and cheap to maintain, and with a low power consumption', and which would be 'as efficient as the best press on the market today'. The new 'Unipress' easily met these criteria. For example, its energy costs were low because it used two motors with a total power output of 18.7 kilowatts, whereas other screw presses used one, with an output of 25 kilowatts. In tests carried out at Ulu Bernam over the four years 1977–81, its operating results proved consistently superior to those of the three outside makes tried earlier. The 'Unipress' duly became the backbone of the new mills built at Seri Pelangi and elsewhere by Bernam Advisory Services. It also sold well as a stand-alone unit.[40]

The development of the 'Unipress' provides a fitting story with which to end this chapter, for it illustrates the qualities of perfectionism and persistence with which Bek built on Lindquist's legacy and underlines the point which Lindquist himself had understood so well, that the pursuit of higher quality at lower cost is never-ending. It also reminds us that while Bek followed Axel in viewing the factory, and indeed the whole production chain from seedlings to shipment, as an integrated whole, yet he never lost sight of the central importance of the screw press itself. Through the introduction of this press, producers throughout Malaysia's palm oil industry became able to exploit the cost-cutting potential of the Tenera palm to the full. Bek's role in developing this key innovation had brought him to prominence within the planting community by the end of the 1960s. In the decade which followed, as the next chapters will show, his career took a new and even more remarkable turn. Moving beyond Lindquist's legacy to make his own distinctive mark, Børge Bek-Nielsen spearheaded the development of new products and new markets to absorb Malaysia's rapidly growing palm oil output. In so doing, he achieved international and not simply local renown.

NOTES

1   Interview with Tan Sri Dato' Seri B. Bek-Nielsen and Axel Lindquist, 15 April 1989. The direct quotations are from Bek. On the concept of strategic innovation, see C. Baden-Fuller and J.M. Stopford, *Rejuvenating the Mature Business: the Competitive Challenge* (London: Routledge, 1992), Ch. 3. On Bek's publications, see Ch. 7 below, footnote 38.

2   First quotation: Z. Phoon, 'Datuk B Bek-Nielsen – good disciplinarian with a heart for all', *The Planter*, vol. LXIII, no. 9, 1987, pp. 424–428, and S. Sakran, 'A planter at heart', *Malaysian Business*, 16 August 2001. Second quotation: Kjeld Ranum, chairman of the board of Aarhus Oliefabrik, in *Messages of Congratulation to Y.Bhg. Tan Sri Dato' Seri B. Bek-Nielsen on the Occasion of his Golden Anniversary with United Plantations Berhad, 15th September 2001* (Jendarata: United Plantations Berhad, 2001), p. 36; 'We Love Bapa UP', p. 48; see also: messages from John Goodwin, managing director of International Plantations and Finance, W.T. Perera, chief executive of the Incorporated Society of Planters, and Mogens Jensen AMN, general manager of International Plantation Services, pp. 21, 30 and 39.

3   Interview, as note 1; personal communication from Axel's son Valdemar Lindquist, 15 August 1997.

4   Interview, as previous note; Carrie Jørgensen, 'United Plantations and Bernam Oil Palms: highlights from a colourful past' (unpublished mss., 1984), Ch. 9 and pp. 136–145.

5   C.W.S. Hartley, *The Oil Palm (Elaeis Guineensis Jacq.)* 3rd edn (London: Longman, 1988), pp. 705 and 714; J.H. Maycock, 'The developments in palm oil factory design since the early 1900s', *The Planter*, vol. LI, no. 8, 1975, pp. 335–354; UBAR, 1933–40.

6   JAR, 1936–40.

7 Jørgensen, 'United Plantations', pp. 144–147; interview with Tan Sri Dato' Seri B. Bek-Nielsen and Axel Lindquist, 20 February 1989; JAR and UBAR, 1946–60.

8 Interview with Tan Sri Dato' Seri B. Bek-Nielsen and Axel Lindquist, 15 April 1989.

9 UBAR, 1946–55.

10 JAR and UBAR, 1949–52.

11 JAR, 1952–54.

12 C. Wilson, *Unilever 1945–65* (London: Cassell, 1968), pp. 161–163 and 178–179; UPCA, 1947–54; Lim Chong-Yah, *Economic Development of Modern Malaya* (Kuala Lumpur: Oxford University Press, 1967), pp. 317 and 337; JAR, 1948–58; Hartley, *Oil Palm*, p. 687.

13 UBAR, 1949–59; Hartley, *Oil Palm*, pp. 684–685.

14 UBAR, 1951–59.

15 BOPDR, 1927; R.L. Grut, 'Harvesting and transport of fruit bunches' in *The Oil Palm in Malaya* (Kuala Lumpur: Ministry of Agriculture and Co-operatives, 1966), pp. 199–212. Source for Map 5: UBAR, 1955. Fields 1–58 and 69 were planted up before 1940, and the railway network ended there. Further spurs were built out to the east as planting resumed after 1946. A slightly different version of this map appears in Harcharan Singh Khera, *The Oil Palm Industry of Malaya: an Economic Study* (Kuala Lumpur: Penerbit Universiti Malaya, 1976), as Fig. IV–1, p. 93.

16 Interviews with Axel Lindquist, 20 February 1989, and Tan Sri Dato' Seri B. Bek-Nielsen, 15 April 1989; UBAR, 1946–61; JAR, 1953–59.

17 Jørgensen, 'United Plantations', pp. 147–165; JAR, 1962–66; UBAR, 1963–65; H.V. Speldewinde, 'Fruit evacuation palm to mill using rail network', *The Planter*, vol. XLI, nos 11–12, 1965, pp. 500–509 and 560–570; and 'Harvesting and harvesting methods', in P.D. Turner (ed.), *Oil Palm Developments in Malaysia: Proceedings of the First Malaysian Oil Palm Conference* (Kuala Lumpur: Incorporated Society of Planters, 1968), pp. 106–117; M.M. Kehoe and L.C. Chan, *Buffalo Draught Power on Oil Palm Estates* (Kuala Lumpur: Incorporated Society of Planters, 1987), esp. Chs 1, 2 and 6. Illustrations from BOPAR, 1963 and 1965, and UPAR, 1966 and 1972.

18 UBAR, 1934 and 1946–58; interview with E.A. Rosenquist, 11 July 1988; W.O. Grut to N. Benzon, 6 April and 18 June 1951, CC, 1948–51.

19 W.O. Grut to N. Benzon, 6 April and 18 June 1951, CC, 1948–51: the quotation is from the June letter.

20 BOP board meetings, 16 May 1956, 7 May 1958, 24 Sept 1959 and 27 March 1960; BOPDR, 1956–61; UBAR, 1951–65. The quotation is from UBAR, 1962.

21 Wilson, *Unilever 1945–65*, pp. 78–79.

22 Maycock, 'Developments in palm oil factory design', pp. 339–342; interview with Keith Hamblin of Unilever Plantations Engineering Department, 20 July 1988.

23 On costs and company policy, D.K. Fieldhouse, *Unilever Overseas: the Anatomy of a Multinational, 1895–1965* (London: Croom Helm, 1978), Ch. 9; on Beirnaert's research and Yaligimba, Unilever Photo Archives: HCB Yaligimba file (1959); see also the section on the Congo in Chapter 5.

24 Maycock, 'Developments in palm oil factory design', pp. 339–342; CONGOPALM, 'Research on production and storage of palm oil: work carried out under the auspices of IRSIA, 1952–1955', 2 vols (mimeoed translation circulated by the Oil Palm Growers' Council, Kuala Lumpur) – henceforth referred to as the Mongana Report – Ch. III, sections 2 and 3.

25 Unilever Photo Archives: HCB Yaligimba file (1959); Fieldhouse, *Unilever Overseas*, pp. 529–31.

26 Mongana Report, pp. 111 and 124.

27 M. Crawford Young, 'Zaire, Rwanda and Burundi', in M. Crowder (ed.), *The Cambridge History of Africa*, Vol. 8 (Cambridge: Cambridge University Press, 1984), pp. 698–730.

28 Fieldhouse, *Unilever Overseas*, pp. 541–545; Unilever Plantations Engineering Department, personal communication, 31 March 1977; personal communication from Leslie Davidson, then chairman of Unilever's Plantations Group, 7 July 1988.

29 Fieldhouse, *Unilever Overseas*, pp. 545–546; interview with J.H. Maycock, 29 August 1987; A. Wolversperges, 'The extraction of palm oil by means of screw presses', *The Planter*, vol. XXXIX, nos. 1–3, 1963, pp. 11–14, 68–71 and 111–113.

30 Interview with Tan Sri Dato' Seri B. Bek-Nielsen, 15 April 1989; UBAR, 1962–65.

31 Quote from interview with Tan Sri Dato' Seri B. Bek-Nielsen, 15 April 1989; on small-scale trials, UBAR, 1962–66; on regular screw press operations, UBAR, 1977–86.

32 UBAR, 1966–69.

33 Hartley, *Oil Palm*, pp. 681–689; symposium proceedings, P.D. Turner (ed.), *The Quality and Marketing of Oil Palm Products* (Kuala Lumpur: Incorporated Society of Planters, 1969); UBAR, 1969.

34 Mongana Report, Chs II, IV and VII.

35 UBAR, 1961–66, including quotation from Bek, 1963; interview with Leslie Davidson, then chairman of Unilever's Plantations Group, 7 July 1988.

36 Interview with Davidson, as previous note; interview with Tan Sri Dato' Seri B. Bek-Nielsen, 15 April 1989; Jørgensen, 'United Plantations', pp. 162–166; BOP board meetings, 4 December 1958 and 23 May 1962; BOPCA, 1965–66; UPAR, 1966–71.

37 Interview with Tan Sri Dato' Seri B. Bek-Nielsen, 15 April 1989; UBAR, 1965–87; BOPCA, 1965–66; UPAR, 1966–87.

38 UPAR, 1971–1998; United International Enterprises Ltd., Annual Report and Accounts, 1992.

39 UBAR, 1963–79; UPAR, 1972–96; Hartley, *Oil Palm*, pp. 722–723.

40 Interview with Tan Sri Dato' Seri B. Bek-Nielsen, 15 April 1989; UBAR, 1967–81; UPAR, 1977–93; Bek is cited as an authority on the screw press by Hartley, *Oil Palm*, pp. 716–717.

CHAPTER SEVEN

The Invisible Ingredient: Catering for New Consumers

A MARKET TRANSFORMED

*A*fter the Second World War a sea-change occurred in the world market for palm oil. The United States, previously the main consumer of high-quality oil, now bought very little. During the wartime era of scarce and costly palm oil supplies, American soap and compound lard manufacturers had found new ways of processing other oils and fats to meet their needs; and after the war, synthetic detergents began to attack the conventional soap industry at its very roots. Malaysian palm oil producers had to look elsewhere, and to work increasingly hard at creating market opportunities, as their own output began to soar in the 1960s. Many looked to the rapidly expanding food-processing and catering industries of Western Europe. These offered the prospect of fresh uses and new customers for palm oil, if only it could be transformed beyond recognition from its natural state. In the 1990s deeply coloured, strongly flavoured vegetable oils began to acquire a positive value among cooks eager for exotic treats, but in the 1960s food manufacturers viewed such characteristics with caution. Vegetable oils were attractive because they were cheap, but in order to become effective substitutes for butter and lard they had to be refined into a bland, pale form: a blank canvas upon which manufacturers could create the desired impression. Developments in refining techniques therefore proceeded apace during the 1950s and 1960s, and palm oil producers gradually became aware that quality improvements were needed within their mills, too, in order to produce new grades of palm oil tailored to the refiners' requirements. Palm oil had a great future as an invisible ingredient, used in a wide range of products ranging from margarine through biscuits and crisps to ice cream. Yet in order to realize this dream, planters and engineers had to pursue the quest for quality at low cost more vigorously than ever before. As shown in the previous chapter, Bek-Nielsen was well placed to do so, and although much of the pioneering research in this area was done outside United Plantations, he was so quick to adopt innovations and so keen to develop them further that his firm's name eventually became synonymous with quality at the highest level.[1]

Britain, the imperial heartland and for many planters in Malaya the home country, was naturally the first market to which they turned when American demand was cut off. During and immediately after the Second World War they had little option, for palm oil demand was high in Britain and the government acted directly to secure supplies. Demand remained high in Britain for two main reasons. First, the British soap industry showed a ten-year delay in following American trends. Cheaper substitutes for palm oil were not widely used in Britain until the early 1950s; and the British soap industry was not severely affected by competition from detergents until the late 1960s. Second, margarine and compound lard gained a new acceptability among British consumers because of acute wartime shortages of animal fats which persisted long into the peace. Marguerite Patten, who worked for the ministry's Food Advice Division during the war, recalls vividly the privations of the time. Family cooks had to use all their ingenuity to produce decent meals and make up for the meagreness of standard rations. Grated potato and oatmeal were used to eke out the fat in pastry, and the resulting dishes had to be cooked in hotter ovens than usual. Cooks were urged to save the fat from frying pans and baking tins, to skim it off the top of cold stews and to follow an elaborate procedure of melting, straining, washing and reheating to preserve the fat for future use. Against this background, British consumers gradually began to overcome their aversion to vegetable-based cooking fats; and the Ministry of Food was driven to pay extremely high prices when buying up Malaya's palm oil between 1946 and 1952.[2]

After 1952, however, British demand for palm oil began to slacken and Malaysian producers had to begin searching for new uses and new markets. The root of the problem in Britain was that cooks had returned with relief to butter and other old favourites once rationing came to an end. In the long run, the growth of the mass-market catering and food-processing industries was to provide palm oil with two vital sources of fresh demand, but the new users set stringent quality standards. Since domestic customers clearly valued the colour, taste and texture of animal fats, industrial food producers felt they should make their cheap vegetable-based substitutes into increasingly effective copies of the originals. Vegetable oils were no longer competing with each other only on price and physical characteristics, for example stability under intense heat. New competitive criteria were emerging, as manufacturers found that some oils were easier than others to disguise. The ideal, invisible ingredient was an oil which could be made colourless and flavourless, ready to blend indistinguishably with other oils and fats and to take on the new tastes and appearances wanted by the manufacturer. Both technical and organizational change was needed within the mills and plantations before new grades of palm oil could be produced to fit this blueprint. Meanwhile, demand for palm oil from the soap industry was falling, not only because of renewed competition from marine oils and animal fats but also because of the rise of detergents. Britain's total net imports of palm oil fell by 12 per cent in volume terms between 1949–51 and 1959–61; and her share of Malaya's palm oil exports fell from 100 per cent in 1949 to 37 per cent in 1961.[3]

While British demand for palm oil was declining during the 1950s, Malaysian producers found that markets were growing elsewhere in Western Europe, where the catering and convenience food industries were emerging just as in Britain, and where there was considerable accumulated demand from the soap industry and other traditional users. Wartime trading restrictions, which had driven the Americans to develop substitutes for palm oil, had a less severe impact on palm oil users in Western Europe. Although Malayan and British West African supplies continued to be cornered by the British Ministry of Food until 1952, other European users were still able to obtain palm oil from French colonies in Africa, from the Belgian Congo and from the Netherlands East Indies. Between 1949 and 1951 the five major mainland European importers of palm oil were Belgium, France, West Germany, Italy and the Netherlands. Their purchases averaged 180,000 tonnes per annum, nearly 80 per cent of the corresponding British figure, which was 230,000 tonnes. British imperial trading restrictions prevented other European users from buying as much palm oil as they would have liked but did not force them to invest heavily in developing fresh processing techniques for alternative oils. Hence, when trading restrictions were lifted at the end of 1952, mainland European imports of palm oil were poised to grow. By 1959–61 the five major buyers listed above had collectively overtaken Britain, taking an average of 230,000 tonnes of palm oil each year as compared with Britain's 180,000, in a neat reversal of the position ten years earlier.[4]

During the 1960s mainland European demand continued to grow, while British palm oil use stagnated. In 1969–71 British imports averaged 170,000 tonnes per annum, while those to the five mainland countries stood at a level 80 per cent higher, that is 310,000 tonnes per year. No other European countries had yet emerged as major new users of palm oil, so that the net impact of these trends on total European demand, both British and mainland, was to keep it stable during the 1950s and allow for a slow rise during the 1960s. Annual average European palm oil imports rose from just over 400,000 tonnes in 1959–61 to almost 500,000 in 1969–71. Over the same period Malaysia's palm oil exports rose from 80,000 to 450,000 tonnes per annum, and total world exports from 580,000 to 830,000 tonnes a year. From the Malaysian planter's point of view, these trends had clear implications. The European market was growing and offered good opportunities for producers who could deliver palm oil of guaranteed quality, especially if they were able to meet the new specifications of the catering and convenience foods industry. However, world palm oil supplies were growing faster than the European market, and Malaysian supplies were growing faster than those in the world as a whole. Malaysian producers needed to perform much better than their rivals if they were to capture market share in affluent Europe, which they needed to do if they were to continue delivering the returns that would keep their shareholders satisfied. Investment, both in research and in machinery, was vital if they were to maintain their pre-war reputation for high quality and continue to prosper in the new post-war world.[5]

UNILEVER AND UNITED PLANTATIONS: CONTRASTING STYLES IN THE QUEST FOR QUALITY

Ironically, the company which came to lead Malaysia's planters in their post-war search for new processing methods and product applications was a relatively new entrant to the local industry. As shown in Chapter 6, Unilever had invested heavily through its Belgian Congo subsidiary in developing mill technology tailored to the characteristics of the Tenera palm, and it will be shown below that this investment in research threw up vital leads in the quest for ways of making higher-grade oil. Meanwhile, Unilever's strong manufacturing and marketing presence in the industrial West gave the European parent company a head start in sensing new food-industry trends and developing products to capitalize on them. The company used these advantages to the full and developed a systematic strategy of market-led scientific research, departing radically from its pre-war policy through which staff developed technical knowledge 'on the job' and made improvements to products whenever they saw an opportunity to do so, while relying on luck to ensure their market success. Charles Wilson, the Cambridge professor and official historian of Unilever, has shown that after 1945 the company moved from owner-management to salaried management and, simultaneously, from management by flair to management by science. The twin disciplines of marketing and 'research and development' (R&D) came to the fore. Cash was invested in ways that did not always bear fruit, but the overall result was to enable the company to continue prospering and growing in a regional market that, at the outset, seemed to be saturated or even in decline.[6]

United Plantations, by contrast, retained strong elements of the owner–manager system throughout the 1950s and 1960s. Even during the period of Niels Benzon's hands-off chairmanship (1949–63), Olof and Rolf Grut effectively played the roles of owner–managers in waiting. From 1963 Olof Grut was fully in charge as chairman and sustained a close relationship of mutual trust with his two key executives in Malaysia: Ole Traugott Schwensen, the general manager, and Børge Bek-Nielsen, the chief engineer. A second important difference between Unilever and United Plantations is that, as a small company, United Plantations could ill spare the financial resources needed to support a systematic marketing initiative, especially one aimed at transforming a large existing market. Hence the innovative strategies developed by Børge Bek-Nielsen, and supported by Schwensen and Grut at United Plantations, differed fundamentally from the policies pursued at Unilever.

Initially, Bek's approach was to watch, learn and follow suit once the technology was developed and the market advantages clear. Through his contacts in Unilever's Pamol (Malaya) subsidiary he became aware of the pioneering 1950s research in the Belgian Congo that by the end of the 1960s had been replicated by Harrisons & Crosfield. Like Unilever, Harrisons had a long-standing presence in the European manufacturing sector, specifically in the chemicals industry, which underpinned the research through which both companies developed high-grade, branded palm oils. Observing these achievements, Bek realized that this was a game which both could and must be joined. Building upon the gains achieved by Axel Lindquist before him, he embarked upon his own distinctive quest for quality. Unilever helped him at the start, but he later continued in characteristic fashion, persisting in the quest over decades and rejecting all standard solutions in favour of his own improved versions. Bek's drive to serve the market took him ever-closer to it, to the ultimate point of direct investment in soap and food processing plants in Europe as well as Asia. In contrast to Unilever, a manufacturing company which had moved into plantations early in the twentieth century as a source of supply, United Plantations moved into manufacturing as a way of getting closer to the market.[7]

AFRICAN APPROACHES

Back in the early 1950s, United Plantations and other Malayan producers were still recovering financially from the tremendous task of post-war rehabilitation, and Unilever, whose operations in the Belgian Congo had been relatively little affected by the Second World War, was leading the way in the quest for new uses of palm oil. Unilever's search focused on the European mass-market catering and convenience foods industries, which were then in their infancy. The quality standards set by palm oil buyers in these industries were relatively unsophisticated. Yet their basic needs were already clear. They valued palm oil chiefly for its physical properties, in particular because it was semi-solid at northern ambient temperatures. In this respect palm oil was unlike sunflower and other competing vegetable oils which, being liquid, were less easy to transport and store and which required expensive hydrogenation to convert them to the solid state. Palm oil also had the natural advantage of remaining stable under high and prolonged thermal stress, making it especially suitable for industrial frying operations. Its only serious drawbacks were its strong colour and taste.[8]

One of the key technical challenges facing European palm oil refiners who wanted to sell to the edible oils market was, therefore, the removal of the oil's distinctive red colour and taste. They tackled this challenge by bleaching and deodorizing the palm oil after they had removed the free fatty acids (FFA) from it by the basic refining process of neutralization. They soon found that oil from different shipments tended to vary in its chemical properties, producing inconsistent results from the bleaching and deodorization processes. Naturally they were keen to minimize such variations by buying palm oil with standard chemical properties, but there was no consensus as to which were the most important properties for their purpose, or how such properties could be measured in the crude palm oil. Still less was there a clear understanding of which aspects of the milling process were linked to variations in the chemical properties of the oil.[9]

In 1952 Unilever's Congo subsidiary began co-operating with the government-sponsored Mongana research station in a comprehensive study of palm oil processing methods. As discussed in the previous chapter, the study's main focus was on the efficiency of alternative presses, but the researchers also made a pioneering attempt to tackle the new quality issues. They were adventurous in their approach and ended by defining quality in a new way. Whereas Axel Lindquist and other contemporary engineers were seeking simply to minimize the FFA, dirt and moisture content of their factories' palm oil, the Mongana researchers urged them to aim at no fewer than nine additional targets. Included in these were three new criteria which were particularly relevant to the Western food industry: low oxidation, high bleachability and low heavy metal content. All three were chemical rather than physical properties, reinforcing the message that from now on, palm oil companies would need to employ chemists as well as engineers in order to get high-quality results.[10]

The Mongana researchers were well aware that their views were ahead of their time. For example, their experiments had shown that it was possible to lower the oxidation (peroxide value) of crude palm oil by using chemical reducing agents. They further indicated that this treatment would not only reduce the rancidity of the oil as it left the African or Asian mill but also improve its keeping quality once refined. Yet the researchers noted that the market was not yet highly selective: refiners remained to be convinced that it was worth paying more for palm oil with a low peroxide value. Apart from anything else, the refiners' own state of knowledge about peroxide values and their practical meaning was extremely limited. They had only recently learnt how to determine the peroxide value of any given batch of palm oil, and they had no idea how to use this measure to predict its keeping qualities, let alone how to compare the keeping qualities of deperoxidized and standard palm oil. The Mongana Report was the first step towards solving these technical riddles, and so creating a new market within which deperoxidized palm oil could sell at a premium.[11]

Just as the Mongana researchers were starting work in 1952, another major research effort was getting under way at the newly founded West African Institute for Oil Palm Research (WAIFOR) near Benin City in Nigeria. The two projects overlapped in the study of bleachability, which had already emerged as a key quality criterion in the minds of refiners but which was poorly understood. Although the original depth of colour of each batch of palm oil could easily be measured using the 13.3 cm Lovibond cell index, the ease with which this colour could be removed was far harder to predict. The two groups of researchers, in the Congo and in Nigeria, initially took radically different approaches to the bleachability problem. The Congo researchers focused on the factors which made it harder to remove the oil's red colour in the refinery and found a link between high iron and copper levels and poor bleachability. They showed that it was possible to measure iron and copper levels in the crude palm oil by spectrographic analysis and indicated that new mill techniques could usefully be developed either to prevent the entry of these metals into the oil, or to remove it at the end of processing.[12]

In contrast, the WAIFOR researchers focused initially on field rather than factory. Knowing that oil from their region had a reputation for poor bleachability, they tried to find out whether genetic differences between the West African and Deli Dura palms included a variation in carotene levels. Carotene is now valued as a source of Vitamin A, but in the 1950s refiners aimed to eliminate it from the crude palm oil, removing with it its distinctive orange-red colour. By the mid-1960s several West African surveys of carotene levels had been carried out. These showed that while carotene levels did indeed vary between Deli Dura and West African Dura fruit, there were even wider variations between different batches of West African fruit and between oils extracted from similar fruit but by different methods. Ultimately, therefore, the West African research led back to the starting-point of the work at Mongana and focused attention on the mill rather than the planting material. A major conclusion of the WAIFOR resarch on processing methods was that there was a direct link between high oxidation and poor bleachability. What had seemed initially to the Mongana researchers to be three separate aspects of quality – that is low oxidation, high bleachability and low heavy metal content – now seemed to be three links in the same chain. Research over the next two decades, in Asia as well as Africa, was to focus on the ways by which exposure to both metals and air could be limited in the course of palm oil extraction, thus limiting oxidation and promoting high bleachability.[13]

NEW BRANDS OF PALM OIL

The first fruit of the post-war African research was the special prime bleach (SPB) brand, developed by chemists in the Congo and publicized by Loncin and Jacobsberg at the oil palm conference held by the Tropical Products Institute

(TPI) in London in 1965. SPB palm oil contained under 2 per cent FFA, very low levels of moisture and dirt, high levels of tocopherol (a natural anti-oxidant) and low levels of iron and copper. Carotene levels were minimized and, after 30 minutes' simple heat-bleaching, the red colour could be reduced to a level of 2.0 on the 13.3 cm Lovibond cell index. For anyone familiar with the refining industry, and able to follow the presentation which Loncin and Jacobsberg made at the London conference, these results would have been startling. As described in a separate paper presented at the same conference by Jasperson and Pritchard of the Liverpool processing firm J. Bibby & Sons Ltd, European refiners expected a good quality crude palm oil to produce a Lovibond 'red' reading of up to 6.0 after simple heat-bleaching. The 2.0 level, now obtainable by heat-bleaching SPB oil, compared very favourably with the readings which they aimed to produce by full refining of the highest-quality crude palm oils previously available. These ranged from a low point of 1.5, which was the required level for use in making 'white' cooking fats, to a high point of 4.0, which was acceptable to users in the margarine industry. In other words, the SPB oil offered refiners the chance of valuable cost savings. By using it they could hope to achieve the same low Lovibond reading through cheap, simple heat-bleaching, as they would otherwise seek through full refining, using a variety of complicated and expensive neutralization and bleaching techniques. Refiners were already used to paying price premiums of between £1 and £2 per ton for good quality crude palm oil from preferred suppliers, and so it was an obvious possibility that the SPB brand would soon command its own distinctive price.[14]

Unfortunately, although they published their work in English, Loncin and Jacobsberg made their presentation to the London audience in French and failed to include any of the key details about the refining industry which might have shown the commercial significance of their technical results. Their paper generated little discussion at the conference, and none of the participants commented on the link which, with hindsight, it is easy to make between this engineering breakthrough and the needs of contemporary refiners serving the Western food industry. Similarly Jasperson and Pritchard, even when revising their paper for publication, failed to incorporate the new information about SPB oil into their survey of the relative processing costs of oils from different sources. The main fact which they emphasized was that Nigerian oil sold at a discount because of its poor bleachability, and they shared the central concern of the conference organizers which was with the problems facing African smallholders. Quality was clearly seen as a long-standing Nigerian problem, rather than a fresh Malaysian opportunity. It would therefore have taken an extremely astute conference participant, with both French and English language skills, and both engineering and marketing expertise, to listen to the two papers and draw what, with hindsight, would seem to be the obvious conclusion: that there was a large premium-price market for SPB oil.[15]

By the time of the TPI conference Olof Grut had become well established as chairman of United Plantations, while still retaining the English connections developed during his years on the Norfolk farm. He recognized that the conference was likely to yield interesting news, but clearly did not expect this news to take the form of announcing an engineering breakthrough, for the two directors whom he sent to observe proceedings were experts in planting and marketing, rather than palm oil processing. Ole Schwensen, the general manager of United Plantations and Bernam Oil Palms, and Benny Olsen, the former company secretary of United Plantations and then managing director of International Plantations and Finance, were well-respected managers with a great depth of Malayan experience. However, there was a long tradition within the sister companies, which Axel Lindquist had encouraged, of planters and other managers leaving the business of engineering to the engineers. In the absence of their colleague Bek-Nielsen, it is possible that Schwensen and Olsen did not feel it was appropriate for them to comment on the report on SPB oil. Certainly, their notes on the event focus on other issues, and the event itself had no visible impact on board debates and company policy.[16]

Nevertheless, once Schwensen returned to Malaysia, the new ideas he had encountered at the conference may well have inclined him to support Bek's quest for quality with renewed enthusiasm. Børge Bek-Nielsen had become chief engineer for the sister companies in 1959 and had gained an early knowledge of developments in the Congo through his friendships within the wider planting community. Through his study of the Mongana project he became aware that chemists as well as engineers would be needed in the quest for quality. In 1964, with Ole Schwensen's support, he hired a new laboratory assistant, Chin Au Wah, to work in premises which had existed at Ulu Bernam since 1949. Chin was to become one of the firm's longest-serving staff and a linchpin of the new research effort. For nine months from July 1967 his work was directed by W.S. Kao, a chemical engineer from Singapore, who flew in for a series of short visits. Such an initiative was low cost and low profile, like Rolf Grut's early experiments with the Tenera palm; it provided a base on which Bek could build quickly, just as soon as the Copenhagen Board could be persuaded to back him.[17]

By the end of 1967 world market developments were clearly supporting Bek's case. The development of branded high-quality palm oil no longer looked like an engineer's dream, of unproven commercial relevance. Instead, it was coming to seem a basic requirement for competition in Western markets. This shift in perception was caused not only by the changing demand structures outlined earlier in this chapter but also by a more sudden transformation of the pattern of palm oil supply. From 1945 to the mid-1960s Nigeria had been the world's biggest single exporter of palm oil, but the outbreak of the Nigerian Civil War in 1967 effectively put an end to that country's export trade, which has never recovered. The only other large-scale African producer by the late 1960s was the Congo (to be known as Zaire from 1971 to 1997), whose palm oil exports were to tail off dramatically over the following ten years. In terms of quality, including bleachability, the standard Congo palm oil was much closer to the Malaysian and Sumatran product than to the Nigerian smallholder version. The disappearance of Nigerian palm oil from the world market therefore changed the rules of competition overnight. Planters in Malaysia now had to measure the quality of their ordinary oil mainly against the higher benchmark provided by the new SPB variety, rather than the lower one provided by the Nigerian smallholder product. Furthermore, they were becoming aware that Western food manufacturers were now measuring the quality of palm oil against that of an ever-widening range of substitutes: animal fats, marine oils and other vegetable oils which, like palm oil itself, were becoming easier to transform into the bland 'blank canvas' which manufacturers prized.[18]

One of the most important oils which had come into competition with palm oil by 1967 was soyabean oil. Soyabeans had long been a staple food crop in China, but their use in the West dates back only to the 1930s, when soyabean cultivation began to grow rapidly in the USA. At first the new crop was valued mainly as a source of animal feed, and the by-product oil was thought to be too fluid for use in making butter or lard substitutes. It also had a peculiar taste, which consumers struggled to describe in words ranging from 'grassy' to 'fishy'. The American compound lard industry, which also sprang up in the 1930s, used palm oil as a preferred ingredient, valuing its quality of being naturally semi-solid in temperate climates and finding its taste less objectionable than that of soyabean oil. However, the outbreak of the Second World War, and the interruption of the palm oil trade to America, stimulated research into the use of hydrogenation to transform soya and other liquid oils into semi-solid fats. After the war ended, the soyabean industry received a further boost from the rise of intensive animal and poultry farming that created a new demand for soya meal. As increasing quantities of soya oil were produced as a by-product of the animal feeds industry, researchers on both sides of the Atlantic began to look seriously at the off-flavours which remained a major obstacle to increased sales. Taste panels were set up by America's government-run Agricultural Research Service to establish a consensus view of how soyabean oil tasted; and in its laboratories at Vlaardingen in the Netherlands, established in 1954, Unilever's scientists used gas chromatography and spectroscopy to isolate the components of specific off-flavours. Further research identified various ways in which oil processors could eliminate these flavours: by removing iron and copper from their factories, adding citric acid to the deodorized oil and removing the oil's naturally high linolenic acid content by partial hydrogenation. The latter technique, developed during the early 1960s, was equally applicable to rapeseed oil, which also has a naturally high linolenic acid content. However, the rapeseed industry did not fully develop until the late 1970s, following a rise in Canadian plantings of a new variety with distinctive nutritional benefits.[19]

Unilever, involved as it was in processing both palm and soyabean oils in both Europe and America, was in an ideal position to anticipate the impact of these technical developments on the world market. An awareness, not only of the fresh opportunities arising within Western food industries but also of the growing threat posed by alternative oils, underpinned its pioneering research and the development of the SPB palm oil brand. For other producers, such an awareness was slower to emerge. As late as 1965, they were providing an appreciative audience for the TPI conference paper presented by the Institute economist, P.C. Cheshire, who argued that palm oil faced no special threat from other vegetable oils on the British market. In soap production, he noticed that lower-grade Nigerian palm oil had been replaced by tallow; but in the production of margarine and compound cooking fats (CCF), higher-grade Malaysian and African palm oils still seemed to be competing strongly against alternative ingredients. Whale oil and lard had eroded the market share of some other vegetable oils in these food industries, but the share of palm oil had proved resilient. Between 1954–56 and 1960–62 the share of palm oil in the volume of oils bought by margarine manufacturers had fallen only slightly, from 20 per cent to 19 per cent; in the CCF industry the corresponding fall was from 25 per cent to 23 per cent.[20]

A closer look at Cheshire's figures, which few of his listeners would have been inclined to undertake at the time, reveals with hindsight an ominous trend. The share of soyabean oil in the British margarine market grew from 3 per cent to 8 per cent , and in the CCF market from 0.3 per cent to 8 per cent, between the mid-1950s and the early 1960s. Cheshire attached no importance to this development in 1965, but by the late 1960s its significance began to become obvious. The share of all vegetable oils in both the margarine and CCF markets continued to fall, and when it began to grow again in the 1970s, it was the producers of soya and rapeseed, rather than palm oil, who reaped most benefit. Between 1966–68 and 1979–81 the share of palm oil in the British market for CCF ingredients rose from 15 per cent to 20 per cent, that is to a level which was still lower than that of the early 1960s. The share of soyabean oil, however, rose from 4 per cent to 18 per cent and of rapeseed oil from 2 per cent to 9 per cent. Palm oil was losing out despite the fact that it had a distinctive advantage in performance, the quality of being relatively stable at high temperatures. Meanwhile in the British market for margarine ingredients, where this quality was irrelevant, palm oil's share dropped from 11 per cent in 1966–68 to 6 per cent in 1979–81, while soyabean oil's share climbed from 8 per cent to 16 per cent and rapeseed oil's from 2 per cent to 11 per cent.[21]

The rise of the soyabean industry was first noticed by Malaysian planters in 1967, when the price of soyabean oil, which had traditionally been above that of palm oil, suddenly dipped below it. In January 1967 *The Planter* carried a small article commenting on the rise of American soyabean plantings which, once attention was focused on them, quickly began to seem alarming. Between 1960–62 and 1966–68 the annual average US soyabean crop rose from 17 to 27 million tonnes per annum, a jump of 58 per cent. World palm oil exports rose by just 8 per cent over the same period. In its first comments on the new supply trends, *The Planter* took a relatively relaxed attitude, forecasting such a growth in world demand for vegetable oils that there would be ample room for all competitors. Yet within six months, in July 1967, the editor was calling for defensive action, asking the government to support fresh palm oil research. By November 1968 his demands were clearly focused on the need for better processing techniques, quality control and marketing support for the industry nation-wide. By November 1969 explicit comparisons were being made between the keen but unco-ordinated efforts of the Malaysian private sector and the systematic, well-funded and successful American marketing of soyabean oil, supported officially by various means including overseas aid programmes.[22]

Olof Grut's annual statements to his Copenhagen shareholders show a similar shift in thinking. In May 1966 he felt confident that the world market for palm oil was expanding, though he warned that Malaysian production might expand even faster. In such a context, efficient production at low cost was the key to business success; he did not mention the need to look outside the palm oil industry in order to set new quality targets. By May 1967, however, possibly alerted by Ole Schwensen who took a keen interest in this matter, Olof was warning the shareholders that palm oil faced stiff competition from other vegetable oils. Malaysian growers needed to make a concerted effort to improve the quality of their palm oil, and then to publicize their achievements, if they were to thrive within the new world trading environment. In May 1968 Olof returned to this theme, warning that the threat from marine oils, Soviet sunflowers and the American 'soybean cornucopia' had now grown because of the closure of the Suez Canal, which had put Malaysian exporters at a transport cost disadvantage. At the same time, Ole Schwensen was becoming so impressed by the rise of the soyabean that he even tried it out as a catch crop under young oil palms on Sungei Bernam Estate, buying specialized mechanical equipment for the purpose. The experiment lasted from 1969 to 1973, and although the beans proved vulnerable to fungus, insect and weevil attacks and yielded poorly, the experience was turned to good use in developing better cultivation methods for the standard ground cover crops, such as the leguminous Pueraria.[23]

Among the other planters who saw that the rules of competition were changing in the mid-1960s was Tom Barlow, Sir Frank Swettenham's successor as chairman of the Highlands & Lowlands Para Rubber Company. Like United Plantations, the Highlands & Lowlands Company had been an early entrant to the Malaysian palm oil industry. Barlow and the Grut brothers were friends, and indeed Olof served as a director of Barlow's company until 1972. In his July 1967 address to his shareholders, Barlow took up the theme of the rising competitive threat from alternative oils, and emphasized the need to find new outlets for Malaysia's rising palm oil output as well as to focus on improved quality and marketing. The manager in charge of his new research department, G.C. McCulloch, played a leading role in organizing the Incorporated Society of Planters' 1969 symposium on palm oil quality and marketing.[24]

Meanwhile, further scientific strides were being made behind the scenes, as a second firm took up the search begun by Unilever and looked for a reliable measure of bleachability. Harrisons & Crosfield had a long-standing involvement in the British chemicals industry, and as its newly planted stands of oil palms came into bearing in the mid-1960s, small laboratories were built into the design of each new oil mill. In 1968 Harrisons set up a central quality control test laboratory in Malaysia that worked in close association with Harrisons' research laboratories in Camberley, Surrey. G. Johansson of the leading Swedish vegetable oil refinery, Karlshamns Oljefabriker, also became involved in the search mounted by these laboratories for a new quality measure for palm oil. A suitable measure was quickly found: anisidine value. When combined with the traditional measure of peroxide value in a new 'Totox' index, this provided the best test yet of oxidation. A low 'Totox' value implied high levels both of bleachability during refining and of keepability for the end product. Using this index, Harrisons were now able to launch a distinctive brand of palm oil: 'Lotox'. This combined a low 'Totox' value with low levels of copper and iron, and only slightly higher levels of FFA (2.5 per cent), moisture and dirt than Unilever's SPB brand.[25]

A CHEMICAL ENGINEER AT UNITED PLANTATIONS

By the end of 1967, world market developments and the responses being made by other firms in Malaysia had clearly strengthened Bek's case for setting up an independent research laboratory at Ulu Bernam. In 1968 he won Ole Schwensen's support in recruiting a full-time chemical engineer to help United Plantations produce 'the best crude palm oil in the world'. They advertised locally and were lucky in attracting the attention of S. 'Krish' Krishnan, a Malaysian who had studied chemistry and chemical engineering on a scholarship in India but was now keen to return. Attracted by the entrepreneurial culture of United Plantations, and by the challenge of starting up an innovative project within the firm, Krish resigned his post with Esso in Bombay. He arrived at Ulu Bernam in July 1968 to begin a successful career and a close personal friendship with Bek which still continues.[26]

United Plantations' choice of Asian rather than European staff for the new project reflected a general shift in company policy. Since 1960 the firm had been making serious efforts to develop a cadre of Asian managers, partly in response to government pressure but also as a reflection of the Grut brothers' genuine interest and confidence in their local staff. Three main means were employed. The highest in profile was the Cadet Scheme, started for field managers in 1964. Promising young men were recruited locally and given a two-year training as planting assistants, based partly at the new training centre and hostel on Kuala Bernam Estate, and partly in Denmark, where they would spend 3 months at a language school and 6 months working on farms as casual labourers. This scheme was an adapted form of the long-established system of European staff recruitment, whereby young men were trained from scratch and expected to give long service. Therein lay its central flaw. By the 1960s, even European planters were beginning to move more freely from firm to firm. Among Asian staff, and in a political context which made all United Plantations' competitors equally keen to recruit them, a training system which assumed long service was almost bound to fail. Nevertheless, the Cadet Scheme had one conspicuous success. Ho Dua Tiam, one of its pioneering members in 1964, went on to have a long and distinguished career with United Plantations. He served as estate manager at Seri Pelangi, 1978–79; at Sungei Bernam, 1979–80; at Jendarata, 1981–87; and finally as group manager at Ulu Bernam, until 1991 when he became general manager of United International Enterprises (Malaysia). Since 1995 he has combined this role with a seat on the board of United Plantations, originally as executive director (planting), then since March 2002 as deputy senior executive director and inspector general (estates).[27]

Some of Ho's fellow recruits to the Cadet Scheme, including Chew Keong Lye and K. Balachandran, also stayed with the firm for several years. However, most stayed only briefly, either because they did not make the grade or because they were lured away by higher salaries once trained. A similar pattern was found in engineering. The first cadet engineer, L.L. Cornelius, who joined the staff of Ulu Bernam in 1967, rose to become resident engineer there in 1974. Yet two more trainees, hired soon afterwards, became fed up with the estate's isolation and resigned within the year. Bek noted in 1969 that it was pointless to train men who could then be poached so easily. He recommended a second strategy, the mirror image of the first: to choose well-trained men and offer them high salaries from the outset. This was effectively the method that was followed with Krishnan.[28]

An alternative means of obtaining Asian managers, and one which produced two of Krish's most highly valued colleagues at Ulu Bernam, was promotion from within. Bek appreciated talent wherever he saw it. On becoming chief engineer in 1959, he immediately introduced a regular tribute in his annual report to 'the keen and loyal service always given by the Asian staff members here at Ulu'. By 1965 11 long-serving staff had been promoted to the rank of assistant, including S. Kandiah, a conductor (field supervisor) who had come over from Sri Lanka before the Second World War, and who ended his career by playing a leading role in the development of the new estate at Changkat Mentri in 1977–78. Kandiah's outstanding ability to get things done, coupled with his widespread popularity among both management and workers, made an immediate impression on the young Krishnan. The second man whom he quickly came to like and respect was T.K. Cherian, a tall and imposing Indian who had joined Bernam Oil Palms as the factory foreman in 1947, and had been promoted to assistant in 1965. Cherian remained at Ulu Bernam for many years and was honoured with the title of factory manager in 1971. He ended his career in the same role at Jendarata (1975–81) and remained in touch with Bek and Krish after his retirement.[29]

Despite the welcome after-hours companionship offered by such colleagues at Ulu Bernam, Krish found himself almost alone in his everyday work. Chin's help was vital in finding out what had been done at Ulu Bernam to date, and Bek was able to tell him about the Mongana research, which was to be his first source of inspiration. Beyond this, Krish had to rely on his own ingenuity in working out what kind of laboratory he should set up and what experiments he should conduct there. Fortunately, he was able to use his university contacts to track down the relevant scientific publications. Krish was also given full support by H.K. Jørgensen, Ulu Bernam's Resident Engineer, in obtaining equipment to fill what had been, on his arrival, an empty room. He turned the isolation of Ulu Bernam to his advantage, spending up to three days at a time completely immersed in his research. In this way he quickly progressed from an advisory role, helping the general manager to respond to customer queries about peroxide values, to a more active research role, in which his recommendations influenced the way the mill was run. One of his most important early findings was that the keeping quality of the crude palm oil could be greatly improved if the palm fruit was not handled in the mill after being sterilized. This highlighted the importance of Axel Lindquist's work on conveyors and elevators during the 1950s. Axel's belief in the importance of designing a mill as an integrated whole could once again be seen not simply as a matter of streamlining and cost reduction but also as part of the quest for quality.[30]

GAINING A LEADING EDGE

From the start of Chin's experiments in 1967, United Plantations had been aiming to match Loncin and Jacobsberg's specifications and produce the SPB grade of palm oil. In 1968 several small batches of oil had been produced and sent to Unilever's Danish plant for testing, but from 1969 Krish was able to do all the necessary work in his new laboratory. United Plantations now began to produce SPB oil in bulk and make special shipments of it direct to Europe from their own bulking installation, which they had set up in 1952 in Penang. Krish used to accompany the oil on the company's tankers from Ulu Bernam to Penang, carefully controlling its shipping environment and taking samples to test its keeping quality on the journey. Axel's distinctive emphasis on control of the whole sequence of operations, from seedlings to shipment, had not been forgotten.[31]

At the other end of the chain stretching from seedlings to shipment, Bek began to press for stricter harvesting controls. In 1969 nearly 2,000 tonnes of SPB oil had been produced, accounting for a quarter of Ulu Bernam's oil sales by weight, but the operation had made a net loss. This was because the FFA level in SPB oil had to be below 2 per cent when it left the factory, and so the extraction rate of palm oil from the harvested fruit tended to be correspondingly low. The trade-off which Axel's factory overhauls had done so much to ease in the 1950s had returned with a vengeance. The extension of Speldewinde's gantry system, allied to the use of tractor-trailers to take the fruit from tree to railside, became an urgent priority. Ecological factors limited the use of this system at Ulu Bernam, but as tractor-trailers took over at Jendarata, more bullocks and carts were released for service on the up-river estate. Better field transport gradually reduced the fruit-bruising that was a root cause of high FFA levels. Beyond this, more accurate identification of ripe fruit was needed so as to minimize both FFA and wastage. From 1970, a new harvesting system was set up at Ulu Bernam, whereby the fruit collectors separated bunches and loose fruit into two categories, and the sub-standard material was kept apart from the main crop for separate processing after arrival at the mill.[32]

In April 1971 Ole Schwensen retired and was succeeded as United Plantations' chief executive by Børge Bek-Nielsen, using the new title of senior executive director. By this time Bek was confident that SPB oil production was a viable venture, and Olof Grut supported him, telling the shareholders that the new oil carried 'a worthwhile premium'. Special production lines had just been built for the venture, using three main means to minimize oxidation. Steel replaced copper and brass in the pipes and valves; temperature was strictly controlled; and contact between the oil and the outside atmosphere was avoided. The same principles were applied to the design of the special tanks used for storage and transportation. The production lines themselves, together with Krish's new quality control laboratory, were shown proudly to the shareholders in a six-page photofeature attached to the Annual Report for 1970, which was written in spring 1971. The feature emphasized the growing variety of edible uses for palm oil, ranging from margarine through bakery shortenings to frying and salad oils. It also showed a keen awareness that the immediate customers for United Plantations' crude oil were the Western refineries which processed it into forms suitable for edible use. Krish's new laboratory included a complete refining unit within which the performance of the oil could be monitored as it went through the successive stages of neutralizing, bleaching and deodorizing. In this way United Plantations aimed to ensure customer satisfaction even before the oil had left the factory.[33]

BEK AT THE HELM

By the time Bek became senior executive director in 1971, he was already a powerful member of the United Plantations board, and from now on he came to dominate the process of company-level policy-making. Bek had first joined the board in 1968, as an alternate for Rolf Grut; and following J.H. Reid's retirement in 1969, he and the company secretary Leo Ebbesen had joined Ole Schwensen as full directors. As of June 1970, the board therefore had eleven members. Olof Grut, who was to remain chairman until June 1978, led the way together with S.T. Westenholz, who remained vice-chairman until September 1972. Other long-standing members included G.D. Craig, Rolf Grut, Benny Olsen, W.J. Huntsman, Eggert Benzon and P.B. Heilmann. However, for the first time there were now three executive directors resident in Malaysia: Schwensen, Ebbesen and Bek-Nielsen. Also for the first time in June 1970, the company's Annual General Meeting was held at Jendarata, rather than in Copenhagen.[34]

The balance of power thus shifted decisively in 1970, and it continued moving away from Copenhagen and towards Jendarata during the next few years. The retirements of Ole Schwensen and Poul Bent Heilmann in 1971 were followed by the election of just one new board member, Ken Stimpson, who became the new executive director (planting). In 1972, S.T. Westenholz and

Benny Olsen left the board, and again just one new member joined: the first Malaysian to do so, Tan Sri Datuk Haji C.M. Yusuf, who tragically died just three years later in a car accident and was succeeded by Datuk Mohammed Pilus bin Yusoh. Finally, when G.D. Craig retired in 1973, the new balance of the eight-man board was settled with the selection of Knud Gyldenstierne Sehested, a Dane based in Malaysia and, as a civil engineer, a long-standing friend and business ally of Bek-Nielsen's. The board now consisted of two men with long personal experience of, and a deep loyalty to, Malaysia (the Grut brothers); three senior executives resident in Malaysia (Bek, Stimpson and, until December 1976, Leo Ebbesen, who then retired and was succeeded in January 1978 by the chief engineer, J. Svensson and then, from 1981, H.K. Jørgensen); two other Malaysian residents (C.M. Yusuf and then Mohd. Pilus; and Sehested); the lawyer W.J. Huntsman and the Danish shareholders' representative, Eggert Benzon. In June 1978, when Olof retired, even the chairmanship of the board shifted to Malaysia, and for the first time the roles of chairman and chief executive were combined in the person of Børge Bek-Nielsen. Knud Sehested was elected as vice-chairman and, again for the first time, both the chairman and vice-chairman of the company had their main homes in Malaysia. The link with Denmark was by no means lost, however, as both men retained homes in that country, too. Even when he became rich through the success of United Plantations under his leadership, Bek remained a man of few extravagances, but there was one striking exception. As soon as he was able, he bought the most beautiful house in the Jutland town of Holstebro which he had always admired and longed to own when delivering newspapers to it in his boyhood.[35]

With Bek at the helm, and following the Ecuadorean misadventure which had inclined the Copenhagen shareholders to look more kindly upon Malaysia, United Plantations began to focus its corporate energies even more clearly upon the challenges of innovation and expansion within the palm oil industry. In 1971 and the years which followed, the quest for quality remained the keynote of company policy, and Bek continued to encourage his engineers to design with high bleachability in mind. Hans Jørgensen's vacuum driers, developed in 1971, proved a highly successful innovation. They enabled the temperature of the palm oil to be strictly controlled, and air exposure to be kept to a minimum, during the final stage of purification. Marshall Pike of Harrisons & Crosfield had been an early advocate of this idea, but United Plantations was the first company to put it into practice. Industry rivals soon followed suit, however, and vacuum driers became the Malaysian norm. Meanwhile, United Plantations' engineers began to use stainless steel for an ever-greater proportion of the machines made within their workshops, including the single-screw press developed at Ulu Bernam in 1976–78. Once again, the practice quickly spread within the industry, but Bek remained its most thorough exponent, and by the late 1980s the extensive use of stainless steel had become a United Plantations' hallmark.[36]

Not content with developing advanced production techniques and rigorous methods of quality control within his factories, Bek encouraged his staff to go further and to consider how their oil's high quality could be made apparent to overseas buyers, who had no chance to see United Plantations' operations at first hand. The measure of peroxide value developed by the Mongana researchers, and the 'Totox' index devised by Harrisons & Crosfield, provided a good foundation on which to build but were not in themselves direct measures of bleachability, one of the most important qualities from the refiner's point of view. J.A. Cornelius of the Tropical Products Institute had done some pioneering work in the late 1960s on such a direct measure, and from 1971 Krish pursued this line of enquiry with vigour. By 1975 he had developed the Bernam Bleachability Test, details of which were published to widespread acclaim in the *Journal of the American Oil Chemists' Society*. Many other tests were developed by both producers and refiners during the mid 1970s, but Krish's was one of only two selected as a possible basis for a national standard method by the Technical Research Committee of the Malaysian Oil Palm Growers' Council in 1979. The second of these two, developed by the International Association of Seed Crushers, represented a slight variation on Krish's basic technique. Clearly Krish had made a fundamental contribution to the development of industry-wide quality standards and test measures, and this was recognized in the 1980s when he was appointed chairman of the Technical Committee on Vegetable Oils of the Standards Industrial Research Institute of Malaysia.[37]

Børge Bek-Nielsen approved heartily of Krish's involvement in developing industry-wide standards and serving on national committees, for he believed strongly that the quest for quality should be not only continuous but also cooperative. He never lost sight of the fact that all of Malaysia's palm oil needed to be of demonstrably high quality, if it were to sell in bulk at high prices on the world market. Like Rolf Grut in his early work on the Tenera palm, Bek also recognized the value of ideas shared with him by colleagues in other firms and was keen to publish findings in his turn. He gave no fewer than three papers at the

Incorporated Society of Planters' 1969 quality conference, and followed these up at the society's 1976 conference with a comprehensive survey of quality preservation and testing methods. The international journal *Oléagineux* republished two of these pieces, which have become classic references on the subject.[38]

These and Bek's other publications contributed strongly to the free exchange of ideas, which he continues to encourage through the work of the Tan Sri Dato' Seri B. Bek-Nielsen Foundation. Set up in 1995, the foundation provides fellowships and grants to individuals and institutions for the promotion of oils and fats science and technology. It is administered by the Malaysian Oil Scientists' and Technologists' Association (MOSTA), which was itself set up in 1989 to promote the professional development of members throughout the Asia-Pacific region by organizing teach-ins, short courses, symposia, workshops and other scientific meetings. MOSTA's role here is very similar to that of the Incorporated Society of Planters (ISP), except that instead of focusing its educational work on the topics of plant breeding and field operations, it focuses on processing technology. Like the ISP, MOSTA encourages its members to exchange ideas not only with one another but also with colleagues abroad. MOSTA is a member of the International Society for Fat Research (ISF) and encourages Malaysian participation in the ISF's annual World Congress and Exhibitions, as well as organizing its own annual Oils and Fats International Congress in Kuala Lumpur, which regularly attracts participants from over 30 countries. A further highlight of the MOSTA calendar is the annual Bek-Nielsen Foundation Lecture Series, at which an eminent policy-maker, economist or food scientist goes on tour to Sabah, Sarawak and Johore, as well as Kuala Lumpur.[39]

In October 2002 MOSTA elected Bek-Nielsen to an Honorary Fellowship, its highest award, presented to him at a special banquet by Dato' Seri Dr Lim Keng Yaik, Malaysia's minister of primary industries. The award was made in recognition of Bek's contribution not only to MOSTA's work but also to the overall development of Malaysia's palm oil industry. Through the foundation, as through the publication of his own findings on palm oil quality, Bek-Nielsen has encouraged the remarkable practice of inter-company research co-operation which has, over many decades, remained one of the hallmarks of Malaysia's innovative plantation industry. He has also strengthened United Plantations' claim to a central place in the history of innovation, not only through his unending quest for quality but also through his bold championing of an initially unpopular cause: the setting up of local refineries.[40]

Although he never stopped looking for ways to improve the quality of United Plantations' crude palm oil, Bek was not content to pursue this strategy to the exclusion of all others. He knew that the development of SPB branded oil was essentially a 'me-too' innovation, and he could never be satisfied with those. Furthermore, there was limited scope for further innovation at mill level following the big breakthroughs of the 1950s and 1960s. In the two decades which followed, Hans Jørgensen of United Plantations was not alone in directing his most innovative efforts towards the processing of bunch waste and mill effluent, rather than of palm oil itself. Industry observers began to notice in the early 1990s that crude palm oil processing had reached a technological plateau. Between 1986 and 1990 the average oil extraction rate for all mills in Peninsular Malaysia had held steady at 19.6 per cent, and worse was to follow. In the early 1990s this rate began to fall, averaging just 18.5 per cent in 1993. This was only a very little better than the rate which Axel Lindquist had achieved at Ulu Bernam in the mid-1950s, using Dura rather than the oil-rich Tenera fruit variety. It began to seem possible that mill operators had become unduly complacent, if not slack.[41]

Researchers quickly responded to these concerns about the efficiency of milling practice, and the results of several detailed surveys were compared at national seminars held in 1993 and 1998. United Plantations' representatives agreed with the majority view that the problems did not, after all, occur at the milling stage. Many researchers highlighted the wide variety of problems reported at field level, especially the acute labour shortages which affected harvesting rounds, loose fruit collection and FFB quality. Falling yields were also reported on ageing stands of palms. Finally, many planters linked low yields to the reduction in sunlight which now occurs every few years, when a smoky 'haze' drifts across from Indonesia. Producers did not feel helpless in the face of these difficulties. As will be shown in Chapter 10, they were actively seeking fresh planting materials and propagation methods, and fresh forms of field mechanization. Some of the results of their search, in particular the possible development of genetically engineered palms in association with cloning, may eventually lead to a demand for new milling techniques to cope with new kinds of palm fruit, in the same way that the Tenera palm became associated with the screw press in the 1950s. However, for the time being, there seems little scope for improving productivity in the mill. Now, as in the late 1960s, it would be only natural for a restless innovator like Bek-Nielsen to look beyond the mill towards the next level of palm oil processing and to begin a fresh quest for quality in the sphere of refining technology and end-product design.[42]

Despite problems with the oil extraction rate, Malaysian palm oil production has continued to grow rapidly during the 1990s, just as it did during the 1970s and 1980s. Back in 1969, Bek-Nielsen and his industry colleagues were well aware that this was likely to happen, and that Malaysian producers would need to look beyond the mill and to find fresh ways of improving their share in the world fats and oils market if they were to continue riding the wave of prosperity. Bek's own solution to the dilemma was both radical and highly influential, as will be shown in the next chapter. He decided to break with the tradition of sending palm oil to Europe for refining and to develop further processing facilities in Perak. Palm oil was now to be transformed into an invisible ingredient on-site, leaving Jendarata in the form of fine toilet soaps, cooking oils and fats and eventually in the highly processed form of cocoa butter equivalent and other speciality fats. Through this strategy Bek took United Plantations into a leading position, not only as a high-quality producer but also as a bold innovator and role model for fellow agricultural exporters.

NOTES

1   Lim Chong-Yah, *Economic Development of Modern Malaya* (Kuala Lumpur: Oxford University Press, 1967), pp. 130–132; Harcharan Singh Khera, *The Oil Palm Industry of Malaya: an Economic Study* (Kuala Lumpur: Penerbit Universiti Malaya, 1976), pp. 228–230; H.A.J. Moll, *The Economics of the Oil Palm* (Wageningen, Netherlands: PUDOC, 1987), p. 159.

2   On British palm oil buying, see Chapter 3. On cooking with rations, Marguerite Patten, *We'll Eat Again: A Collection of Recipes from the War Years* (London: Hamlyn, 1990; first published in London by Reed International, 1985), pp. 6–9, 21, 29 and 106–109.

3   M. Leeming, *A History of Food: from Manna to Microwave* (London: BBC, 1991), pp. 154–169; Bernard Davis, *Food Commodities* (London: Heinemann, 1978), Chs 3 and 10; Lim, *Economic Development*, pp. 130–132 and 137; Khera, *Oil Palm Industry*, pp. 228–233.

4   Lim, *Economic Development*, p. 132.

5   Lim, *Economic Development*, p. 336; Khera, *Oil Palm Industry*, pp. 185 and 262–263.

6   Charles Wilson, *Unilever 1945–65* (London: Cassell, 1968), Chs I and II.

7   On the role and character of Unilever: D.K. Fieldhouse, *Unilever Overseas: the Anatomy of a Multinational, 1895–1965* (London: Croom Helm, 1978), pp. 10–13;

interview with Leslie Davidson, then chairman of Unilever's Plantations Group, 7 July 1988. On Harrisons & Crosfield: Peter Pugh *et al.*, edited by Guy Nickalls, *Great Enterprise: a History of Harrisons & Crosfield* (London: Harrisons & Crosfield, 1990), pp. 52–54 and Ch. 7.

8   On Unilever and the Belgian Congo: M. Crowder, 'The Second World War: prelude to decolonization in Africa', in M. Crowder (ed.), *The Cambridge History of Africa*, Vol. 8 (Cambridge: Cambridge University Press, 1984), pp. 15–22; and Fieldhouse, *Unilever Overseas*, pp. 529–531. On food uses of palm oil: Davis, *Food Commodities*, pp. 42–47; Anuwar Mahmud, 'The palm oil industry', *PORIM Occasional Papers*, 1 (1982), pp. 6–7.

9   CONGOPALM, 'Research on production and storage of palm oil: work carried out under the auspices of IRSIA, 1952–1955', 2 vols (mimeoed translation circulated by the Oil Palm Growers' Council, Kuala Lumpur) – henceforth referred to as the Mongana Report – pp. 200–201.

10 Mongana Report, Ch. VI.

11 Mongana Report, pp. 200–201, 221–240 and 327.

12 Mongana Report, p. 250; Hartley, *Oil Palm*, pp. 29 and 685.

13 Hartley, *Oil Palm*, pp. 685–687.

14 Hartley, *Oil Palm*, pp. 685–688; M. Loncin and B. Jacobsberg, 'Research on palm oil in Belgium and the Congo' and H. Jasperson and J.L.R. Pritchard, 'Factors influencing the refining and bleaching of palm oil', in Tropical Products Institute, Ministry of Overseas Development, *The Oil Palm: Papers Presented at the Conference, 3–6 May 1965* (London: TPI, 1965), pp. 85–95 and 96–104. Loncin and Jacobsberg published an earlier version of their findings in America: 'Studies on Congo palm oil', *Journal of the American Oil Chemists' Society*, vol. 40, no. 6, 1963, pp. 18–19, 40 and 45.

15 Sources as previous note. See also S.C. Nwanze and C.W.S. Hartley, 'Factors responsible for the production of poor quality oils'; and 'Final session: general discussion', TPI, *Oil Palm*, pp. 68–72 and 153–160.

16 Carrie Jørgensen , 'United Plantations and Bernam Oil Palms: highlights from a colourful past' (unpublished mss., 1984), pp. 147–164; UPDR and BOPDR, 1946–65 and personal communication from Knud Sehested, 19 December 1999. Report by O.T. Schwensen on the Tropical Products Institute Conference, 3–6 May 1965 and comment by B. Olsen on clipping from the *Straits Echo*: 'Bleachability test for palm oil' 14 September 1967, CC, 1965–67.

17 Interview with Leslie Davidson, 7 July 1988; UBAR, 1966–8; Jørgensen , 'United Plantations', pp. 162–177.

18 Hartley, *Oil Palm*, pp. 24–25; on African events, see S.M. Martin, *Palm Oil and Protest: an Economic History of the Ngwa Region, South-Eastern Nigeria, 1800–1980* (Cambridge: Cambridge University Press, 1988), Ch. 10; and M. Crawford Young, 'Zaire, Rwanda and Burundi', in M. Crowder (ed.), *The Cambridge History of Africa*, Vol. 8 (Cambridge: Cambridge University Press, 1988), pp. 698–754.

19 Lim, *Economic Development*, pp. 130–132; T.L. Mounts, 'Bailey's legacy is decades of fats and oils research', in Y.H. Hui (ed.), *Bailey's Industrial Oil and Fat Products*, 5th edn (New York: Wiley, 1996), pp. xiii–xv of each of the 5 vols; Wilson, *Unilever 1945–65*, pp. 6, 12 and 67–71; K.G. Berger, 'Dynamics of supply and demand for oils and fats', *PORIM Bulletin Special Issue*, November 1984, pp. 21–26.

20 P.C. Cheshire, 'The market for oil palm products with particular reference to the United Kingdom market', TPI, *Oil Palm*, pp. 126–127 and 145–147.

21 As note 20 and, for figures on 1966–68 and 1979–81, Yusof Basiron, D. Moore and Law Kia Sang, 'The UK market for palm oil', in *Proceedings of Workshop on Palm Oil Technical Promotion and Market Development, 15 June 1982* (Kuala Lumpur: PORIM, 1983), pp. 68 and 71.

22 Production figures from *Oil World 1958–2007*, Commodities-Past Section, pp. 20 and 77, adjusted for palm oil as in note 5 above; price figures from *International Financial Statistics Yearbook 1987* (Washington: International Monetary Fund, 1987), pp. 180–181; E.M. Stewart, 'Palm oil – production and consumption', *The Planter*, vol. XLIII, no. 1, 1967, pp. 33–34; editorial, 'Oil palm conference', *The Planter*, vol. XLIII, no. 7, 1967, pp. 290–291; editorial, 'The second Malaysian oil palm conference', *The Planter*, vol. XLIV, no. 11, 1968, pp. 567–568; editorial, 'Palm oil quality and marketing', *The Planter*, vol. XLV, no. 11, 1969, pp. 575–576.

23 UPCA and BOPCA, 1966; UPAR, 1966–72. Each UPAR contains the Chairman's Statement for the meeting held in the following calendar year. Ole Schwensen's role was confirmed by Knud Sehested, who joined the board of United Plantations only in 1973 but who had been involved with the company for many years beforehand as a long-standing resident of Malaysia and executive with United Engineers; personal communication, 19 December 1999.

24 'Company meetings: Highlands & Lowlands Para Rubber Company Limited', *Malaysia*, vol. IV, no. 8, 1967, p. 41; vol. V, no. 7, 1968, p. 36; vol. VI, no. 7, 1969, p. 37; vol. VII, no. 9, 1970, p. 37; and vol. IX, no. 9, 1972, pp. 29–30. Personal background from interview with Henry S. Barlow, 18 April 1989. Symposium proceedings published in P.D. Turner (ed.), *The Quality and Marketing of Oil Palm Products* (Kuala Lumpur: Incorporated Society of Planters, 1969).

25 'Company meetings: The Pataling Rubber Estates Limited', *Malaysia*, vol. V, no. 3, 1968, p. 39; 'Company meetings: Golden Hope Plantations Limited', *Malaysia*, vol.

VI, no. 1, 1969, p. 34; Pugh, *Great Enterprise*, pp. 52–54 and Chs 7 and 9; interview with Marshall Pike, who was involved in work at Camberley on the 'Lotox' brand, 15 April 1987; Hartley, *Oil Palm*, p. 689; G. Johansson and P.O. Pehlergard, 'Aspects on quality of palm oil', in D.A. Earp and W. Newall (eds), *International Developments in Palm Oil* (Kuala Lumpur: Incorporated Society of Planters, 1977), pp. 203–223.

26 UBAR, 1968; quote from interview with S. Krishnan, then production manager, Unitata Berhad, 16 April 1989. Krishnan moved on to the associated company of Aarhus Olie, for which he worked throughout the 1990s.

27 Jørgensen, 'United Plantations', pp. 163–177; UPCA, 1966; UPAR, 1978–2001.

28 UBAR, 1966–69.

29 Jørgensen, 'United Plantations', pp. 174–176; UBAR, 1959–78.

30 Interview with S. Krishnan, 16 April 1989; on Axel Lindquist, see Ch. 7 above.

31 UBAR, 1952–53 and 1967–69; interview with S. Krishnan, 16 April 1989. United Plantations referred to its oil as 'Stabilized Prime Bleachable Oil' but its specifications were identical to those of Unilever's 'Special Prime Bleach': UPAR, 1970 and Hartley, *Oil Palm*, p. 688.

32 UBAR, 1969–75; on Axel and Speldewinde, see Ch. 7 above.

33 Information, and quote from Olof Grut, in UPAR, 1970.

34 UPAR, 1968–70.

35 UPAR, 1971–78; interview with Tan Sri Dato' Seri B. Bek-Nielsen and Axel Lindquist, 15 April 1989. Datin Gadys Bek-Nielsen kindly entertained me for a weekend in her Holstebro home in September 1989.

36 Interview with Marshall Pike, director of technical research, Harrisons & Crosfield, 15 April 1987; UBAR, 1971–78; UPAR, 1989; Hartley, *Oil Palm*, p. 687.

37 On Cornelius's work: clipping from the *Straits Echo* with comment by B. Olsen, 'Bleachability test for palm oil', 14 September 1967, CC, 1965–67; later publications by Cornelius cited by Hartley, *Oil Palm*, p. 741. On the Bernam Test: interview with S. Krishnan, 16 April 1989; S. Krishnan, 'Bernam bleachability test method for palm oil', *Journal of the American Oil Chemists' Society*, vol. 52, no. 2, 1975, pp. 23–27, cited by M.L. Yong, 'Recent developments in the Malaysian palm oil industry', *The Planter*, vol. LIII, no. 1, 1977, pp. 26–33; A.H.G. Chin, 'Palm oil standards in relation to marketing and refining behaviour', *The Planter*, vol. LV, no. 9, 1979, pp. 414–439.

38 B. Bek-Nielsen, papers on peroxides, palm kernels and extraction plants in Turner (ed.), *Quality and Marketing*, pp. 86–105, 161–168 and 169–200; the first of these also published in *Oléagineux*, vol. XXVII, no. 7, 1972, pp. 379–383 and vol. XXVII,

nos 8–9, 1972, pp. 443–446. Bek's contribution to the 1969 conference is described as outstanding by C.W.S. Hartley, review of Turner (ed.), *Quality and Marketing,* in *The Planter,* vol. XLVI, no. 7, 1970, pp. 227–228. B. Bek-Nielsen, 'Quality preservation and testing of Malaysian palm oil from FFB to the oil refinery', in D.A. Earp and W. Newall (eds), *International Developments in Palm Oil* (Kuala Lumpur: ISP, 1977), pp. 159–168, and in *Oléagineux,* vol. XXXII, no. 10, 1977, pp. 437–441; the latter paper is cited as the key authority on quality by Moll, *Economics,* p. 40.

39 Information directly from MOSTA; this organization does not currently have a website but may be contacted by e-mail at malsci@tm.net.my .

40 Bek's championing of the Malaysian palm oil industry has also been recognized in the USA. In 1996 the National Institute of Oilseed Products, based in Washington,DC, awarded him its B.T. Rocca, Sr. Award for outstanding leadership. He is one of only five recipients of this award since its inception in 1985. In keeping with his role of leadership within the palm oil industry, Bek's later publications have often taken the form of overviews of industry trends. See, for example, the keynote address in the 'Milling refining and processing' section of the 1987 joint PORIM/ISP conference: *Proceedings of Conference II: Technology* (Kuala Lumpur: PORIM, 1988), pp. 137–154; and the paper, 'Techno-economic status of the Malaysian palm oil industry' in K. Ragupathy (ed.), *Facing 2020: the Challenges to the Plantation Industry* (Kuala Lumpur: Institute of Strategic and International Studies, 1992), pp. 85–103.

41 Lim Kang Hoe, 'Current technological developments and trends in the palm oil processing industry', *PORIM Bulletin,* vol. 20, May 1990, pp. 1–12; Chow Chee Sing, 'The age effect of oil palms on oil extraction rate in peninsular Malaysia', *PORIM Bulletin,* vol. 29, November 1994, pp. 31–39.

42 Chong Chiew Let, 'Crude palm oil quality – a survey over the last two decades', *PORIM Bulletin,* vol. 22, May 1991, pp. 27–32; T.S. Toh and Y.P. Tan, 'United Plantations Berhad's experience in palm oil mill processing', in Ariffin Darus and B.S. Jalani (eds), *Proceedings of National Seminar on Palm Oil Extraction Rate, 21–22 December 1993* (Kuala Lumpur: PORIM, 1994), pp. 115–28; A.R. Zulkifli and M. Ravi, 'Case studies on the factors affecting oil extraction rate in palm oil mill', in Ariffin Darus *et al* (eds), *Proceedings of the National Seminar on Opportunities for Maximizing Production through Better OER and Offshore Investment in Oil Palm, 14–15 December 1998* (Kuala Lumpur: PORIM, 1999), pp. 257–261.

CHAPTER EIGHT

Adding Value: Realizing an Asian Vision

A BREAK WITH TRADITION?

*B*y the time he became chief engineer for United Plantations and Bernam Oil Palms in 1959, Børge Bek-Nielsen had already become dissatisfied with the established range of strategic options pursued by European plantation companies in Malaysia. To acquire more land and plant more trees, in Malaysia or abroad; to introduce new crops, to improve yields in field and factory, and to improve oil quality so as to meet the requirements of new Western buyers: all these aims were still worth pursuing, but they were not new. As the decade of the 1960s wore on, Bek and his key allies, the Grut brothers together with Ole Schwensen and Leo Ebbesen, felt increasingly strongly that new avenues should be explored. Rapidly expanding Malaysian palm oil output, rising competition from alternative vegetable oils and the obvious limits to overall market growth in mature European economies, all suggested to them that fresh markets should be sought in Asia and new products should be developed to suit them. If the existing European refineries and trade networks could not meet this challenge, Bek felt that producers in Malaysia should waste no time in setting up their own.

In deciding to look beyond the established Western markets, Bek was breaking with post-war tradition, but at the same time he was following in the footsteps of United Plantations' earliest pioneer, Aage Westenholz, who had made his fortune supplying transport and power services to Bangkok. Bek's actions were also rooted more directly in the past through the 1930s experiments of Olof Grut. Olof had tried out a range of further oil-processing techniques at Ulu Bernam, including fractionation and air-bleaching. His sales of bleached oil in drums to soapmakers in India and the Middle East soon grew to such a level that they caused friction within the palm oil producers' selling pool. However, all these initiatives had to be abandoned during the Second World War, and there was no possibility of resuming them in the late 1940s, once the British Ministry of Food had contracted to buy Malaya's entire palm oil output in its normal crude form. By the time the final Ministry of Food contract expired at the end of December 1952, Olof Grut had retired from the East and the Emergency was crowding most other concerns from the planters' minds. Only after the end of the Emergency in 1960 did the time seem right for renewed experimentation.[1]

Now it was Bek's turn to take up the baton and bring Olof's ideas to full commercial fruition. He did so through a whole set of changes – in United Plantations' technology, organization and external relations – which took 15 years to complete but which finally created a new way of competing within the palm oil industry. Just as in Stopford and Baden-Fuller's model of strategic innovation, Bek's actions brought new life to the industry as a whole. Encouraged both by United Plantations' example and by government industrialization policy, many other firms built palm oil refineries in Malaysia in the mid-1970s. Together they developed fresh types of cooking oils and fats designed to appeal to Eastern rather than Western palates and opened up much-needed new Asian markets, ensuring that the country's rapidly increasing output of palm oil could still be sold profitably. Their success has become a source of national and not just corporate pride, providing a rare example from the tropics of industrial growth working to enhance, rather than undermine, the process of agricultural development.[2]

SELLING TO INDIA: BEYOND THE BOUNDS OF THE POOL

Bek's first move towards Asian markets came through the revival of bleached oil production. From 1960 to 1972, his engineers produced substantial quantities of air-bleached oil at Ulu Bernam. The venture had enthusiastic support from Rolf Grut, who was general manager of United Plantations and Bernam Oil Palms from 1956 to 1963, and Leo Ebbesen, who had succeeded Benny Olsen as company secretary to both firms in 1959. Olof Grut also took a personal interest, urging Niels Benzon to sanction the project at the outset:

> A premium of about £4 per ton can now be obtained for air-bleached palm oil. The process which I personally introduced in pre-war days at Ulu Bernam is being revived by Bek Nielsen, and by using the old equipment which is mainly intact, we can now start production at any time.[3]

Just as in the case of Rolf's experiments with the Tenera palm, the revival of bleached oil production was thus presented in Copenhagen as a small step, a matter of seizing a current market opportunity at low risk and low cost; its strategic significance was played down. Nevertheless, it was a potentially revolutionary move, which bucked the main industry trends of the 1960s while asserting the value of ideas unique to United Plantations in three main ways. First, bleached oil production involved the use of a pioneering technique which had been developed in-house; in no sense was it a 'me-too' innovation. Second, the product was non-edible, going against the SPB trend of tailoring products to meet the needs of food-processing companies. Third, the associated sales effort was aimed initially at India, rather than at the established markets of Europe and the United States. In reaching out to this new market, Ebbesen and his sales team immediately found themselves reviving a bitter pre-war controversy. In order to establish a direct sales network, they had to break the boundaries of the powerful Malayan Palm Oil Pool.

During the 1930s and 1940s it would have been inconceivable for a single firm to break up the pool, and even in the 1960s it was essential to proceed with caution. The original co-operative selling arrangements for Malayan palm oil had been underpinned, not only by the protectionist ideas of the 1930s and later by the need to have a common voice in the post-war price negotiations with the Ministry of Food but also by the fact that the firms were committed to co-operation in storage and shipping. In 1932, as detailed in Chapter 2, they had formed the Malayan Palm Oil Bulking Company to lease and operate a bulk oil installation in Singapore Harbour. By making his initial shipments of bleached oil in drums, Olof had avoided the need to use this installation, but his experiments with volatile Indian and Middle Eastern markets had still been viewed with deep suspicion by the other European firms.

At the end of 1952 two fresh developments had significantly weakened the power of the pool, paving the way for United Plantations' eventual drive towards independence. The first was the expiry of the Ministry of Food's final buying contract, which brought an end to central negotiations on palm oil prices. The second was the expiry of the Malayan palm oil producers' lease on the Singapore bulking installation. In 1951, they had already tried and failed to set up a fresh co-operative bulking facility at Port Swettenham, and so United Plantations and Bernam Oil Palms decided to make their own arrangements. They leased a site from the Penang Harbour Board in 1952, and began construction of a custom-built installation which they took into use in February 1953. Guthries decided to continue operating in Singapore, through a subsidiary called the Palm Oil Bulking Co. Pte Ltd, and Socfin set up an independent facility in Port Swettenham. From this point onwards a division emerged between Guthries, which had been entirely happy with the workings of the pool system up to 1952, and United Plantations and Socfin, who were willing to try more independent arrangements.[4]

Charles Mann, a London director of Guthries, quickly perceived the risk of a split and acted to pre-empt it. As soon as the new arrangements for Guthries' management of the Singapore Installation had been finalized in November 1952, he organized a new pooling agreement among the various companies who would still be sending their palm oil there. He suggested that United Plantations and Bernam Oil Palms should make a similar agreement among users of their installation, and then join with Guthries in co-ordinating sales in Europe. This co-operation worked well during 1953, and in April 1954 Socfin decided to join the pool. In November that year a formal agreement was made among all the companies involved.

Under the 1954 agreement, all companies shipping palm oil through the three bulking installations were members of the pool and bound by its rules, but only the three Shipping Parties – Guthries, Socfin and the Danes – had representatives on the Joint Selling Committee (JSC) which determined its strategy. The JSC was based in London and the Danish sister companies were represented on it by G.M. Smyth of the trading firm of Czarnikow, who served as a director of both United Plantations and Bernam Oil Palms from 1947 to 1962. All palm oil sales had to be authorized by the JSC, which kept a record of the terms of each contract. Guthries, as secretaries of the pool, would calculate the average price received at the end of each quarter and arrange for cheques to be passed between member companies to cancel out the variations in actual prices paid. Members were free to make their own arrangements for fulfilling their contracts, but Guthries were keen to organize sales to countries like India through their own channels, taking a commission on each sale. United Plantations' managers disliked Guthries' dominance from the outset but accepted it during the 1950s because of the overwhelming advantages of dealing with large northern European customers like Unilever through a centralized London-based committee.[5]

Meanwhile, in Malaysia the Danish firms spent the 1950s consolidating their relationship with the independent Penang trading house of Grumitt, Reid &

Company. F.H. Grumitt had become a founding director of Bernam Oil Palms in 1927, having first got to know United Plantations as an auditor with McAuliffes, of London and Penang. In 1940 he joined the wartime board of United Plantations and remained a director of both companies until his death in 1946. Two years later his brother Corey Grumitt took his place on each board, serving for 10 years until 1 January 1959. He was succeeded in this role by his business partner J.H. Reid, who served in turn for 10 years before retiring from the board, aged 70, in June 1969. The links between the palm oil producer and the trading house were thus close and long-lasting, with a high degree of trust on both sides. Throughout the 1950s Grumitts handled negotiations on all palm oil export sales, in consultation with G.M. Smyth in London. They also handled sales to local buyers, gaining the JSC's approval for the contract before authorizing the buyer to fill his drums with red palm oil from the Penang Installation.[6]

This system was adapted in 1960 to cater for United Plantations' new bleached oil business, but it was immediately obvious that the adaptations were inadequate. If a large-scale direct trade with India were to develop, it would never be enough to bend the rules of the pool. Sooner or later they would have to be broken altogether. As a founding member of the pool under the 1954 agreement, United Plantations had the power to initiate its dissolution, which Bek-Nielsen famously did in October 1971. In the short term, and at the outset of experimental marketing in 1960, however, neither he nor Olof nor Ebbesen were willing to go this far. Instead, they agreed on a compromise solution: to buy red palm oil from the pool, process it and put it into drums at Ulu Bernam. When Grumitts eventually sold the bleached oil at Penang, they had no need to consult the pool. The new venture therefore brought a limited degree of independence.[7]

The limited value of this compromise solution soon became painfully apparent. Most palm produce was sold on a 3-month forward contract, and all forward sales of palm kernels and red palm oil had to be made through Czarnikow's and Guthries' London offices. The London agents charged a commission on every deal, even if the sale was to an Eastern buyer who would have been willing to negotiate direct with Grumitts. Meanwhile, potential sales to local buyers who lacked London contacts were being lost altogether, as very little produce remained once forward contracts had been fulfilled. One such wasted opportunity was an early contact which Leo Ebbesen made with Manilal & Sons of Penang, who offered a price premium of £2 to £3 per ton for palm oil shipped to Calcutta. From the pool's point of view, the post-war compromise eliminated the knock-on effects of Indian market volatility that had so much irritated Bernam Oil Palms' pre-war selling partners, but for United Plantations, it posed a clear conflict between pool membership and any serious attempt to develop direct trade with India.[8]

United Plantations' interest in India was heightened in 1961 when Olof Grut was approached by J. Jenk, the managing director of Swiss operations for Tata, India's largest business group. Leo Ebbesen had already made contact with Tata Oil Mills Company (TOMCO) of Bombay, reputed to be India's biggest kernel-crushers; and J. Jenk now explained that Tata was considering setting up a joint-venture oil palm plantation in their home country. Olof sent his brother Rolf on two visits to India and, while they eventually decided not to co operate in the plantation scheme, both agreed that there was scope for United Plantations to assist Indian growers through technical consultancy. It was clear at the outset that Indian palm oil production would be designed to serve the local market and so would have to go beyond crude oil processing to yield a range of fully refined products. With this in mind, Olof and Leo arranged for six drums of United Plantations' crude palm oil to be sent to two existing Scandinavian refineries, run by A.B. Separator in Stockholm and Basts Talgsmelteri in Copenhagen. Their aim was to find out whether red palm oil could easily be converted into an edible oil suitable for the Indian market.[9]

Nothing came of this experiment in the short run, but Olof remained convinced that United Plantations should develop closer ties with India. By 1963 the company had managed to negotiate a fresh arrangement with the pool, allowing for forward local sales of crude palm oil. Sales could be made to buyers either in Malaysia, using drums, or in India, through bulk shipment. The pool secretaries in London had to be consulted on each bid, and the proceeds had to be pooled as before, but at least the bids themselves could be made directly in the East. Ebbesen quickly established relations with four Indian buyers: Hindustan Lever, Swastik Oil Mill, Godrej Soap and TOMCO. Sales of both red and bleached oil to Indian buyers continued until 1965, when protectionism halted the trade. Pending its revival, Ebbesen concentrated on developing new trading contacts in Africa and the Middle East.[10]

A NEW VISION: REFINING FOR ASIA

Although India had proved a disappointment as a market, Bek and Olof retained a keen interest in the idea of developing new refining techniques to suit the needs of edible oil users there. They also retained an interest in the House of Tata, which had some striking cultural similarities with their own firm. Founded in 1868 by Jamsetji Nusserwanji Tata, a Bombay merchant-banker's son who had added to his fortune by trading in textiles, the central holding company Tata Sons retained the ethos of a family firm. Like Aage Westenholz, Jamsetji and his successors had a strong social conscience and provided their employees with living and working conditions that met the highest standards of their day. Various philanthropic trusts were set up over the years, returning a share of the Tata group's profits to the surrounding community. The strong emphasis which the Tata group's leaders placed on welfare and community relations appealed to Bek and Olof, who were also impressed by the group's breadth of business interests, encompassing steel and chemicals as well as consumer goods production. Tata had a long history of diversification by means of joint ventures and much experience of working with foreign partners. A final attraction, especially during the 1960s when many African economies were thriving, was that as an Indian company, Tata was well placed to develop links with the Indian trading networks which were important throughout Eastern, Central and Southern Africa. For Bek, to begin palm oil refining with such a partner was to make a conscious bid for independence from the established trading and manufacturing networks of Western Europe. Asian skills and business contacts were to be combined with United Plantations' resources and expertise to produce an enterprise uniquely well designed to develop both African and Asian markets.[11]

Bek and Olof's interest in palm oil refining gained renewed strength in 1968, when the Malaysian government passed the Investment Incentives Act. Unlike the Pioneer Industries Ordinance of 1958, the new act aimed to encourage capital-intensive innovation in old as well as new sectors of the Malaysian economy by means of tax credits in the case of firms which did not qualify for pioneer status. Whereas the 1958 ordinance had stimulated the growth of import-substituting industries, the government hoped that the 1968 act would encourage production using local raw materials and selling to the wider export market.[12]

The act was supported by a range of other measures, including tariff exemptions. Since 1947 all palm oil exports had been subject to an export duty of 5 per cent *ad valorem*, rising to 7.5 per cent from 1965. This tax had originally been designed purely as a revenue-raising device, but from 1968 it was used to reinforce industrial policy. Processed palm oil exports were exempted from the duty, a concession whose impact was only partly diluted by the fact that Western countries tended to impose higher import tariffs on processed than on crude palm oil. For example, palm oil imported into the EEC by industrial users in the early 1970s was subject to an *ad valorem* duty of 8 per cent if it had already been refined but only 4 per cent if it was still in crude form. Malaysian tariff policy therefore cancelled out the effects of EEC discrimination, while providing a modest positive incentive for export-orientated palm oil refining. The policy was certainly needed, for when it was initiated in 1968 only two refineries existed in Malaysia, operated by Unilever and by the Malaysian-Singaporean firm of Lam Soon. Both produced soap, margarine, vanaspati (vegetable ghee) and cooking oil for the local market. There was very little precedent for an initiative of the type which soon took shape in Bek's mind, through which a wide range of processed oils could be produced in bulk, alongside end-use consumer products, for the world market rather than for Malaysia alone.[13]

THE VIEW FROM DENMARK

Seen from the perspective of 1969, the decision which confronted the Copenhagen Directors was by no means an easy one. Should they back Olof, Bek and Ebbesen in pursuing their admittedly risky Asian vision, or could they find a more sensible use of shareholders' funds? The Asian vision rested on two main assumptions: first, that Malaysian palm oil production would go on rising as fast as it had in the previous decade; and second, that the Western market would continue to grow more slowly than Malaysian exports, despite the technical breakthrough represented by SPB oil. As shown in Chapters 5 and 7, both assumptions proved accurate, but this could not have been assured at the time.

The Malaysian riots of 13 May 1969 provided further cause for hesitation. Initial fears of a renewed Emergency were quickly calmed but then replaced by the growing certainty that government policy would never be the same again. The New Economic Policy was finally unveiled by the Department of National Unity in its Directive of 18 March 1970. United Plantations then discovered that, like all the other foreign plantation firms, it would have to accept a short-term curb on its plans for land acquisition and a long-term commitment to share its ownership with Malaysians. As shown in the previous chapter, preparations were already well under way for the Malaysianization of the firm's management, but to share ownership and control was a far more radical step. The decision which was still confronting the Copenhagen directors, of whether or not to back the local refineries scheme, suddenly acquired a more profound dimension. Should the Danish shareholders be encouraged to deepen their financial commitment to a company in which Malaysians would soon be joining them as equal partners at the very highest level? Many of the British Agency House directors balked at a similar prospect, but Olof decided to press on regardless.[14]

In putting his case to the Copenhagen board, Olof had three main advantages. First, by 1969 he had acquired considerable authority in his own right, being firmly established as the chairman of six years' standing who had successfully organized the unification of United Plantations and Bernam Oil Palms in 1966. Second, he was dealing with people who had either a long commitment to Asia, or an intimate knowledge of the pitfalls of investing elsewhere. In January 1969, United Plantations' Board of Directors had ten members. In addition to Olof, his brother Rolf and United Plantations' General Manager Ole Schwensen were committed oil palm enthusiasts. G.D. Craig, J.H. Reid and W.J. Huntsman were all well placed to assess the industry's trading prospects and the Malaysian business climate. Meanwhile, Benny Olsen, S.T. Westenholz, P.B. Heilmann and Eggert Benzon were already beginning to reassess their earlier enthusiasm for African and Latin American ventures, in the light of the experiences recounted in Chapter 4. Finally, from mid-1968 Olof was able to call upon a third, and decisive advantage. He appointed Børge Bek-Nielsen as an alternate director for Rolf Grut, and Bek quickly proved to be a boardroom battler of unrivalled forcefulness and skill.[15]

Bek was under no illusions about the seriousness of the political situation in Malaysia. He had happened to be in Kuala Lumpur on 13 May 1969, attending the Annual General Meeting of the Royal Selangor Flying Club, and had been shocked by the violence, which surpassed any he had seen during the Emergency. Yet he kept his nerve and his will to find a constructive way forward. A quotation from one of his own Chairman's Statements, made in April 1979 immediately after he had succeeded Olof, may serve to illustrate both his eloquence and his enduring faith in an Asian future:[16]

> The investment environment in Malaysia continues to be one of the best in the world ... The rate of inflation in respect of 1978 was kept at 4.9 per cent ... the GNP between 1979 and 1990 is expected to grow by an average of 8.5 per cent per year. The trade surplus has shown a substantial positive balance for many years, altogether a situation which nowadays is foreign to many of the industrialized countries of the Western world

where the consumption seems to race ahead of the production without regard to the long-term consequences.

Malaysia has proven its ability to overcome the lengthy onslaught of the communist guerrillas, confrontation with Indonesia, the internal tension after the 1969 election as well as the upheaval created by the debacle in Vietnam.

The formation of ASEAN, which no doubt will prove to be a worthy and important trade partner to the EEC, should further strengthen the socio-economic development of this strategically central area of South-East Asia, which has the resources and manpower to create an increasingly strong commercial and manufacturing centre for the world to reckon with.

The Copenhagen Directors were convinced; they accepted not only the process of Malaysianization but also the concept of recommitting to fresh investment in Asia within a fresh political context. In February 1970, 'Krish' Krishnan departed on a study tour that was to lay the technical foundations for the Unitata refinery; and in June 1970, United Plantations held its Annual General Meeting for the first time at Jendarata rather than in Copenhagen. In the same year, the Board of Directors began its slow transition from being a Copenhagen board to being a Malaysian board. Børge Bek-Nielsen and Leo Ebbesen became full board members, and together with Ole Schwensen they were given the freshly created title of executive director. The stage was set for United Plantations to embark on the most innovative phase in its history.[17]

REFINING THE VISION

In pursuing their innovative vision, Olof, Bek and Ebbesen relied heavily on their Tata partners; but they were not lacking in technical strengths from within their own firm and its European contacts. The contribution made by United Plantations to the refinery project rested especially on the work of four men: within the firm, 'Krish' Krishnan and John Svensson; and as independent allies, Florent Tirtiaux and his son Alain.

Krish's role was especially vital in the early stages, when he used his own Indian contacts and United Plantations' European links to organize an extensive study tour, lasting from February to May 1970. The primary aim of this tour was 'to study the various aspects of palm oil and palm kernel quality' and find out

236

what the refiners were looking for in the crude product; but Krish also seized the opportunity to investigate the refiners' own processing methods and end products. While in Bombay he was able to gain plenty of information about the making of vanaspati, a shortening which provided a vegetable-based alternative to butterfat ghee. However, once he arrived in Europe he found the refiners more secretive. Many were happy to take him on a short guided tour of their existing facilities but unwilling to discuss techniques in depth or to share their views on future possibilities. His experiences were entirely consistent with those of Olof and Bek in their own contacts with the London owners of Malaysian estates and with European refiners. At this stage, Olof and Bek would have been eager to co-operate in the construction of a big co-operative palm oil refinery at one of the main Malaysian ports, but it was quite clear that neither the British-owned plantations nor the European refineries would join in. The firms concerned were determined to maximize the value of their existing investment in plant and to retain control of further processing within Europe itself.[18]

Krish was not to be put off by the European refiners' guarded welcome. He was determined to find out more about the technique of fractionation, in particular, which he already knew was likely to transform the range of palm oil uses in the following decade. Through fractionation manufacturers could split a fat into solid and liquid parts. The technique had been developed for butterfat in the mid-nineteenth century and had been applied to palm oil by Unilever scientists when searching for a cheaper version of cocoa butter in the mid-1950s. By the time of his tour Krish was certain that almost all the major palm oil refiners were experimenting with the technique, but the topic was 'surrounded by a cloud of secrecy'. One possible means of dispelling the cloud was to deal directly with the manufacturers of fractionation equipment. Krish had time to visit only one, Alfa Laval's plant near Stockholm, but noted that several others existed: for example the Belgian firm of De Smet and the Italian firm of Bernardini. He strongly recommended the purchase of small-scale apparatus so that he could make his own assessment of the new process in the laboratory at Ulu Bernam.[19]

Florent Tirtiaux then came on the scene through the efforts of Bek-Nielsen and Olof Grut, who had long had a personal interest in fractionation and now supported a series of visits to the various European equipment manufacturers. Apart from the big firms, which were developing a range of 'wet' fractionation methods involving the use of detergents or chemical solvents, United Plantations' engineers were intrigued to discover Tirtiaux, an enterprising individual who was building experimental machinery in a couple of barns beside his Belgian farm-house. Tirtiaux based his design for a 'dry' band filter on techniques he had developed for fractionating butter while working as an engineer in the dairy industry.[20]

The Tirtiaux method involved the same initial steps as all the others: the palm oil was heated to a temperature of 70 degrees centigrade to make it completely liquid and then cooled slowly until the hard fraction (stearin) had crystallized. At this point, in the 'wet' processes, detergent or solvent would be added to aid the separation of the stearin from the liquid olein in a centrifuge. By contrast, in Tirtiaux's 'dry' process, no additives were required. The oil was passed over a fine-meshed drum, the band filter, and the olein was sucked through the mesh by a vacuum, leaving a layer of stearin ready to be scraped off the surface. This method involved less waste, less pollution and less hazardous work than the various 'wet' methods. It also had relatively low capital requirements and running costs, benefits which were eventually to make it extremely popular with palm oil refiners world-wide. Bek and Olof were among the first to see its appeal, and they played a key role in encouraging Tirtiaux to develop a full-scale version of his design. The collaboration proved so pleasant that Tirtiaux eventually sent his son Alain out to Malaysia to help with the construction of the fractionation plant at Unitata and to learn from the firm's experience in operating it. As in the case of the screw press, Bek's enthusiasm for innovation as a continuous process, and his ability to work effectively with equipment manufacturers, enabled United Plantations to play a leading role in developing new technology for the palm oil industry as a whole.[21]

By 1971 United Plantations' board was convinced that it would be both possible and commercially valuable to build a palm oil refinery in Malaysia. Bek and his team had developed a complete vision, which went well beyond the simple refining of palm oil – that is, the three basic steps of neutralization, bleaching and deodorization. Bek's vision embraced the use of the latest fractionation technology – to produce high-quality olein for frying and other edible uses, and to incorporate the stearin, together with palm kernel oil and the fatty-acid by-products of the refining process itself, into a wide range of end products, from toilet soap to vanaspati. Bek, Olof and Leo felt confident that this range of products would find a ready market in India and other Asian or African countries; and they knew that, as a founding member of the selling pool, United Plantations had the power to break down the only barrier which could stand in its way.

The Federal Industrial Development Authority, which was responsible for registering companies for tax credits and tariff exemptions, agreed that the new venture was worth supporting. Unitata Sdn Bhd was therefore incorporated on 27 May, as a joint venture between United Plantations and the Tata Oil Mills Company (TOMCO). The Board of Directors, which was chaired by Tun Azmi bin Haji Mohamad, included three TOMCO directors: A.B. Bilimoria, S.Z. Varcie and Dar S. Seth. Bek and Olof represented United Plantations on the board. Finally, there was one independent member, the civil and structural engineer Knud Gyldenstierne Sehested, who was to be responsible for designing and building the refinery. He joined the board of United Plantations itself in 1973.[22]

Under the joint venture agreeement, TOMCO undertook to supply trained personnel from its six well-established Indian vegetable-oil refineries, while United Plantations agreed to make its own engineering skills available and negotiated the purchase of a suitable site from the owners of Teluk Buloh Estate, which adjoined Jendarata. Unitata's authorized share capital was M$5 million, with ownership divided equally between the two founding partners. The government helped to arrange additional finance through loans on favourable terms, with repayment due to begin in 1977, by which time Unitata was indeed making a healthy profit. It was understood that once the firm's financial position was secure, a public share issue would be made through which a third of the share capital could be acquired by *Bumiputeras* (Malays, literally 'sons of the soil').[23]

As soon as the arrangements for setting up Unitata were finalized, Olof, Bek and Leo began to plan further organizational changes to support their strategy. Two new subsidiaries were set up: Bernam Advisory Services, the wholly owned engineering consultancy described in Chapter 6, through which the services of Jendarata's Chief Engineer John Svensson could now be made available to the refinery; and Berta Services, a second joint venture in which TOMCO and United Plantations held equal shares, which was to play a vital role in marketing Unitata's products from 1974. A review of the Penang Bulking Installation was undertaken, and since there was no scope for further expansion on the existing site, a fresh site was found at the Butterworth wharves on the mainland opposite Penang. Construction of a new installation began in 1971, and in 1973 a fresh subsidiary, the Butterworth Bulking Installation Sdn Bhd, was set up to run it. The Malayan Sugar Manufacturing Co. Ltd took a 20 per cent share in this subsidiary, as four tanks within the installation were to be given over to molasses.[24]

On 1 October 1971 the final essential step was taken, when United Plantations served notice of its intention to leave the Malayan Palm Oil Pool. By this action, Bek ensured the dissolution of the pool itself, which took place on 1 January 1972. Several other Malaysian palm oil producers, in particular the FELDA small-holder organization, were delighted with this outcome since it gave them the scope to activate their own embryonic selling organization. The West Malaysian Palm Oil Producers' Association (WMPOPA) had been planned in 1970 and formally registered in May 1971 on the understanding that it would remain a dormant body while the pool arrangements continued. As soon as the pool was dissolved, the WMPOPA set up its own Sales Policy Committee, based in Kuala Lumpur, to replace the pool's London-based Joint Selling Committee. United Plantations joined the new body but had left again by January 1973, dis-appointed by its failure to break with the established marketing methods of the old pool. The other users of United Plantations' Bulking Installations followed this lead. FELDA, while remaining within the WMPOPA, reserved the right to make direct sales to any foreign government or official foreign government buying agency. The WMPOPA itself was dissolved and replaced by the Malaysian Palm Oil Producers' Association (MPOPA) in 1974, under which the monolithic character of the old marketing system broke down still further. In 1980 the in-corporation of the Kuala Lumpur Commodity Exchange was to usher in a new era of competitive trading.[25]

UNITATA IN ACTION

When Unitata was first set up in 1971, it was hoped that production would begin two years later. In the event the project was plagued by delays and cancel-lations. The site chosen for the factory turned out to have extremely fragile soils of recent alluvial origin. After a career in civil engineering spanning five decades, Knud Sehested recalled that 'they had found the softest of all the soft spots which I had come across'. A great deal of time-consuming piling and other measures had to be undertaken in order to make the foundations secure, and only then could the factory itself take shape. No sooner were the walls and roof completed, than the Middle East War and oil embargoes of 1973–74 began to disrupt supplies of machinery from overseas.[26]

These early setbacks cast a shadow over the venture that was never entirely dispelled. The task of making the refinery work profitably proved to be unexpectedly difficult for a whole series of reasons. Yet the venture was immensely worthwhile, not only because it enabled United Plantations to reach new customers but also because it gave inspiration to other entrepreneurs within Malaysia, whose collective effort in creating a bulk edible-oils' refining industry has underpinned the nation's spectacular 1980s and 1990s success in Asian markets.

Production at Unitata eventually began in October 1974, although intractable problems remained with the boiler installation, and the plant was only finally completed in 1976. John Svensson and Alain Tirtiaux played an invaluable role in resolving all the teething problems, working in close association with Dr K.C. Dandona and P.T. Bhide, who had been seconded from TOMCO to serve as director-in-charge and process plant manager, respectively. The Tirtiaux fractionation plant was an immediate success, and further specialized equipment was bought from Gerstenberg and Agger, for making vanaspati and margarine; and from Mazzoni, for making soap. In spring 1975 the manufacture of consumer products began. However, the Indian market was still closed to all refined palm oil products from abroad, so that the venture was unable to make the best use of TOMCO's contacts. Leo Ebbesen, who had been working full-time as managing director of Berta Services since 1974, struggled to find Malaysian buyers instead. In the meantime, he fell back on his European and American contacts and managed to find plenty of willing buyers in these markets. American food manufacturers were especially appreciative of Unitata's high-quality output. Once again United Plantations had managed to make a virtue out of smallness: located just next to the Jendarata mill and within 30 miles of all the firm's other estates, Unitata was able to get its palm oil fresh, and quality was still managed in an integrated fashion through the whole production chain from seedlings to shipment.[27]

In 1975, the first full year of production, Unitata made a profit of M\$7.7 million. Olof reported proudly to his shareholders that the new refinery had been able to take up United Plantations' entire output of palm oil, and that it had built up its own dedicated fleet of road tankers which, in conjunction with the parent company's 'Ulu Bernam' motortanker, had been able to handle all shipments to the Butterworth and Penang Bulking Installations. The only fly in the ointment was that the refinery, for which plans had changed repeatedly in the course of construction and which now had three times the capacity envisaged in 1971, could only count on United Plantations to supply about 40 per cent of the crude palm oil which it required. In 1976 further extensions were made to the plant, but purchases of palm oil from outside suppliers fell well short of the amount needed.[28]

Unitata's turnover, which had been just under 100,000 tonnes in 1976, rose slightly to average 105,000 tonnes a year during the five years which followed. Operating profits revived as well, reaching M$11 million in 1977, and an all-time high of M$13 million in 1978. However, after this the refinery's troubles began in earnest. Profits fell gradually in 1979 and 1980, paving the way for four consecutive years of operating losses from 1981 to 1984. The essential problem was that Bek's vision had been too attractive, too quickly, to people outside United Plantations. Capacity had grown too fast within the Malaysian palm oil refining industry as a whole.[29]

NEW PLAYERS IN A CHANGING GAME

The growth of Malaysia's palm oil refining industry occurred at an explosive rate, very soon after the formation of Unitata. In 1975, Unitata's first full year of production, its output of 84,000 tonnes of processed palm oil products represented approximately 30 per cent of the national total; by 1977 this proportion had dwindled to just 13 per cent. By 1980 Unitata was one of 44 refineries in operation in Peninsular Malaysia, with a combined installed capacity of about 2.8 million tonnes. Peninsular Malaysia's total production of crude palm oil in the same year was just 2.4 million tonnes.[30]

Inevitably, given the unwillingness of the Agency Houses and the European refiners to co-operate in the construction of a few big coastal plants, the development of Malaysia's palm oil refining industry had occurred relatively haphazardly, the fruit of grassroots initiative rather than big-business planning. Such a process was possible partly because of the breakdown of the monolithic pool marketing structure from January 1972 onwards, partly because of the availability of finance from Malaysian Chinese and Japanese investors, and partly because the Malaysian government was determined to encourage industrialization in general, and the local refining of palm oil, in particular.[31]

Under the Second and Third Malaysia Plans (1971–75 and 1976–80) the government renewed its support for export-orientated industrialization using local raw materials, and applied this policy to the palm oil industry with increasing finesse. In 1972 a variable surcharge was levied, above and beyond the basic export duty of 7.5 per cent on the f.o.b. price of palm oil. For every increase of

M$50 above the baseline price level of M$350 per tonne, the duty rate would rise by 2.5 per cent: for example, at an export price of M$400 it would be 10 per cent, and so on, to a maximum rate of 30 per cent at M$700 per tonne. Also in 1972, the export duty on palm kernels was raised from 10 per cent to 20 per cent, which brought an immediate halt to exports of kernels rather than palm kernel oil and cake. United Plantations immediately began to plan their own palm kernel crushing plant at Jendarata, which began operations in 1975. Throughout the period 1968–75, processed palm oil remained completely exempt from export duty, though in practice this did not lose the government much money, as there were virtually no exports from palm oil refineries until Unitata began its overseas sales in late 1974. In 1975, Malaysia exported 960,000 tonnes of crude palm oil and just 220,000 in refinery-processed form, of which 38 per cent came from Unitata alone.[32]

Then, in 1976, as exports of processed palm oil rose to 460,000 tonnes (a full third of all Malaysia's palm oil exports for the year), the government announced a further change in the export duty system. The main industry association, the Malaysian Oil Palm Growers' Council, was allowed to advise the government annually of the current production cost levels for crude palm oil. This would determine the baseline f.o.b. price level below which duty would not be payable. However, above this level the duty rate would start at 30 per cent and rise on a sliding scale as before to a maximum of 50 per cent. This gave an extremely powerful incentive for crude palm oil producers to sell to neighbouring refineries rather than to shippers, and for local entrepreneurs to build fresh refineries. The government also attempted to influence the kind of refining carried out to maximize the value added to the oil within Malaysia. From July 1976, exported palm oil was to be divided into five categories. Crude palm oil (CPO) would be taxable at the full rate. If the oil had simply been neutralized, it would attract a duty of half the full rate. If it had been bleached as well, just 35 per cent of the full rate would apply. The further processing stage of deodorization, which created the fully refined (RBD) palm oil, would bring the rate down to 20 per cent of the CPO charge. Finally, the fractionated forms of RBD oil (olein, stearin and the products made from them) would continue to be completely duty free.[33]

This duty structure favoured Unitata, which could and did undertake the full range of processing operations. However, Unitata was not at all favoured by the pattern of development which now emerged within the local refining industry: that is, by the proliferation of stand-alone businesses, producing straightforward

RBD palm oil for export in bulk. A few of the palm oil refining companies which were set up in 1975–77 did have ties to planting operations. For example, Kempas Edible Oil was part of the Sime Darby Group, which already had close ties to local Chinese and other Malaysian, as well as British, capital; Jomalina was part of the Harrisons & Crosfield Group; Soctek was linked to Socfin; and FELDA had its own refining subsidiary, FELDA Oil Products. However, Jomalina was the only one of these to join Unitata in locating its operations near the estates and their palm oil mills, rather than in Johor's vast Pasir Gudang industrial area, or near the main north-western sea-ports of Penang, Kelang and Melaka.[34]

In the shakeout which occurred once the problem of overcapacity had surfaced in 1980, a further difference appeared between Unitata and its main competitors. Unitata, with its capacity of just over 100,000 tonnes per annum, had been a relatively large-scale operator in 1980, when the average capacity of plants within the Malaysian industry as a whole was 60,000 tonnes. However, in 1981 four of the smaller refineries went out of business, leaving the average capacity of the survivors at 70,000 tonnes. In 1982 ten new plants, with a similar average capacity, came on-stream; but in 1983 the industry suffered a further shakeout, losing 14 of its smaller plants (average capacity: 55,000 tonnes). By 1984–85, the average capacity of each installation had risen to 140,000 tonnes, substantially bigger than that of Unitata. The Malaysian refining industry's total capacity of 5.2 million tonnes was also substantially higher than the nation's total production for 1985 of 4.1 million tonnes of crude palm oil.[35]

Against this background, it is hardly surprising that Unitata made losses throughout the early 1980s. After a brief recovery in 1985–86 when profits of over M$5 million a year were made on its operations, the refinery lapsed into the red again in 1987–89. Nor was it alone in its difficulties. A further three of the smaller plants had closed down in 1986, leaving the average capacity of the survivors at 230,000 tonnes per annum; and several new refinery construction projects which had received government approval were now postponed. Despite this bleak picture, Bek was steadfast in his support for Unitata throughout the 1980s. He perceived the problem essentially as one of too many plants being built ahead of demand, and he was certain that demand would carry on growing and so resolve the problem. Throughout Unitata's darkest times, Bek retained his faith in the strategic importance of the Malaysian refineries sector and in the future of the edible oil and consumer products market within Asia. As the following survey of trade figures will show, that faith was amply justified.[36]

SUCCESS IN ASIAN MARKETS: MEETING THE
CHALLENGE OF SHIFTING SANDS

The long-standing Indian import ban, which was only finally lifted at the start of 1977, taught the Malaysians one extremely valuable lesson: in marketing to Asia it was essential to maintain the ability to switch quickly between countries as some markets closed and new ones opened. Selling to Asia was hard, risky work. Nevertheless, the effort was to prove well worthwhile, for the developing economies of Asia, and later Africa and Eastern Europe, offered growth opportunities on a scale which dwarfed those of Japan and the United States, which had been the refineries' best customers before the Indian trade re-opened.[37]

Just as the Malaysian refineries needed the Indian and other Asian markets, so too did the Asian market need the local refineries. Processed palm oil became much cheaper to import once transport costs to and from the refineries of Western Europe had been removed, and once Malaysian producers began to forge direct links with Asian end users, cutting out commission payments to London agents. Bek lobbied strongly at an early stage to persuade industry colleagues and the government to provide centralized support for such marketing efforts as well as for technical research. The Incorporated Society of Planters put its weight behind the campaign in 1976. Finally, in 1979, the Palm Oil Research Institute of Malaysia (PORIM) was set up. It was financed initially by voluntary contributions from the industry and from 1980 by a tax of M$4 per tonne of palm oil ex-mill.[38]

One of PORIM's first recruits was an experienced food scientist, Kurt Berger, who had previously worked for Lyons of London. Berger was charged with establishing PORIM's Technical Advisory Service, whose officers travelled regularly to different countries, visiting current and prospective customers to get feedback and to offer technical support in their use of palm oil products. New customers could be invited to attend one of PORIM's annual Palm Oil Familiarization Programmes, which from 1984 could be held at the fine new headquarters at Bangi, near Kuala Lumpur, which contained a full range of purpose-built laboratories. The first two permanent Technical Advisory Service bases were also opened in 1984. One was in England, at the Malaysian Rubber Producers' Research Association centre at Brickendonbury. The other was in Karachi, in Pakistan. A further point of contact for American end users was established at the Malaysian Embassy in Washington. Similar arrangements were made with Malaysia's diplomatic missions in Hong Kong, in 1992; in Egypt, in 1995; and in Iran, in 2000. The net result of all these private and public-sector initiatives was that existing Asian customers quickly began to buy more palm oil, and the trade spread to many more countries.[39]

By 1980 the success of the new strategy was already obvious. India bought 400,000 tonnes directly from Malaysia in that year alone, with Japan taking a further 140,000 and Pakistan 120,000 tonnes. The sum total of the three countries' imports of Malaysian palm oil was even greater than these figures suggest: for nearly 30 per cent of Malaysia's palm oil exports, or 650,000 tonnes per annum, were still being channelled through Singapore, apparently to the same pattern of destinations as exports made from Malaysia itself. India and Pakistan may therefore have bought as much as 720,000 tonnes of Malaysian palm oil between them and Japan as much as 200,000 tonnes in 1980. Other Asian buyers bought a further 180,000 tonnes directly from Malaysia and approximately 70,000 tonnes re-exported from Singapore in the same year. Asian buyers therefore accounted for almost 1.2 million tonnes, or slightly over one-half of Malaysia's total palm oil exports for 1980. The corresponding proportion in 1975 had been just a sixth.[40]

Tables 5 and 6 illustrate how the strategy of developing Asian markets continued to work well throughout the 1980s and 1990s. In order to remove the confusing effect of the re-export trade from Singapore, which continued to be important during this period, the exports from Malaysia to Singapore have not been counted as exports to Asia. Instead, they have been reallocated among the various importing regions according to their respective shares of Malaysia's direct export trade. This method has produced a fair approximation of the total quantity of Malaysian palm oil imported to each region. It should also be noted that the figures given refer only to processed palm oil, because the crude palm oil trade from Malaysia had dwindled almost to nothing by 1980. Malaysia exported less than a thousand tonnes of crude palm oil each year in 1982–85, and although this trade began to grow again in the late 1980s, its volume in the period 1992–95 averaged just 50,000 tonnes a year to all destinations, including Singapore.[41]

Within the broad regional trends illustrated in Table 5, a few points of detail should be highlighted. The first is the meteoric rise of Eastern Europe, a region which had not figured at all in Malaysia's export figures for 1975 but where processed palm oil opened up the market in the early 1980s. Sadly, the collapse of the Soviet Union brought the collapse of this market. Growing demand in Egypt, the Sudan and sub-Saharan Africa – like Eastern Europe, regions which lacked

Table 5: Export destinations of Malaysian processed palm oil, 1982–2000
Annual Average (1,000 Tonnes)

Destination	1982–1985	1992–1995	1999–2000
South Asia	1,090	1,570	3,540
Middle East	340	760	820
East Asia	330	1,750	1,750
South-East Asia	70	400	370
ALL ASIA	*1,830*	*4,480*	*6,480*
Western Europe	390	730	1,150
Eastern Europe	270	20	80
ALL EUROPE	*660*	*750*	*1,230*
N. AMERICA	140	200	170
S. AMERICA	0	160	40
AFRICA	120	640	930
OTHERS (includes Australia and Oceania)	150	120	150
WORLD TOTAL	**2,900**	**6,350**	**9,000**

Note: The regions have been defined as follows: South Asia has been taken to include Afghanistan, Bangladesh, India, Nepal, Pakistan and Sri Lanka. The Middle East includes Bahrain, Cyprus, Iran, Iraq, Jordan, Kuwait, Lebanon, Oman, Saudi Arabia, Syria, Turkey, the United Arab Emirates and Yemen. All the other buying countries listed in the Asian section of the *Oil World* statistics have been grouped under East and South-East Asia. Fiji and Papua New Guinea have been grouped with Australia and New Zealand within the category 'Others'. See also note 41.

Sources: Figures for 1982–85 were calculated from the raw data in S. Mielke (ed.), *Oil World Annual 1987* (Hamburg: ISTA Mielke GMBH, 1987), Countries Section, West Malaysia, p. 182. Figures for 1992–95 were calculated from T. Mielke (ed.), *Oil World Annual 1995* (Hamburg: ISTA Mielke GMBH, 1995), Countries Section, Asia: Malaysia, p. 49 and from T. Mielke (ed.), *Oil World Annual 1997* (Hamburg: ISTA Mielke GMBH, 1997), Countries Section, Asia: Malaysia, pp. 51–53. Figures for 1999–2000 were calculated from the Table 'Export volume and value of palm oil by destination: 1999 and 2000' available on the Malaysian Palm Oil Board website, http://www.mpob.gov.my.

Table 6: Regional shares in Malaysia's export trade in processed palm oil, 1982–2000 (percentage of world total)

Destination	1982–1985	1992–1995	1999–2000
South Asia	38	25	39
Middle East	12	12	9
East Asia	11	28	20
South-East Asia	2	6	4
ALL ASIA	*63*	*71*	*72*
Western Europe	14	12	13
Eastern Europe	9	0	1
ALL EUROPE	*23*	*12*	*14*
N. AMERICA	5	3	2
S. AMERICA	0	3	0
AFRICA	4	10	10
OTHERS (includes Australia and Oceania)	5	1	2
WORLD TOTAL	**100**	**100**	**100**

Note and sources: as per Table 5.

a domestic capacity for edible oil refining – filled the gap. Meanwhile, within Asia it was China, rather than India, which seemed to be emerging during the early 1990s as the national market with most potential. Between 1992 and 1995 China absorbed over 1 million tonnes per annum of Malaysian palm oil, completely overshadowing India's annual average of 330,000 tonnes. However, having reached this point, Chinese demand began to slacken, and in 1999–2000 China took just 910,000 tonnes of Malaysian palm oil each year, less than Pakistan which accounted for 1.1 million tonnes, and under half the Indian level of 2.2 million tonnes.

The clear message which emerges from these highly complex trade figures is that demand growth from Asia and Africa was the vital force underpinning the successful growth of Malaysia's palm oil industry during the 1980s and 1990s.

However, specific national markets within these regions, as within Eastern Europe, were highly volatile. Malaysian palm oil sellers had to be able to negotiate the shifting sands of developing-country demand with sure-footed skill if their spectacular success was to continue.

The following chapter will show how Malaysian refiners hedged the risks implied in their dependence on volatile emerging markets by revitalizing their trade with Western Europe. This was achieved through a further series of product and market developments, which for Unitata in particular proved the springboard to fresh success. From the mid-1980s Malaysian refiners began exploring the options of oleochemical and speciality fats production. These activities built upon their core strengths in high-quality bulk oils processing, while adding further value to the output. Often they involved the creation of new joint-venture partnerships with European firms that gave Malaysian manufacturers access both to foreign technology and to new kinds of customer in Western Europe.

At a time when many Malaysian palm-oil companies were loosening their links with European parents under the New Economic Policy, United Plantations was in an exceptionally strong position to build new bridges between the two regions, because Bek-Nielsen stayed on throughout the 1980s and 1990s, working in an extremely harmonious partnership with Tan Sri Dato' Seri Haji Basir bin Ismail, his own replacement as company chairman. Bek-Nielsen was therefore able to continue playing an inspirational role for Malaysian palm oil refiners as they sought to develop new speciality fats at the top end of their product range. He also found himself playing a role which was possibly even more important for the nation as a whole: helping the Malaysian government respond to a fresh Western propaganda campaign that threatened the position of palm oil in its competition with soyabean oil in the key markets of the East. Having achieved national recognition through his technical work on palm oil quality and further processing, Bek now came to international prominence doing something new: speaking up for an emerging Southern-hemisphere nation under attack from the protectionist North.

NOTES

1   On Aage Westenholz and Olof Grut, see Chs 1 to 4 above. On the obstacles to bleached oil sales in the period 1945–50, Møller to Olof Grut, 6 November 1945;

Olof to Grumitt, 1 February 1946; and Olof to Calcutta Chemical Co. Ltd, 26 February 1946, all in BOPMC, 1945–46; Rolf Grut to Benzon, 10 June 1950 and Mann, of Guthrie & Co., to Benzon, 1 August 1950 and 6 October 1950, CC, 1948–51.

2   C. Baden-Fuller and J.M. Stopford, *Rejuvenating the Mature Business: the Competitive Challenge* (London: Routledge, 1992), Ch. 3; T. Kemp, *Industrialization in the Non–Western World* (London: Longman, 1983), Ch. 8.

3   Quote from Olof Grut to Benzon, 24 February 1960, CC, 1959–60. On Grut and Ebbesen: UPDR and BOPDR, 1956–63. On bleached oil: pre-war production volumes are given in BOPDR, 1933–46, but unfortunately there are no matching figures for the later period, only incremental cost statistics in UBAR, 1960–72.

4   Sources for this and the next paragraph: correspondence file in UP's Copenhagen office, 'Formation of Malayan Palm Oil Pool, 1952–60'. See also BOPDR, 1932; UPCA, 1950–55; UBAR, 1952–53.

5   Sources as previous note and, on Smyth: BOPAR and UPAR, 1947–62, and BOPCA, 1964; on Guthries in India: Olof Grut to S. Pontoppidan Møller, 26 January 1954, CC, 1952–58. The number of shipping parties grew in the 1960s. Harrisons & Crosfield, which at first used United Plantations' Penang Installation, opened its own facility at Port Swettenham in 1960 and then gained the full status of shipping party within the pool: UBAR, 1960 and BOP board meetings, 7 December 1960 and 22 March 1961. In 1968 United Plantations formed a subsidiary company, Bernam Agencies Sdn. Bhd., to run the Penang installation and distribution facilities: UPAR, 1968. By 1969 Barlows had also become a shipping party. These developments produced the list of JSC members given by Harcharan Singh Khera, *The Oil Palm Industry of Malaya: an Economic Study* (Kuala Lumpur: Penerbit Universiti Malaya, 1976), p. 278.

6   UPDR, 1920–60; BOPDR, 1927–60. On palm oil sales: Leo Ebbesen, Secretary's Handing-Over Notes, 21 June 1960.

7   Leo Ebbesen, Secretary's Handing-Over Notes, 21 June 1960; Khera, *Oil Palm Industry*, pp. 278–281.

8   Ebbesen to Benzon, 6 January 1960 and Olof Grut to Benzon, 24 February 1960, CC, 1959–60.

9   On TOMCO, see Ebbesen to Benzon, 6 January 1960, CC, 1959–60; on the Tata proposal, see BOP Board Meetings, 11 October 1961, 13–14 December 1961, 21 March 1962, 12–13 December 1962 and 2 October 1963.

10 Leo Ebbesen, Secretary's Handing-Over Notes, 2 July 1963; Ebbesen's strategy in the late 1960s was recalled in an interview with S. Krishnan, 16 April 1989. Unfortunately, the records of UP and BOP, both in Perak and Copenhagen, contain no direct information on Ebbesen's sales methods and contacts after 1963, although

the establishment of UPSA (see Chapter 4) would have given him one easy way of making contacts in Southern Africa. He continued to serve as company secretary of UP and BOP until 1974, and as managing director of Unitata's marketing arm, Berta Services Sdn Bhd, from 1971; but in December 1976, owing to illness, he retired from Berta Services, and as a non-executive director of United Plantations, and was not available to be interviewed for this study. BOPAR, 1963–65, and UPAR, 1963–76.

11 'Transforming Tata', *International Business Week*, 21 March 1994; *Unitata: an Introduction* (Teluk Anson, Perak: Unitata, 1978); interview with S. Krishnan, 16 April 1989; B. Bek-Nielsen, 'Techno-economic status of the Malaysian palm oil industry', in K. Ragupathy (ed.), *Facing 2020: the Challenges to the Plantation Industry* (Kuala Lumpur: Institute of Strategic and International Studies, 1992), especially p. 96.

12 David Lim, *Economic Growth and Development in West Malaysia, 1947–1970* (London: Oxford University Press, 1973), pp. 254–268.

13 Fong Chan Onn, *Technological Leap: Malaysian Industry in Transition* (Singapore: Oxford University Press, 1986), pp. 26–36; H.S. Khera, 'Production and consumption pattern of oil palm products in Malaysia', in ITC, *Market Development of Palm Oil Products: Seminar Proceedings, 27 March–1 April 1978* (Geneva: United Nations, International Trade Centre UNCTAD/GATT, 1978), pp. 38–39; Khera, *Oil Palm Industry*, p. 41; Lim Chong-Yah, *Economic Development of Modern Malaya* (Kuala Lumpur: Oxford University Press, 1967), p. 268.

14 On the New Economic Policy, see John H. Drabble, *An Economic History of Malaysia, c.1800–1990: the Transition to Modern Economic Growth* (London: Macmillan, 2000), Ch. 10 and J. Faaland, J.R. Parkinson, and R. Saniman, *Growth and Ethnic Inequality: Malaysia's New Economic Policy* (London: C. Hurst, 1990). On Agency House responses, see N. J. White, *Business, Government and the End of Empire: Malaya, 1942–1957* (Kuala Lumpur: Oxford University Press, 1996), Ch. 6 and D.J.M. Tate, *The RGA History of the Plantation Industry in the Malay Peninsula* (Kuala Lumpur: Oxford University Press, 1996), Ch. 40.

15 UPAR, 1968.

16 Poul Kragelund, *Aarhus Olie 1871–1996* (Aarhus, Denmark: Aarhus Oliefabrik A/S, 1996), pp. 171–173; quotation from UPAR, 1978.

17 UPAR, 1969–70.

18 S. Krishnan, 'Report on the study tour of India, Egypt and the UK', 20 June 1970; B. Bek-Nielsen, letter to Tan Sri Sir Claude Fenner of the RGA, 11 September 1974; on Fenner himself, see Tate, *RGA History*, pp. 588–590.

19 Krishnan, 1970 'Report'; interview on fractionation with K.G. Berger, 15 September 1995; Unilever's UK patent specification for COBERENE cocoa-butter equivalent, No. 827,172 filed 20 February 1956; Charles Wilson, *Unilever 1945–65* (London: Cassell, 1968), pp. 80–81.

20 Interview with K.G. Berger, 15 September 1995. See also Y.H. Hui (ed.), *Bailey's Industrial Oil and Fat Products*, 5th edn, Vol. 4, *Edible Oil and Fat Products: Processing Technology* (New York: Wiley, 1996), pp. 41–45 and 307–313.

21 Interviews with A. Tirtiaux, 10 April 1989, and S. Krishnan, 16 April 1989. The comparative merits of various refining processes are well surveyed by Hui, as previous note, and J.A. Cornelius, *Processing of Oil Palm Fruit and its Products*, TPI Report G149 (London: Tropical Products Institute, 1983), Ch. 7.

22 *Unitata – an Introduction*; UPAR, 1973.

23 UPAR, 1971.

24 UPAR, 1971–73.

25 UPAR, 1971–74; Khera, *Oil Palm Industry*, pp. 280–284; H.A.J. Moll, *The Economics of the Oil Palm* (Wageningen, Netherlands: PUDOC, 1987), pp. 155 and 161–162. D.H.N. Allott and I.C.H. Wong, 'Price determination', in ITC *Market Development Seminar*, pp. 60–66.

26 Personal communication from Knud Sehested, 15 September 2001; UPAR, 1971–74.

27 UPAR, 1974–76; *Unitata – an Introduction*.

28 UPAR, 1975–76.

29 UPAR, 1977–84. The problem was anticipated by Leong Khee Seong, soon to become the Malaysian minister of primary industries, in his Opening Address to the ITC *Market Development Seminar*, p. 2.

30 UPAR, 1975–77; compare Table 13.1 of R.M. Todd, 'Malaysia's experience in the export of processed palm oil', in ITC *Market Development Seminar*, p. 72. For 1980, see Palm Oil Registration and Licensing Authority, *Directory, Oil Palm Industry 1980* (Kuala Lumpur: PORLA, 1980), esp. p. 2; and Ministry of Primary Industries, *Statistics on Commodities 1986* (Kuala Lumpur: MPI, 1986), pp. 38–41.

31 On the attitudes of investors from different nations, see J.T. Lindblad, *Foreign Investment in South-East Asia in the Twentieth Century* (London: Macmillan, 1998), Chs 2 and 5, esp. pp. 116–118; on government policy, see Drabble, *Economic History*, Ch. 12, and Abdul Samad Hadi, 'Agriculture and industry: towards vertical integration', in H. Brookfield (ed.), *Transformation with Industrialization in Peninsular Malaysia* (Kuala Lumpur: Oxford University Press, 1994), pp. 49–62. Japanese investors were already strongly involved in the Malaysian palm oil refining

industry by 1974: Malaysian Oil Palm Growers' Council, 'Report on Further Processing of Palm Oil in Malaysia', September 1974 (unpublished report; copy supplied by Bek).

32 J.T. Thoburn, *Primary Commodity Exports and Economic Development: Theory, Evidence and a Study of Malaysia* (London: John Wiley & Sons, 1977), p. 165; Moll, *Economics*, pp. 141–142; Malaysian Palm Oil Board, *Malaysian Oil Palm Statistics 1999* (Kuala Lumpur: MPOB, 2000), p. 41.

33 Moll, *Economics*, pp. 156–157; Khera, 'Production and consumption pattern', in ITC *Market Development Seminar*, pp. 38–39.

34 The Palm Oil Refiners' Association of Malaysia (PORAM), *Annual Report, Year Ending 31 May 1989* (Kuala Lumpur: PORAM, 1989); and *Technical Brochure* (Kuala Lumpur: PORAM, 1989). Unitata and Kempas were among the eight founding members when this association was set up in September 1975.

35 Ministry of Primary Industries, *Statistics on Commodities 1986*, pp. 38–41.

36 UPAR, 1981–89; Ministry of Primary Industries, *Statistics on Commodities 1988* (Kuala Lumpur: MPI, 1988), p. 51.

37 On Japan and America, see UPAR, 1974–76, and Table 13.3 in R.M. Todd, 'Malaysia's Experience', p. 75. On Malaysia's palm oil trade with Asia before 1977, see Lim, *Economic Development*, p. 132 and 137; Khera, *Oil Palm Industry*, p. 262; T. Mielke (ed.), *Oil World 1963–2012* (Hamburg: ISTA Mielke GMBH, 1994), Commodities-Past Section, p. 81.

38 B. Bek-Nielsen, 'Techno-economic status of the Malaysian palm oil Industry', in K. Ragupathy (ed.), *Facing 2020: the Challenges to the Plantation Industry* (Kuala Lumpur: Institute of Strategic and International Studies, 1992), pp. 85–103; 'Editorial', *The Planter*, vol. LII, no. 8, 1976, pp. 308–310; *Laws of Malaysia*, Act 218: *Palm Oil Research and Development Act 1979*; 'PORIM –then and now', *Palm Oil Developments*, vol. 11, 1989, pp. 1–6 and '20 Years of PORIM (1979–1999)', vol. 30, 1999, pp. 32–33.

39 Interview with Kurt G. Berger, 15 September 1995; updated listing of TAS offices, *Palm Oil Developments*, vol. 33, 2000, p. 39. PORIM's journal *TAS News* (1986 onwards), relaunched in 1995 as the *Palm Oil Technical Bulletin*, effectively disseminated information from TAS visits to the Malaysian industry as a whole. PORIM also organized workshops and conferences at which information could be shared and later published: for example, *Proceedings of Workshop on Palm Oil Technical Promotion and Market Development, 15 June 1982* (Kuala Lumpur: PORIM, 1983); and *Proceedings of the International Seminar on Market Development for Palm Oil Products, 23–27 January 1984* (Kuala Lumpur: PORIM, 1984).

40 Moll, *Economics*, p. 159. Singapore's role as a bulking centre for palm oil exports to other regions is further explored in W.G. Huff, *The Economic Growth of Singapore: Trade and Development in the Twentieth Century* (Cambridge: Cambridge University Press, 1994), pp. 77, 148, 189, 310 and 372–385.

41 Between 1982 and 1985 Singapore took an average of 670,000 tonnes of Malaysian palm oil for re-export each year; and from 1992 to 1995, an average of 560,000 tonnes. In 1999–2000 the corresponding figure was 380,000 tonnes.

CHAPTER NINE

Building Bridges between Nations:
Two Tan Sris

NATIONALIZATION AND THE NEW ECONOMIC POLICY

*I*n 1982, the moment which United Plantations' directors had been expecting ever since the dark days of the Emergency in the 1950s, and the unveiling of Malaysia's New Economic Policy in 1970, finally arrived. One-third of the company's shares (a controlling interest) was sold by the Danish shareholders to the Malaysian state-owned company Food Industries of Malaysia Berhad (FIMA), and Bek-Nielsen handed over the chairmanship of UP to FIMA's executive director, Dato' Haji Basir bin Ismail. This event was by no means the disaster which Danish shareholders might have feared in the 1950s. The shareholders were paid a fair and mutually acceptable price for their assets, and the company was not even subjected to a 'dawn raid' on the stock market, in contrast to the well-documented cases of Sime Darby in 1976 and Guthrie's in 1981. United Plantations experienced no hostility in the takeover, and no wholesale transformation of its board and top management. On the contrary, the Malaysians were extremely keen to retain an active connection with the Danish shareholders, and a continuing involvement by Bek and his team in the firm's operations. As will be shown in this chapter and the one which follows, Bek and Basir forged an excellent working partnership which lasted 20 years and produced fresh developments, not only in products and markets but also in the field.[1]

As argued in the Introduction, nationalization had been on the agenda for Malaysian politicians ever since James Puthucheary spoke out in favour of it while in Changi jail in the 1950s, and it had been feared by the Agency Houses

Tan Sri Børge Bek-Nielsen

Tan Sri Haji Basir bin Ismail

and other European businesses for just as long. The fact that it was so long delayed can be interpreted in many different ways. Krozewski and Jones' findings on the positive economic and business developments of the 1950s and 1960s imply that moderate Malaysian leaders may simply have shown straightforward good sense in recognizing the real contribution which expatriates could still make in their independent country. Other studies of the political process, for example by Harper and Furedi, suggest that pragmatism on the Malaysian side, and the continuing desire of Britain to exercise power within the region, may have been equally important. [2]

While this debate continues, however, relatively little attention has been paid to the issue of what happened to the businesses built up by the Agency Houses and other formerly European-controlled firms, after they finally underwent nationalization under the New Economic Policy in the late 1970s and early 1980s. Geoff Jones's study of the Agency Houses ends with this event, while Lindblad's survey of foreign investment in Malaysia during the late 1980s and 1990s concentrates on the inflow of capital from new American and Japanese entrants. The capital assets created by earlier generations of foreign investors, and now being managed under Malaysian control, have disappeared from the picture. Yet if these assets were worth nationalizing – as Puthucheary argued – and worth creating in the first place – as Jones has shown – then surely the following question is worth asking. How can the continued value of these assets be ensured, and the successful creation of the next generation of assets be achieved, once ownership and control have been transferred? [3]

One possible answer, which is only one of many but which emerges powerfully from the United Plantations' story as told below, is through continued co-operation. European managers and consultants can learn, as Bek-Nielsen has done, to work with and for Asian owners, as good guests in a foreign country. Many Europeans have continued to be involved with Malaysia's Palm Oil Research Institute (now the Malaysian Palm Oil Board), with plantation and refinery enterprises and with university and business education in Malaysia and Singapore since the ownership changes of the 1980s. The process of co-operation has not ended, even though Malaysians have taken an ever-greater share in the leadership of it. Both sides have much to gain, and both sides can be recognized as valuable contributors in their own right. This certainly happened to Bek and Basir. Both now hold the title of Tan Sri, the highest honour which can be awarded to a non-royal in Malaysia.

BEK AND BASIR: A MEETING OF MINDS

Tan Sri Dato' Seri Haji Basir bin Ismail, who has served for many years as chairman of the Palm Oil Research Institute of Malaysia (and now of the Malaysian Palm Oil Board), first met Bek-Nielsen in 1980, when they were both involved in the inaugural meetings of PORIM's Program Advisory Committee. Both men were of a similar age; Basir had been born in Johor in 1927. Both shared an affection for Britain. Bek's wife Gladys came from Scotland, and Basir had studied agro-economics at Wye College in Kent, after taking his BSc in agriculture at Durham University. He retained a lively friendship with a college colleague, Whittaker, who regularly entertained Basir and his family while they were on their annual touring holiday in Europe. Like Bek, whose marriage to Gladys was exceptionally close and strong, and whose sons have matured into close friends and colleagues of their father, Basir has placed a high value on his family life. Like another long-standing friend, Prime Minister Dato' Seri Dr Mahathir bin Mohamad, he chose not to play golf or to undertake hobbies in isolation from his wife and children. In the 1980s one of his favourite pastimes was working with his son on a small durian plantation close to home.[4]

Beyond these personal similarities, Bek and Basir were united in their passion for Malaysian development in general, and the agricultural sector in particular. After leaving college, Basir served in the Colonial Agricultural Service in Kelantan and Trengganu, and became a lecturer at the College of Agriculture Malaya. This college had been founded in 1931 and was located conveniently close to the Agricultural Department's Experimental Station at Serdang, the site of Rosenquist's pioneering experiments with the Tenera palm. In 1962 the college became a part of the University of Malaya and in 1971 gained full status as the independent Universiti Pertanian Malaysia, with Faculties of Forestry and Animal Science as well as Agriculture, and branches in Serawak and Terengganu. Since the 1980s the Universiti has broadened its scope to include the full range of subjects in science and technology and changed its name in 1997 to the Universiti Putra Malaysia. Basir has retained an interest in its development, and in that of the University of Malaya itself, where he served for many years on the Board of Directors.[5]

By 1970 Basir had moved back from agricultural theory to practice and had shown that he could perform well in the role of state agriculture officer in his home state of Johor. He was then promoted to executive director of the loss-making Johor State Economic Development Corporation, which he soon managed to turn around, acquiring a strong reputation as an effective 'Mr Clean' in the process. He then helped the central government resolve corruption problems within the Rice Marketing Board, and his reputation grew. Soon after Mahathir became prime minister in 1981, he appointed Basir to the bigger role of executive director of FIMA, a government-owned firm which had grown rapidly from its modest origins operating a pineapple cannery in 1972, to embrace a wide range of plantation, processing and other agro-based business activities. FIMA's central aim to apply the most advanced technology and management methods to the business of food production, was to prove well suited both to Basir's own education and temperament and to the relationship with United Plantations as it was soon to develop. Basir settled in quickly at FIMA, where he took on the role of executive chairman in 1985. Meanwhile, the Rubber Growers' Association had entrusted him with the delicate task of managing their transfer from London to Kuala Lumpur. In 1982 Basir became only the second person who was neither British, nor of British descent, to serve as chairman of the RGA. The first had been a Dane, H.T. Karsten, who had served in 1956–57.[6]

By the time that Bek and Basir met, both were therefore well known as effective and honest operators in their respective fields. Basir was directly involved in the nationalization programme under the New Economic Policy, serving along with another conspicuously honest man, Tun Ismail bin Mohamed Ali, on the management board of Permodalan Nasional Berhad (Pernas). Pernas, which eventually came to hold a 5 per cent stake in United Plantations, is the National Equity Fund which was set up by the Malaysian government to invest on behalf of the *Bumiputeras*, and which was responsible for the hostile take-overs of Sime Darby and Guthrie's. As he got to know Bek-Nielsen, Basir became convinced that while United Plantations clearly fell within the general category of foreign-owned plantation enterprises in which Pernas was keen to take a stake, it was a very special case which deserved a special approach. As a relatively small and geographically concentrated operation, it risked being swamped if taken over directly by Pernas in the same way as the much bigger Agency Houses. Meanwhile, United Plantations' distinctive management style held a strong personal appeal for Basir, especially because of its strong emphasis on work-force welfare and on the personal involvement of top managers in all field and mill activities, backed up by the attractive tradition of self-piloted flying visits. Basir quickly realized that the small size and strong engineering skills of the company, together with Unitata's recent focus on food industry product-market development, made it a strong candidate for a friendly approach from his own firm, FIMA. Meanwhile, Tun Ismail steered Pernas towards a similarly friendly approach to the last remaining Agency House concern, Harrisons & Crosfield. In 1982, while FIMA was negotiating its purchase of a controlling stake in United Plantations, Pernas was making the final arrangements for the creation of Harrisons Malaysian Plantations Berhad (HMPB), in which Pernas was to hold a 59 per cent stake and the London-based Harrisons & Crosfield the remainder.[7]

The Harrisons' takeover was handled far more amicably than were those of Sime Darby and Guthrie's. Yet still there was a lingering feeling of loss on the British side, and a growing emotional gulf between London and Kuala Lumpur, which resulted in a change in the direction of fresh capital flows initiated by Harrisons' London board in the 1980s. New Harrisons' plantations were set up, and old ones expanded, in Indonesia and Papua New Guinea, forming part of a trend which, by the year 2000, was threatening Malaysia's position as the world's biggest palm oil exporter. Meanwhile, by the mid-1980s Harrisons' London board was beginning to doubt the wisdom of a plantations-based strategy in general, and in 1989 their remaining 41 per cent stake in HMPB was offered for sale and taken up by a combination of Malaysian, Kuwaiti and other Islamic investors. Harrisons' in London retained its stake in its wholly owned Indonesian plantations subsidiary and refocused its European operations to emphasize the production of food including animal feed, timber and chemicals. By 1997 the strategy had narrowed still further, and Harrisons had sold off its remaining plantation interests to focus on speciality chemicals. Back in Malaysia, HMPB has acquired a new name, Golden Hope Plantations Berhad, and has continued to flourish in Malaysian hands. However, like Sime Darby and Guthrie's, during the 1990s Golden Hope gained an increasing proportion of its profits from the conversion of plantation land to housing and other uses. Recently, Guthrie's has even begun to redirect its own plantation investment flows towards Indonesia, which by the year 2000 was producing 7 million tonnes of palm oil per year, as compared with Malaysia's 11 million tonnes and the world total of 22 million tonnes. These trends stand in striking contrast to the path that was to be chosen by Bek and Basir.[8]

After becoming chairman of United Plantations, Basir refocused his own professional interests more than once. He took on another turnaround challenge as executive chairman of Bank Bumiputra Malaysia Berhad from 1985, and in 1988 he became chairman of the bank's parent company, the Malaysian National Oil Corporation (Petronas). An interest in petroleum led naturally on to an interest in aviation and motor sports and so to the chairmanship of Malaysia Airports Berhad and of its subsidiary, the Sepang International Formula One Racing Circuit. Yet Basir remained an active and interested chairman of United Plantations, as well as of the Malaysian Agricultural Producers' Association, the Malaysian Palm Oil Board and the University of Malaya. He derived much pleasure from his association with all these agricultural and academic bodies.[9]

At United Plantations, Basir was sensitive to Bek's feelings as outgoing chairman, and made it easy for him to continue in his new role as senior executive director. Bek remained in overall charge of the engineering side of the firm's operations, while Basir took on Rolf Grut's old executive role as inspector general (estates). They worked in close conjunction with the two other executive directors, K.M.S. Stimpson who was in charge of planting, and H.K. Jørgensen who was responsible for technical matters. When these two retired in 1983 and 1984 respectively, Bek-Nielsen took over the role of technical director while Peter Cowling was recruited from Harrisons, like Stimpson before him, to take charge of field operations. This team lasted 10 years, until the time came for Cowling, too, to retire in 1994. Basir felt that, of all the many top teams to which he had belonged, this was one of the best because it was exceptionally united and disciplined in implementing its decisions. Differences of opinion would be expressed openly in their meetings and conflicts resolved before the decisions were made. This process was made much easier by the fact that all three were united by a common management philosophy, as well as by their active interest in the details of operations. None of them was ever satisfied with second best, and all believed that honesty and team work were essential. None were afraid of working in tough conditions, and all shared a lively interest in the culture of the various races who inevitably find themselves working together in any given Malaysian field or factory setting. Peter Cowling has enjoyed a long and happy marriage to Frances, a Malaysian of Indian background, the very kind of union which was frowned upon within the Agency Houses but which fitted in perfectly with the culture of United Plantations under Bek and Basir. The Cowlings' son has since married Gladys Bek-Nielsen's daughter.[10]

Apart from these key executive directors, the new Board of United Plantations Berhad, as established when FIMA acquired its controlling interest on 9 July 1982, had two non-executive directors. Tuan Haji (Tan Sri since 1996)

Ahmad Azizuddin bin Haji Zainal Abidin, a mineral engineer by profession who was speaker of the Perak State Legislative Council from 1978 to 1982 and state assemblyman of Belanja District during the four following years, joined Tan Sri Basir in representing the interests of *Bumiputera* shareholders. Meanwhile, Fouad Khaled Jaffar represented the interests of the Kuwait Investment Office, a minority shareholder which held between 20 and 28 per cent of United Plantations' share capital during the mid-1980s. Finally, in 1984 a third non-executive director joined the board, taking the place vacated by H.K. Jørgensen. This was Tan Sri (Dato' since 1996) Hashim bin Aman, currently the Pro Chancellor of the Universiti Putra Malaysia and an experienced government administrator. These directors continued to guide United Plantations through-out the 1980s, a period during which there was a very active trade in United Plantations' shares in Kuala Lumpur. Other significant Malaysian shareholders emerged including Pernas, with about 5 per cent of the company's total equity in 1989; the Employees' Provident Fund Board, with 8 per cent; the Lembaga Tabung Angkatan Tentera (Armed Forces Savings Board), also with 8 per cent; and the Lembaga Urusan dan Tabong Haji (Pilgrims' Fund Board), at 3 per cent. United Plantations' own Jendarata Bernam Provident Fund and Workers' Benevolent Fund held a further 3 per cent between them.[11]

Børge Bek-Nielsen found it very easy to work with his new Board of Directors. Basir, in particular, proved to have a character after Bek's own heart – friendly, relaxed, honest and astute, with a flair for business and an eager eye for new crops and technologies. For his part, Bek proved to be not just able but willing and even enthusiastic to stay on. He entered wholeheartedly into the process of building and defending an independent Malaysian economy under *Bumiputera* rule; and his sense of loyalty to the Malaysian people has extended not just to his colleagues on the board but also to his staff and to the work-force. Furthermore, with Basir's backing, he made sure the company retained friendly and co-operative links with the original Danish shareholders. Like HMPB, United Plantations Berhad became in 1982 a joint Malaysian-European venture; but unlike HMPB, it has stayed that way, and has attracted new investment partners from Europe as well as from within Asia. In the remainder of this chapter, the history of United Plantations' links with its European shareholders since 1982 will be traced, and it will be shown how those links have influenced the business. Finally, in the chapter which follows, the story will return to the Malaysian plantations and will show how the era of successful collaboration between Bek and Basir has also been an era of field expansion, during which fresh ecological and economic challenges have been confronted at estate level. Difficulties remain, but United Plantations is at the forefront of the struggle to overcome them.

THE AARHUS ALLIANCE

The years of successful co-operation between Bek and Basir have also been years of increasingly close ties between United Plantations Berhad and the Danish firm of Aarhus Oliefabrik A/S (Aarhus Olie), which Bek had first visited in 1971. Aarhus Olie had been founded exactly one hundred years before, as a palm kernel-crushing operation supplying cattle feed to Danish farmers. A market was found in Lithuania for palm kernel oil, the main by-product of this operation, and the firm shifted its operations there in the 1880s to get behind newly imposed tariff barriers. It returned to Denmark in the 1890s to begin oil production for the infant margarine industry. Before the First World War the firm became involved in joint-venture operations in England and Germany and set up a network of trading agencies in Asia through which it obtained copra, which was then its main raw material. These international ventures were badly disrupted by the war and by the world trading fluctuations of the early 1920s. In 1928 the firm was reconstructed as a purely Danish processing concern with just two trading agencies, in Ceylon and Celebes, specializing in copra. Four decades of modest prosperity followed, but by the time of Bek's visit the management of Aarhus Olie were feeling ready for more adventures. They had already begun to engage in vegetable oil refining, going beyond the simple operation of copra crushing, and were keen to experiment with new raw materials. They had tried and liked Harrisons & Crosfield's Lotox brand of palm oil, and Bek convinced them that United Plantations could match and even supersede this quality. Thus began a trading relationship which was later to lead to close co-operation in manufacturing and ultimately to co-ownership through a complex set of interlocking shareholdings.[12]

Bek's 1971 visit to Aarhus Olie coincided with his own advance to the helm of United Plantations, as described at the end of Chapter 7. At that time changes had just taken place in the top management of Aarhus Olie, too. In 1970 S. Christian Mellerup, an engineer who had joined the firm in 1944, had become managing director; and Henning F Andersen, who had been involved in the firm's Asian trade since 1947, joined the board as commercial director. Together with their chairman, Georg Loeber, they were ultimately to forge a close working relationship with Bek which was to last right through until Loeber's retirement in 1988. Under Loeber's successor Poul Jensen, the former chief executive of Bruun & Sørensen Energiteknik, the relationship would become even closer, as shown below. However, at the outset Henning Andersen was Bek's main ally, and he had to use all his tact and negotiating skill in order to bring the parties into agreement. In May 1973 Thorkild Bjerglund Andersen, whose wife Mette is the granddaughter of United Plantations' early Director Thorkil Knudtzon, joined the Aarhus Olie Board and he, too, was to play a vital intermediary role at a later stage of the negotiations.[13]

The key strength within Aarhus Olie, which was of interest to both Olof and Bek, was its long-standing experience of linking the process of fractionation to the business of specialty fats production. The inspirational early technical director, Dr M.C. Holst, a chemical engineer who stayed with Aarhus Olie until 1940, had begun applying the process of fractionation to coconut oil immediately on his arrival at the firm, aged just 21 and fresh from college, in 1896. He produced a coconut stearin which he called CEBES, reflecting his hopes that it would become a cocoa-butter substitute (C-B-S) of use to chocolate and confectionery manufacturers. Like the engineers of United Plantations from the 1940s, Holst engaged in a continuous process of experimentation, both with machinery and with different raw materials. By 1930 he had discovered that, when trying to produce CEBES, the fractionation process gave best results if applied to Borneo tallow (*Shorea robusta* or *S. stenoptera;* marketing name, Illipe butter). Aarhus Olie therefore built a new, specialized plant for this activity.[14]

Holst's successor, C.O. Gravenhorst, had worked closely with him at Aarhus Olie since 1913 and so was able to pass on directly to Mellerup the lessons learnt from two lifetimes' experience of fractionation and CEBES production. The two men followed with keen interest the progress of Unilever's 1950s experiments with palm oil fractionation and COBERENE. Mellerup was eager to raise Aarhus Olie's profile within the international oil processing community and so agreed to host the 1971 International Association of Seed Crushers' (IASC) Congress, in co-operation with a neighbouring soya-crushing firm, Dansk Soja-Kagefabrik. Two years later, in 1973, he and Henning Andersen attended the IASC Congress in Monaco, and Andersen introduced him to Bek, who immediately mooted the idea of technical collaboration but was rebuffed, as was Olof when he made a more formal approach early in 1978.[15]

Olof retired from the board of United Plantations in June 1978, but remained chairman of International Plantations and Finance (IPF) for one further
year. He, Bek, and Leo Ebbesen now began the pursuit of Aarhus Olie in earnest.
Following an August meeting between Bek, Leo, Mellerup, Loeber and Henning
Andersen – which was only just saved from total disaster by Andersen's diplomacy
– Olof, Bek and Leo swiftly changed tactics. They applied the lessons learnt in
1976 from the case of Sime Darby, the first of the European plantation firms to
come under Malaysian control, whose directors had been shocked to discover
after the event that the Malaysian State trading corporation, Pernas, had been
conducting a large-scale share-buying campaign on the London markets. Bek
and his allies now embarked on a similar campaign against Aarhus Olie. By the
end of August, IPF had accumulated a shareholding of 25 per cent in Aarhus
Olie, completely eclipsing the firm's previous major shareholder, Provinsbankens,
which now retained its original stake of 12 per cent. Thorkild Bjerglund Andersen
was entrusted with the delicate task of communicating this news to Georg
Loeber.[16]

Loeber's reaction to the news proved remarkably warm and sportsmanlike,
setting the scene for a fruitful collaboration between him and Bek in the years
which followed. In the early summer of 1979 Olof retired as chairman of IPF,
leaving Bek to add this role to his chairmanship of United Plantations; and Bek,
Leo and Erland Thrane joined the board of Aarhus Olie. Erland Thrane, a
director of the leading steel company Det Danske Staalvalseværk, had become
a board member of IPF in 1976. This pattern of co-directorships was eventually
to be completed when Thorkild Bjerglund Andersen and his fellow Aarhus Olie
director, Mogens Absalonsen, joined the board of IPF in October 1981. The
stage was now set for Krish, by now production manager at Unitata, to begin
co-operating with the Danes of Aarhus Olie in developing a fresh speciality oils
and fats production and marketing strategy. The era of Bek and Basir was thus,
from its very start, also the era of the Aarhus alliance.

REVITALIZING WESTERN MARKETS: FROM SOAP
TO SPECIALITY FATS

The underlying reason why Bek wanted to pursue the Aarhus alliance was that
Unitata was still having difficulty sustaining its profits in the face of recurring
problems of overcapacity within Malaysia's rapidly growing palm-oil refineries

sector. As shown in Chapter 8, Malaysia's oil palm industry as a whole had gained immensely from the establishment of refineries, which had underpinned the expansion of palm oil sales into new Asian markets. This expansion had been essential to the success of United Plantations' core business of estate and milling operations, as well as to that of other estate operations and smallholder schemes, as their collective output grew by leaps and bounds in the 1970s. However, the process of capacity expansion within the refineries sector tended to run ahead of itself, outpacing the growth of crude palm oil supplies.

Unitata suffered especially acutely from the recurring crises which arose from this cause throughout the late 1970s and 1980s. The rise of larger-scale refineries closer to the Malaysian coast (especially in Johor) had left this relatively small, inland operation with an enduring competitive weakness in the price-conscious Asian and African markets. The losses made in 1981–84 and 1987–89 reflected a fundamental problem. The big trade that was emerging within Asian markets was in bulk oils, for which only the basic refining processes of neutralization, bleaching and deodorization were required. Unitata's ability to produce high-quality soap, vanaspati and other finished products was of benefit to a narrower range of customers. When the first national statistics of Malaysia's export trade in finished oil palm products were made available in the late 1980s, this trade amounted to just 34,000 tonnes a year, smaller even than the export trade in crude palm oil, which averaged 70,000 tonnes per annum over the same period, 1987 to 1989. Both trades were tiny by comparison with the processed palm oil export trade, which averaged 4,500,000 tonnes a year at that time.[17]

Although the strategy of producing high-quality finished, or end products was not enough to make Unitata profitable in the 1980s, it remained intrinsically well suited to United Plantations' identity as an innovative, tightly focused producer and to Unitata's distinctive strengths of close integration with a high-quality supplier of raw materials and of access to dedicated transport facilities and well-run coastal storage installations at Butterworth and Penang. Unitata had the edge over many of its competitors in its ability to achieve a sustained control of quality, stretching through the whole chain from seedlings to shipment. Unitata's use of fractionation gave it a further competitive strength: the ability to produce a wide range of liquid and semi-solid raw materials, as well as end products like soap and vanaspati, the quality of which could be precisely specified to meet the needs of particular customers. If the Asian market for such products was not large enough to ensure Unitata's success, one obvious option remained: to diversify geographically and develop fresh premium-price niche markets in Europe.

Aarhus Olie proved to be an ideal ally in this strategy, especially because its existing ties were with continental Europe rather than with Britain. In developing his relationship with Aarhus Olie throughout the 1970s, Bek-Nielsen was well aware that the regional market was changing profoundly. Refiners in Britain were reeling from the shock of Malaysia's success in asserting its economic independence. They, and the brokers who supplied them, continued to be appalled, partly at their own loss of power over suppliers – in a neat reversal of colonial trends – and partly because of worries about quality. They were concerned that palm oil refined in Malaysia would deteriorate in storage and on the long sea journey to Europe, so that it would be unfit to meet the needs of their core customers in the food industry unless they engaged in costly further refining within Europe. Concerned that rising costs would put them at a competitive disadvantage, they searched desperately for alternative sources of crude palm oil.[18]

At first, the brokers serving the UK market simply switched their custom from Peninsular Malaysia to Singapore, where they bought crude palm oil from various sources within the region. Immediately, however, this influx of custom provoked a soaring of the local price for crude palm oil (CPO) and unscrupulous local dealers began importing RBD palm oil from Malaysia, mixing it with the scarce CPO from other sources, and selling it on as a 'cocktail' of which the quality was highly unstable. British refiners were highly dissatisfied with this unpredictable product, and brokers quickly found they had to switch to direct purchases of CPO from Indonesia, where oil palm acreages were also expanding rapidly during the 1970s. However, here too they found it hard to buy as much oil as they wanted. The rapid growth in palm oil output that took place in Indonesia – from 0.2 to 0.7 million tonnes per annum between 1970 and 1980 – turned out to be largely absorbed by domestic demand. Seventy per cent of Indonesian palm oil was consumed locally in the early 1980s, and as the refining industry which processed this oil for the domestic market began to suffer from over-capacity, an increasing proportion of the oil destined for export was processed locally as well. Only 50 per cent of the 260,000 tonnes of palm oil exported by Indonesia in 1982 was shipped out in crude form. For this reason, British imports of palm oil from Indonesia never rose sufficiently to fill the gap left by falling imports from Malaysia. Malaysian supplies of palm oil to Britain fell gradually between 1975 and 1982, from 180,000 to 120,000 tonnes of palm oil per annum, and then took a further sharp drop to a new level of 40,000 tonnes per annum, which was maintained throughout the period 1983–85. Yet British imports of palm oil from Indonesia remained static, at an annual average of 60,000 tonnes, from 1982 to 1985. Instead of switching to alternative suppliers of palm oil, British refiners were apparently switching to alternative vegetable oils. As noted in Chapter 7, soyabean and rapeseed oil were gaining ground in the British margarine and compound cooking fat industries.[19]

These trends have been mirrored in the history of the United Plantations Group, since they took the decision in 1981 to establish Anglia Oils, a vegetable oil and oilseeds processing plant based in Hull, England. Anglia Oils was originally set up as a joint venture between United Plantations and Aarhus Olie but has been under Aarhus Olie's sole ownership since 1988. Anglia Oils became extremely successful, and had captured a 40 per cent share of the British palm and lauric oils market by 1999. The only problem was that this market was still small. In 1999–2000 the UK's total annual imports of palm oil from Malaysia averaged just 30,000 tonnes. In order to thrive and grow, Anglia Oils has had to draw on a wider variety of raw materials. It now produces a range of over a hundred different speciality oils and vinegars, organic oils and dressings, derived from sources ranging from apricot kernels through grapeseeds and pistachios to olives and walnuts. These new product lines have been successful both in Britain and abroad, enabling Anglia Oils to win the British 'Grocery Exporter of the Year' Award in 2001.[20]

Meanwhile, in continental Europe, where buyers had never shared in the British feeling of personal affront at the rise of Asian competition, many now came to accept that Malaysia's shift to local processing was both permanent and successful; and European imports of Malaysian palm oil began to revive. Buyers were especially willing to welcome Malaysian palm oil if it came from reliable high-quality refiners, capable of using segregated port storage facilities and dedicated shipping.[21]

The statistics for individual European countries are complicated by the dominance of Rotterdam as an entrepot for continental European trade. However, the picture for Western Europe as a whole is clear. As shown in Table 5, imports of processed palm oil from Malaysia were rising in absolute terms throughout the 1980s and 1990s, and from Table 6 it may be seen that between 1995 and 2000 they even rose slightly in relative terms too. Imports to Denmark, even without taking into account any oil brought overland from Rotterdam, rose steadily from an annual average of 30,000 tonnes in 1982–85, to 40,000 in 1992–95, and 60,000 (double the British figure) in 1999–2000. At least part of this increase may be directly attributed to the success of the collaboration between Unitata and Aarhus Olie.[22]

One of the first fruits of this collaboration was the development of a fresh range of fully packed products which Unitata was able to sell to the growing local urban market. Cooking oil, margarine and shortening were supplemented by top-quality soaps, using the soapstock produced as a by-product of edible oil refining. By 1987, Unitata had obtained the Cussons Imperial Leather franchise and was supplying soap to the hotels of Singapore, Bangkok and Hong Kong. Meanwhile, Krish was collaborating with the Aarhus chemical engineers on the provision of suitable ingredients for a renewed development of their CEBES product line. The Tirtiaux fractionation plant at Unitata was turned to a new use, producing a palm mid-fraction, half-way between olein and stearin, which was ideal for manufacturing a direct equivalent of cocoa butter – even better than a substitute. Meanwhile, experiments began in the local manufacture of CEBES, using the palm kernel oil which could now be supplied direct from Jendarata.[23]

In December 1985 the House of Tata exchanged its 50 per cent shareholding in Unitata for a 3.5 per cent stake in United Plantations Berhad. This transaction fulfilled the original promise made to the Federal Industrial Development Authority in 1971, that 30 per cent of Unitata's share capital would eventually pass into *Bumiputera* ownership; for Unitata now became wholly owned by United Plantations, in which *Bumiputera* interests had already acquired a controlling stake. Yet, because of the Aarhus alliance, the transaction also cleared the way for Unitata's operations to be more fully aligned with those in Denmark. A formal production agreement was negotiated, and in 1987 a fresh plant came into operation, producing CEBES, coffee-whitener and coconut powder in a purpose-built setting. The new products immediately began to earn good profits, and in 1990 the operation was expanded.[24]

The positive results of Bek and Basir's alliance with Aarhus Olie did not pass unnoticed by the Malaysian government. Since 1986 there had been a progressive relaxation of the New Economic Policy's rules on *Bumiputera* share ownership, especially for companies which exported more than 80 per cent of their output. From August 1989 this had been reinforced by a move to encourage privatization, with the aim of encouraging productive investment by both local and foreign entrepreneurs. FIMA was among the first companies to undergo a management buyout under the new policy, in 1991. Tan Sri Basir decided to take the company into new fields including stockbroking and property development, and while raising funds to support these new ventures, he was allowed to sell the remaining FIMA stake in United Plantations back to the Danes. By 1991 the FIMA stake in United Plantations had already fallen to 19 per cent, with other *Bumiputera* interests including Pernas and the Employees Provident Fund Board accounting for a further 30 per cent of the company's total equity capital. The Kuwait Investment Office, another Islamic interest, held a further 17 per cent. However, in an apparently minor trend which only acquires its significance with hindsight, shortly before 1991 the firm's original Danish shareholders, both individually and through International Plantations and Finance, had rebuilt their holdings to approximately 12 per cent of all United Plantations' shares. In 1991, the Malaysian government publicly set its seal of approval on this trend, as Aarhus Olie was allowed to buy up and consolidate the Danish holdings along with FIMA's remaining stake, providing a controlling interest of 31 per cent. Although a variety of *Bumiputera* organizations have retained a substantial collective interest in United Plantations, the Kuwaitis have gradually reduced their stake from 17 per cent to 2 per cent, and Aarhus Olie has been the single biggest shareholder since 1991.[25]

Under the new dispensation, the old partnership between Bek and Basir continued as before, and the pace of change within the Board of Directors was slow. The Kuwait Investment Office retained a representative until 1994, when their stake finally fell below 10 per cent and Khaled Nasser Al-Sabah, who had replaced his compatriot Fouad Khaled Jaffar in 1990, stepped down from the board at the Annual General Meeting. Peter Cowling also retired in 1994, and from 1 January 1995 two new executive directors joined the board: Ho Dua Tiam, who was responsible for planting, and Peter Selvarajah, who had been the company secretary since 1980 and now became the director responsible for finance. The board now contained four executive directors, including Bek and Basir; together with the two established non-executive directors, Tan Sri Ahmad Azizuddin and Tan Sri Hashim. This team remained in place until the year 2000, when Bek and Basir began preparing to hand over their interests to their sons. Carl Bek-Nielsen joined the board in January, to be followed by his younger brother and fellow Danish University graduate in agriculture, Martin,

271

Tan Sri Dr Johari bin Mat

in August. Ahmad Riza Basir, a barrister trained at Lincoln's Inn and an experienced businessman, currently the executive chairman of FIMA and director of several other Malaysian enterprises, was appointed in June. In March 2002 the handover continued with the retirement of three Tan Sris: Basir, Azizuddin and Hashim. Three new non-executive directors were recruited to take over their role in representing the interests of *Bumiputeras* and minority shareholders. Jeremy Diamond, a long-standing Malaysian resident and experienced planter from Socfin, joined along with Dr Sharifuddin bin Abdul Hamid, who retired as a full professor from Universiti Putra Malaysia in 1998, and Tan Sri Datuk Dr Johari bin Mat, who became United Plantations' new chairman. Like Tan Sri Hashim, Tan Sri Johari is a distinguished civil servant with a special interest in university management, having served on the boards of seven Malaysian universities since 1995.[26]

The main effect of all these changes at board level during the 1990s was to reinforce the authority of those with management experience within United Plantations and to consolidate the firm's Malaysian identity. The board built, and maintained, strong links with universities and especially with the two disciplines of agriculture and management studies, including finance. The Aarhus alliance continued to be of vital importance, however, in providing fresh ideas about palm oil processing and new end uses. Unitata continued to focus on finished products to supplement the trade in bulk oils and to support its quest for profitable value added niche markets.

In 1992, further experiments with fractionation, using the very latest Tirtiaux membrane press filters, yielded yet another pathbreaking product. United Plantations' 'Golden Palm Oil', later to be brand-named Nutrolein, retains the original rich colour of crude palm oil while being free of its impurities and saturated fats. The successful commercial development of this 'super-olein', rich in beta-carotene and in Vitamin E, once again put United Plantations at the leading edge of innovation within the industry. More recently, further experimental work on a 'prime olein' has held forth the prospect of a red palm oil which stays completely liquid, even in temperate climates, eliminating the problem of clouding which has so far stood in the way of direct sales to Northern domestic consumers. Other companies have been keen to take up these ideas, especially the J.C. Chang group in Johor, which co-operated with PORIM in launching the Carotino brand in 1997; and Golden Hope Plantations, which has not only launched its own super-olein but has also followed United Plantations' example in developing business alliances abroad. In 1996 a consortium within the British food industry set up a purpose-built plant in Yorkshire, very similar to Anglia Oils and even employing some of Anglia's former managers. Golden Hope's Malaysian refinery, Jomalina, which like Unitata is estate-based and places a strong emphasis on quality, supplies its red palm super-olein and other products to Britannia Foods. Recently, Golden Hope has committed itself even more firmly to European enterprise by buying up Unilever's Dutch vegetable-oil-refining subsidiary, Unimills BV, following on from its acquisition of refineries in Vietnam, China and Bangladesh. While analysing this latest move, M.R. Chandran, the chief executive of the Malaysian Palm Oil Association, identified it as part of a trend headed by United Plantations and Aarhus Olie, with their chain of refineries now extending from Malaysia through Denmark and the United Kingdom to the USA and Mexico.[27]

Table 7: Export volume and export value of Malaysian oil palm products, 1999–2001 (volume: 1,000 tonnes per annum; value: 1,000 Ringgit per tonne)

	Volume				Value
	1999	2000	2001	average p.a. 1999–2001	average p.a. 1999–2001
Crude palm oil	260	400	1280	647	0.9
Processed palm oil	8,650	8,680	9,340	8,890	1.2
Crude palm kernel oil	80	20	70	57	1.8
Processed palm kernel oil	470	500	600	523	2.0
Palm kernel cake	1,250	1,350	1,810	1,470	0.2
Oleo-chemicals	1,010	1,140	1,200	1,117	2.5
Soap	1	2	1	1	2.3
Vanaspati	49	132	156	112	1.6
Margarine	3	6	6	5	2.3
Shortening	45	91	102	79	1.4
Dough fats	2	4	2	3	1.5
Cocoa butter substitute/ equivalent	6	4	13	8	3.0
Red olein	1	1	1	1	3.0
Other finished products	7	11	9	9	1.6
Oil-processing by-products	10	30	40	27	0.6

Note: By-products include sludge oil, industrial-grade palm oil, high acid oils, palm fatty acid residue and other residue.

Sources: Malaysian Palm Oil Board, *Oil Palm Statistics 2000* and *2001* (Kuala Lumpur: MPOB, 2001 and 2002), Tables 4.1 to 4.13; for updated figures as they appear, see the MPOB website (http://mpob.gov.my).

In 1999 Malaysian exports of red palm olein reached a thousand tonnes per annum and stayed around this level for the next two years. Although small, this niche has proved to carry an extremely high level of value added. During this period red palm olein was worth, on average, 3,000 Malaysian ringgit per tonne, as compared with 900 ringgit per tonne of crude palm oil, and 1,200 ringgit per tonne of processed palm oil. Meanwhile, exports of other finished products, especially vanaspati and shortening, have finally taken off, and a substantial oleochemicals industry has developed. The new, and highly complex, structure of the Malaysian oil palm export sector is illustrated in Table 7.

Unitata's success in developing new products with higher value added, and in exporting finished goods like vanaspati and soap to Asian as well as European niche markets, was reflected in the fact that from 1990 to 2001, the refinery consistently made a profit. The segment data provided in United Plantations' Annual Reports, permitting a comparison between the Unitata refinery and the parent company's estate-and-milling operations, makes it clear just how modest this profit was: Unitata's pre-tax profit averaged just 2.6 per cent of turnover, whereas for the plantations' segment the corresponding figure was 38.3 per cent. However, given the industrial context, what is most remarkable about these figures is that Unitata had not only survived but even reached a steady state of modest profitability, averaging M$4 million a year in pre-tax profits through-out the period 1990–2001. The strict financial and organizational controls put in place by Haji Mohd Nordin Abas, Unitata's company secretary, and by the financial controller, Kerk Choon Keng, played a vital part in achieving this outcome.[28]

Unitata's turnaround demonstrates the enduring value of a strategy built on United Plantations' long-established identity: that of a small and agile player. Bek did not even attempt to follow other entrepreneurs in scaling up to enter the oleochemicals industry, a heavily promoted sector within Malaysia's Industrial Master Plans of 1986 and 1996. Recent expansion has brought Unitata's capacity up to 175,000 tonnes of CPO per annum, but this is still small by industry standards: among the 37 palm oil refineries in operation within Peninsular Malaysia at the end of December 2000, the average capacity was 300,000 tonnes per annum. Despite its small size, Unitata has continued to be profitable and has become a showpiece operation of which the whole nation, and not only United Plantations itself, is justly proud. Unitata has figured in PORIM's publicity materials on the industry, and during my stay there in 1989, I found that it was being used regularly by the Palm Oil Refining and Licensing Authority as a model in its training courses on quality management. The refinery which at one time struggled to survive is now an icon of excellence for the industry as a whole. United Plantations, too, has remained an icon of excellence, both within

Malaysia and abroad, featuring for example in *Forbes Global Magazine*'s list of 'The 300 Best Small Companies' in 1999. Meanwhile, Bek-Nielsen himself became increasingly well known, not only as a businessman but also as a spokesman for Malaysia's palm oil industry as a whole in an increasingly bitter war of words with its main foreign competitors: the soyabean producers of North America.[29]

THE 'WAR OF OILS'

As shown in Chapter 7, the discovery of processing methods to remove the peculiar natural taste of soyabean oil had revolutionized the market for this commodity in the mid-1960s. From then on, soyabean oil competed directly with palm oil in edible-oil markets throughout the world. On the home territory of each commodity, the other held only a tiny share. North American imports of Malaysian palm oil fluctuated around a declining trend from 300,000 to 80,000 tonnes a year between 1986 and 1995, while Malaysian imports of North American soyabeans fluctuated around a rising trend, from 30,000 to 300,000 tonnes a year. However, on the European, African and Asian markets the two oils competed fiercely. As Malaysian production grew, and the nation's Asian sales campaigns became increasingly successful during the 1980s, the powerful American Soybean Association (ASA) decided to strike back.[30]

The ASA was well aware of the emotive power of health issues, especially those relating to the growing threat of heart disease in the affluent, over-fed West. Although the incidence of heart disease within America could hardly have borne any relation to palm oil consumption – which was negligible – the ASA decided in 1986 to launch an intensive domestic media campaign designed to brand palm oil as an unhealthy tropical grease. The campaign purported to be focused on the American Food and Drug Administration, which was petitioned to label all 'tropical oils' as saturated fats, but its ultimate targets were the opinion formers of India and other Asian nations, who naturally followed with interest the scientific and media debates of the West. The campaign focused on the characteristics of unfractionated palm and palm kernel oils, blurring the boundaries between them in a way which highlighted the worst nutritional characteristics of palm kernel oil and then implied that these attached to palm oil too. Since, in fact, palm kernel oil has a distinctive chemical composition and a much higher saturated fat content than palm oil, this was a distinctly underhand tactic.[31]

The Malaysian government and the plantation companies were united in their outrage at the campaign. They quickly found that detailed explanations of the difference between palm and palm kernel oils – let alone between the relatively solid, saturated palm stearin and the liquid, relatively unsaturated palm oleins, super-oleins and prime oleins – simply served to bring a glazed expression to the eyes of their listeners. They decided to commission an alternative group of nutritional scientists to look afresh at the qualities of palm oil as a generic food-stuff. Over the years that followed, these scientists have gradually established that the specific type of fatty acids contained in palm oil have a benign effect on blood cholesterol and that the relative solidity of palm relative to soya oil has a positive nutritional benefit. Palm oil does not need to be hydrogenated for use in the margarine or compound cooking fats industries. Unlike soya oil, therefore, it contains no trans isomers when it enters the consumer's mouth. Trans isomers, a distinctive group of fatty acids created as an unavoidable consequence of hydro-genation, have a similar effect to saturated fats on blood cholesterol and may have further undesirable effects on health. Experiments are still continuing to establish the full extent of the health risks posed by trans isomers, but that such risks exist is now widely accepted by Western scientists and equally widely publicized by the Malaysian Palm Oil Board (formerly PORIM) and the Malaysian Palm Oil Promotion Council.[32]

Meanwhile, back in 1986, the Malaysians had to act quickly, without the benefit of detailed research findings or a dedicated organizational support structure. Dato' Seri Dr Lim Keng Yaik, the newly appointed minister for primary industries, relied heavily on the support of Professor Tan Sri Datuk Dr Augustine Ong, then director-general of PORIM, who had in turn been supported by Bek in the early 1970s, when he first began his involvement with the industry. Bek was now called upon to help again. As a prominent member of the Malaysian Oil Palm Growers'Council, which he served as chairman in 1976, 1980, 1984 and 1988, he threw himself energetically into the defence campaign. He joined the Malaysian team which toured America to speak in defence of their product; and on returning home to Malaysia, he conducted a hurried campaign within the private sector to fund the counter-attack. The campaign remained his passionate interest throughout the years 1987–89. In 1988, after the governments of Indonesia and the Philippines had petitioned the Reagan Administration of the USA in support of the Malaysian position, it became clear that no action would be taken to lend American government support to the ASA's labelling campaign.

However, the ASA responded with a fresh media campaign, designed to fix the 'tropical grease' smear more firmly in consumers' minds. Bek joined Lim Keng Yaik in making a series of powerful speeches at American industry meetings which eventually forced the ASA to concede defeat in July 1989. The whole saga was followed with intense interest within Malaysia, where observers relished the spectacle of David defeating Goliath once again.[33]

THE COMPASSIONATE FACE OF CAPITALISM

By the time the 'War of Oils' had drawn to a close, Bek was confirmed in his status as a popular hero within Malaysia. Years of successful innovation and entrepreneurship had already brought him numerous accolades. The Sultan of Perak had awarded him the decoration Ahli Mahkota Perak as early as 1972, which was followed in 1976 by the title of Dato'. HRH Queen Margrethe II of Denmark made him a Knight of Dannebrog the following year, and in 1981 he was appointed Honorary Danish Consul for the States of Penang, Perlis, Kedah and Perak. Further royal recognition came in 1983, when the king of Malaysia awarded Bek the decoration Johan Setia Mahkota in his Birthday Honours. The greatest honours, however, were yet to come. At the conclusion of the 'War of Oils', in 1989, he became Y.B. Dato' Seri B. Bek-Nielsen, and in 1996 he was awarded the highest honour open to a non-royal, the title of Tan Sri.

In Denmark, too, Bek's achievements continued to gain greater recognition. In 1990 he was raised to the rank of Knight of First Grade of the Royal Danish Dannebrogordenen, and in March 2002, by which time he was serving as president of the Malaysian-Danish Business Council, Queen Margrethe awarded him the Commander's Cross of the same order. Forty-five years after *Merdeka* it is a remarkable tribute, both to Bek-Nielsen and to the spirit of tolerance and co-operation which characterizes Danes and Malaysians alike, that it was possible for the same man to achieve the highest honours available to a commoner in both countries. The citation for Bek's Commander's Cross aptly sums up the twin foundations of this remarkable achievement. First come his 'outstanding accomplishments as a businessman', realizing a 'dare to win...*Malaysia Boleh*' [Malaysia can-do] vision of 'prevailing by excelling' – not only for United Plantations but also for the Malaysian palm oil industry as a whole. Second, the citation highlights an achievement which is possibly even rarer: Bek 'has remained true to his high human principles and service to the benefit of both Malaysian and Danish interests'.[34]

Bek's honours may thus be seen as a reward, not only for his concrete achievements but also for his generosity of spirit, his courage, his energy and loyalty and his ability to be a good guest in a nation emerging from colonial rule. He often jokes that in his youth he was 'politically to the right of Genghis Khan', but in the decades since independence he has consistently supported Malaysia's leaders, both in their vision of creating a refining industry catering for an Asian market and in their defence of an emerging tropical economy against the propaganda power of the rich, protectionist West. While always alive to the political risks inherent in his position as a foreign entrepreneur in a newly independent country, Bek stayed on and stuck with Malaysia, as with Unitata, through thick and thin: through years of share swap and shakeout, Emergency, riots and economic reform.

Above and beyond all these virtues, perhaps the most important of all is the compassion which was recognized by his work-force, and their representatives in the National Union of Plantation Workers, when they pronounced Bek the 'Workers' Guardian' in 1982 and awarded him the title of 'Bapa UP' in 1986. They have used these titles to sum up their appreciation of his firm but fair management style, his high visibility on the estate – he continues to live and have his office at Jendarata – and his active concern for their welfare.[35]

Since the mid-1970s, although work-force living conditions have been improving on plantations throughout Malaysia, United Plantations has consistently gone well beyond the industry norm: for example in running an in-house bakery, and an Old Folks'Home with full medical facilities. The company Benevolent Fund, which Bek set up in 1981, provides workers retiring at 55 with a handsome bonus. Free transport to secondary school and scholarships for university studies are also provided for the workers' children, while the quality of the housing, free drinking water, crèches, primary schools, leisure and medical facilities provided on the estates has been nationally acclaimed. For example, in 1997 the workers' quarters on the United Plantations' new Sungei Erong and Sungei Chawang Estates received a national award for excellence. In the same year, the Malaysian Ministry of Health inspected 23 hospitals on a wide range of estates, and only two were judged worthy to continue holding full hospital status, rather than being redesignated as estate health clinics. Both of the outstanding performers were owned by United Plantations: they were the long-established hospitals at Jendarata and Ulu Bernam.[36]

Today, as it passes out of the era of Bek and Basir and welcomes a third Tan Sri – Datuk Dr Johari bin Mat – as its new chairman, United Plantations remains just as proud of its record on welfare as it is of those on profitability and innovation. Bek's successors seem likely to continue to present the compassionate face of capitalism to the world. In the next chapter, we will return to the field and focus on the issues of growth and innovation at plantation level; but the theme of ethics in business will not be forgotten, for in the agricultural growth of the early twenty-first century, issues of environmental sustainability and 'playing God' will be seen to be moving to centre stage.

NOTES

1   UPAR, 1982; J. Faaland, J.R. Parkinson and R. Saniman, *Growth and Ethnic Inequality: Malaysia's New Economic Policy* (London: Hurst, 1990), pp. 139–145; J.T. Lindblad, *Foreign Investment in South-East Asia in the Twentieth Century* (London: Macmillan, 1998), pp. 108–109.

2   J.J. Puthucheary, *Ownership and Control in the Malayan Economy* (Singapore: Donald Moore for Eastern Universities Press, 1960); G. Krozewski, *Money and the End of Empire: British Economic Policy and the Colonies, 1947–1958* (London: Palgrave, 2001); G. Jones, *Merchants to Multinationals: British Trading Companies in the Nineteenth and Twentieth Centuries* (Oxford: Oxford University Press, 2000); see also N.J. White, *Business, Government and the End of Empire: Malaya, 1942–1957* (Kuala Lumpur: Oxford University Press, 1996); T.N. Harper, *The End of Empire and the Making of Malaya* (Cambridge: Cambridge University Press, 1999); F. Furedi, *Colonial Wars and the Politics of Third World Nationalism* (London: I.B. Tauris, 1994).

3   Lindblad, *Foreign Investment*, Chs 6 and 7; Jones, *Merchants to Multinationals*, p. 346.

4   Interview with Tan Sri Dato' Seri Haji Basir bin Ismail, 21 April 1989; *Messages of Congratulation to Y.Bhg. Tan Sri Dato' Seri B. Bek-Nielsen on the Occasion of his Golden Anniversary with United Plantations Berhad, 15th September 2001* (Jendarata: United Plantations Berhad, 2001), contribution by Basir, p. 5.

5   Interview, as previous note; on UPM, see its website (http://www.upm.edu.my).

6   Interview, as note 5; additional details on FIMA from its website (http://www.fima.com.my) and on Basir from D.J.M. Tate, *The RGA History of the Plantation Industry in the Malay Peninsula* (Kuala Lumpur: Oxford University Press for the Rubber Growers' Association (Malaysia) Berhad, 1996), p. 576 note 30, p. 598 note 46, and pp. 600 and 619.

7   Interview as previous note; Lindblad, *Foreign Investment*, pp. 108–109.

8   Peter Pugh *et al.*, edited by Guy Nickalls, *Great Enterprise: a History of Harrisons & Crosfield* (London: Harrisons & Crosfield, 1990), pp. 265–272; Jones, *Merchants to Multinationals*, p. 339. On property development, see M Shanmugam, 'Blessings of a golden harvest', *Malaysian Business*, 1 February 1998; and, on Guthrie's in Indonesia, S. Jayasankaran and Sadanand Dhume, 'Betting the farm', *Far Eastern Economic Review*, 26 April 2001.On production figures: Malaysian Palm Oil Board, *Review of the Malaysian Oil Palm Industry 2000* (Kuala Lumpur: MPOB, 2001), Appendix 53.

9   N. Seaward, 'Malaysia's oil giant', *Far Eastern Economic Review*, 26 October 1989; D. Tsuruoka, 'Slick transition', *Far Eastern Economic Review*, 31 January 1991; 'Basir steps down as executive chairman of Malaysia Airports Holdings Berhad', *Business Times* (Kuala Lumpur), 4 October 2000.

10 UPAR, 1982–94. Peter Cowling was my guide on my first visit to United Plantations in 1987 and has done much both to enthuse and to enlighten me about the company's culture over the years since then.

11 UPAR, 1982–89; further details on Tan Sri Ahmad Azizuddin and Tan Sri Hashim bin Aman from the websites http://www.ijm.com and http://www2.moe.gov.my.

12 Interviews with Marshall Pike, a member of the original Lotox development team and then director of technical research for Harrisons & Crosfield, 15 April 1987; and with Henning F. Andersen, who served from 1970 to 1988 as commercial director of Aarhus Olie, 29 August 1989. See also Kragelund, *Aarhus Olie*. More up-to-date information can be found on the company's website (http://www.aarhus.com).

13 Interviews with Henning Andersen, 29 August 1989 and with Thorkild and Mette Bjerglund Andersen, 30 August 1989; Kragelund, *Aarhus Olie*, pp. 143–159 and 171–210.

14 Kragelund, *Aarhus Olie*, pp. 17–20, 65–67 and 88.

15 Kragelund, *Aarhus Olie*, pp. 109, 148–150 and 175; on COBERENE, see footnote 19 to Chapter 8, above.

16 Kragelund, *Aarhus Olie*, p. 176; *Story of Sime Darby: 75th Anniversary* (Kuala Lumpur: Sime Darby, 1985), pp. 11–12; UPAR and IPFAR, 1978.

17 UPAR, 1981–89; Palm Oil Registration and Licensing Authority, *PORLA Palm Oil Statistics*, No. 8 (Kuala Lumpur: PORLA, 1988), Tables 24 and 30–33 and No. 9 (1989), Tables 33 and 39–42.

18 Interview with Marshall Pike, 15 April 1987; C. Dunn, 'Economics of further processing: the markets', in ITC *Market Development Seminar*, pp. 67–71; Yusof B., D. Moore and Law K.S., 'The UK market for palm oil', *Workshop Proceedings: Palm Oil Technical Promotion, 1982*, pp. 61–83.

19 Yusof, Moore and Law, 'UK market', pp. 68 and 71; B.A. Chapman, 'Commercial importance of palm oil and current problems', *PORIM Bulletin*, vol. 2, 1981, pp. 25–32; Moll, *Economics*, pp. 113–115, 126–128 and 157–159; S. Mielke (ed.), *Oil World Annual 1987* (Hamburg: ISTA Mielke GMBH, 1987), Countries Section, pp. 170 and 182.

20 UPAR, 1981; Kragelund, *Aarhus Olie*, pp. 185–188; 'Company profile: Anglia Oils', *Oils and Fats International*, August 1999, pp. 26–29; 'Local speciality oil company wins export award', Press Release, 12 December 2001, on http://www.foodfrombritain.com with additional information from http://www.angliaoils.co.uk.

21 Interview with Marshall Pike, 15 April 1987; B. Bek-Nielsen, 'Technical aspects of marketing quality palm oil', in ITC *Market Development Seminar*, pp. 86–95.

22 Sources as Tables 5 and 6, Chapter 8, above.

23 UPAR, 1981–87.

24 UPAR, 1971 and 1985–90.

25 Lindblad, *Foreign Investment*, pp. 116–118; Faaland *et al.*, *Growth and Ethnic Inequality*, pp. 144–145; UPAR, 1985–2001; Nazatul Izma, 'Basir's baby turns behemoth: Kumpulan Fima makes tracks to the KLSE', *Malaysian Business*, 1 October 1996; Kragelund, *Aarhus Olie*, pp. 216–217.

26 UPAR, 1991–2001, especially the biographies of all directors provided in UPAR, 2001.

27 UPAR, 1992–96; Marc J. Kokken, 'Super oleins from palm oil fractionation', *PORIM Bulletin*, vol. 20, 1990, pp. 13–20; on Carotino, 'Well-oiled', *Malaysian Business*, 16 September 2000, p. 31; on Britannia Foods, http://www.britanniafood.com and on Golden Hope and Unimills, Seelen Sakran, 'Hoping for a golden pay-off', *Malaysian Business*, 1 March 2002.

28 UPAR, 1977–2000.

29 Interview with J.R. Santhiapillai who worked on both of the Industrial Master Plans, 22 September 1995; UPAR, 1997; MPOB, *Review of the Malaysian Oil Palm Industry 2000* (Kuala Lumpur: MPOB, 2001), p. 51; 'United Plantations (Unitata) – a company profile', *Palm Oil Developments*, vol. 21, 1994, pp. 40–43; 'The 300 best small companies', *Forbes Global Magazine*, 1 November 1999.

30 Figures for 1992–95, as Tables 1 and 2. For earlier years, T. Mielke (ed.), *Oil World Annual 1991* (Hamburg: ISTA Mielke GMBH, 1991), Countries Section, pp. 274–276.

31 Interviews with Dennis Gilbert of the Tropical Growers' Association, 2 August 1988, and with Kurt Berger, 25 March 1987; K. Gurunathan, *The War of Oils* (Penang: Principal Quest Sdn. Bhd., 1995), Chs 1 and 7.

32 'Fats and oils in human nutrition', *FAO Food and Nutrition Papers*, 57 (United Nations: Food and Agriculture Organization, Rome, 1994), p. 5; Y.H. Hui (ed.), *Bailey's Industrial Oil and Fat Products*, Vol. 2, *Edible Oil and Fat Products: Oils and Oil Seeds*, 5th edn (New York: Wiley, 1996), pp. 33–34, 211, 355–363 and 563–581. Regular features on nutrition appear in the MPOB journal *Palm Oil Developments*, in the MPOB's regularly updated *Pocketbook of Palm Oil Uses* and in the MPOPC's booklets, aimed at specific groups of users. All can be obtained from MPOB Europe, Brickendonbury, Hertford SG13 8NL. The MPOPC, incorporated in January 1990, now has its own website (http://www.mpopc.org.my).

33 Gurunathan, *War of Oils*, Chs 3–8; Pamela Sodhy, *The US-Malaysian Nexus: Themes in Superpower –Small State Relations* (Kuala Lumpur: ISIS, 1991), pp. 446–455. Dato' Seri Lim and Tan Sri Datuk Ong have expressed their thanks very fully in their contributions to *Messages of Congratulation*, pp. 2–3 and 8.

34 UPAR, 1972–2001; first and fourth quotes are from the Citation for the Commander's Cross, presented on 7 March 2002; further quotes: on 'dare to win… *Malaysia Boleh*', from Bek himself in an interview on 'Pushing Forward into New Frontiers' with Malaysia's *The Star* newspaper, 13 December 2001; and on 'prevailing by excelling', from Ambassador Lasse Reimann's speech at Bek's 75th birthday celebration, 1 December 2000.

35 The title of 'Bapa UP' is untranslatable but carries overtones of respect, as in 'Big Boss', combined with affection, as in 'Papa'. Z. Phoon, 'Datuk B. Bek-Nielsen – good disciplinarian with a heart for all', *The Planter*, vol. LXIII, no. 9, 1987, pp. 424–428; 'Bek-Nielsen – a life's work' in Malaysia's *New Sunday Times*, 4 September 1994; and song, 'We Love Bapa UP', in *Messages of Congratulation*, p. 49. On 'dawn raids', see Lindblad, *Foreign Investment*, pp. 108–109.

36 Feature on Bek-Nielsen, 'An able manager of men', in *The Star*, 23 January 1989; UPAR, 1997–98; and contributions by Tan Sri Dato' Hashim bin Aman (a UP director since 1984), Jeremy Diamond of Socfin, W.T. Perera of the Incorporated Society of Planters and General Ismail Ibrahim, in *Messages of Congratulation*, pp. 10, 27, 30 and 34–35.

Table 8: Oil palm planted area, United Plantations, United International Enterprises and Malaysia, 1981–2001 (1,000 ha)

Year	United Plant'ns	United Internat'l Enterprises	Malaysia: Estate Sector	Peninsular Malaysia	All Malaysia	UP + UIE as % of all Malaysia
1981	13		591	983	1,108	1.2
1982	13		646	1,048	1,183	1.1
1983	14		657	1,100	1,253	1.1
1984	15		700	1,144	1,330	1.1
1985	17		755	1,292	1,482	1.1
1986	20	1	778	1,410	1,599	1.3
1987	21	1	793	1,461	1,673	1.3
1988	22	4	858	1,557	1,806	1.4
1989	23	7	893	1,644	1,947	1.5
1990	23	9	912	1,698	2,029	1.6
1991	22	9	952	1,745	2,094	1.5
1992	23	9	991	1,776	2,198	1.5
1993	24	9	1,054	1,832	2,306	1.4
1994	24	9	1,154	1,858	2,412	1.4
1995	24	9	1,255	1,903	2,540	1.3
1996	23	9	1,402	1,926	2,692	1.2
1997	23	9	1,498	1,959	2,893	1.1
1998	23	9	1,751	1,987	3,078	1.0
1999	23	9	1,942	2,052	3,313	1.0
2000	23	9	2,024	2,046	3,377	1.0
2001	23	9	2,079	2,097	3,499	0.9

Sources: UPAR, 1980–2001; UIEAR, 1988–2001; K.S. Law, 'Development of palm oil industry in Malaya', *Revue Française des Corps Gras*, vol. 35, nos 6–7, 1988, pp. 287–292; Malaysia: Palm Oil Registration and Licensing Authority, *PORLA Palm Oil Statistics 1988–98* (Kuala Lumpur: PORLA, 1989–99), Tables 1.2 and 1.3; Malaysian Palm Oil Board: *Malaysian Oil Palm Statistics 1999–2001* (Kuala Lumpur: MPOB, 2000–2002), Tables 1.2 and 1.3.

CHAPTER TEN

Growing with the Country

THE PLANTATIONS EXPAND

*T*he era of Bek and Basir brought renewed expansion to United Plantations just as the development of Asian markets was bringing renewed growth to Malaysia's oil palm industry as a whole. In 1980, as shown in Chapter 5, United Plantations had 13,000 hectares planted to oil palm, and accounted for 1 per cent of Malaysia's total area of this crop. By the year 2000, as shown in Table 8, United Plantations' oil palm area had expanded to 23,000 hectares, and a sister company, United International Enterprises, had created a fresh estate in Perak on which a further 9,000 hectares had been planted up with high-yielding oil palms. Plans were announced in May 2002 to merge the two firms, creating a unit which will still account for 1 per cent of Malaysia's total oil palm land.

In this chapter it will be shown how United Plantations maintained its tradition of excellent field management and state-of-the-art plant breeding practice throughout these decades of rapid growth. As in previous years, the firm gained from the co-operative spirit which continued to flourish among oil palm researchers in Malaysia and abroad, but increasingly from the 1970s onwards, United Plantations began to lead the way in specific fields of research. The company was beginning to gain a reputation for originality and ingenuity in the field to match its existing renown for engineering and marketing innovation.

Such qualities were no less vital at the end of the twentieth century than they had been in earlier decades. Pre-war planters had been forced to grapple with all the unpredictable technical challenges involved, first in creating estates from jungle and then in introducing a new species – the oil palm itself – to Malaysia from abroad. After the Second World War a fresh set of challenges arose, as oil palm planters switched from the Dura to the Tenera variety. By the 1970s, the switch to the Tenera palm was complete, and planters had become aware that although the Tenera palm had given them a tremendous jump in productivity, it by no means solved all their problems in the field. The old questions of how to save labour in field operations, how to combat pests like bagworms and how to get the fruit quickly and in pristine condition to the mill, continued to vex them. Meanwhile, as replanting gathered pace, new diseases like Ganoderma became a menace and new problems of soil exhaustion required increasingly complex scientific solutions. Finally, from the mid-1970s planters began to confront fresh ecological challenges. A relaxation of government restrictions in the 1980s meant that estate owners in Peninsular Malaysia could look forward to cultivating new land, while smallholder schemes also expanded, especially in Sabah and Sarawak during the 1990s, as shown in Table 8. Yet in both cases the new land taken into cultivation was more fragile than before and was usually waterlogged and peaty.

United Plantations led the way in developing new fertilizer and water management regimes to get the best out of such marginal land, and the company's managers also continued to keep well abreast of developments elsewhere. In addition to the old informal links cultivated by Rolf Grut, new links were developed through conferences and written papers and through formal exchange visits to the research stations run by the government and by other firms within the oil palm industry. United Plantations set up its own Research Department which helped in the search for solutions to the field managers' problems and which also contributed to the industry-wide drive to find fresh planting materials.

Through this final drive Malaysian oil palm researchers now began to lead the world in a search for fresh inventions that took three main forms. Plant breeders sought to improve the basic Tenera palm by prospecting for fresh materials and developing more sophisticated selection methods to isolate high-yielding trees. Nursery managers sought to find ways of bringing young palms into production more quickly. Finally, and more controversially, researchers laid the foundations for a second 'big leap' in productivity through cloning and, potentially, genetic engineering.

So far the prospect of a genetically engineered oil palm remains within the realm of speculation, and United Plantations has remained detached from it. Instead, the firm has linked itself, through Unitata, Anglia Oils and Aarhus Olie, with the development of organic product lines. This may be seen partly as a reflection of the growing commitment to 'green' issues within Danish society and political life, but it is also a reflection of United Plantations' own history and culture. The company's managers have consistently shown an interest in 'green' issues, such as recycling, long before it became fashionable to do so. Finally, the managers are keenly aware that in European markets, if not in America or elsewhere, the fact that the oil palm has not been genetically modified gives it a distinct competitive advantage over two of its main rivals, soyabean and oilseed rape.[1]

While remaining aloof from the speculation over genetic engineering, United Plantations' field managers and researchers have been actively involved in a remarkably large number of other developments, both through their own discoveries and by the swift application of ideas developed by researchers in larger units elsewhere. In the new era of explosive growth, the speed with which new ideas have continued to spread within the industry is quite remarkable and shows that the early spirit of co-operation among the palm oil pioneers was not lost once the industry became big business. Ideas often spread particularly quickly to United Plantations, partly through the wide network of personal friendships built up earlier by the Grut brothers, and partly as a reflection of the new respect felt for Tan Sri Dato' Seri B. Bek-Nielsen and his fellow engineers. However, from the 1970s a further factor came into play. This was the growing reputation being won by United Plantations' agricultural research staff, especially Tan Yap Pau. The company was beginning to win a name for agronomic advances in its own right.

RESEARCH BEGINS AT JENDARATA

In 1963 Olof Grut took the first step towards setting up United Plantations' own Research Department by commissioning a visit from Dr C.G. Lamm of the Copenhagen Polytechnic School for Scientific and Technical Studies. Dr Lamm's report was presented to the 1964 Annual General Meetings of United Plantations and Bernam Oil Palms, and on the strength of this it was agreed to hire a specialized researcher to work on the use of fertilizers, the combat of pests and diseases, and the breeding and selection of hybrid crop varieties. H. Mollegaard duly arrived at Jendarata Estate towards the end of the year, and by May 1965 work was well under way on soil classification, oil palm genetics and the rationalization of the fertilizer trials and foliar analyses which individual estate managers had previously been carrying out in their spare time. Mollegaard's most pressing task, however, was the large-scale production of Tenera seedlings to support the new planting programmes at Jendarata and Ulu Bernam and of coconut seedlings for use on the other United Plantations' estates. By the time he left in 1972 these production lines were well established and a number of locally recruited staff had been trained to keep them going, led by Field Officers Edward Chan for coconuts and Tan Yap Pau for oil palms.[2]

Both Chan and Tan stayed with United Plantations for many years and developed their roles well beyond the core task of seedling production. Chan stayed until 1984, working simultaneously on cocoa and coconuts, which were then being developed by United Plantations as complementary crops. As mentioned in Chapter 4, Olof Grut took a personal interest in the cocoa trials. He encouraged Chan and Arne Nygaard Rasmussen, the estate manager at Jendarata, to extend the trials from coconut to oil palm stands in the mid-1970s. Initially, the cocoa trees were planted in fields of established oil palms, which were thinned out to varying degrees to provide extra light for the young cocoa plants. These experiments built upon earlier work in the Belgian Congo but were highly innovative within the Malaysian context. The early field trials proved successful and the system of intercropping was extended to cover 4,000 hectares of oil palms and coconuts as part of United Plantations' replanting programme for these taller crops. For about ten years cocoa growing provided the firm with a profitable sideline, although as labour costs rose and world cocoa prices fell in the 1990s, the venture became uneconomic and was phased out. Despite its sad end, it remains a modestly successful example of the distinctive United Plantations' policy of moving beyond monocrop plantations wherever new opportunities can be seen.[3]

Chan also contributed to the mainstream trend of research within Malaysia's plantation sector by developing a plant breeding programme to produce a new hybrid variety of coconuts. Like the programme which had produced the Tenera palm, this involved international co-operation: from 1971, United Plantations was exchanging planting materials with the Institut de Recherches pour les Huiles et Oléagineux (IRHO) of Paris and the Ivory Coast, and the Department of Agriculture of the British Solomon Islands. These exchanges brought remarkably quick results: by 1974 United Plantations was able to make trial plantings of the now famous MAWA palm, combining the short stature of Malaysian palms with the high yields of their West African counterparts. Sales of these coconut seednuts soon began and helped to finance further research. Tan continued where Chan left off in 1984 and by the early 1990s had produced the improved MATAG hybrid. At Kuala Bernam and Sungei Bernam Estates, managers A. Arikiah and Loh Hang Pai led a team which made full productive use of the new coconut varieties throughout the 1980s and 1990s, while sales of seed to other growers continued to help finance fresh research. Meanwhile, United Plantations continued to sell Tenera oil palm seeds and seedlings. In the mid-1990s the company was Malaysia's fifth largest oil palm seed producer, a position held jointly with Applied Agricultural Research Sdn Bhd behind FELDA, Guthries' Chemara and Highlands Units and Harrisons' Golden Hope Plantations Berhad. Through its sales of both coconut and oil palm planting materials, United Plantations' Research Department furthered the development of Malaysia's agricultural sector as a whole.[4]

HYBRID OIL PALMS

Tan Yap Pau's work on oil palms covered a wide range of issues from plant breeding to nursery and field practice, and his breadth of outlook eventually received full recognition when he was appointed as United Plantations' overall research controller in 1980, a post which he held until his retirement in 1997. However, his key achievement is undoubtedly the pioneering *Oleifera guineensis* breeding programme, which could help take the Malaysian palm oil industry into a new era. As will be shown in Chapter 8, the market for palm oil as an edible fat became increasingly important in the 1960s and 1970s. In the late 1980s Malaysian producers became the target of a propaganda campaign waged by their major rivals in this market, the American soyabean producers, who alleged that palm oil was an unhealthy saturated fat. Malaysian producers have been attempting to set the record straight – for the soyabean growers vastly overstated their case – but in the long term their best weapons may well prove to be new strains of oil palm, yielding oil with a high iodine value and low unsaturated fat content. One such strain is the *Oleifera guineensis* hybrid, which aims to blend the high yields of the standard *Elaeis guineensis* palm with the high unsaturated fat content of the South American *Elaeis oleifera* species.[5]

Jaap Hardon of the Oil Palm Genetics Laboratory (OPGL) had been the first to publicize the qualities of the *Oleifera guineensis* hybrid in an article published in 1969. However, at that time his group's main aim was to develop the standard

Elaeis guineensis palm through prospecting for fresh material, testing for genetic variations in yield and developing improved breeding methods for selected palms. The *Elaeis oleifera* seemed to be a curious byway unworthy of exploration, because its fruit was extremely awkward to process. Each bunch contained many small fruitlets that took a wide variety of fruit forms even on the same bunch, ranging from no kernel to three kernels per fruit and with correspondingly thin or thick pulp. At United Plantations, though, Hardon's observations were read with interest, because Olof Grut's pre-war experiments with bleached oil had established a company tradition of developing distinctive oils for new markets. As it happened, Jendarata Estate already possessed a small stand of *Oleifera guineensis* palms which had been planted in 1959 under the Co-Operative Breeding Scheme. In 1970 a sample of oil from these palms was sent to Sweden for laboratory analysis, and when the analysis confirmed the qualities found in Hardon's samples, a new hybrid breeding programme was born.[6]

Even within United Plantations the *Oleifera guineensis* programme was a maverick scheme, and it ran on a small scale compared to the Research Department's staple work in selecting and breeding from high-yielding trees of the *Elaeis guineensis* variety. Nevertheless, it persisted throughout the two decades which were needed to bring solid results. This demonstrates not only the continued willingness of United Plantations' top management to invest for the distant future but also the importance of individual staff – in this case Tan Yap Pau – in spotting potentially winning schemes and carrying them through. Tan gained support for the scheme by pointing out that the hybrid offered the prospect not only of a new oil for new markets but also of help with two of the field managers' most pressing agronomic problems. He could see from the existing plot of hybrids that the trees were short, easing the problem of harvesting mature stands; and resistant to the Ganoderma disease, which has since developed into a major scourge of Malaysia's oil palm industry but was then just beginning to invade replanted stands.[7]

On the strength of these arguments, United Plantations imported fresh supplies of *Elaeis oleifera* seeds and pollen in 1973 and 1974. New stands of pure *Elaeis oleifera* as well as the *Oleifera guineensis* hybrid were planted at Jendarata and observed carefully over the following six years. The pure stands showed very poor growth, and the hybrids could thrive only on the best soils. The hybrids also had very few male inflorescences, which meant that many bunches might fail to produce fruit. These were grave problems, but Tan did not give up; indeed he organized a fresh prospecting expedition to Latin America with Charles Hartley in 1980–81.[8]

By this time the Malaysian Government had begun to show an interest in breeding palms yielding oil with a high iodine value and low saturated fat content. They had already taken over the OPGL and expanded it to become the Palm Oil Research Institute of Malaysia (PORIM). In 1979 Kurt Berger, a chemical engineer with long experience in the British food industry, joined PORIM and began a series of experiments analysing the oil from each of the African palms originally planted by the colonial Agricultural Department at Serdang. A further collection of Nigerian planting material had been made in 1973, as a joint effort by the Malaysian Agricultural Research and Development Institute (MARDI) and the Nigerian Institute for Oil Palm Research (NIFOR). PORIM inherited MARDI's germplasm from this collection too, and as a result has been able to produce three new types of Dura x Pisifera planting materials: PS1 for dwarfness; PS2 for high iodine value; and PS3 for high kernel content. United Plantations was among the companies invited to make trial plantings of these materials, which are now bearing fruit and being carefully assessed by comparison with standard Deli x AVROS (Malaysian/Indonesian) planting stock.[9]

Within this wide-ranging government research programme, two specific *Elaeis guineensis* palms have proved to be of special value: they yield oil with an iodine value of 66–68, as compared with a typical value for *Elaeis guineensis* Tenera palms of 53 and for *Elaeis oleifera* palms of 89. Not content with its efforts to breed from these two palms, however, PORIM decided in 1980 to send Dr N. Rajanaidu to make an *Elaeis oleifera* prospection in Latin America. Travelling at the same time as Tan and Hartley, Rajanaidu kept in friendly contact with them, continuing a time-honoured tradition within the plant breeding community.[10]

At United Plantations, yield recording of Tan's new *Oleifera guineensis* planting material could not begin until 1986, but it then became clear that his prospection had been a success. Some of the new hybrid progenies had an impressively high fruit yield, and United Plantations immediately began an accelerated breeding programme using this material. By 1989 hybrid palms accounted for 1 per cent of the firm's total palm oil output – some 750,000 tonnes per year. As originally intended, this oil had a distinctively low saturated fat content – just 30 per cent as compared with 44 per cent for the oil from the standard *Elaeis guineensis* Tenera palm. Its unsaturated fat content was correspondingly high – 68 per cent as compared with 49 per cent for the Tenera. Finally, it had a high iodine value of 72, making it ideal for the cooking oil market in the temperate zone. In short, the *Oleifera guineensis* hybrid did indeed yield a new oil for new markets, and after 20 years of patient breeding it was beginning to do so with an acceptable yield of oil per hectare. United Plantations' early start and persistence in research on the hybrid have placed it well ahead of the competition. As with PORIM's work on the selected African palms, United Plantations' hybrid project may soon begin to produce seedlings for wider sale, thus generating income for further research as well as spreading the benefits of the work done to date.[11]

IDEAS EXCHANGED

In all his work, whether on the major *Oleifera guineensis* breakthrough or on the steady improvement of nursery and field practice, Tan Yap Pau co-operated extensively with other researchers. Yet this co-operation was especially important in two main areas: in the drive to increase yields in the early years of an oil palm's life and in the drive to cut field labour costs. Both these drives were vital to keep up producers' profitability in an era of declining palm oil prices, and both required patient work on a number of small improvements rather than one striking breakthrough. Exchanges of ideas between the members of different firms helped not only to spread the benefits of research more quickly throughout the planting community, but also to sustain the enthusiasm of researchers. Each apparently small advance could be seen in its full glory when put together with the other innovations which would complement it, and each lone researcher could bask briefly in the praise of his peers.

From the late 1960s, as the Malaysian research effort began to gather pace, awareness of new research findings began to spread increasingly rapidly. This spread occurred partly through the informal contacts which had always been vital but now also through a new network of conferences and specialist publications. The Malaysian Agricultural Department published a new version of its handbook on oil palms in 1966 with the significant change that it was written not by departmental officials but by a wide range of private-sector planters including Rolf Grut. In 1967 Charles Hartley published the first edition of his classic textbook on the crop, drawing not only on his Malaysian experience but also on his 10 years' work at the West African Institute for Oil Palm Research. Meanwhile, the Incorporated Society of Planters took on a new lease of life. Apart from publishing its long-standing journal, *The Planter*, it began to cater for the needs of a new wave of Malaysian members just starting careers in plantation management, extending its Technical Education Scheme and publishing handbooks on specific topics. Four handbooks on the oil palm alone were published by the ISP between 1966 and 1974, and at the same time the society held a series of four oil palm conferences, the papers from which were also published. The ISP could justly pride itself on being 'the leading organization to disseminate knowledge concerning oil palm planting' in a decade during which many of its long-standing members were trying this crop for the first time.[12]

These publications and conferences helped to create a feeling among young planters and research staff that they were joining an increasingly united and professional group. The tremendous *esprit de corps* within this group helped to sustain and invigorate potential inventors and innovators in what Leslie Davidson, the former chairman of Unilever's Plantations Group, has described as a 'Renaissance' period. Young men were entering a booming industry in a newly independent country and were being let loose to experiment by employers who felt that oil palm was the crop of the future. Even an apparently small discovery could be recognized as exciting and important within this context, seen as part of a wave of changes which were sweeping the industry rapidly along towards full development.[13]

The way in which discoveries were made and ideas exchanged can be illustrated by the examples of the polybag and the weevil. The first helped transform nursery practice in the 1960s; the second did the same for one key aspect of field practice in the 1980s. Both ideas arose as a result of travel, as individuals observed how things were done differently in various countries, but neither represented the simple application to Malaysia of practices in use elsewhere. The Malaysian oil palm industry had now come of age. Its field managers and researchers were able to develop fresh ideas instead of simply importing a fully-developed innovation like the Tenera palm.

The use of the black polythene bag, or polybag as it soon became known, was the brainchild of Harrisons & Crosfield's Brian Gray. When Gray arrived in Malaysia in the 1950s he found that it was standard practice to plant germinated oil palm seeds in beds in a pre-nursery and then to transplant the young seedlings directly into the ground of a field nursery before moving them again to a permanent site. When he visited Sumatra soon afterwards he was struck by the way in which Harrisons' planters there used small bamboo baskets to grow the seedlings. Trials in Malaysia showed that this practice greatly reduced transplanting shock, which meant that field planting could go on all year round regardless of 'drought' periods. However, the handwoven baskets were expensive both to make and to store. Then Gray had his inspiration: why not try polythene? Trials at the Banting nursery gave good results, especially at the prenursery stage where root development was exceptionally fast. Indeed, Gray soon found that by planting the germinated seed directly into a large polybag, it was possible to cut out the pre-nursery stage altogether and transplant the seedling directly from its first bag into its final position in the field. Although the polybags had to be kept well watered, leading to years of further work by various firms on irrigation systems, their use finally cut nursery labour costs while ensuring a more rapid growth for the young plants. Once these benefits had been demonstrated at Banting the practice spread rapidly, though a few planters resisted the idea on the grounds that polythene was 'unnatural'.[14]

A similar resistance was encountered by Leslie Davidson when he first had the idea of using insects to pollinate oil palms. Since 1980 the use of the pollinating weevil *Elaeidobius kamerunicus* has become a staple feature of the Malaysian oil palm industry, yet the idea had not even been thought of when Davidson arrived to run the Pamol estate in Sabah in the early 1960s. Beforehand while working in West Africa he had encountered the spontaneous insect pollination of oil palms. However, in Malaysia the local insects were so poor at the job that planters believed wind pollination was the only 'natural' way, requiring expensive human assistance. Sabah's high rainfall meant that wind pollination was even less effective there than usual, requiring much manual labour to ensure a good fruit set on the palms; even so, for several years Davidson found it impossible to raise the funds needed to try introducing new insects. Most local researchers and planters seemed to have an unshakeable belief that no insect could be capable of pollinating a palm. Finally Davidson rose to become vice-chairman of Unilever's Plantations Group in 1976, and in this position he was able to pursue his idea. In 1979 the Commonwealth Institute of Biological Control co-funded a visit to Cameroun by a Malaysian agricultural officer, R.A. Syed, whose research conclusively proved the value of weevils and identified a suitable variety for introduction to Malaysia.[15]

The weevils were released on the Pamol estate at Kluang in February 1981, and United Plantations was among the first to purchase supplies of the insects once permission had been given for their general release that September. By the following summer it had become evident that the weevils were flourishing and that their presence both removed the need for assisted pollination and ensured an exceptionally high fruit set. These results were no mere flash in the pan, as the experience of later years has shown, and mill engineers now had to adapt in their turn, finding ways to strip the fruit from larger, fully packed bunches. The net result was a rise in returns, less to land or to the capital employed in the mill, than to the increasingly scarce productive resource of harvesting labour. Fruit yields per tree, and hence per hectare, were not dramatically boosted by the weevil, as each palm now produced fewer bunches. Meanwhile, within the mill the amount of palm oil extracted from each tonne of fruit may actually have fallen, as each weevil-pollinated bunch contained a larger number of smaller fruits, with a higher ratio of kernel to oil content in each fruit. However, planters flocked to adopt the weevil because it made the harvesters' work so much more productive: each bunch cut so painstakingly by hand was now more valuable. Like the introduction of the polybag, that of the weevil was a small innovation compared with the great breakthrough of the Tenera palm, but when combined with the many other small advances of the period, it had immense significance. It was through changes like these that Malaysian producers were able to maintain their leading position world-wide.[16]

THE CHALLENGE OF DEEP PEAT

United Plantations made its greatest contribution to the industry-wide drive to improve planting practices through researching the use of fertilizers and through developing appropriate water management techniques for marginal areas with deep peaty soils. The firm had a special interest in research of this kind, for both Olof Grut and his successor as chairman, Børge Bek-Nielsen, remained dedicated to the ideal of expanding the planted area around a central core at Jendarata and Ulu Bernam. Unlike the other European firms, which were content to manage estates scattered around Malaysia, United Plantations wanted to keep its highly personal, hands-on style of top management and therefore to keep all its estates within a short ride by light plane from the administrative centre. This meant that further expansion could only be achieved by buying out the few neighbouring rubber estates, a strategy of limited scope which had effectively been exhausted by 1973, or by developing the jungle areas nearby which contained a high proportion of deep peaty soils. United Plantations was thus confronted early on with a challenge which has since become more pressing for other Malaysian producers as the area cultivated by both smallholders and estates expands to embrace more marginal soils.

In dealing with this topic we enter a zone of fierce controversy. Marginal soils cannot be cultivated fruitfully using fertilizer- and pesticide-free 'organic farming' techniques. Furthermore, recent campaigns to save the rainforests have highlighted the issue of whether the rich diversity of the jungle should be allowed to give way to the profitable uniformity of the plantation. In areas where the soil is marginal for agricultural purposes, and the profits therefore limited, the case for retaining the original forest is probably at its strongest. Nevertheless, in many areas of South-East Asia the driving force behind jungle felling is not the planter but the logger. In this case the key question becomes, not whether the jungle should be replaced but what should replace it. On my first visit to United Plantations in 1987 I saw from the air the devastation which had resulted from felling alone in areas neighbouring the company's new estates. The contrast between the newly planted fields and the neglected wasteland was unforgettable. Like many of his fellows, the planter who flew me that day liked living near the jungle and would go into it for pleasure in his spare time; he would not wish to see it disappear. Yet he was proud of the firm's achievement in creating wealth from an environment which, in its natural form, could support very few people. He was proud of the clean water supply, the decent housing, clinics and schools which the firm could now afford to provide for its work-force. In his view, the battle to make marginal land fruitful was well worth winning.[17]

For United Plantations this battle began in earnest in the early 1970s. As shown in Chapter 5, oil palm expansion in the 1960s had been achieved largely by purchasing small rubber estates near Jendarata and replanting them, together with Jendarata's own old rubber stands. Luckily for the company, just as its scope for expansion of this kind began to be exhausted, Malaysian government policy towards new land concessions underwent a radical change. The shift is all the more surprising because it ran counter to the main trend of the economic policy review provoked by the riots of 13 May 1969. The New Economic Policy was in general unfavourable towards foreign ownership of Malaysian assets, because the politicians' main concern was to reduce inequality between Malaysia's ethnic groups and in particular to give the Malays and other *Bumiputeras* ('Sons of the Soil') a greater share in the ownership of profitable concerns. However, they were also concerned to promote economic growth and in the agricultural sector this led them to give fresh approval to the operations of foreign companies. As shown in Chapter 5, since the 1940s state-run smallholder resettlement schemes had been the main vehicle of new land development in Malaysia. But the New Economic Policy statement issued by the Department of National Unity in March 1970 openly stated that estates had played a valuable role in raising agricultural productivity during the same period. It followed that: 'There is now a clear responsibility on Government to ensure that estate development does in fact play an active role in the much needed acceleration of new land development.' While state-run schemes continued to be important, it now became much easier for private companies to gain limited amounts of fresh jungle land.[18]

United Plantations took swift advantage of the policy change, acquiring 3,000 hectares of jungle adjoining Jendarata and Ulu Bernam Estates in 1970–72. In 1973 it gained the right to develop a new 1,000 hectare estate at Seri Pelangi, adjoining the Bidor River just east of Teluk Anson; and in 1979 it gained a further jungle land concession of 1,700 hectares at Changkat Mentri, directly to the south and east of Ulu Bernam. Following the sale of a large share-holding to the *Bumiputera* food conglomerate Kumpulan Fima in 1982 the company acquired 10,742 hectares of land adjoining Changkat Mentri, which has since been developed to form the estates of Ulu Basir, Sungei Erong and Sungei Chawang (see Map 6). Meanwhile, all the pre-war oil palm fields at Ulu Bernam itself had been replanted by 1975, and in 1976 a second round of replanting began. The company was beginning to confront the challenge of cultivating depleted as well as marginal soils.[19]

In their battle to make the most of depleted soils, United Plantations' field managers were not alone. From the early 1960s onwards the Malaysian planting community had been mounting an urgent search for ways of boosting soil nutrient levels, spurred on by the more exhaustive demands of the Tenera palm as well as by the general trend towards replanting. The key innovation which they were now adopting and refining was the use of chemical fertilizers. Field upkeep costs, of which fertilizers were the major element, climbed steeply in the 1960s and 1970s. At Ulu Bernam, for example, they accounted for nearly 30 per cent of all production costs by 1980, as compared with 15 per cent in the early 1960s.[20]

At Ulu Bernam the first fertilizer trials had been made as early as 1931, but at that time the estate managers were more concerned with improving the structure of the soil to prevent erosion than with boosting its nutrient content. They tried out a few artificial fertilizers but quickly came to prefer bunch manuring. By

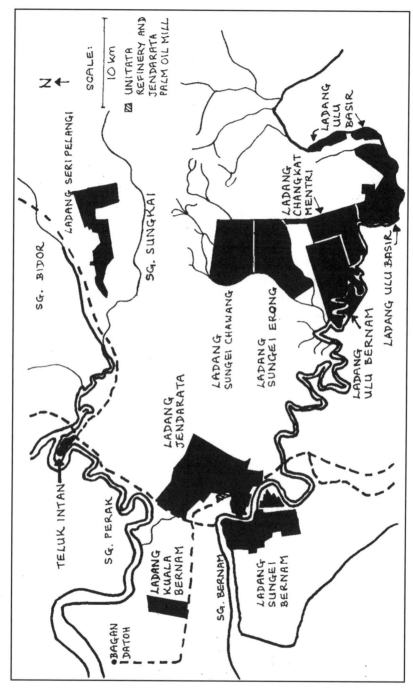

Map 6: United Plantations' estates, 2001

recycling the empty palm fruit bunches from their own factory they hoped to add valuable organic matter to the soil as well as putting back nutrients cheaply. This approach served them well until the 1950s, but like the other planters in Malaysia they then began to feel that more concentrated doses of chemical nutrients were needed. Once they began to spend money on artificial fertilizers, they wanted to make sure that they were choosing the right ones and applying no more than was strictly necessary. Hence, in United Plantations as elsewhere, a demand arose for specialized scientific staff who could use soil analysis to identify the strengths and weaknesses of specific zones within each estate and leaf analysis to determine how well the vital nutrients were being absorbed by the palms themselves.[21]

During the 1960s United Plantations relied largely on outside agencies like Guthries' Chemara Research Station and the Agricultural Department to conduct leaf analyses and small-scale fertilizer trials at Ulu Bernam. At Jendarata, Mollegaard's trials produced no clear results. After his departure Olof Grut decided that work on fertilizers should be the new research controller's first priority, and so in October 1972 Dr Ng Siew Kee, a professional soil scientist and a man of vigour and imagination, was appointed to the post. He quickly drew up fresh maps of the soils on each estate and set up varied and complex experiments with different fertilizer mixes. These experiments, which were modified by Ng's successor Kanapathy and then continued throughout the 1970s and 1980s, eventually brought good results. Their most spectacular success was in dealing with the condition known as 'peat yellows', a withering of the leaves of young palms planted on deep peat soils. Ng found that zinc and copper sulphate sprays could prevent this, and his successors built on this discovery to develop a mix of sprays and surface applications of a wide range of fertilizers so that finally it became possible not only to grow healthy palms on deep peat but also to achieve a healthy yield of fruit.[22]

Important though such work on fertilizers was, the deep peat case high-lights the fact that it had to be done in co-operation with the field managers, who in turn had to adapt their cultivation methods to ensure that the new nutrients were successfully absorbed. Water control was an especially vital task within the new dispensation, as field managers strove to keep the palms well sup-plied with water without washing away their newly applied, expensive chemicals. In deep peat areas there were additional challenges: loose, waterlogged soils had to be firmly compacted and drained without destroying their capacity to support life. These challenges became of immediate relevance to managers at Jendarata and Ulu Bernam in the early 1970s, following the Malaysian government's change of policy on jungle land: a significant part of the new land acquired by United Plantations was deep peat.[23]

Ken Stimpson, who had been recruited as manager of Ulu Bernam Estate in 1966, played a pivotal role in United Plantations' campaign to meet these challenges. Stimpson was the first Scot to join United Plantations, although Scots were predominant elsewhere in Malaysia's planting industry. He had first encountered United Plantations while managing the neighbouring Sungei Samak Estate for Harrisons and Crosfield in the early 1960s. Rolf Grut welcomed his relatively isolated neighbour to the Ulu Bernam Club, where he soon struck up lasting friendships with both Rolf and the young Bek-Nielsen. Like Rolf, Ken Stimpson was a keen sportsman, and when based in Selangor as a young planter just after the war had been allowed three afternoons off to play rugby each week. Like Bek-Nielsen, he enjoyed telling tales about the more comic side of the Emergency, for example about the occasion when he was driving down a lonely road on the Dunedin Division of Kajang rubber estate. He was carrying the first firearm he had been issued with, a single-barrelled shotgun. A branch became stuck under the wheels of the car and he leapt out to remove it, only to be startled by a tremendous explosion. Wriggling hastily out from under the chassis he dived for cover into the nearest ditch, expecting to find himself in the middle of a terrorist ambush. After several minutes of silence he peered cautiously out, only to see smoke billowing from the car itself. The vibration of the engine had set off the shotgun! Both car and driver survived, but the upholstery was never the same again.[24]

On a professional level, the Ulu Bernam managers were interested in Stimpson's earlier experience at the Carey Island Estate, where Harrisons had inherited an extensive system of bunds on purchasing the plantation in 1960. Bunds, or embankments, were vital at Carey Island to prevent salt water flooding, though their use had traditionally been limited on freshwater sites like Ulu Bernam. In 1931 the Ulu Bernam planters had constructed a small bund where two big creeks flowed into the Bernam River, extending it to border the two neighbouring fields following severe floods two years later. But attacks by elephants combined with water erosion to make this embankment very expensive to maintain, and the system was not developed further before the war. Estate managers at Ulu Bernam concentrated instead on developing a distinctive system of trench drainage and watergates, in which Stimpson and other Harrisons managers later became interested in their turn.[25]

When Stimpson joined United Plantations he quickly began an overhaul of Ulu Bernam's entire system of water control, desilting and weeding the field drains and extending the pre-war bunds to cover the whole estate. The task was completed very rapidly, aided by the new tools for efficient earthworks which had recently come to hand. The cumbersome, costly bulldozers, excavators and tractors tried out at Ulu Bernam in 1948 had now been replaced by an equally expensive but more effective second generation, and Olof Grut's personal enthusiasm for machinery ensured that United Plantations would be willing to try it out. One of Stimpson's first acts was to purchase a 'Beaver' excavator at a cost of M$54,000, and this proved ideal for making river bunds. The whole estate was protected by the end of 1967, and the system worked well for a decade.[26]

When the bunds were eventually rebuilt it was not because they had proved faulty but because of the construction of yet more bunds upriver. The new bunds of the late 1970s were designed to protect fresh smallholder developments being carved out of the jungle by government agencies, although they also benefited the new estate which United Plantations was to create at Changkat Mentri from 1979. Useful though they were to these upriver developments, the new bunds created problems at Ulu Bernam and neighbouring regions down-river. Water from the eastern upriver regions, which would previously have spread out under the trees during the heavy rains, was now being channelled into the main river. Even though rainfall levels were falling at Ulu Bernam during the late 1970s, with an annual average of 74 inches in 1974–78 as compared with 96 in the immediate post-war years of 1946–55, the peak river levels were now rising well above those of the earlier period. Hence the building of ever-higher bunds was required, and still closer attention had to be paid to the system of drains and watergates controlling water levels on the fields behind them.[27]

All this experience with water control served Stimpson well when it came to considering the special planting challenges posed by deep peat. Swampy, peaty land needed to be drained skilfully in order to avoid irreversible drying, a process through which the soil loses its capacity to retain moisture and vital nutrients are leached away. This process had already occurred on the eastern fields of Ulu Bernam Estate when they were cleared and planted in the late 1940s. Although the water table had gradually been raised by M. Alsing, who was manager of Ulu Bernam from 1957 to 1961, his successor Finn Klastrup was

301

dismayed to find that large deposits of sulphurous compounds had accumulated near the surface as a result. The water table was lowered yet again and calcium fertilizers applied; ground cover crops like calopogonium and centrosema, the use of which had previously been unpopular at United Plantations, were then planted in an attempt to prevent further drying of the topsoil. Stimpson learnt from this experience when setting the initial water table levels in newly drained jungle areas. He was also greatly helped by being able to work with Ejnar Dissing Pedersen, who had been recruited as a planting assistant to Jendarata in 1961 and had a wealth of practical field experience on the full range of United Plantations' estates. As manager of Ulu Bernam Estate from 1979 to 1983, Dissing Pedersen was Stimpson's right-hand man in the pioneering work of clearing and planting up the deep peat land of Changkat Mentri. Dissing was a sound and reliable planter and a talented pilot but also an extremely modest man who shunned the limelight and was always glad to give others credit for innovative ideas. He co-operated well with Stimpson and made successful use, not only of the latest machinery in constructing bunds and drainage channels, but also of leguminous cover crops, which were new to United Plantations but which had long been popular at Harrisons & Crosfield.[28]

Ken Stimpson's personality, as Dissing appreciated, was almost as great an asset to United Plantations as his practical experience. A hot-tempered but hospitable Scot whose wife Morag had joined Rothes Grut as a pillar of the local Women's Institute, Stimpson was well liked and widely respected. In negotiations with trades unions he had a reputation for being tough but fair, and in dealings with individuals he shared Bek-Nielsen's knack of giving praise where it was due, not in a formal manner but with great personal warmth. This gave him a distinctive ability to pull senior managers together into an enthusiastic team. Such qualities were especially vital in managing a project like deep peat, which called for close communication between people who would normally have worked apart.[29]

Stimpson's own collaborative relationship with Ng Siew Kee set the first example of fruitful co-operation between Research Department staff and field managers, yielding useful guidelines on how to link water table control with fertilizer use. Later on, Kanapathy and Dr Gurmit Singh drew on these results in developing specific fertilizer regimes for deep peat areas. Meanwhile Arne Nygaard Rasmussen, the manager of Jendarata Estate from 1968 to 1981, was making pioneering trials using heavy machinery to compact deep peat soils. In his role as executive director (planting) for the whole United Plantations Group from 1971 to 1983, Stimpson took a keen interest in this work. He encouraged Dissing Pedersen, together with Rasmussen and his energetic deputy Norman Santa Maria, to keep in close touch with Kanapathy and Gurmit Singh. At first this was done informally and then, from 1980, through discussion papers circulated for the annual meetings of a new Planting Practices Committee. Following Kanapathy's departure in 1980, Gurmit Singh also co-operated with the field managers in writing a Company Management Manual, designed to inform new assistants of the best planting practices on deep peat and on other soils. This was produced on the eve of Stimpson's departure in 1983. News of the team's progress spread outside the company, too, through the conferences of the Incorporated Society of Planters. Gurmit Singh became a well-respected figure within Malaysia's oil palm research community and within United Plantations, succeeding Tan Yap Pau on his retirement as research director in 1997.[30]

The deep peat project did not just require collaboration; it also required great patience. Ng Siew Kee had been interested in deep peat since his arrival at United Plantations in October 1972, just at the time when Rasmussen, Dissing and Stimpson were assessing the challenges posed by newly acquired jungle land adjoining their estates. Yet even in 1976 Olof Grut was still warning the shareholders that their deep peat reserves should be considered 'unsuitable for any crop' and should not be counted on for future income. It was not until 1980 that a new chairman, Børge Bek-Nielsen, was able to reveal that respectable palm fruit yields had finally been obtained 'on peat 10 feet deep and more'. An extensive planting programme now began on the 1,000 hectares of deep peat reserve at Jendarata and Ulu Bernam. Having carried the work at Jendarata to a successful conclusion, Norman Santa Maria then moved on to consolidate Dissing's work on the even more extensive deep peat plantings of Changkat Mentri Estate, 1983–87, and finally to open up the new 4,500-hectare Ulu Basir Estate from 1987. In both these projects Santa Maria had two effective mentors: Peter Cowling, who succeeded Ken Stimpson as executive director (planting) in 1984 and Ho Dua Tiam, who had been with United Plantations since 1964. Ho had run the estates of Seri Pelangi, Sungei Bernam and Jendarata in turn before becoming group manager at Ulu Bernam with responsibility for both old and new estates, in 1987. Like Stimpson and Dissing, Cowling and Ho made a good complementary team. Peter Cowling had spent many years with Harrisons & Crosfield before joining United Plantations; together, he and Ho encouraged Santa

Maria to make optimal use of the planting traditions of both firms. A man of great calmness and charm, Peter Cowling used different managerial techniques to achieve essentially the same results as Ken Stimpson: a fruitful collaboration between researchers and field managers in overcoming tough ecological challenges.[31]

When Peter Cowling retired in 1994, Ho succeeded him as United Plantations' executive director (planting), but by this time he was also serving as the general manager of yet another jungle development, the Gula Perak Estate of United International Enterprises (Malaysia). (See Map 1, before the Introduction, above.) In practice, responsibility for planting operations at United Plantations now fell directly on the shoulders of two other men. In 1994, Norman Santa Maria became group manager (Ulu Bernam), in overall charge both of Ulu Bernam Esatate and of the four new estates of the 'jungle development': Ulu Basir, Sungei Chawang, Sungei Erong and Changkat Mentri. Meanwhile, Loh Hang Pai, who had made his name within the company for his work on coconuts in the 1980s, continued to serve throughout the 1990s as group manager (Jendarata), a post he had taken up in 1987. In this role, Loh was responsible for coconut production at Kuala Bernam and Sungei Bernam, as well as for oil palm production at Jendarata and Seri Pelangi. He and Santa Maria received additional support from A. Arikiah, who became manager (industrial relations) in 1994, taking the increasingly difficult business of labour recruitment and management off their hands. They also worked closely with S. Manoharan and Toh Tai San, the experienced group engineers at Ulu Bernam and Jendarata respectively, both of whom were long-serving company men. When Bek asked them to work with Axel Lindquist, who was employed as a consultant on the construction of the new palm oil mills at Seri Pelangi and Ulu Basir, they responded with friendly enthusiasm and found themselves agreeing wholeheartedly with his key ideas. Hence, although Lindquist is no longer with them, the new generation of engineers at United Plantations continue to look for new ways of improving their mill design, to make machinery in-house and to see the value of integrating the whole production process – from seedlings to shipment.[32]

UNITED INTERNATIONAL ENTERPRISES

While the teams led by Loh and Santa Maria at United Plantations continued to uphold the best in-house traditions of mill and field management throughout the 1990s, Ho Dua Tiam was returning to the era of the pioneers. The Gula

Perak project involved a fresh venture into deep-peat jungle territory where elephants still roamed. Politically, too, it symbolized a revival of the past relationship between the Danes, as friendly foreign investors, and a welcoming host government. In this case, however, the government was no longer colonial, but securely independent; and the welcome to be offered was clearly conditional on productive performance, rather than on race.

Shortly after United Plantations' original Danish shareholders had sold a controlling interest in the company to FIMA and other *Bumiputera* interests in 1982, Bek-Nielsen had set up a fresh company, United International Enterprises Limited. UIE has its registered office in the Bahamas and is listed on the Luxembourg and Copenhagen Stock Exchanges. Many of the original shareholders chose to invest in this new company, a choice made easier by the involvement of Mogens Jensen in its administration. Jensen, the experienced Copenhagen office manager for United Plantations and a personal friend of many shareholders, now became general manager of International Plantation Services Ltd (IPS) in Copenhagen. IPS was set up to ensure the smooth running of relationships between the shareholders and the various companies in what was rapidly becoming a complex group. By the year 2002 Plantagegruppen, as it had become known, comprised four major companies: United Plantations Berhad, Aarhus Oliefabrik A/S, International Plantations & Finance Ltd and United International Enterprises Ltd, together with their subsidiaries in Malaysia, Denmark, England, Norway, Mexico, the USA, the Bahamas, Sri Lanka, Australia, Swaziland, Benin, Ghana, the Ivory Coast, France and Russia.[33]

The trading and financial relationships between the various companies within Plantagegruppen were extremely complicated, characterized by interlocking shareholdings, ties of normal trading credit and, occasionally, more substantial loans. A clear head was required to manage them, and Bek was fortunate in having found one in the mid-1970s, in the person of a British mechant banker, John Goodwin. Born in 1945, Goodwin qualified as a chartered accountant and worked as a banker in London, Malaysia and Australia before becoming the managing director of International Plantations and Finance on the retirement of Leo Ebbesen in early 1983. Goodwin had already advised United Plantations and the Danish shareholders for several years in his capacity as a merchant banker. Knowing that a *Bumiputera* takeover must happen soon, in 1981 United Plantations Berhad had sold its own stake in International Plantations & Finance (IPF) back to the Danish shareholders and had reinvested the proceeds in the 15,000-hectare Gordon Downs property in Central Queensland, Australia. John Goodwin carried through the arrangements both for purchasing the property and for setting up the new company that has run Gordon Downs ever since. United Plantations (Australia) Pty Ltd has been owned jointly by United Plantations Berhad (30 per cent) and IPF (70 per cent) and has established a high-quality organic wheat-growing operation. However, its profitability has been marred by a long-running dispute over damages from mining operations underneath the land and more recently by rainfall problems, a difficulty with which Plantagegruppen's investors have long been familiar from their experiences in Southern Africa. Both in Africa and in Australia, therefore, John Goodwin's skills have also been invaluable in managing the financial affairs of highly volatile operations.[34]

John Goodwin also advised the Danish shareholders throughout the delicate negotiations leading up to the *Bumiputera* takeover of United Plantations Berhad in 1982, and was thus extremely well placed to help them in their search for fresh uses for their capital after the takeover. He became a founding Director of United International Enterprises when it was incorporated in May 1983, together with Ken Stimpson, Knud Sehested, Torkild Bjerglund Andersen and Nils Peter Grut, Olof's son; and Børge Bek-Nielsen, the founding chairman. Their original intention was to invest in a spread of tropical agricultural enterprises and they investigated possibilities in Nigeria, Thailand, the Philippines and Australia. However, mindful of the difficulties which IPF had encountered elsewhere in Africa and in Latin America, they adopted a cautious approach and kept much of their capital in relatively liquid form. Then, in October 1986, the Malaysian government announced a further policy shift, amending its laws to allow foreigners to own land once again. Within a month Bek had opened negotiations with Gula Perak Berhad, the owners of a failed sugar plantation at Pantai Remis, near the deep-water port of Lumut, 55 kilometers to the northwest of Teluk Intan.[35]

Gula Perak had obtained 7,200 hectares of land from the Perak State government in 1968, but the soil had turned out to be unsuitable for the company's purpose of sugar cane cultivation. The company eventually went into receivership, and Bek-Nielsen saw an opportunity. The land was flat and well suited to oil palm cultivation, as the owners proved by planting up 400 hectares with young palms in 1986. The Perak State Agricultural Development Corporation (PSADC) was keen to encourage the estate's conversion to this new use and was willing to make a further 3,200 hectares of adjoining land available on long lease to the right partner. Bek-Nielsen was the ideal man to seal a deal; not only was he well known in Perak as a long-standing and eminent figure within the oil palm planting community but he also held a commanding position within United International Enterprises, as the founding chairman and major shareholder. By this time Bek-Nielsen and his family collectively owned just over a quarter of UIE's shares.[36]

In October 1987 an agreement was concluded between UIE, PSADC and Gula Perak for the acquisition of the full 10,400 hectares of land, at a total price of M\$32 million. Part of this sum was paid in cash to Gula Perak and PSADC, with the remainder being paid to PSADC in the form of shares in the newly formed United International Enterprises (Malaysia) Berhad, the firm which was to own and run the estate. The deal absorbed about 75 per cent of the net tangible assets of United International Enterprises Limited, in return for which the Bahamas-based parent company would own 85 per cent of the newly created Malaysian subsidiary. In January 1988 the deal was approved by the parent company's shareholders, and in November 1988 the Malaysian High Court provided the final ratification. A contract was then concluded whereby United Plantations would provide top management for the new venture for at least the first three years, by seconding its own staff, just as had once been done when setting up Bernam Oil Palms. The stage was now set once more for bringing into play three of United Plantations' most distinctive strengths. First, as about a third of the new estate's total area consisted of deep peaty soil, the expertise of Dr Gurmit Singh and Ho Dua Tiam was essential. Second, because the area was flat, it lent itself easily to reproducing the renowned United Plantations railway system for transporting fresh fruit bunches from field to mill, including the use of Speldewinde's gantry lifting mechanisms. Indeed, Speldewinde was the new firm's first managing director. Finally, the conversion of the old sugar factory into a state-of-the-art palm oil mill gave plenty of scope for the skills, first of the 'old Viking', Axel Lindquist, and then, after his death, of two men who had known him well: S. Manoharan and Poul K. Vestergaard.[37]

By the year 2000 it was clear that the new venture was a spectacular success. Table 9 illustrates the high yields of palm oil obtained from the land at Pantai Remis. United Plantations had always been a high-yielding producer compared with other Malaysian growers: in 1981–90, United Plantations' yields of palm oil averaged 4.3 tonnes per mature hectare per annum, as compared with the

Table 9: Oil palm mature area (1,000 ha) and crude palm oil output (1,000 tonnes per annum), United Plantations, United International Enterprises and Malaysia, 1981–2001

Year	United Plantations area	United Plantations output	UIE (Malaysia) area	UIE (Malaysia) output	Malaysia total area	Malaysia total output
1981	11	49			850	2,820
1982	11	53			890	3,510
1983	11	42			1,010	3,020
1984	12	46			1,070	3,710
1985	11	51			1,200	4,130
1986	11	48			1,360	4,540
1987	13	49			1,370	4,530
1988	14	59			1,530	5,030
1989	16	75			1,670	6,060
1990	18	87			1,750	6,090
1991	19	93	3	6	1,830	6,140
1992	20	103	8	18	1,890	6,370
1993	21	107	9	33	2,020	7,400
1994	20	100	9	50	2,140	7,220
1995	20	102	9	54	2,240	7,810
1996	19	104	9	59	2,350	8,390
1997	19	107	9	61	2,510	9,070
1998	20	98	9	50	2,600	8,320
1999	20	110	9	53	2,860	10,550
2000	19	109	9	55	2,940	10,840
2001	20	99	9	59	3,010	11,800

Note: Figures for mature (rather than planted) areas are not available for earlier periods.

Sources: UPAR, 1981–2001 and UIEAR, 1991–2001; Malaysia: Palm Oil Registration and Licensing Authority, *PORLA Palm Oil Statistics 1988–98* (Kuala Lumpur: PORLA, annual editions), Tables 1.2, 1.3 and 3.1; Malaysian Palm Oil Board, *Malaysian Oil Palm Statistics 1999* (Kuala Lumpur: MPOB, 2000), Tables 1.2, 1.3 and 3.1; MPOB, *Review of the Malaysian Palm Oil Industry 2000* and *2001* (Kuala Lumpur: MPOB, 2001 and 2002), Chapters 1.2, 1.3, 1.4 and 3.1.

Malaysian average of 3.4 tonnes. However, over the decade 1991–2000, as the trees at Pantai Remis matured, United International Enterprises' yields rose steadily, from 2 tonnes per mature hectare in 1991, to 5.6 tonnes in 1994. Over the period 1995–2001, yields for Malaysia as a whole averaged 3.6 tonnes of palm oil per mature hectare per annum, whereas yields at United Plantations averaged 5.3 tonnes and at United International Enterprises, 6.2 tonnes.[38]

These differences in yields may be explained partly by the close and effective integration between field and mill operations and by the excellent methods of mill design and management used by both United International Enterprises and United Plantations. For Malaysia as a whole, the oil extraction rate (OER: the yield of crude palm oil, expressed as a percentage of the weight of fresh fruit bunches used by the mill in making it) averaged 18.8 per cent during the period 1995–2001. At United Plantations the average OER achieved over the same period was 20.5 per cent, while at United International Enterprises it was 20.7 per cent.

Of even greater importance than this difference in mill efficiency, however, was the gap that had opened up in field performance between the two Plantage-gruppen firms and the rest of the Malaysian growers. The average Malaysian yield of fresh fruit bunches (FFB) from oil palms was 18 tonnes per hectare per annum in 1995–2001; over the same period, United Plantations was harvesting 26 tonnes of FFB per hectare, and United International Enterprises, 29. While the difference in OER gave the Plantagegruppen firms a 10 per cent lead over their Malaysian competitors, the difference in FFB yields gave them a further lead of 44 per cent, in the case of United Plantations, and 61 per cent, in the case of United International Enterprises.

At the beginning of the twenty-first century, the pre-requisites for success in Malaysia's palm oil industry are thus strikingly similar to those which were evident 50 years before. Mill operations must be well managed, but above all to ensure quality standards, rather than in the hope of making massive gains in productivity. The extent to which the OER can be raised through innovation is very limited. The key to productivity gains, now as in the 1950s, lies in the im-provement of field operations and planting materials. The enduring importance of the planter within the oil palm industry may be seen in the continuing rise of Ho Dua Tiam, who in 2002 became the deputy senior executive director of United Plantations; and of Loh Hang Pai, who then inherited Ho's position as general manager of United International Enterprises, while retaining his responsibilities within United Plantations as the group manager (Jendarata). Meanwhile, the industry as a whole is focusing its attention once again on the search for improved planting materials, as the need to replant the many stands of oil palms established in the 1970s and 1980s becomes acute. Can a modern equivalent of the Tenera palm be found, or has the industry reached maturity at last? Malaysian oil palm planters obviously hope that maturity is still a long way away and, as the next section will show, they continue to search valiantly for fresh innovations, pinning their highest hopes on the technology of cloning.

CLONING THE OIL PALM

The introduction of cloning was possibly the most important innovation which United Plantations adopted from elsewhere in the 1980s, although it has yet to fulfil its promise as the greatest breakthrough since the Tenera palm. Cloning in the form of bud-grafting had enabled rubber producers to cut their costs dramatically in the early 1930s. As compared with plants grown from selected seed, bud-grafted plants were cheaper and quicker to bring to the yielding stage and were more reliable reproductions of the original stock. Unfortunately this form of cloning, known as vegetative propagation, is impossible for oil palms because each palm has only one growing point. However, in the 1960s a new cloning technique was developed. Tissue was cut from the living plant and used to develop a cell culture in laboratory conditions. Placed in the right growing medium, the cells would develop into a callus on which embryoids capable of generating new plantlets would appear. Once the plantlets, known as ramets, began producing true leaves they could be transferred to the nursery and treated in the same way as ordinary seedlings.[39]

In 1970 the French plant breeder Jean-Pierre Gascon of IRHO set up a pioneering oil palm tissue culture programme. The British were not far behind, and soon Unilever and Harrisons had set up a Malaysian programme through their specialized joint venture Bakasawit. The Malaysian government research agency PORIM also set up an oil palm tissue culture laboratory at the end of the decade. Top managers at United Plantations watched these ventures with interest, though it was not until 1985 that they thought it worth constructing a laboratory of their own. By this time the methods and equipment needed had been well tried and tested by the pioneers, an important point for United Plantations, which as a relatively small company needed to take special care over such high-budget, lumpy investments. While waiting for the right moment to build their laboratory, however, Tan Yap Pau and Bek-Nielsen had not been idle. They had developed close working relationships with the pioneers at both Bakasawit and PORIM, who from 1982 were supplying United Plantations with clonal plantlets and using tissue from high-yielding United Plantations palms in their laboratories.[40]

Seventy Bakasawit plantlets were raised in the nursery at Jendarata and transplanted to the field in September 1983. By December 1985 they were yielding their first fruit. It was at this stage, just as United Plantations was poised to join the other companies in a full-scale transition from conventional to clonal oil palm breeding, that a shadow was cast over the whole project. Most of the Jendarata plantlets yielded abnormal bunches, in which a ring of six fleshy outgrowths surrounded each fruit. Such 'mantled' fruit had previously been very rare. At one time it had been valued by Sumatran plant breeders for its high mesocarp, or oily pulp, content, but it soon dropped out of favour when it was realized that mantled fruit was often seedless, failing to ripen normally and rotting on the bunch instead. Hence its appearance in the clonal plantlets was both mysterious and alarming. Furthermore, other trials revealed that the Jendarata result was no freak aberration. Early clonal plantings made in 1977–80 by Harrisons and Pamol had produced perfectly normal fruit, but the plantlets produced in 1983 had given abnormal results not only at Jendarata but also on the other companies' estates in Johor, Selangor and Trengganu.[41]

It took years of fine tuning of the tissue culture process, not just at United Plantations but in other private-sector laboratories, at PORIM and at the Indonesian Oil Palm Research Institute, before researchers even came close to solving the mystery of the mantled fruit. During the late 1980s and early 1990s their efforts focused on finding ways of identifying, and so weeding out, abnormal plantlets while they were still at the *in-vitro* stage, thus eliminating the waste involved in nursing them along until they bear fruit. By 1992 United Plantations' Research Manager for Tissue Culture, Ho Yuk Wah, felt sufficiently confident of her success in this endeavour that fresh field trials were begun. By 1998 the company had planted out a total of 220 clones of elite Tenera and *Oleifera guineensis* hybrids, covering an area of 341 hectares. The early results of these trials showed that less than 5 per cent of the plants were bearing mantled fruit.[42]

Meanwhile, research continues throughout the industry into the fundamental science and future uses of cloning. At United Plantations and elsewhere, strategists continue to hope that cloning will eventually provide higher-yielding oil palms even if it never fulfils its early promise as a cheap and reliable method of propagation. Even bolder hopes are held by a few pioneering researchers in the field of genetic engineering. As early as 1992 the French specialist J. Meunier explained to an interested audience of oil palm breeders that a reliable cloning method was an essential aid to genetic engineering of the oil palm, because only through such a method could each expensively transformed plant be faithfully reproduced. His point was reiterated at the same conference by Hereward Corley of Unilever and his colleagues from Plant Breeding International of Cambridge, England, who reported some early success in using the 'gene gun' to produce a fleeting impression on oil palm cells in immature spear leaf tissue. Since then researchers in the clonal laboratories of PORIM and of the John Innes Centre in Norwich, England, have conducted further successful experiments, applying the particle bombardment method of gene transfer to oil palm callus tissues. They are still a long way from developing a commercially usable technique, but they have developed a vision which may eventually take them there.[43]

Many people, especially in England, have doubts about the ethics of genetic engineering, and about the wisdom of opening a fresh Pandora's Box for the oil palm, which to date has remained untouched by the controversy raging over field trials of rapeseed, and infiltration of genetically modified soya into supplies of the unmodified product. Certainly, United Plantations has shown no signs of enthusiasm for genetic engineering as yet. Rather than pushing Ho Yuk Wah to develop her tissue culture laboratory into an ever more sophisticated scientific enterprise conducting fundamental research, the firm's chairman from 1982 to 2002, Tan Sri Dato' Seri Haji Basir bin Ismail, encouraged her to follow two long-established company traditions. The first is that of applied research, experimenting with new uses of fundamental techniques invented elsewhere; while the second is that of crop diversification. During the late 1980s, while refining her methods of oil palm plantlet selection, Ho Yuk Wah also succeeded in producing a wide range of other plantlets, from roses to bananas. The bananas, Tan Sri Basir's personal favourite among the new clonal crops, offer especially good prospects for commercial cultivation and could also prove useful as a rotation crop in between plantings of oil palms.[44]

Recent ecological developments within South-East Asia have highlighted the wisdom of this approach. The recurring climatic problem of the 'haze',

which the Malaysian government found particularly embarrassing during the
Commonwealth Games year of 1998, was linked by many observers to the large-
scale open burning of felled trees on Indonesian plantations. Such burning,
whether in the course of replanting or of jungle clearance for new estates, has
been banned in Malaysia for over 20 years under the Environmental Quality
Acts of 1974 and 1978. As Malaysian planters began to comply with this legislation, for example by interplanting new palms among old trees, or by windrowing felled palms, that is, piling them in avenues beside each stand of young
trees, so they found themselves facing fresh problems of pests and disease.
When it was first transported to South-East Asia in seed form from Africa, the
oil palm had left most of its original pests and diseases behind. However, local
pests such as bagworms and nettle caterpillars had caused sporadic problems,
for example at Ulu Bernam in 1938 and 1956–57. When United Plantations
began extensive replantings at Ulu Bernam in the late 1950s and 1960s, using
the windrowing technique well in advance of the national clean air legislation,
field managers quickly encountered two fresh problems: the Oryctes rhinoceros
beetle, which feeds on growing palms and breeds in decaying coconut or oil
palm trunks; and the rampant root disease Ganoderma, caused by a fungus
which spreads from the felled trunks and stumps of old oil palms to the young
palms replanted among them. By the 1980s, with zero-burning replanting
techniques becoming widespread within the Malaysian oil palm industry, the
control of Ganoderma and the rhinoceros beetle had become pressing national
problems. By the late 1990s, a consensus was emerging that the intercropping
of young oil palms with other crops, for example thickly growing legumes,
could be one of the best possible weapons in this battle. Against this background, Ho Yuk Wah's experiments with bananas, and United Plantations' oil-
palm field managers' trials of other complementary crops including rice, take
on a wider significance.[45]

BEYOND CLONING?

The story of cloning illustrates once again the speculative and long-term nature
of investment in innovation within the oil palm industry. Because the tree itself
takes several years to begin yielding fruit, the virtues of new selected seeds or
clones take a long time to prove. The Tenera palm took two decades to become
a reliable breed, and the development of reliable clones is taking even longer.

Such investment is risky not just in technical but also in political terms, as the planters and government researchers of the Belgian Congo found to their cost: by the time they had achieved results, the Congo no longer provided a stable environment for applying their findings in the field. Yet in the context of the oil palm industry world-wide, the investment in Tenera proved well worth making, and tissue culture still holds forth the prospect of a second major leap in productivity in the future.

Meanwhile, small advances on other fronts are as eagerly sought as ever. The search for ways of saving labour in field operations continues and seems unlikely to be resolved by any single breakthrough, despite the high hopes held by researchers who have seen what can be achieved by robots and computers at factory level within other industries. Unpredictable factors like the weather militate against the routine computerized control of field operations, while no single robot could possibly tackle the full range of tasks from bunding to harvest. Nevertheless, each new machine that tackles a fresh task can help in a small way to ease the strains of labour shortage. Similarly, new ways of approaching tasks, like the use of polybags and the weevil, can lighten the workers' overall load. Yet there is a constant tension between this drive to save labour and cut manpower requirements, and the equally strong drive to increase productivity and extend planting to more marginal areas. New chemicals, especially in the area of pest and disease control, promise to increase productivity for the 1990s in the same way that fertilizers did in the 1960s and 1970s, but they can be extremely labour-intensive to apply. One especially significant innovation may therefore be United Plantations' recent introduction of aerial fertilizer application; if successful, this technique could well be used with other chemicals. As in the case of mechanized bunding, however, the final result of this innovation may not be to reduce the company's wage bill but to enable it to take on new tasks, which would have seemed impossibly expensive if done by hand.[46]

In all these areas, from the big 'breakthrough' projects to the patient search for small improvements, the process of innovation in the oil palm industry continues to be marked by the struggle to do new things, and not simply to do existing things more cheaply. United Plantations maintains its place in the forefront of the struggle, not only in the sphere of engineering in which Bek-Nielsen has personally excelled but also in the sphere of agronomy just surveyed. In this struggle today's planters are working for the future, but they are also maintaining the traditions of the past: those of men like Aage Westenholz and

Lennart Grut, inspired by the vision of creating settled prosperity in the pirates' lair and willing to invest even when prices tumbled and the jungle fought back.

NOTES

1   A succinct summary of the European marketing issues has been made by Britannia Food Ingredients Ltd, 'Genetic engineering: implications for oils and fats supply' (Technical Communication 3, March 1999) available on their website (http://www.britanniafood.com).

2   BOPCA, 1964; UPCA, 1965–66; UPAR, 1966–72; UPRDAR, 1964–72.

3   UPAR, 1978–79 and 1996; C.W.S. Hartley, *The Oil Palm (Elaeis guineensis Jacq.)* 3rd edn (London: Longman, 1988), pp. 567–571.

4   Interview with Tan Yap Pau, 3 September 1987; UPRDAR, 1971–88; UPAR, 1996–97; A. Kushairi, B.S. Jalani, D. Ariffin and N. Rajanaidu, 'Seed production and export of Malaysian oil palm planting materials', *The Planter*, vol. LXXIII, no. 4, 1997, pp. 185–200.

5   Hartley, *Oil Palm*, pp. 681–683; UPAR, 1988; interviews with K.G. Berger of PORIM, 25 March 1987, Dennis Gilbert of the Tropical Growers' Association, 2 August 1988, and Tan Sri Dato' Seri B. Bek-Nielsen, 31 March 1989. Strictly speaking the name of the new hybrid should be *Elaeis oleifera guineensis*, but in practice the short form is always used.

6   J.J. Hardon, 'Interspecific hybrids in the genus Elaeis. II. Vegetative growth and yield of F1 hybrids *E. Guineensis x E. Oleifera*', *Euphytica*, vol. 18, 1969, p. 380; interview with Dr H. Corley, formerly of OPGL, 11 July 1988; Hartley, *Oil Palm*, pp. 87–89; UPRDAR, 1968–70; UPAR, 1970.

7   Hartley, *Oil Palm*, pp. 608–611; UPRDAR, 1969–73.

8   UPRDAR, 1978–82.

9   Interviews with K.G. Berger, 18 May 1993 and C.W.S. Hartley, 10 August 1988; A. Kushairi, N. Rajanaidu *et al.*, 'PORIM oil palm planting materials', *PORIM Bulletin*, vol. 38, May 1999, pp. 1–13; M. Sharma, 'Utilization of Nigerian PS1 and PS2 selection in oil palm breeding programmes at UP Berhad' in N. Rajanaidu and B.S. Jalani (eds), *Proceedings of Seminar on PS1 and PS2 Planting Materials, 1 June 1999* (Kuala Lumpur: PORIM, 1999), pp. 18–29.

10 N. Rajanaidu, V. Rao and B.K. Tan, 'Analysis of fatty acid composition in *Elaeis guineensis, Elaeis oleifera* and hybrids', in *Oil Composition in Oil Palm: Task Force Report to Director-General of PORIM* (Kuala Lumpur: PORIM, 1985), pp. 81–94; N. Rajanaidu and V. Rao, 'Oil palm genetic collections: their performance and use

to the industry', in Abdul Halim b. Hj. Hassan, P.S. Chew, B.J. Wood and E. Pushparajah (eds), *Proceedings of the 1987 International Oil Palm/Palm Oil Conferences, I: Agriculture* (Kuala Lumpur: PORIM/ISP, 1987), pp. 59–85; N. Rajanaidu, '*Elaeis oleifera* collection in Central and South America', in *Proceedings of International Workshop on Oil Palm Germplasm and Utilization, 26–27 March 1985* (Kuala Lumpur: ISOPB/PORIM, 1986), pp. 84–94.

11 UPRDAR, 1986; UPAR, 1987–89.

12 Interview with Tan Yap Pau, 3 September 1987; *The Oil Palm in Malaya* (1st edn, by B. Bunting, C.D.V. Georgi and J.N. Milsum, Kuala Lumpur: Department of Agriculture, 1934; 2nd edn, no editor named, Kuala Lumpur: Ministry of Agriculture and Co-Operatives, 1966); Hartley, *Oil Palm,* was first published 1967; quotation about the ISP from commemorative programme for the official opening of Wisma ISP, 30 December 1982; handbooks published in Kuala Lumpur by the ISP: J.W.L. Bevan, T. Fleming and B.S. Gray, *Planting Techniques for Oil Palms in Malaysia* (1966), B.J. Wood, *Pests of Oil Palms in Malaysia and their Control* (1969), J.W.L. Bevan and B.S. Gray, *The Organization and Control of Field Practice for Large-Scale Oil Palm Plantings in Malaysia* (1969), P.D. Turner and R.A. Gillbanks, *Oil Palm Cultivation and Management* (1974). A handbook based on these publications is C.N. Williams and Y.C. Hsu, *Oil Palm Cultivation in Malaya: Technical and Economic Aspects* (Kuala Lumpur: University of Malaya Press, 1970). ISP Conference publications: *Oil Palm Developments in Malaysia* (1968); *Progress in Oil Palm* (1969); *The Quality and Marketing of Oil Palm Products* (1969); *Advances in Oil Palm Cultivation* (1973). A study of the extensive bibliography in Hartley, *Oil Palm* (3rd edn, 1988) shows how important the ISP publications continued to be, alongside those of WAIFOR (now NIFOR) and the French journal *Oléagineux,* as sources of information on the best oil palm planting practice.

13 Interview with Leslie Davidson, 7 July 1988.

14 Interview with Dr B.S. Gray, 6 June 1989; Hartley, *Oil Palm* (3rd edn, 1988), pp. 336–343. Baskets were recommended by A. Bybjerg Pedersen, then at Ulu Bernam, in 'Some notes on oil palms', *The Planter*, vol. XXXIV, no. 7, 1958, pp. 389–392. Polybags were popularized by J.E. Duckett of Malayan Estate Agencies Group Ltd in 'The use of perforated polythene bags in the oil palm pre-nursery', *The Planter*, vol. XL, no. 8, 1964, pp. 384–389, and were adopted at Ulu Bernam in the same year: UBAR, 1964.

15 Interview with L. Davidson, 7 July 1988; Hartley, *Oil Palm* (3rd edn, 1988), pp. 174–178.

16 UPRD: Minutes of the second planting practices committee meeting, 12 May 1982. On the long-term impact of the weevil on bunch patterns, see T.P. Pantzaris, 'Palm

oil, palm kernels and *Elaeidobius* – Parts 1 and 2', *Palm Oil Developments*, vol. 3, December 1985, pp. 7–9, and vol. 4, January 1986, pp. 1–3; Chin Cheuk Weng, Foong S.F. and Mohd. Hussin M.S., 'FFB production, oil and kernel yields over a 14-year period (1982 to 1995) for FELDA's lysimeter and two surrounding palms' in N. Rajanaidu, I.E. Henson and B.S. Jalani (eds), *Proceedings of International Conference on Oil and Kernel Production in Oil Palm, ISOPB and PORIM, 27–28 September 1996* (Kuala Lumpur: PORIM, 1998), pp. 55–77.

17 Interview with P.G. Cowling, 3 September 1987.

18 New Economic Policy statement, 18 March 1970, reprinted in J. Faaland, J.R. Parkinson and R. Saniman, *Growth and Ethnic Inequality: Malaysia's New Economic Policy* (London: Hurst, 1990), p. 312.

19 UBAR, 1950–82; UPAR, 1970–90. Source for Map 6: UPAR, 2001.

20 B.S. Gray, 'A study of the influence of genetic, agronomic and environmental factors on the growth, flowering and bunch production of the oil palm on the west coast of West Malaysia' (unpublished PhD thesis, University of Aberdeen, 1969), pp. 399–441; J.T. Thoburn, *Primary Commodity Exports and Economic Development: Theory, Evidence and a Study of Malaysia* (London: Wiley, 1977), p. 172.

21 UBAR, 1931–40 and 1946–80.

22 Interviews with Tan Yap Pau, 3 September 1987, and C.W.S. Hartley, 10 August 1988; Hartley, *Oil Palm* (3rd edn, 1988), pp. 495 and 546–547; UPRDAR, 1972–88; UBAR, 1960–80.

23 Interviews with K.M.S. Stimpson, 19 July and 10 November 1988; UPAR, 1970–72; UPRDAR, 1978.

24 Interviews as previous note; 'The Planter interview: K.M.S. Stimpson', *The Planter*, vol. LXII, no. 6, 1986, pp. 247–254. The Scots connection with Malayan planting goes back to Ceylon, from which many of the pioneering British Malayan planters came: Daniel Green, *A Plantation Family* (Ipswich: The Boydell Press, 1979), Ch. 2; K.M.S. Stimpson, 'Malayan estates – the Scots connection', *Selangor St Andrew's Society 1887–1986* (Kuala Lumpur: SSAS Centenary Committee, 1986), pp. 44–46.

25 Interview with Stimpson, 10 November 1988; UBAR, 1930–40.

26 UBAR, 1946–78; General manager's summary of UP and BOP's internal annual reports, 1949.

27 UBAR, 1946–78.

28 UBAR, 1957–62; interviews with D.M. Gold, formerly of Harrisons & Crosfield, 9 August 1988; and K.M.S. Stimpson, 19 July 1988. In his retirement, since 1983, Dissing has become the owner of three farms in England and Denmark, one of which is close to Ole Schwensen's estate. The ties of friendship within United

Plantations' planting community have often endured in this way: personal communication from Knud Sehested, 29 June 2000.

29 Interviews with Mrs R. Grut, 21 April 1988; K.M.S. Stimpson, 19 July 1988; and M. Rajadurai, executive secretary, ISP, 18 April 1989.

30 Interview with K.M.S. Stimpson, 10 November 1988; Carrie Jørgensen , 'United Plantations and Bernam Oil Palms: highlights from a colourful past' (unpublished mss, 1984), pp. 156–167; UPRDAR, 1980–88; UPAR, 1997; papers by Gurmit Singh, S. Manoharan, K. Kanapathy, Tan Yap Pau, E. Mohan, H. Jørgensen, A.N. Rasmussen and N. Santa Maria in E. Pushparajah and P.S. Chew (eds), *The Oil Palm in Agriculture in the Eighties*, Vol 2 (Kuala Lumpur: ISP, 1982), pp. 367–378, 623–636 and 641–652.

31 Interview with Peter Cowling, 3 September 1987; UPAR, 1964–87.

32 UPAR, 1975–2001; interviews with Toh Tai San, 3 September 1987, and S. Manoharan, 20 February 1989.

33 Interview with Mogens Jensen, 27 August 1989; IPFAR, 2001.

34 Interviews with John Goodwin, 30 August 1988 and 21 December 2000; UPAR, 1981; IPFAR, 1983–2001.

35 United International Enterprises, Explanatory Memorandum and Circular Letter to UP and IPF Shareholders, 9 May 1983; J. T. Lindblad, *Foreign Investment in South-East Asia in the Twentieth Century* (London: Macmillan, 1998), p. 117; Wong Sulong, 'Danes cash in on NEP *volte-face*', *Financial Times* (London), 23 March 1988.

36 United International Enterprises Ltd, Prospectus for 1989 Rights Issue.

37 UIE Ltd, Annual Reports, 1988–2001.

38 Sources for the two following paragraphs as for Table 9.

39 S. Cunyngham-Brown, *The Traders: a Story of Britain's South-East Asian Commercial Adventure* (London: Newman Neame, for Guthrie & Co., 1971), pp. 294–295; P.T. Bauer, *The Rubber Industry: a Study in Competition and Monopoly* (London: Longman, 1948), Appendix E; Hartley, *Oil Palm* (3rd edn, 1988), pp. 281–284; interview with Dr R.H.V. Corley of Unifield Tissue Culture Ltd, 11 July 1988.

40 UPAR, 1981–85; UPRDAR, 1983; 'Jean-Pierre Gascon: biographical notes', *Newsletter of the International Society for Oil Palm Breeders*, vol. IX, no. 1, 1992, pp. 2–3.

41 UPRDAR, 1983–85; Hartley, *Oil Palm* (3rd edn, 1988), pp. 80, 238–239 and 284–286; R.H.V. Corley, C.H. Lee, I.H. Law and C.Y. Wong, 'Abnormal flower development in oil palm clones', *The Planter*, vol. LXII, no. 6, 1986, pp. 247–254.

42 Hartley, *Oil Palm* (3rd edn, 1988), pp. 607–611; N. Rajanaidu, O. Rohani and B.S. Jalani, 'Oil palm clones: current status and prospects for commercial production', *The Planter*, vol. LXXIII, no. 4, 1997, pp. 163–184; G. Ginting, C. Mollers and K.

Pamin, 'Somatic embryogenesis in oil palm for the *in-vitro* propagation of elite clones', *Jurnal Pusat Penelitian Kelapa Sawit (Indonesian Journal of Oil Palm Research)*, vol. 4, no. 1 1996, pp. 11–16; UPAR, 1998.

43   N. Rajanaidu and B.S. Jalani (eds), *Proceedings of the Symposium on The Science of Palm Oil Breeding, 30 June–2 July 1992* (Kuala Lumpur: PORIM, 1999) – J. Meunier, 'Developments in the field of biotechnology and their applications to oil palm breeding', pp. 1–7, and R.H.V. Corley, S.G. Hughes, P.L. Jack, N.P. Batty and S. Mayes, 'Future prospects for oil palm breeding: new techniques, new strategies, new products', pp. 274–299; Ghulam Kadir A. Parveez and Paul Christou, 'Biolistic-mediated DNA delivery and isolation of transgenic oil palm (*Elaeis guineensis* Jacq.) embryogenic callus cultures', *Journal of Oil Palm Research* (PORIM), vol. 10, no. 2, 1998, pp. 29–38.

44   UPRDAR, 1988; UPAR, 1990.

45   Sources as previous note, and UBAR, 1938 and 1956–61; Hartley, *Oil Palm*, Ch. 13; 'Zero burning techniques for oil palm development', in Ariffin Darus, Ahmad Hitam and Ahmad Zamri Md. Yusof (eds), *Proceedings of the National Seminar on Mechanization in Oil Palm Plantation, 30 June–1 July 1998* (Kuala Lumpur: PORIM, 1999), Session V, pp. 99–126.

46   On researchers' hopes, see Sessions I to IV in Ariffin Darus *et al.* (eds), *Proceedings of the National Seminar on Mechanization, 1998*, and Wan Ishak Wan Ismail and Mohd. Zohadie Bardaie, 'Automation and robotic in agriculture: with special reference to the oil palm industry', in *Proceedings of the 1999 PORIM International Palm Oil Congress: Agriculture* (Kuala Lumpur: PORIM, 1999), pp. 89–94; on planes and fertilizers, see UPAR, 1992–93.

Conclusion

The end of the year 2002 provides a good moment for taking stock of the two success stories told in this book: the development of Malaysia's palm oil industry since the Second World War, and the survival and growth of United Plantations through almost a century of peace and wartime, British imperial rule and independent government. As the year moved towards its close, Malaysia's long-serving prime minister, Dr Mahathir Mohamad, began to prepare the way for his retirement. So, too, did Tan Sri Bek-Nielsen, following in the footsteps of his friend and colleague, Tan Sri Haji Basir bin Ismail. Meanwhile, United Plantations and United International Enterprises (Malaysia) stood on the brink of merger, as did International Plantations and Finance and United International Enterprises (Bahamas). The last two firms were already owned by essentially the same group of shareholders: namely, the descendants of United Plantations' original Scandinavian shareholders and founders, together with the families of Tan Sri Bek-Nielsen and the other key European executives of the post-war era. This group now faces the same challenge as in the 1950s and the 1980s: how best to invest the proceeds of successful oil palm planting. Malaysia, meanwhile, faces the challenge of how best to build on the success of economic policies that have promoted goals of growth and equity together. In both cases, an understanding of the reasons for past success may prove of value in informing current decisions.

In the case of Malaysia's palm oil industry, success depended critically on the application of numerous inventions, most of which had been made elsewhere. Each of these inventions may best be seen as a cog or wheel that gained its full value only when combined with the others to make a whole. Innovation took place in plant breeding, field cultivation, harvesting and transport methods, in

320

specific items of factory machinery and in the arrangement of workflows within the mill. As Axel Lindquist saw in the 1950s, and as Bek-Nielsen has continued to impress upon his managers ever since, the production process for palm oil must be managed in a fully integrated way throughout the value chain leading from seedlings to shipment if quality is to be raised and costs driven down effectively. This integrated approach to nursery, field and factory operations, when combined with a constant attention to detail and an unceasing quest for small improvements as well as big technical leaps, help to explain the competitive edge which United Plantations has maintained throughout the era of Bek and Basir.

For Malaysia as a whole, the ability of the planting community to share ideas about new techniques and management methods has been another key reason for success. Ideas came into colonial Malaya across imperial as well as regional boundaries, from the Netherlands East Indies and the Belgian Congo, from Europe and America, from India and Japan. From the earliest years of commercial palm oil production in the 1920s, these ideas began to encompass the spheres of marketing and new product development without which the spectacular development of Malaysia's palm oil industry after *Merdeka* (Independence) would have been impossible. The planting community provided a vehicle whereby local commodity producers could have a window on the world, first through the trading ties of the Agency Houses, and second through the vertical integration of companies like Unilever in the 1940s, and then United Plantations itself through its investment in Aarhus Oliefabrik.

The success since 1950 of Malaysia's planters, in eclipsing the West African smallholders who had initially supplied palm oil to the world, has been shown in this way to rest not on any intrinsic superiority of planters to peasants but on two specific features of Malaysia's planting community: its openness to new ideas and its ability to manage planting, processing and product placement in an integrated way. Malaysia's planters also benefited from a stroke of luck in that oil palm yields are highly sensitive to soils and climate, and the conditions found in Peninsular Malaysia and neighbouring Sumatra have proved to be ideal. Finally, the development in the 1940s of reliable breeding techniques for the Tenera hybrid variety, the one innovation which stands out as the cornerstone of all the rest, immediately removed the main advantage which West African farmers had previously enjoyed over their competitors: their access to semi-wild palms which grew in symbiosis with cultivated food crops. Once a cultivated palm became available which offered dramatically higher yields and easier harvesting, dependence on semi-wild varieties became a drawback rather than an asset.

Meanwhile, Malaysia's rubber planters were experiencing the reverse trend: as the artificial restrictions on smallholder competition came to an end in the 1940s, and as the world market for rubber was transformed by the development of synthetics, so plantation rubber production became less profitable. The palm oil planters, both at United Plantations and elsewhere, were now able to expand quickly by converting rubber stands and to benefit from the hard work of earlier generations in clearing dense jungle and constructing road and river transport links to the ports. This windfall gain of low start-up costs combined with the high yields from the Tenera palm to give the Malaysian planters a strong competitive edge over their West African smallholder counterparts. One indicator of this fundamental contrast in yields could be seen in the living standards of the mid-twentieth century. Plantation managers in Malaysia were able to offer their workers a higher standard of living, cleaner water, better medical facilities and schools than those available to smallholder palm oil producers in Nigeria. For United Plantations' founder, Aage Westenholz, and subsequent generations of managers who remained true to his ideals, high standards of welfare provision were a point of principle. Yet such principles remained affordable because of the high yields offered by the plantations' palms. United Plantations and its sister firm, Bernam Oil Palms, continued to make a handsome profit for their shareholders, even after they began paying substantial taxes to the government in 1952.

High yields, however, are only part of the story. United Plantations, as an early entrant to the palm oil industry and an early investor in the Tenera palm, reaped the full benefit of high yields from the mid-1940s to the 1960s. Yet in order to keep its leading edge as other companies, and state-sponsored group smallholdings, entered the palm oil business thereafter, United Plantations had to develop fresh forms of innovation, moving from the field to the factory and beyond to the world market itself. As in the case of plant breeding, the search for engineering and marketing innovations was being carried out by many different firms and government agencies. The remarkable co-operative spirit within the industry, encouraged by the existence of organizations like the Incorporated Society of Planters, the Tropical Products Institute in London and, from 1979, the Palm Oil Research Institute of Malaysia, allowed ideas to spread quickly. Bek-Nielsen, as chief engineer of United Plantations from 1959 onwards, was therefore able to build not only on the company's in-house traditions of experimentation but also on the new approaches of engineers at Unilever's Pamol operation and at Harrisons & Crosfield, who were benefiting from their parent companies' close ties to the Western market.

The common thread uniting the work of the post-war engineers with the ideas of pre-war pioneers like Olof Grut, the son of Bernam Oil Palms' inspirational founder, was an appreciation of the versatility of palm oil. During the nineteenth and early twentieth centuries, Westerners had been well aware that palm oil was used as a foodstuff in West Africa but regarded this as, at best, an entertaining curiosity. Within the British imperial economic order, palm oil had its niche as an industrial commodity, used as a flux in tin-plating; as an ingredient in soap and candle-making; and only to a very limited extent for edible purposes. The margarine and compound lard industries, which were in any case better developed in the USA than in Europe, required bland, pale oils – and palm oil in its natural state is dark red, strongly flavoured and heavily aromatic. Olof Grut was regarded as a troublesome eccentric when he developed a method of air-bleaching the oil in the 1930s and began selling the product directly to India, bypassing the highly organized hub-and-spoke trading network focused on England that was favoured by his Agency House peers.

In the immediate aftermath of the Second World War, Olof's experiments were put aside while Axel Lindquist concentrated on rebuilding and renovating the factories, laying the foundations for a formidable in-house machine-making capability in the process. This capability proved vital after the introduction of the Tenera palm for its oil-rich fruit required fresh kinds of processing machinery, developed on the spot by trial and error. Similar experiments were going on throughout Malaya, building on Unilever's early trials at Mongana in the Belgian Congo; but those carried out by Bek-Nielsen, following Axel's retirement, were conspicuously successful and laid the foundations of an international reputation.

Meanwhile, far more radical work was going on in Europe and North America, where the chronic shortage of animal fats during and after the Second World War had prompted the development of new refining techniques for palm oil and other vegetable based alternatives to butter and lard. By the 1960s it had become possible to transform palm oil into an 'invisible ingredient,' flavourless and colourless. The oil could then be split down into fractions, making it as soft or hard, as liquid or solid, as the Western manufacturer desired. By adding flavours, colours, other blended oils and nutritional supplements, palm oil could be turned into a convincing replica of almost any other oil or fat. From now on it became known primarily as an edible, rather than an industrial, commodity and the quality of the crude oil supplied by growers became all-important. The mill-and-plantation system, within which quality could be tightly controlled, now acquired an unbeatable competitive advantage over the individual small-holder. Group smallholdings, modelled on the mill-and-plantation managerial system but with shared ownership, could still compete, and indeed gained market share within Malaysia as a result of official land policy from the mid-1950s onwards. However, the West African farmers who had dominated the world palm oil trade since the nineteenth century were now completely eclipsed, as local political instability and heavy taxation compounded the effects of these underlying competitive trends.

Once palm oil became established as an edible commodity within Western markets, world demand for it began to grow rapidly. However, Bek-Nielsen was among the first to realize that Western demand alone would not be enough to absorb the massive increase in supplies which could be expected from Malaysia by the 1970s. Even though the Indonesian and Congo palm oil industries had fallen into disarray, and West African smallholder production systems were becoming uncompetitive, so much land was still being turned over to oil palms by rubber planters and government planners in Malaysia that the market could easily have been swamped. This risk appeared especially acute once new processing methods were developed for soyabean oil, and American plantings of this crop increased dramatically in the late 1960s.

The spectacular success of Malaysia's palm oil industry since 1970 is, therefore, not least a story of pro-active product and market development. Bek-Nielsen and his colleagues at United Plantations have been at the forefront of this saga. Like Olof Grut in the 1930s, they were viewed initially as troublesome eccentrics, especially by the Agency Houses when they broke up the cosy cartel arrangements through which palm oil prices were determined, and sales agreed, in London. In breaking up the cartel, United Plantations opened the way for all Malaysian producers to seek buyers for their palm oil directly in Japan, India, Pakistan, North Africa, the Gulf States and China. These regions have since become key growth markets for Malaysia. The rigid imperial hub-and-spoke has been replaced by a flexible web-like pattern of world trade. The web has many advantages over the former system, especially in its ability to spread the risks of demand fluctuation within the notoriously volatile commodity trade.

It is worth reflecting here on the advantages of Malaysia's own post-colonial social and political system. The ability of successive administrations to contain ethnic tensions and keep the peace, while allowing space for each of Malaysia's ethnic communities to retain its distinctive identity within the plural society, is surely the most important reason for the economic success of the country and, within it, of the palm oil industry. Peace and political stability are essential conditions for the success of any long-term investment: and oil palms require four to seven years to reach maturity. Beyond this, the involvement of South Asian, Chinese and Muslim Malay executives as co-operative colleagues within United Plantations, as within Malaysia's palm oil industry as a whole, has been of immeasurable value both in developing new products to suit various Asian tastes and in cultivating the market contacts which are needed in selling them.

Bek-Nielsen realized very early on that if Malaysia's palm oil producers were to be successful in penetrating Asian markets, they would have to refine their oil locally into a form that end users would value. Before 1970, almost all refining of Malaysian crude palm oil was carried out in Europe, and United Plantations was at the forefront of the struggle to break this pattern. In so doing, the firm spearheaded the application to the palm oil industry of the Malaysian government's overall strategy of export-led industrialization. The Unitata refinery, opened in 1974, has become a model of best practice in high-quality production. It has turned its major weaknesses – relatively small size and inland location – into strengths by focusing on profitable niche products such as the vitamin-rich red palm oil. Through its link with the Danish firm Aarhus Oliefabrik, it has continued to channel new product ideas and technologies into Malaysia, and through Anglia Oils, it has even refreshed Malaysia's old trading ties with the British market.

The continued ability of United Plantations to make a positive contribution to the Malaysian development process, together with the ability of other European and Japanese firms to help build a palm-oil-based oleochemicals industry from the 1980s onwards, highlights another reason for Malaysia's overall success in the field of export-led industrialization. Successive Malaysian governments have continued to welcome foreign investors, provided they show a proper understanding of their role as guests in an independent state. Europeans, too, have their niche within the plural society. Greatly though the old Agency House managers may have dreaded life after *Merdeka*, the actual experience of Bek-Nielsen, and the managers from other firms who were interviewed for this study, has been rich and invigorating. Certainly, the Europeans who stayed found that they had to share authority and ownership with Asians, but as the experience of Bek and Basir has shown, this could produce excellent results for both the individuals and their firms. Nationalization and localization, implemented in the Malaysian case with careful pacing and evident fairness, need not mean economic disruption and the waste or destruction of the capital assets so painfully created during the imperial era. On the contrary, in the case of Malaysia's palm oil industry, the period of the New Economic Policy has also been a time of rapid innovation and growth, in which existing assets have been fully used and further developed for the benefit of future generations.

As the new generation of Asian managers prepares to take control, they will readily appreciate the value of the physical assets, the fields, factories, refineries and oleochemicals plants, created by the hard work described in this book. Yet an even more valuable legacy, as they prepare to find fresh solutions to the challenges of the new millennium, will be the culture and spirit of the palm oil pioneers. In the case of United Plantations, many individual strands have combined to produce the quirky, adventurous yet warm and welcoming culture which characterizes the modern firm. Bek and Basir have nurtured many of the qualities of earlier leaders: the patience and compassion of Aage Westenholz, the passion for performance of Commander Grut, the love of diversity and experimentation shown by the visionary Olof Grut, the love of talk and good company through which his brother Rolf brought in new practical solutions and the toughness and ingenuity of Axel Lindquist. To this, they have added a genuine fascination with palm oil in all its varied uses and a passionate belief in its value as an edible oil for the world. For such a passionate belief in the intrinsic interest of one's work there is no substitute. Without this belief, quality standards cannot be pushed higher and innovation will not happen. Fortunately for Malaysia, it is a nation full of belief, and the palm oil industry is full of young people who find their work exciting. There is every reason for hope in the future.

Local Processing of Malaysian Palm Oil: The Bek-Nielsen View

*I*n September 1974, Børge Bek-Nielsen first put down on paper what he has since come to regard as the classic expression of his views on this subject. His letter, reproduced below, was addressed to Tan Sri Sir Claude Fenner, then the Special Representative of the Rubber Growers' Association in Kuala Lumpur. The governing Council of the RGA was still based in London at the time, and Bek's letter highlights the differences in attitude between United Plantations, which had already embraced the principle of localization, and the British Agency Houses.

In a further letter to the present author, dated 26 February 2003, Tan Sri Bek-Nielsen adds:

Tan Sri Sir Claude Fenner

> Tan Sri Sir Claude Fenner was my personal friend, whose whole official career was associated with the police, which he joined as a probationary ASP in 1936. During the Second World War, having managed to escape from Singapore in February 1941, he joined the Special Operations Executive (SOE) of South-East Asia Command and as a member of the Force 136 landed in Malaya on two occasions (once by submarine and once by air) behind Japanese lines. After the war, Fenner resumed his career in the Malaysian Police, being appointed Inspector General in 1963. After retirement he was actively involved as a member of the Malaysian Oil Palm Growers' Council.

UNITED PLANTATIONS BERHAD-

(Incorporated in the States of Malaya)

REGISTERED OFFICE:
Jendarata Estate
Teluk Anson.

~~TELEPHONE~~
Teluk Anson 621800 (10 lines)

ESTATES
Jendarata
Kuala Bernam
Sungei Bernam
Ulu Bernam

TELEGRAMS
UNITED, Teluk Anson
TELEX
MA 46061

Teluk Anson
Malaysia

PERSONAL

11th September 1974

Tan Sri Sir Claude Fenner,
The Rubber Growers' Association Ltd.,
Peti Surat 1094
KUALA LUMPUR.

Dear *Claude,*

Local Processing of Malaysian Palm Oil

With reference to the above mentioned subject which has been analysed in the London produced paper "The Malaysian Palm Oil Industry", I should like to submit the following comments for your personal information.

You know I have, for some years, strongly advocated a more active approach to the question of further local processing of Malaysian Palm Oil. I have done so not to further U.P.'s interest because we have long ago taken the initiative to create the plants required for fully integrated production of such items as refined oil, vanaspati, margarine, glycerine and soap because we did not expect the palm oil producers would be able to agree that a common interest would justify the construction of a few big plants at the ports of export.

However, I have for quite some time been able to judge the future development by grass root connections, and it is for this reason I have raised my voice on several occasions, because I have seen the danger of the palm oil industry being overpowered by the initiative taken by outsiders. The proliferation of further processing plants will in time to come make it extremely difficult to control the orderly selling and distribution of the Oil Palm Growers' products. Time will soon prove this to be a realistic view.

The British people, for whom I have such high regard and eternal admiration, nowadays seem to show very little of the spirit which during the second world war commanded the respect of all freedom loving people. It is no good at all that the boys in London are sticking their heads together, and producing a well written paper on why it is not advisable to go in for local processing of palm oil in excess of what can be sold locally or to nearby markets.

To add that local refining would seriously aggravate the effluent problem can only be taken as an ill concealed proof that further local processing of palm oil is something which the ex-colonial masters in London will try to prevent, if at all possible.

It is therefore appropriate to ask what it is London wishes to achieve by trying to suppress a natural urge by a new and comparatively dynamic nation like Malaysia, which instead of remaining plain producer of primary products now aspires to obtain a little more of the cake by having a part of the more-added value done in this country. This in turn will help to increase the G.N.P., and it does not necessarily mean that London will loose out. On the contrary the investment benefits given by Malaysia are more attractive than obtained anywhere else, and if British firms are not interested, Japanese business houses are.

The paper submitted by London reflects the same attitude which Henry Ford often met in the infancy of the car industry. The story goes that he frequently found many of his brilliant engineers telling him why a new idea could not be produced or adopted. If he then subsequently went to the skilled craftsmen on the shop floor with his problem, they quickly found a solution in spite of their comparative ignorance.. It is something similar which is now taking place within the palm oil industry. The good experts in London tell us out here why it is not feasible or advisable to go in for further processing at local level, which the Chines, Japanese, Indians and even the Danes rush into such ventures.

The answer to this could of course be that we are all fools, and those who disagree with our views could be right. There is however strong evidence that those who could have taken the initiative with the greatest chances of success have chosen to be inactive, and thereby run the risk of one day no longer being the master of their own products.

About 50,000 tons of refined oil has already been sold, and all the talk about it being inadvisable to ship refined oil, does not ring very convincingly when it is common knowledge that refined coconut oil has been shipped from the Philippine to the U.S.A. over many years. Similarly refined oil can be bought ex tanks at various terminals throughout the world. The problem of oxidation is not at all impossible to overcome if a blanket of an inert gas is applied; and it is strange that it has not been mentioned that several refining plants in Europe now refine, bleach and deodorise high quality palm oil in one operation. Even Unilever apply such operation at several plants. It would therefore be natural to use semi-refined and even bleached palm oil in such plants because a small build up of F.F.A. in semi-refined oil would be distilled over during deodorising.

It is perhaps a natural inclination to fight to maintain status quo, and when Prof. M. Locin and Miss. Jacobsberg make great effort to promote the production of high grade palm oil, it is understandable because they pay great attention to what Unilever would prefer.

My personal view is in strong conflict with such attitude, and it will be Europe's downfall if the people in the old world continue to allow themselves to live under the mis-apprehension that the resources of the under-developed nations must be available at cheap rates in order to allow the trade union dictatorship, we have, to continue to win wage claims which will only further widen the gap between Europe and the developing world of which Malaysia is a more advanced member. Even if we accepted the idea that it would not be possible to ship refined oil to Europe on account of import duty; would it not then have been a wise move if London based palm oil producers had taken the initiative to build a bridge between such organisations as Unilever, Bibby's and others. By doing this it would have been possible to forestall the losses Unilever now will suffer in the Persian Gulf area, because they have failed to make an entrance through the back door by making a joint venture with for instance 1/3 Bumiputra, 1/3 Unilever and 1/3 London controlled palm oil producers.

It is incredible that London has shown so little foresight and forgotten about the old saying "if you cannot beat them join them". To do so would have shown that London accepted the policy of Bumiputra participation. It is now left to Orang Nippon to replace the British in yet another field of commercial activity, and I am afraid this will not be the last time such a thing happens.

You may for instance know that Datuk Harris is in the course of having erected a palm kernel extraction plant at Labuan. When it is ready, I think it will be obvious that the producers in Sabah can expect an export ban on kernels. Would the producers' interest not have been better served by having arranged for one or two co-operative kernel oil extraction plants? I think time will supply a convincing answer to this question.

I trust the above has given you an idea of how we in U.P. look upon the question of further processing in Malaysia, and I personally have no doubt that events will prove we have not been entirely wrong.

With best wishes.

Yours sincerely,

Bibliography

INTERVIEWS

Mr Henning F. Andersen, former commercial director of Aarhus Olie, 29 August 1989

Mr Henry Barlow, historian and son of the veteran Highlands & Lowlands planter, Tom Barlow, 18 April 1989

Tan Sri Dato' Seri Haji Basir bin Ismail, chairman of United Plantations, 21 April 1989

Tan Sri Dato' Seri Børge Bek-Nielsen, senior executive director of United Plantations, 31 March 1989 onwards

Mr Kurt Berger, formerly of the Palm Oil Research Institute of Malaysia, 3 March 1987 onwards

Mr Thorkild Bjerglund-Andersen, long-standing investor, and Mrs Mette Bjerglund-Andersen, granddaughter of Thorkil Knudtzon, early legal adviser to United Plantations, 30 August 1989

Dr Hereward Corley, of Unifield Tissue Culture Ltd, Unilever Plantations & Plant Science Group, 11 July 1988

Mr Peter Cowling, executive director (planting) of United Plantations, 4 September 1987 onwards

Mr Leslie Davidson, chairman, Unilever Plantations Group, 7 July 1988

Mr Jeremy Diamond, formerly chief executive officer of Socfin in Malaysia, currently chairman of Socfin's Management Committee and since 2001 an independent non-executive director of United Plantations, interviewed at the Maison des Palmes, 30 August 1987

Mr Thomas Fleming, based in Sumatra 1939–64 with Harrisons and Crosfield, 4 October 1988

Ms Bente Flensborg, Danish radio journalist, 12 April 1989

Mr Dennis Gilbert, of the Tropical Growers' Association, 2 August 1988

Mr Douglas Gold, formerly of Harrisons and Crosfield, 9 August 1988

Mr John Goodwin, managing director of International Plantations and Finance, 30 August 1988 onwards

331

Dr Brian Gray, formerly of Harrisons and Crosfield, 6 June 1989

Mr Erling Grut, compiler of the Grut and Hansen family trees, 3 September 1989

Mr Rolf Lennartson Grut, nephew of Aage Westenholz and former general manager of United Plantations and Bernam Oil Palms; and Mrs Rothes Grut, 19 and 21 April 1988

Mr Keith Hamblin, of Unilever Plantations Engineering Department, 20 July 1988

Mr C.W.S. Hartley, author and former colonial agricultural officer in Lower Perak, and Mrs Hartley, 10 August 1988

Mrs Carrie Jørgensen, historian of United Plantations, 24 August 1988

Mr Hans Jørgensen, former executive director (technical) of United Plantations, 24 August 1988

Mr S. Krishnan, production manager of Unitata, and Mrs Andal Krishnan, 16 April 1989

Mr Axel Lindquist, former chief engineer of United Plantations and Bernam Oil Palms, 20 February and 6 April 1989

Mr S. Manoharan, group engineer (Ulu Bernam), 20 February 1989

Mathalamuthu, chef and entrepreneur, based since 1926 at Jendarata, 8 April 1989

Mr J.H. Maycock, pioneering oil palm mill designer with Unilever, 29 August 1987

Miss Marianne Mayntz-Clausen, daughter of the Ulu Bernam planter, Theodor Mayntz-Clausen, 11 June 1998

Mme Renganayagi Ganapathy, retired estate worker who first came to Ulu Bernam in 1940, to join her brother and sister-in-law, 24 February 1989

Residents of the Jendarata Old Folks' Home: group interview with 20 long-serving estate workers, Jendarata Old Folks' Home, 22 March 1989

Residents of the Jendarata Old Folks' Home: group interview with Muthama, Vallathi, Amirtham, Pasupathu, Rajamma, Pakiam and Muniamna, 5 April 1989

Mr Preben Sten Petersen, son-in-law of United Plantations' director, Sven Torben Westenholz, 2 September 1989

Mr Marshall Pike, director of technical research, Harrisons and Crosfield, 15 April 1987

Mr M. Rajadurai, executive secretary, Incorporated Society of Planters, 18 April 1989

Mr Eric Rosenquist, formerly of the Malayan Agricultural Department and of Guthries' Chemara Research Station, 11 July and 11 August 1988

Mr Joseph R. Santhiapillai, oleochemicals specialist with the Palm Oil Research Institute of Malaysia, 22 September 1995

Mr H.V. Speldewinde, general manager of United International Enterprises (Malaysia), 9 April 1989

Mr Ken Stimpson, former executive director (planting) of United Plantations, 19 July 1988 onwards

Mr Tamaya, retired estate worker then aged c. 90, in Jendarata Hospital, 22 March 1989

Mr Tan Yap Pau, research controller of United Plantations, 3 September 1987

Mr Toh Tai San, group engineer (Jendarata), 3 September 1987

Mr Alain Tirtiaux, designer of fractionation plants, 10 April 1989

Mr Poul K. Vestergaard, chief engineer of United International Enterprises (Malaysia), 10 April 1989

Mrs Shirley Young, formerly of the Carmen Curler Company, 24 May 1991

CORRESPONDENTS

Mr Christian Flemming Heilmann and Mr John Heilmann, sons of United Plantations' general manager, Poul Bent Heilmann

Mr Mogens Jensen, general manager of International Plantation Services Ltd, which runs United Plantations' and its associated companies' Copenhagen office

Mr Kerk Choon Keng, financial controller, Unitata

Dr Valdemar Lindquist, son of United Plantations' chief engineer, Axel Lindquist

Mrs Inge Asboe Mitchell, who was attached to the Ingemann household from 1945 to 1952, during the formative years of United Plantations (South Africa)

Mr Knud Sehested, former vice-chairman of United Plantations

DOCUMENTARY SOURCES PROVIDED BY UNITED PLANTATIONS

Bek-Nielsen, B., letter to Tan Sri Sir Claude Fenner of the Rubber Growers' Association, 11 Sept. 1974

BOPCA, 1928–66: Chairman's Address, made at the Annual General Meeting of Bernam Oil Palms

BOP Board Meetings, 1952–65: Minutes of Bernam Oil Palms' Board Meetings

BOPCM, 1948–54: Minutes of Directors' Committee Meetings, Bernam Oil Palms

BOPDR, 1927–65: Directors' Report on the Annual Accounts of Bernam Oil Palms

BOPMC, 1945–46: Correspondence between the general manager, Bernam Oil Palms, and the general manager, United Plantations

CB, 1928–33: Correspondence between the Copenhagen and Bangkok offices of United Plantations

CC, 1935–67: Chairman's Correspondence, Bernam Oil Palms and United Plantations

Correspondence file in Copenhagen office, 'Formation of Malayan Palm Oil Pool, 1952–60'

Ebbesen, Leo, United Plantations' Company Secretary's Handing-Over Notes, 21 June 1960 and 2 July 1963

General manager's summary of UP and BOP's internal annual reports, 1949

Heilmann, P.B., 'An outline of the history of United Plantations South Africa Limited and United Plantations (Swaziland) Limited, 1950–1971' (unpublished mss., 1972)

IPF files: International Plantations and Finance Limited, 'Memoranda on formation', 1956–57; 'Ecuador', 1960–74; and 'John P. Chase', correspondence with a Boston investment consultant, 1961–64.

IPFAR, 1972 onwards: Annual Report, International Plantations and Finance

JAR, 1936 onwards: Annual Report, Jendarata Estate

Jendarata Rubber Co., Ltd: Statutes, November 1907

Jørgensen, Carrie, 'United Plantations and Bernam Oil Palms: highlights from a colourful past' (unpublished mss., 1984)

Krishnan, S., 'Report on the study tour of India, Egypt and the U.K.', 20 June 1970

Malaysian Oil Palm Growers' Council, 'Report on further processing of palm oil in Malaysia' (unpublished mss., September 1974)

Messages of congratulation to Y.Bhg. Tan Sri Dato' Seri B. Bek-Nielsen on the occasion of his golden anniversary with United Plantations Berhad, 15 Sept. 2001

Report by Major A.C. Smith on visit to Bernam Oil Palms, 11–14 July 1947

Share Registers for Bernam Oil Palms, 1927–39 and 1947–48, and United Plantations, 1947–48, held in Copenhagen office

Siam Electricity Co., Ltd, 13th Directors' Report (on the 1906 Accounts).

Souvenir booklet produced by the Veteran Security Association of Malaysia when Bek-Nielsen received the title of Darjah Seri Paduka Mahkota Perak, 8 July 1989

Souvenir programme for the opening of Jendarata's new temple building, 25 November 1987, written in Tamil by Munusamy and Ramalu, with English translation of historical section by Mrs Andal Krishnan.

UBAR, 1927 onwards: Annual Report, Ulu Bernam Estate

UIEAR, 1987 onwards: Annual Report, United International Enterprises

Unitata, 'Unitata: an introduction', 1978

United International Enterprises, Explanatory memorandum and circular letter to UP and IPF Shareholders, 9 May 1983

United International Enterprises, Prospectus for 1989 Rights Issue

United Plantations Africa Ltd, 'Introduction to the Stock Exchange', 28 May 1987

UP Africa AR, 1987–2001: Annual Report, United Plantations Africa

UP Extraordinary General Meetings, 1955–57: United Plantations, Minutes of Meetings

UPAR, 1966 onwards: Annual Report (including Directors' Report and Chairman's Statement) for United Plantations (in Malaysia: previously two separate companies, Bernam Oil Palms and United Plantations)

UPBM, 1958–65: Minutes of United Plantations' Board Meetings

UPCA, 1928–66: Chairman's Address, made at the Annual General Meeting of United Plantations

UPDR, 1917–65: Directors' Report on the Annual Accounts of United Plantations

UPRDAR, 1964–88: United Plantations Research Department Annual Report

Westenholz, A., 'Memorandum angaaende Danmarks Forsvar' [Memorandum concerning Denmark's defence] (printed for private circulation, Holte, Denmark, 1907)

SERIAL PUBLICATIONS

Annual Reports of the RGA (Rubber Growers' Association): 12th, 13th and 14th, 1920–22 (London: RGA, 1921–23)

Bulletin of the RGA, 1919–38 (London: Rubber Growers' Association)

Business Times, 1980 onwards (Kuala Lumpur: New Straits Times Press)

Far Eastern Economic Review, 1980 onwards (Hong Kong: Review Publishing)

International Financial Statistics Yearbooks 1987–96 (Washington, DC: International Monetary Fund)

Malaya, 1952–64, and *Malaysia*, 1964–73 (London: Association of British Malaya/ Malaysia)

Malaysian Business, 1990 onwards (Kuala Lumpur: Berita Publishing)

Malaysian Oil Palm Statistics, 1999 onwards (Kuala Lumpur: Malaysian Palm Oil Board, 2000 onwards); earlier years published by PORLA, see below

Oil World Annual, 1987 onwards (Hamburg: ISTA Mielke GmbH)

Palm Oil Developments, 1985 onwards (Kuala Lumpur: Palm Oil Research Institute of Malaysia, 1985–99; Malaysian Palm Oil Board from 2000)

Palm Oil Technical Bulletin, 1995–2001 (Kuala Lumpur: Palm Oil Research Institute of Malaysia, 1985–99; Malaysian Palm Oil Board from 2000)

The Planter, 1920 onwards (Kuala Lumpur: Incorporated Society of Planters)

PORLA Palm Oil Statistics, 1980–98 (Kuala Lumpur: Palm Oil Registration and Licensing Authority, published annually in the following year, 1981–99); later years published by Malaysian Palm Oil Board

Review of the Malaysian Palm Oil Industry, 2000 onwards (Kuala Lumpur: Malaysian Palm Oil Board, published annually, 2001 onwards)

The Star, 1989 onwards (Kuala Lumpur: Star Publications)

Statistics on Commodities, 1986 onwards (Kuala Lumpur: Ministry of Primary Industries)

BOOKS AND ARTICLES

Abdul Halim b. Hj. Hassan, P.S. Chew, B.J. Wood and E. Pushparajah (eds), *Proceedings of the 1987 International Oil Palm/Palm Oil Conferences, I: Agriculture* (Kuala Lumpur: Palm Oil Research Institute of Malaysia / Incorporated Society of Planters, 1987)

Allen, G.C. and A.G. Donnithorne, *Western Enterprise in Indonesia and Malaya: a Study in Economic Development* (London: Allen & Unwin, 1957)

Amin, Mohamed and Malcolm Caldwell (eds), *Malaya: the Making of a Neo-Colony* (Nottingham: Spokesman Books, 1977)

Ampalavanar, R., *The Indian Minority and Political Change in Malaya, 1945–57* (Kuala Lumpur: Oxford University Press, 1981)

Anciaux, L., *La Participation des Belges à l'Oeuvre Coloniale des Hollandais aux Indes Orientales* (Brussels: Académie Royale des Sciences d'Outre-Mer, 1955)

Andaya, B.W., *Perak, the Abode of Grace* (Kuala Lumpur: Oxford University Press, 1979)

—— and Andaya, L.Y., *A History of Malaysia*, 2nd edn (London: Palgrave, 2001)

Anon, 'The 300 best small companies', *Forbes Global Magazine*, 1 November 1999

Anon, 'Company profile: Anglia Oils', *Oils and Fats International*, August 1999, pp. 26–29

Anon, *The Oil Palm in Malaya* (Kuala Lumpur: Ministry of Agriculture and Co-Operatives, 1966; 2nd edn of work listed under Bunting, B. below)

Anon, *Story of Sime Darby: 75th Anniversary* (Kuala Lumpur: Sime Darby, 1985)

Anon, 'Transforming Tata', *International Business Week*, 21 March 1994

Anuwar Mahmud, 'The palm oil industry', *PORIM Occasional Papers*, 1 (1982)

Ariffin Darus, Ahmad Hitam and Ahmad Zamri Md. Yusof (eds), *Proceedings of the National Seminar on Mechanization in Oil Palm Plantation, 30 June–1 July 1998* (Kuala Lumpur: Palm Oil Research Institute of Malaysia, 1999)

Ariffin Darus and B.S. Jalani (eds), *Proceedings of National Seminar on Palm Oil Extraction Rate, 21–22 December 1993* (Kuala Lumpur: PORIM, 1994)

Ariffin Darus, K. Sivasothy *et al.* (eds), *Proceedings of the National Seminar on Opportunities for Maximizing Production through Better OER and Offshore Investment in Oil Palm, 14–15 December 1998* (Kuala Lumpur: PORIM, 1999)

Baden-Fuller, Charles and Martyn Pitt (eds), *Strategic Innovation: an International Casebook on Strategic Management* (London: Routledge, 1996)

Baden-Fuller, Charles, and John M. Stopford, *Rejuvenating the Mature Business: the Competitive Challenge* (London: Routledge, 1992)

Barlow, C., *The Natural Rubber Industry: Its Development, Technology and Economy in Malaysia* (Kuala Lumpur: Oxford University Press, 1978)

——, S. Jayasuriya and C. Suan Tan, *The World Rubber Industry* (London: Routledge, 1994)

Barlow, H.S., *Swettenham* (Kuala Lumpur: Southdene Sdn. Bhd., 1995; also available from Dekalb, Illinois: Southeast Asia Publications, Northern Illinois University, 1997)

Basri Wahid, Mohd and Hj. Abdul Halim bin Hj. Hassan, 'The effects of Elaeidobius kamerunicus Faust on rat control programmes of oil palm estates in Malaysia', *PORIM Occasional Papers*, 14 (1985)

Bauer, Peter, *The Rubber Industry: a Study in Competition and Monopoly* (London: Longmans, Green & Co., 1948)

Beasley, W.G., *Japanese Imperialism, 1894–1945* (Oxford: Clarendon Press, 1987)

Beirnaert, A., and R. Vanderweyen, 'Contribution a l'étude génétique et biométrique des variétés d'Elaeis guinéensis Jacquin', *Série Scientifique*, no. 27 (Brussels: Publications de l'Institut National pour l'Etude Agronomique du Congo Belge, 1941)

Bek-Nielsen, B., keynote address, 'Milling, refining and processing', in PORIM/ISP, *Proceedings of Conference II: Technology* (Kuala Lumpur: PORIM, 1988), pp. 137–154

——, 'Techno-economic status of the Malaysian palm oil industry' in K. Ragupathy (ed.), *Facing 2020: the Challenges to the Plantation Industry* (Kuala Lumpur: Institute of Strategic and International Studies, 1992), pp. 85–103

Berger, K.G., 'Palm oil', in H.T. Chan (ed.), *Handbook of Tropical Foods* (New York and Basel: Marcel Dekker, Inc., 1983), pp. 433–468

——, 'Dynamics of supply and demand for oils and fats', *PORIM Bulletin Special Issue* (November 1984), pp. 21–26

——, 'Dr Lewkowitsch and early palm oil technology', *Chemistry and Industry*, 17 April 1989

—— and S.M. Martin, 'Palm oil', in K.F. Kiple and K. C. Ornelas (eds), *The Cambridge World History of Food*, Vol. 1 (Cambridge: Cambridge University Press, 2000), pp. 397–411

Bevan, J.W.L., T. Fleming and B.S. Gray, *Planting Techniques for Oil Palms in Malaysia* (Kuala Lumpur: Incorporated Society of Planters, 1966)

—— and B.S. Gray, *The Organisation and Control of Field Practice for Large-Scale Oil Palm Plantings in Malaysia* (Kuala Lumpur: Incorporated Society of Planters, 1969)

Bird, Isabella, *The Golden Chersonese and the Way Thither* (London: Murray, 1883; reprinted Kuala Lumpur: Oxford University Press, 1967 and 1980).

Birmingham, D. and P.M. Martin (eds), *History of Central Africa*, Vol. II (London: Longman, 1983)

Blixen, Karen, *Letters from Africa, 1914–1931*, edited by Frans Lasson (London: Weiden-feld, 1982 and Picador, 1983)

Boje, Per, *Danmark og de multinationale virksomheder før 1950* [Denmark and the multinational enterprises before 1950] (Odense: Odense Universitetsforlag, 2000)

Boomgaard, P. and I. Brown (eds), *Weathering the Storm: the Economies of Southeast Asia in the 1930s Depression* (Leiden and Singapore: KITLV Press and ISEAS, 2000)

Booth, Anne, *The Indonesian Economy in the Nineteenth and Twentieth Centuries* (London: Macmillan, 1998)

Boulle, Pierre, *Sacrilege in Malaya* (Kuala Lumpur: Oxford University Press, 1983; first edn 1958)

Brealey, R., and S. Myers, *Principles of Corporate Finance* (Singapore: McGraw-Hill, 1984)

Brookfield, H. (ed.), *Transformation with Industrialization in Peninsular Malaysia* (Kuala Lumpur: Oxford University Press, 1994)

Brown, I.G., *The Elite and the Economy in Siam, c. 1890–1920* (Singapore: Oxford University Press, 1988)

——, *Economic Change in South-East Asia, c.1830–1980* (Kuala Lumpur: Oxford University Press, 1997)

Bunting, B., C.D.V. Georgi and J.N. Milsum, *The Oil Palm in Malaya* (Kuala Lumpur: Agricultural Department, 1934)

Burns, P.L. (ed.), *The Journals of J.W.W. Birch, First British Resident to Perak, 1874–1875* (Kuala Lumpur: Oxford University Press, 1976)

—— and C.D. Cowan (eds), *Sir Frank Swettenham's Malayan Journals, 1874–1876* (Kuala Lumpur: Oxford University Press, 1975)

Burroughs, P. and A.J. Stockwell (eds), *Managing the Business of Empire: Essays in Honour of David Fieldhouse* (London: Frank Cass, 1998)

Cain, P.J. and A.G. Hopkins, *British Imperialism*, 2 vols (London: Longman, 1993)

Carr, E.H., *The Bolshevik Revolution, 1917–1923*, Vol. I (London: Macmillan, 1950 and Pelican, 1966)

Chapman, B.A., 'Commercial importance of palm oil and current problems', *PORIM Bulletin*, vol. 2, May 1981, pp. 25–32

Cheah Boon Kheng, *Red Star over Malaya: Resistance and Social Conflict during and after the Japanese Occupation of Malaya, 1941–1946* (Singapore: University Press, 1983)

Chong Chiew Let, 'Crude palm oil quality – a survey over the last two decades', *PORIM Bulletin*, vol. 22, May 1991, pp. 27–32

Chow Chee Sing, 'The age effect of oil palms on oil extraction rate in Peninsular Malaysia', *PORIM Bulletin*, vol. 29, November 1994, pp. 31–39

Clarence-Smith, W.G., *Cocoa and Chocolate, 1765–1914* (London: Routledge, 2000)

Clutterbuck, R., *Conflict and Violence in Singapore and Malaysia, 1945–1983* (Singapore: Graham Brash, 1984)

Coates, A., *The Commerce in Rubber: the First 250 Years* (Singapore: Oxford University Press, 1987)

Colonial Office, UK: Colonial No. 211, *Report of the mission appointed to enquire into the production and transport of vegetable oils and seeds produced in the West African Colonies* (London: HMSO, 1947)

CONGOPALM, 'Research on production and storage of palm oil: work carried out under the auspices of IRSIA, 1952–1955', 2 vols (Brussels, 1955; mimeoed translation circulated in the 1980s by the Oil Palm Growers' Council, Kuala Lumpur: widely known as the Mongana Report)

Corley, R.H.V. and P.B.H. Tinker, *The Oil Palm* (Oxford: Blackwell Science, forthcoming); see Hartley, C.W.S. for previous edition

Cornelius, J.A., *Processing of Oil Palm Fruit and its Products*, TPI Report G149 (London: Tropical Products Institute, 1983)

Courtenay, P.P. 'The plantation in Malaysian economic development', *Journal of Southeast Asian Studies*, vol. XII, no. 2, 1981, p. 333

Creutzberg, P. (ed.), *Changing Economy in Indonesia*, Vol. I, *Indonesia's Export Crops, 1816–1940* (Amsterdam: Royal Tropical Institute, 1975)

Cunyngham-Brown, S., *The Traders: a Story of Britain's South-East Asian Commercial Adventure* (London: Newman Neame, for Guthrie & Co., 1971)

Davis, Bernard, *Food Commodities* (London: Heinemann, 1978)

Department of Agriculture, Straits Settlements and Federated Malay States, *Guide to the Experimental Station, Serdang* (Serdang: Government Printer, 1931)

Drabble, J.H., *Rubber in Malaya 1876–1922: the Genesis of the Industry* (Kuala Lumpur: Oxford University Press, 1973)

——, *Malayan Rubber: the Interwar Years* (London: Macmillan, 1991)

——, *An Economic History of Malaysia, c. 1800–1990: the Transition to Modern Economic Growth* (London: Macmillan, 2000)

——, P.J. Drake, and R.T. Stillson, debate on 'The financing of Malayan rubber, 1905–1923', *Economic History Review*, vol. XXIV, no. 4, 1971, pp. 589–598, and vol. XXVII, no. 1, 1974, pp. 108–123

Dumett, R.E. (ed.), *Gentlemanly Capitalism and British Imperialism: the New Debate on Empire* (London: Longman, 1999)

Dyke, F.M., *Report on the Oil Palm Industry in British West Africa* (Lagos: Government Printer, 1927)

Earp, D.A., and W. Newall (eds), *International Developments in Palm Oil* (Kuala Lumpur: Incorporated Society of Planters, 1977)

Faaland, J., J.R. Parkinson and R. Saniman, *Growth and Ethnic Inequality: Malaysia's New Economic Policy* (London: Hurst, 1990)

Fauconnier, H., *The Soul of Malaya* (London: Penguin, 1948)

Fieldhouse, D.K., *Unilever Overseas: the Anatomy of a Multinational, 1895–1965* (London: Croom Helm, 1978)

Fischer, Wolfram, R. Marwin McInnis and Jürgen Schneider (eds), *The Emergence of a World Economy, 1500–1914. Beiträge zur Wirtschafts- und Sozialgeschichte*, Band 33–2 (Wiesbaden: Franz Steiner, 1986)

Flynn, D.O., L. Frost and A.J.H. Latham (eds), *Pacific Centuries: Pacific and Pacific Rim History since the Sixteenth Century* (London: Routledge, 1999)

Fong Chan Onn, *Technological Leap: Malaysian Industry in Transition* (Singapore: Oxford University Press, 1986)

Friedman, Thomas, *The Lexus and the Olive Tree* (London: HarperCollins, 2000 edition)

Furedi, Frank, *Colonial Wars and the Politics of Third World Nationalism* (London: I.B. Tauris, 1994)

Ghulam Kadir A. Parveez and Paul Christou, 'Biolistic-mediated DNA delivery and isolation of transgenic oil palm (Elaeis guineensis Jacq.) embryogenic callus cultures', *Journal of Oil Palm Research* (Palm Oil Research Institute of Malaysia), vol. 10, no. 2, 1998, pp. 29–38

Ginting, G., C. Mollers and K. Pamin, 'Somatic embryogenesis in oil palm for the in-vitro propagation of elite clones', *Jurnal Pusat Penelitian Kelapa Sawit (Indonesian Journal of Oil Palm Research)*, vol. 4, no. 1, 1996, pp. 11–16

Graham, Edgar, with Ingrid Floering, *The Modern Plantation in the Third World* (London: Croom Helm, 1984)

Gray, B.S., 'A study of the influence of genetic, agronomic and environmental factors on the growth, flowering and bunch production of the oil palm on the west coast of West Malaysia' (unpublished PhD thesis, University of Aberdeen, 1969)

Green, Daniel, *A Plantation Family* (Ipswich: Boydell Press, 1979)

Grut, R.L., 'Harvesting and transport of fruit bunches', in *The Oil Palm in Malaya* (Kuala Lumpur: Ministry of Agriculture and Co-Operatives, 1966), pp. 199–212

Gullick, J.M., *Malaysia: Economic Expansion and National Unity* (London: Ernest Benn, 1981)

——, *Malay Society in the Late Nineteenth Century: the Beginnings of Change* (Singapore: Oxford University Press, 1987)

Gurunathan, K., *The War of Oils* (Penang: Principal Quest Sdn. Bhd., 1995)

Haddon, A.V. and Y.L. Tong, 'Oil palm selection and breeding: a progress report', *Malayan Agricultural Journal*, vol. 42, 1959, pp. 124–156

Hardon, J.J., 'Interspecific hybrids in the genus Elaeis. II. Vegetative growth and yield of F1 hybrids E. Guineensis x E. Oleifera', *Euphytica*, vol. 18, 1969, p. 380

Harper, T.N., *The End of Empire and the Making of Malaya* (Cambridge: Cambridge University Press, 1999)

Hartley, C.W.S. *The Oil Palm (Elaeis guineensis Jacq.)* 3rd edn (London: Longman, 1988); see Corley, R.H.V. for 4th edn

——, 'Reflections on a career in tropical agriculture', Rhodes House Oxford, mss. British Empire s. 476, Box III

Havinden, M., and D. Meredith, *Colonialism and Development: Britain and Its Tropical Colonies, 1850–1960* (London: Routledge, 1993)

Hayes, R.H., 'Why Japanese factories work', *Harvard Business Review*, vol. 59, no. 4, 1981, pp. 64–65

Headrick, D.R., *The Tentacles of Progress: Technology Transfer in the Age of Imperialism, 1850–1940* (New York: Oxford University Press, 1988)

Hitching, Claude, and Derek Stone, *Understand Accounting!* (London: Pitman, 1984)

Hogendorn, J., 'The East African groundnut scheme: lessons of a large-scale agricultural failure', *African Economic History*, vol. 10, 1981, pp. 81–115

Hopkins, A.G., 'Back to the future: from national history to imperial history', *Past and Present*, vol. 164, 1999, pp. 198–243

Huff, W.G., *The Economic Growth of Singapore: Trade and Development in the Twentieth Century* (Cambridge: Cambridge University Press, 1994)

Hui, Y.H. (ed.), *Bailey's Industrial Oil and Fat Products*, 5 vols, 5th edn (New York: Wiley, 1996)

Innes, Emily, *The Chersonese with the Gilding Off*, Vol. II (London: Richard Bentley & Son, 1885; reprinted Kuala Lumpur: Oxford University Press, 1974)

ITC (United Nations, International Trade Centre UNCTAD/GATT), *Market Development of Palm Oil Products: Seminar Proceedings, 27 March–1 April 1978* (Geneva: ITC, 1978)

Jackson, J.C., *Planters and Speculators: Chinese and European Agricultural Enterprise in Malaya, 1786–1921* (Kuala Lumpur: University of Malaya Press, 1968)

Jain, R.K., *South Indians on the Plantation Frontier in Malaya* (New Haven: Yale University Press, 1970)

Jones, G., *Merchants to Multinationals: British Trading Companies in the Nineteenth and Twentieth Centuries* (Oxford: Oxford University Press, 2000)

—— and J. Wale, 'Diversification strategies of British trading companies: Harrisons & Crosfield, c. 1900–c. 1980', *Business History*, vol. 41, no. 2, 1999, pp. 69–101.

Jones, W.G., *Denmark: a Modern History* (London: Croom Helm, 1986)

Kaur, Amarjit, *Bridge and Barrier: Transport and Communications in Colonial Malaya, 1870–1957* (Singapore: Oxford University Press, 1985)

Kehoe, M.M. and L.C. Chan, *Buffalo Draught Power on Oil Palm Estates* (Kuala Lumpur: Incorporated Society of Planters, 1987)

Kemp, T., *Industrialization in the Non-Western World* (London: Longman, 1983)

Kepner, C.D., *Social Aspects of the Banana Industry* (New York: Columbia University Press, 1936)

Khera, Harcharan Singh, *The Oil Palm Industry of Malaya: an Economic Study* (Kuala Lumpur: Penerbit Universiti Malaya, 1976)

Kirby, D.G., *Finland in the Twentieth Century* (London: Hurst, 1979)

341

Kokken, Marc J., 'Super oleins from palm oil fractionation', *PORIM Bulletin,* vol. 20, May 1990, pp. 13–20

Kragelund, Poul, *Aarhus Olie 1871–1996* (Aarhus, Denmark: Aarhus Oliefabrik A/S, 1996)

Kratoska, Paul H., *The Japanese Occupation of Malaya 1941–1945: a Social and Economic History* (London: Hurst, 1998)

Krishnan, S., 'Bernam bleachability test method for palm oil', *Journal of the American Oil Chemists' Society,* vol. 52, no. 2, 1975, pp. 23–27

Krozewski, G., 'Sterling, the 'minor' territories, and the end of formal empire, 1939–1958', *Economic History Review,* vol. XLVI, no. 2, 1993, pp. 239–265

——, *Money and the End of Empire: British Economic Policy and the Colonies, 1947–1958* (London: Palgrave, 2001)

Kushairi, A., N. Rajanaidu *et al.,* 'PORIM oil palm planting materials', *PORIM Bulletin,* vol. 38, May 1999, pp. 1–13

Lange, Ole, *Den hvide Elefant: H.N. Andersens Eventyr og ØK, 1852–1914* [The white elephant: H.N. Andersen's ventures and the East Asiatic Company, 1852–1914] (Copenhagen: Gyldendal, 1986)

——, *Jorden er ikke større … H.N. Andersen, ØK og storpolitikken, 1914–1937* [The Earth is no bigger… H.N. Andersen, the East Asiatic Company and affairs of state, 1914–1937] (Copenhagen: Gyldendal, 1988)

Lass, R.A. and G.A.R. Wood (eds), *Cocoa Production: Present Constraints and Priorities for Research,* Technical Paper No. 39 (Washington, DC: World Bank, 1985)

Latham, A.J.H. and H. Kawakatsu (eds), *Asia-Pacific Dynamism 1550–2000* (London: Routledge, 2000)

Laugesen, Mary, Poul Westphall and Robin Dannhorn, *Scandinavians in Siam* (Scandinavian Society of Thailand, Bangkok, 1980)

Laurent, M., 'Notes sur l'Elaeis au Congo Belge', *Bulletin Agricole du Congo Belge,* vol. IV, 1913, pp. 700–701

Law, K.S. 'Development of palm oil industry in Malaya', *Revue Francaise des Corps Gras,* vol. 35, nos 6–7, 1988, pp. 287–292

Leech, H.W.C., 'About Slim and Bernam', *Journal of the Straits Branch of the Royal Asiatic Society,* vol. 4, 1879, p. 38

Leeming, M., *A History of Food: From Manna to Microwave* (London: BBC, 1991)

Leplae, E., *Le palmier à huile en Afrique: son exploitation au Congo Belge et en Extrème-Orient,* Mémoires Tome VII (Brussels: Institut Royal Colonial Belge, Section des Sciences Naturelles et Médicales, 1939)

Lim Chong-Yah, *Economic Development of Modern Malaya* (Kuala Lumpur: Oxford University Press, 1967)

Lim, David, *Economic Growth and Development in West Malaysia, 1947–1970* (Kuala Lumpur: Oxford University Press, 1973)

Lim Kang Hoe, 'Current technological developments and trends in the palm oil processing industry', *PORIM Bulletin*, vol. 20, May 1990, pp. 1–12

Lim Teck Ghee, *Peasants and their Agricultural Economy in Colonial Malaya, 1874–1941* (Kuala Lumpur: Oxford University Press, 1977)

Lindblad, J. Thomas, *Foreign Investment in South-East Asia in the Twentieth Century* (London: Macmillan, 1998)

Loncin, M. and B. Jacobsberg, 'Studies on Congo palm oil', *Journal of the American Oil Chemists' Society*, vol. 40, no. 6, 1963, pp. 18–19, 40 and 45

Lulofs, M.H., *Rubber* (Kuala Lumpur: Oxford University Press, 1987)

MacFadyen, Eric and Violet MacFadyen, *Eric MacFadyen, 1879–1966* (Barnet, Herts: The Stellar Press, 1968)

Malaysia: Palm Oil Registration and Licensing Authority, *Directory, Oil Palm Industry 1980* (Kuala Lumpur: PORLA, 1980)

Malaysia: Palm Oil Research and Development Act 1979 (Kuala Lumpur: Laws of Malaysia, Act 218, 1979)

Malek bin Mansoor and Colin Barlow, 'The production structure of the Malaysian oil palm industry with special reference to the smallholder subsector', *PORIM Occasional Papers*, 24 (1988)

Mathieu, Dato' Malcolm E., *I Lived By The Spear: an Autobiography, 1941–1945* (Ipoh: Rajan & Co., 1987)

Markides, Constantinos C., *All the Right Moves: a Guide to Crafting Breakthrough Strategy* (Harvard: Harvard Business School Press, 2000)

Martin, S.M., *Palm Oil and Protest: an Economic History of the Ngwa Region, South-Eastern Nigeria, 1800–1980* (Cambridge: Cambridge University Press, 1988).

McNair, F., *Perak and the Malays: Sarong and Kris* (London: Tinsley Bros., 1878)

Mielke, S. (ed.), *Oil World 1958–2007* (Hamburg: ISTA Mielke GMBH, 1988)

Mielke, T. (ed.), *Oil World 1963–2012* (Hamburg: ISTA Mielke GMBH, 1994)

Miller, S.M., A.J.H. Latham and D.O. Flynn (eds), *Studies in the Economic History of the Pacific Rim* (London: Routledge, 1998)

Moll, H.A.J., *The Economics of the Oil Palm* (Wageningen, Netherlands: PUDOC, 1987)

Mongana Report: see CONGOPALM

Neerbek, Hans, *Ridder uden Kors: Aage Westenholz og Danmarks Forsvar* [Knight without a cross: Aage Westenholz and Denmark's defence] (Odense: Odense Universitetsforlag, 1996)

Parmer, J.N., *Colonial Labor Policy and Administration: a History of Labor in the Rubber Plantation Industry in Malaya, c. 1910–1941* (New York: Association for Asian Studies, 1960)

Patten, Marguerite, *We'll Eat Again: a Collection of Recipes from the War Years* (London: Hamlyn, 1990; first published in London by Reed International, 1985)

Pedersen, Erik Helmer, *Pionererne* [Pioneers] (Copenhagen: Politikens Forlag A/S, 1986)

Petrow, R., *The Bitter Years: the Invasion and Occupation of Denmark and Norway, April 1940–May 1945* (London: Hodder and Stoughton, 1974)

PORAM (The Palm Oil Refiners' Association of Malaysia), *Annual Report, Year Ending 31 May 1989* (Kuala Lumpur: PORAM, 1989)

——, *Technical Brochure* (Kuala Lumpur: PORAM, 1989)

PORIM (Palm Oil Research Institute of Malaysia), *Proceedings of Workshop on Palm Oil Technical Promotion and Market Development, 15 June 1982* (Kuala Lumpur: PORIM, 1983)

——, *Proceedings of the International Seminar on Market Development for Palm Oil Products, 23–27 January 1984* (Kuala Lumpur: PORIM, 1984).

Pugh, Peter *et al.*, edited by Guy Nickalls, *Great Enterprise: a History of Harrisons & Crosfield* (London: Harrisons & Crosfield, 1990)

Pushparajah, E., and P.S. Chew (eds), *The Oil Palm in Agriculture in the Eighties* (Kuala Lumpur: Incorporated Society of Planters, 1982)

Puthucheary, J.J., *Ownership and Control in the Malayan Economy* (Singapore: Donald Moore for Eastern Universities Press, 1960)

Rajanaidu, N., 'Elaeis oleifera collection in Central and South America', in *Proceedings of International Workshop on Oil Palm Germplasm and Utilisation, 26–27 March 1985* (Kuala Lumpur: International Society of Oil Palm Breeders / PORIM, 1986), pp. 84–94.

——, I.E. Henson and B.S. Jalani (eds), *Proceedings of International Conference on Oil and Kernel Production in Oil Palm, ISOPB and PORIM, 27–28 September 1996* (Kuala Lumpur: PORIM, 1998)

—— and B.S. Jalani (eds), *Proceedings of the Symposium on The Science of Palm Oil Breeding, 30 June–2 July 1992* (Kuala Lumpur: PORIM, 1999)

—— and B.S. Jalani (eds), *Proceedings of Seminar on PS1 and PS2 Planting Materials, 1 June 1999* (Kuala Lumpur: PORIM, 1999)

——, V. Rao and B.K. Tan, 'Analysis of fatty acid composition in Elaeis guineensis, Elaeis oleifera and hybrids', in *Oil Composition in Oil Palm: Task Force Report to Director-General of PORIM* (Kuala Lumpur: PORIM, 1985), pp. 81–94

Rasmussen, A. Kann, *Danske i Siam, 1858–1942* [Danes in Siam, 1858–1942] (Copenhagen: Dansk Historisk Håndbogsforlag, 1984)

Ravnholt, Henning, *The Danish Co-Operative Movement* (Copenhagen: Det Danske Selskab, 1947)

Reader, W.J., *Unilever Plantations* (London: Unilever, 1961)

Rosenquist, E., 'The genetic base of oil palm breeding populations', in *Proceedings of International Workshop on Oil Palm Germplasm and Utilisation, 26–27 March 1985* (Kuala Lumpur: ISOPB/PORIM, 1986), pp. 27–56

——, 'Post war food and cash crop production in former colonial territories', Rhodes House Oxford, mss. British Empire s. 476, Box IV

The Royal Danish Ministry of Education, *Thai–Danish Relations: 30 Cycles of Friendship* (Copenhagen, 1980)

Rubber Growers' Association, *Fourth Annual Report, 1912–1913* (London: Rubber Growers' Association, 1913)

Sadka, E. (ed.), 'The journal of Sir Hugh Low, Perak, 1877', *Journal of the Malayan Branch of the Royal Asiatic Society*, vol. 27, no. 4, 1954, pp. 7, 28–31 and 90

——, *The Protected Malay States 1874–1895* (Kuala Lumpur: University of Malaya Press, 1968)

Sandhu, Kernial Singh, *Indians in Malaya: Some Aspects of their Immigration and Settlement, 1786–1957* (Cambridge: Cambridge University Press, 1969)

Schodt, D.W., *Ecuador: an Andean Enigma* (Boulder and London: Westview Press, 1987)

Seelen Sakran, 'A planter at heart', *Malaysian Business*, 16 August 2001.

Seymour, S., *Anglo–Danish Relations and Germany, 1933–45* (Odense: Odense University Press, 1982)

Short, A., *The Communist Insurrection in Malaya, 1948–1960* (London: Muller, 1975)

Singam, S. Durai Raja, *Port Weld to Kuantan: a Study of Malayan Place Names*, 3rd edn (Singapore: Kwok Yoke Weng & Co., 1957; 1st edn 1939)

Sodhy, Pamela, *The US–Malaysian Nexus: Themes in Superpower–Small State Relations* (Kuala Lumpur: ISIS, 1991)

Sopiee, Mohamed N., *From Malayan Union to Singapore Separation: Political Unification in the Malaysia Region, 1945–65* (Kuala Lumpur: Penerbit Universiti Malaya, 1974)

Stimpson, K.M.S., 'Malayan estates – the Scots connection', in *Selangor St Andrew's Society 1887–1986* (Kuala Lumpur: SSAS Centenary Committee, 1986), pp. 44–46.

Stockwell, A.J., *British Policy and Malay Politics during the Malayan Union Experiment, 1942–1948* (Kuala Lumpur: Malaysian Branch of the Royal Asiatic Society, 1979)

—— (ed.), *Malaya: British Documents on the End of Empire* Series B, Vol. 3 (London: HMSO, 1995)

Swettenham, F.A., 'From Perak to Slim, and down the Slim and Bernam Rivers', *Journal of the Straits Branch of the Royal Asiatic Society*, vol. 5, 1880, pp. 54–61

——, 'Journal kept during a journey across the Malay Peninsula', *Journal of the Straits Branch of the Royal Asiatic Society*, vol. 15, 1885, pp. 1–2

Szekely, L., *Tropic Fever: the Adventures of a Planter in Sumatra* (Kuala Lumpur: Oxford University Press, 1979)

Tate, D.J.M., *The RGA History of the Plantation Industry in the Malay Peninsula* (Kuala Lumpur: Oxford University Press for the Rubber Growers' Association (Malaysia) Berhad, 1996)

Thambipillay, R., *God's Little Acre 1948–1960* (Batu Gajah: Perak Planters' Association, 1998)

Thoburn, J.T., *Primary Commodity Exports and Economic Development: Theory, Evidence and a Study of Malaysia* (London: Wiley, 1977)

Thomas, Brinley and B.N. Thomsen, *Anglo–Danish Trade, 1661–1963: a Historical Survey* (Aarhus: Aarhus University Press, 1966)

Thurman, Judith, *Isak Dinesen: the Life of Karen Blixen* (London: Wiedenfeld, 1982 and Penguin, 1984)

Tomaru, Junko, *The Postwar Rapprochement of Malaya and Japan, 1945–61: the Roles of Britain and Japan in South-East Asia* (London: Macmillan, 2000)

Tropical Products Institute, UK Ministry of Overseas Development, *The Oil Palm: Papers Presented at the Conference, 3–6 May 1965* (London: TPI, 1965)

Turner, P.D. (ed.), *Oil Palm Developments in Malaysia: Proceedings of the First Malaysian Oil Palm Conference* (Kuala Lumpur: Incorporated Society of Planters, 1968)

—— (ed.), *The Quality and Marketing of Oil Palm Products* (Kuala Lumpur: Incorporated Society of Planters, 1969)

—— and R.A. Gillbanks, *Oil Palm Cultivation and Management* (Kuala Lumpur: Incorporated Society of Planters, 1974)

Upton, A.F., *The Finnish Revolution, 1917–1918* (Minneapolis: University of Minnesota Press, 1980)

Urquhart, D.H., *Cocoa* (London: Longmans, 1956)

Westenholz, Aage, 'Samarbejde mellem Kapital og Arbejdere' [Co-operation between capital and labour], *Borups Hoejskole 1922*, pp. 20–22

White, Nicholas J., *Business, Government and the End of Empire: Malaya, 1942–1957* (Kuala Lumpur: Oxford University Press, 1996)

——, *Decolonization: the British Experience since 1945* (London: Longman, 1999)

——, 'The business and the politics of decolonization: the British experience in the twentieth century', *Economic History Review*, vol. LIII, no. 3, 2000, pp. 544–564.

Williams, C.N. and Y.C. Hsu, *Oil Palm Cultivation in Malaya: Technical and Economic Aspects* (Kuala Lumpur: University of Malaya Press, 1970)

Wilson, C., *Unilever 1945–65* (London: Cassell, 1968)

Wong Sulong, 'Danes cash in on NEP volte-face', *Financial Times* (London), 23 March 1988.

Wood, B.J., *Pests of Oil Palms in Malaysia and their Control* (Kuala Lumpur: Incorporated Society of Planters, 1969)

Young, M. Crawford, 'Zaire, Rwanda and Burundi', in M. Crowder (ed.), *The Cambridge History of Africa*, Vol. 8 (Cambridge: Cambridge University Press, 1984), pp. 698–754

Yusof Basiron, D. Moore and Law Kia Sang, 'The UK market for palm oil', in *Proceedings of Workshop on Palm Oil Technical Promotion and Market Development, 15 June 1982* (Kuala Lumpur: PORIM, 1983), pp. 68–71

Index